BOOKS
THAT
HAVE
CHANGED
MAN'S
THINKING

CHEKHOV
PLAYS

Anton Chekhov

ANTON CHEKHOV

CHEKHOV PLAYS

*With an Introduction
and Appreciation
by*
ARNOLD B. McMILLIN

*Original Illustrations
by*
METTE IVERS

Distributed by
HERON BOOKS

CONTENTS

LIST OF ILLUSTRATIONS

EDITOR'S FOREWORD

The photographs one most often sees of Anton Chekhov, the famous writer, were taken in his last years, when he was dying of tuberculosis. They show a man who, with his worn face, scraggly beard and pince-nez, looks more like a timid schoolmaster than the author of the magnificent plays, instinct with life, which are here reprinted. The frontispiece of this volume shows a less well-known photograph of Chekhov, taken in 1897 when he had begun to write his greatest plays. The face is handsome and strong, the mouth subtle and generous, the eyes penetrating. Here one sees the real Chekhov, not yet too wasted by disease. He was witty and gay, he loved people and parties, nature and beauty in all its forms — and yet because the younger years of this grandson of a serf were spent in poverty and struggle and his later life was blighted by sickness, there were to his character depths upon depths of sadness and frustration at the aimless cruelty of life.

He was essentially humble and would always rather listen than talk. He kept his real self well hidden, and many people felt his inner detachment; no one ever knew him really well.

Yet, despite his constant troubles, he reverenced life: "It is death that needs nothing," he wrote. "The living man needs everything, the whole world ... God created man in order that he should live, and know joy and anguish . . ."

All of this was reflected in his plays — and stories too. The stories came easily; but the plays, mostly written during the last, sick years of his life, were a torture: "dramatic writing," he said, "is like a noisy, showy, impertinent and tiresome mistress." Several of the early productions were disastrous failures, but the real difficulty was that Chekthov was arduously creating an entirely new form of drama, which required new methods of acting and stagecraft — and these simply did not exist until Stanislavsky's Moscow Art Theatre, formed in 1898, undertook to learn how to master Chekhov's new art. And a new art it was. Chekhov's plays have no heroes, no villains, and nobody is a success, nor yet a total failure. The characters talk as one does in life, striving, usually at cross purposes, to break out of their private dreams, to communicate with each other. There is no larger "meaning," no moral in these plays, yet when properly produced they can project an intensity of emotion, drawn from the interplay of the characters, that can hold an audience spellbound. "Don't invent sufferings you have not experienced" Chekhov wrote to his brother, "and don't paint pictures you have not seen, for a lie in a story is much more boring than a lie in conversation." Chekhov's characters were real, and their emotions were taken from life.

In a word, in Chekhov's plays one finds life itself set upon a stage in all its complexity and inconsistency. Chekhov does not write tragedies or comedies but something of both, for life is both tragic and comic. Indeed, it is significant that Chekhov actually called a number of his plays comedies. It is this new dramatic art that Chekhov has willed to the theatre of our day, and many of our modern playwrights are still trying to achieve, *in new ways, what Chekhov accomplished so well. For to present life-as-it-is in compelling form on the stage, without moralizing, without artifice, bombast, or over-simplification is difficult at best. In so doing, Chekhov not only influenced countless authors who came after him but opened our own eyes—the eyes of the audience—to the many plays and by-plays that life presents all around us.*

COURTLANDT CANBY
EDITOR OF THE SERIES

INTRODUCTION

Chekhov's plays occupy a unique position in modern drama. Lacking the intellectual power of Ibsen, the passionate intensity of Strindberg or the verbal brilliance of Shaw, Chekhov makes a more lasting impression on modern audiences than any of his contemporaries or successors, thanks largely to his plays' all-pervasive and immediately recognizable emotional atmosphere. Depending less on what is said than on what remains unsaid, they inevitably evoke a strong personal response from the audience, which becomes intimately involved in the strivings, longings and disappointments of the protagonists. If this fails to happen, thanks, for example, to a bad production, then the spectators will be disappointed and possibly indignant, for Chekhov's drama is above all one of emotional involvement; without this element little remains.

If, however, we respond, we will find the author's great humanity drawing us deeply into the characters' moods, and into the atmosphere, intangible but very real, surrounding their lives. And it is this atmosphere that remains with us long after Ibsen's ideological strivings and Shaw's brilliant paradoxes have been forgotten; this atmosphere that continues to inform Chekhov's plays with life on the stage today, over fifty years after they were written.

In the context of Russian literature's dazzlingly swift development in the nineteenth century, drama had a hesitant, not to say stunted growth, compared with the novel or short story. Certainly most of the novelists and poets of the last century attempted the dramatic form, some of them with outstanding success, like, for example, Gogol in The Government Inspector; *but of all the major writers only Griboyedov and Ostrovsky owe their fame today to plays, as opposed to narrative prose or poetry. Pushkin, Turgenev, Tolstoy and Gorky, to name but a few, all wrote successful plays, but are nonetheless chiefly remembered for their other works, and thus it is not surprising that the theatre followed closely the main stream of Russian literature as a whole, from imitation of foreign, particularly French, neo-classical models at the end of the eighteenth century towards the expansive realism, with its emphasis on social and moral problems, that finds its greatest expression in Dostoyevsky, Turgenev and Tolstoy.*

One of the first landmarks in Russian nineteenth century drama is Griboyedov's brilliant verse comedy Woe from Wit *(1823-24), and already here we can see the classical style and framework being streched almost beyond recognition to express in highly topical terms the conflict between progressive youth, represented by Chatsky, the hero, and, on the other hand, the conservative, patriarchal Moscow society, represented by all the other characters in the play: a very real and actual conflict that was to culminate in the Decembrist rising of 1825.*

The next outstanding comedy to appear, Gogol's The Government Inspector *(1836), was interpreted by contemporary audiences as a biting social satire against the corruption inherent in the bureaucratic officialdom of tsarist Russia. We may today see the play as a moral satire against the vices in man's nature rather than as a social satire against any vices inherent in the system, but the fact remains that Gogol's contemporaries, led by the influential critic Belinsky, drew great social and political significance from this "slap in the face."*

Perhaps the most important, although not the most talented of Chekhov's predecessors was Ostrovsky (1823-1886) who stands apart from the other writers in that his literary career was almost entirely devoted to writing plays. Forty-eight in number, they are mostly naturalistic scenes from the life of the merchant classes (a section of society receiving relatively little attention from thè front rank of Russian writers) and show the problems arising from the backwardness, conservatism and greed characteristic of this milieu. None of his plays has anything to do with art for art's sake, the tragedies arising from the social conditions, and the comedies being highly satirical. Ostrovsky looks forward to Chekhov in the atmospheric quality of some of his plays, for example The Storm *(1860), and in his attempts to reduce aimless theatricality by increasing the naturalness of life shown on the stage; but the setting and language of his plays is too localized and specific for him to find an audience outside Russia; his plays lack the spiritual and intellectual qualities that could rank him with the major dramatists of the modern world.*

Perhaps even closer to Chekhov is Turgenev. From his novels and stories one would expect his few plays to be charged with atmosphere and poetry, as indeed they are, although, curiously, these qualities are not as strongly felt here as in his prose works. The setting of the plays is that of the novels and is also, basically, that of Chekhov's plays, but more important than the common theme of dissatisfied and unhappy estate life is Turgenev's use of 'emotional signals' and simple, apparently insignificant remarks to reveal the intimate moods of his characters. He called for the use of "the simple, unexpected movements in which the human soul finds clear expression." Like Chekhov he is concerned with inner action and the undercurrents of feeling, but even in his best plays, like

INTRODUCTION

A Month in the Country *(1850), the psychological tensions are less subtle and the comedy more obvious; nor do we feel the great compassion that informs Chekhov's mature work. But nonetheless it is, of all his fellow-countrymen, to Turgenev that the later playwright is closest, both in style and in subject matter.*

Thus despite the brilliance of individual works like Woe from Wit *or* The Government Inspector *there existed no large body of Russian plays, apart from those of Ostrovsky, on which to build a national repertoire and establish sound acting traditions. At the end of the nineteenth century foreign plays dominated the stages of both St. Petersburg and Moscow, and theatres, in Chekhov's words, seemed more like ale houses or Tatar restaurants—a situation that was not helped by the relatively small interest shown by writers like Turgenev and Tolstoy in the actual production of their own plays. It was for Chekhov to breathe fresh air into the stale atmosphere of the Russian theatre at the end of the nineteenth century, to insist on naturalness on the stage and to raise the prestige of both actors and dramatists to a level more in keeping with the new status literature had earned through novelists like Dostoyevsky and Tolstoy.*

The modern Russian theatrical tradition is closely based on the work of Chekhov and the Moscow Art Theatre, with whom he collaborated, whilst, on the other hand, trends in modern European drama have been greatly influenced by his work, which is still regularly performed in almost every country of the world.

Arnold B. McMILLIN

University of London

London, June 1968

XVIII

THREE SISTERS

First performed in 1902

CHARACTERS IN THE PLAY

ANDREY SERGEYEVITCH PROZOROV.

NATALYA IVANOVNA, *also called* NATASHA (*his fiancée, afterwards his wife*).

OLGA
MASHA } (*his sisters*).
IRINA

FYODOR ILYITCH KULIGIN (*a High-school Teacher, husband of Masha*).

LIEUTENANT-COLONEL ALEXANDR IGNATYEVITCH VERSHININ (*Battery-Commander*).

BARON NIKOLAY LVOVITCH TUSENBACH (*Lieutenant*).

VASSILY VASSILYEVITCH SOLYONY (*Captain*).

IVAN ROMANITCH TCHEBUTYKIN (*Army Doctor*).

ALEXEY PETROVITCH FEDOTIK (*Second Lieutenant*).

VLADIMIR KARLOVITCH RODDEY (*Second Lieutenant*).

FERAPONT (*an old Porter from the Rural Board*).

ANFISA (*the Nurse, an old woman of eighty*).

The action takes place in a provincial town.

ACT I

In the house of the PROZOROVS. *A drawing-room with columns beyond which a large room is visible. Mid-day; it is bright and sunny. The table in the further room is being laid for lunch.*

OLGA, *in the dark blue uniform of a high-school teacher, is correcting exercise books, at times standing still and then walking up and down;* MASHA, *in a black dress, with her hat on her knee, is reading a book;* IRINA, *in a white dress, is standing plunged in thought.*

OLGA. Father died just a year ago, on this very day—the fifth of May, your name-day, Irina. It was very cold, snow was falling. I felt as though I should not live through it ; you lay fainting as though you were dead. But now a year has passed and we can think of it calmly ; you are already in a white dress, your face is radiant. (*The clock strikes twelve.*) The clock was striking then too (*a pause*). I remember the band playing and the firing at the cemetery as they carried the coffin. Though he was a general in command of a brigade, yet there weren't many people there. It was raining, though. Heavy rain and snow.

3

IRINA. Why recall it !

(BARON TUSENBACH, TCHEBUTYKIN *and* SOLYONY *appear near the table in the dining-room, beyond the columns.*)

OLGA. It is warm to-day, we can have the windows open, but the birches are not in leaf yet. Father was given his brigade and came here with us from Moscow eleven years ago and I remember distinctly that in Moscow at this time, at the beginning of May, everything was already in flower ; it was warm, and everything was bathed in sunshine. It's eleven years ago, and yet I remember it all as though we had left it yesterday. Oh, dear ! I woke up this morning, I saw a blaze of sunshine. I saw the spring, and joy stirred in my heart. I had a passionate longing to be back at home again !

TCHEBUTYKIN. The devil it is !

TUSENBACH. Of course, it's nonsense.

(MASHA, *brooding over a book, softly whistles a song.*)

OLGA. Don't whistle, Masha. How can you ! (*a pause*). Being all day in school and then at my lessons till the evening gives me a perpetual headache and thoughts as gloomy as though I were old. And really these four years that I have been at the high-school I have felt my strength and my youth oozing away from me every day. And only one yearning grows stronger and stronger. . . .

IRINA. To go back to Moscow. To sell the house, to make an end of everything here, and off to Moscow. . . .

4

OLGA. Yes! To Moscow, and quickly.

(TCHEBUTYKIN *and* TUSENBACH *laugh*.)

IRINA. Andrey will probably be a professor, he will not live here anyhow. The only difficulty is poor Masha.

OLGA. Masha will come and spend the whole summer in Moscow every year.

(MASHA *softly whistles a tune*.)

IRINA. Please God it will all be managed. (*Looking out of window*) How fine it is to-day. I don't know why I feel so light-hearted! I remembered this morning that it was my name-day and at once I felt joyful and thought of my childhood when mother was living. And I was thrilled by such wonderful thoughts, such thoughts!

OLGA. You are radiant to-day and looking lovelier than usual. And Masha is lovely too. Andrey would be nice-looking, but he has grown too fat and that does not suit him. And I have grown older and ever so much thinner. I suppose it's because I get so cross with the girls at school. To-day now I am free, I am at home, and my head doesn't ache, and I feel younger than yesterday. I am only twenty-eight. . . . It's all quite right, it's all from God, but it seems to me that if I were married and sitting at home all day, it would be better (*a pause*). I should be fond of my husband.

TUSENBACH (*to* SOLYONY). You talk such nonsense, I am tired of listening to you. (*Coming into the drawing-room*) I forgot to tell you, you will receive a visit to-day from Vershinin, the new commander of our battery (*sits down to the piano*).

OLGA. Well, I shall be delighted.

IRINA. Is he old ?

TUSENBACH. No, nothing to speak of. Forty or forty-five at the most (*softly plays the piano*). He seems to be a nice fellow. He is not stupid, that's certain. Only he talks a lot.

IRINA. Is he interesting ?

TUSENBACH. Yes, he is all right, only he has a wife, a mother-in-law and two little girls. And it's his second wife too. He is paying calls and telling everyone that he has a wife and two little girls. He'll tell you so too. His wife seems a bit crazy, with her hair in a long plait like a girl's, always talks in a high-flown style, makes philosophical reflections and frequently attempts to commit suicide, evidently to annoy her husband. I should have left a woman like that years ago, but he puts up with her and merely complains.

SOLYONY (*coming into the drawing-room with* TCHEBUTYKIN). With one hand I can only lift up half a hundredweight, but with both hands I can lift up a hundredweight and a half or even a hundredweight and three-quarters. From that I conclude that two men are not only twice but three times as strong as one man, or even more. . . .

TCHEBUTYKIN (*reading the newspaper as he comes in*). For hair falling out . . . two ounces of naphthaline in half a bottle of spirit . . . to be dissolved and used daily . . . (*puts it down in his notebook*). Let's make a note of it ! No,

6

mette ivers

I don't want it . . . (*scratches it out*). It doesn't matter.

IRINA. Ivan Romanitch, dear Ivan Romanitch !

TCHEBUTYKIN. What is it, my child, my joy ?

IRINA. Tell me, why is it I am so happy to-day ? As though I were sailing with the great blue sky above me and big white birds flying over it. Why is it ? Why ?

TCHEBUTYKIN (*kissing both her hands, tenderly*). My white bird. . . .

IRINA. When I woke up this morning, got up and washed, it suddenly seemed to me as though everything in the world was clear to me and that I knew how one ought to live. Dear Ivan Romanitch, I know all about it. A man ought to work, to toil in the sweat of his brow, whoever he may be, and all the purpose and meaning of his life, his happiness, his ecstasies lie in that alone. How delightful to be a workman who gets up before dawn and breaks stones on the road, or a shepherd, or a schoolmaster teaching children, or an engine-driver. . . . Oh, dear ! to say nothing of human beings, it would be better to be an ox, better to be a humble horse and work, than a young woman who wakes at twelve o'clock, then has coffee in bed, then spends two hours dressing. . . . Oh, how awful that is ! Just as one has a craving for water in hot weather I have a craving for work. And if I don't get up early and work, give me up as a friend, Ivan Romanitch.

TCHEBUTYKIN (*tenderly*). I'll give you up, I'll give you up. . . .

OLGA. Father trained us to get up at seven o'clock. Now Irina wakes at seven and lies in bed at least till nine thinking. And she looks so serious! (*laughs*).

IRINA. You are used to thinking of me as a child and are surprised when I look serious. I am twenty!

TUSENBACH. The yearning for work, oh dear, how well I understand it! I have never worked in my life. I was born in cold, idle Petersburg, in a family that had known nothing of work or cares of any kind. I remember, when I came home from the school of cadets, a footman used to pull off my boots. I used to be troublesome, but my mother looked at me with reverential awe, and was surprised when other people did not do the same. I was guarded from work. But I doubt if they have succeeded in guarding me completely, I doubt it! The time is at hand, an avalanche is moving down upon us, a mighty clearing storm which is coming, is already near and will soon blow the laziness, the indifference, the distaste for work, the rotten boredom out of our society. I shall work, and in another twenty-five or thirty years every one will have to work. Every one!

TCHEBUTYKIN. I am not going to work.

TUSENBACH. You don't count.

SOLYONY. In another twenty-five years you won't be here, thank God. In two or three years you will kick the bucket, or I shall lose my temper and put a bullet through your head, my angel (*pulls a scent-bottle out of his pocket and sprinkles his chest and hands*).

8

TCHEBUTYKIN (*laughs*). And I really have never done anything at all. I haven't done a stroke of work since I left the university, I have never read a book, I read nothing but newspapers . . . (*takes another newspaper out of his pocket*). Here . . . I know, for instance, from the newspapers that there was such a person as Dobrolyubov, but what he wrote, I can't say. . . . Goodness only knows. . . . (*A knock is heard on the floor from the storey below.*) There . . . they are calling me downstairs, someone has come for me. I'll be back directly. . . . Wait a minute . . . (*goes out hurriedly, combing his beard*).

IRINA. He's got something up his sleeve.

TUSENBACH. Yes, he went out with a solemn face, evidently he is just going to bring you a present.

IRINA. What a nuisance !

OLGA. Yes, it's awful. He is always doing something silly.

MASHA. By the sea-strand an oak-tree green . . . upon that oak a chain of gold . . . upon that oak a chain of gold (*gets up, humming softly*).

OLGA. You are not very cheerful to-day, Masha.

(MASHA, *humming, puts on her hat.*)

OLGA. Where are you going ?

MASHA. Home.

IRINA. How queer ! . . .

TUSENBACH. To go away from a name-day party !

MASHA. Never mind. . . . I'll come in the evening. Good-bye, my darling . . . (*kisses* IRINA). Once again I wish you, be well and happy. In old days, when father was alive, we always had thirty or forty officers here on name-days; it was noisy, but to-day there is only a man and a half, and it is as still as the desert. . . . I'll go. . . . I am in the blues to-day, I am feeling glum, so don't you mind what I say (*laughing through her tears*). We'll talk some other time, and so for now good-bye, darling, I am going. . . .

IRINA (*discontentedly*). Oh, how tiresome you are. . . .

OLGA (*with tears*). I understand you, Masha.

SOLYONY. If a man philosophises, there will be philosophy or sophistry, anyway, but if a woman philosophises, or two do it, then you may just snap your fingers !

MASHA. What do you mean to say by that, you terrible person ?

SOLYONY. Nothing. He had not time to say "alack," before the bear was on his back (*a pause*).

MASHA (*to* OLGA, *angrily*). Don't blubber !

(*Enter* ANFISA *and* FERAPONT *carrying a cake*.)

ANFISA. This way, my good man. Come in, your boots are clean. (*To* IRINA) From the Rural Board, from Mihail Ivanitch Protopopov. . . . A cake.

IRINA. Thanks. Thank him (*takes the cake*).

FERAPONT. What ?

IRINA (*more loudly*). Thank him from me !

OLGA. Nurse dear, give him some pie. Ferapont, go along, they will give you some pie.

FERAPONT. Eh ?

ANFISA. Come along, Ferapont Spiridonitch, my good soul, come along . . . (*goes out with* FERA-PONT).

10

MASHA. I don't like that Protopopov, that Mihail Potapitch or Ivanitch. He ought not to be invited.

IRINA. I did not invite him.

MASHA. That's a good thing.

(*Enter* TCHEBUTYKIN, *followed by an orderly with a silver samovar ; a hum of surprise and displeasure*).

OLGA (*putting her hands over her face*). A samovar ! How awful ! (*goes out to the table in the dining-room*).

IRINA. My dear Ivan Romanitch, what are you thinking about !

TUSENBACH (*laughs*). I warned you !

MASHA. Ivan Romanitch, you really have no conscience !

TCHEBUTYKIN. My dear girls, my darlings, you are all that I have, you are the most precious treasures I have on earth. I shall soon be sixty, I am an old man, alone in the world, a useless old man. . . . There is nothing good in me, except my love for you, and if it were not for you, I should have been dead long ago. . . . (*To* IRINA) My dear, my little girl, I've known you from a baby . . . I've carried you in my arms. . . . I loved your dear mother. . . .

IRINA. But why such expensive presents?

TCHEBUTYKIN (*angry and tearful*). Expensive presents. . . . Get along with you ! (*To the orderly*) Take the samovar in there . . . (*mimicking*) Expensive presents . . . (*The orderly carries the samovar into the dining-room*).

ANFISA (*crossing the room*). My dears, a colonel is here, a stranger. . . . He has taken off his greatcoat, children, he is coming in here. Irinushka, you must be nice and polite, dear . . . (*as she goes out*). And it's time for lunch already . . . mercy on us. . . .

TUSENBACH. Vershinin, I suppose.

(*Enter* VERSHININ.)

TUSENBACH. Colonel Vershinin.

VERSHININ (*to* MASHA *and* IRINA). I have the honour to introduce myself, my name is Vershinin. I am very, very glad to be in your house at last. How you have grown up! Aie-aie!

IRINA. Please sit down. We are delighted to see you.

VERSHININ (*with animation*). How glad I am, how glad I am! But there are three of you sisters. I remember—three little girls. I don't remember your faces, but that your father, Colonel Prozorov, had three little girls I remember perfectly, and saw them with my own eyes. How time passes! Hey-ho, how it passes!

TUSENBACH. Alexandr Ignatyevitch has come from Moscow.

IRINA. From Moscow? You have come from Moscow?

VERSHININ. Yes. Your father was in command of a battery there, and I was an officer in the same brigade. (*To* MASHA). Your face, now, I seem to remember.

MASHA. I don't remember you.

IRINA. Olya! Olya! (*calls into the dining-room*) Olya, come!

(OLGA *comes out of the dining-room into the drawing-room.*)

12

IRINA. Colonel Vershinin is from Moscow, it appears.

VERSHININ. So you are Olga Sergeyevna, the eldest. . . . And you are Marya. . . . And you are Irina, the youngest. . . .

OLGA. You come from Moscow ?

VERSHININ. Yes. I studied in Moscow. I began my service there, I served there for years, and at last I have been given a battery here—I have come here as you see. I don't remember you exactly, I only remember you were three sisters. I remember your father. If I shut my eyes, I can see him as though he were living. I used to visit you in Moscow. . . .

OLGA. I thought I remembered everyone, and now all at once . . .

VERSHININ. My name is Alexandr Ignatyevitch.

IRINA. Alexandr Ignatyevitch, you have come from Moscow. . . . What a surprise !

OLGA. We are going to move there, you know.

IRINA. We are hoping to be there by the autumn. It's our native town, we were born there. . . . In Old Basmanny Street . . . (*both laugh with delight*).

MASHA. To see some one from our own town unexpectedly ! (*Eagerly*) Now I remember ! Do you remember, Olya, they used to talk of the " love-sick major " ? You were a lieutenant at that time and were in love, and for some reason everyone called you " major " to tease you. . . .

VERSHININ (*laughs*). Yes, yes. . . . The love-sick major, that was it.

MASHA. You only had a moustache then. . . . Oh, how much older you look! (*through tears*) how much older!

VERSHININ. Yes, when I was called the love-sick major I was young, I was in love. Now it's very different.

OLGA. But you haven't a single grey hair. You have grown older but you are not old.

VERSHININ. I am in my forty-third year, though. Is it long since you left Moscow?

IRINA. Eleven years. But why are you crying, Masha, you queer girl? . . . (*through her tears*) I shall cry too. . . .

MASHA. I am all right. And in which street did you live?

VERSHININ. In Old Basmanny.

OLGA. And that's where we lived too. . . .

VERSHININ. At one time I lived in Nyemetsky Street. I used to go from there to the Red Barracks. There is a gloomy-looking bridge on the way, where the water makes a noise. It makes a lonely man feel melancholy (*a pause*). And here what a broad, splendid river! A marvellous river!

OLGA. Yes, but it is cold. It's cold here and there are gnats. . . .

VERSHININ. How can you! You've such a splendid healthy Russian climate here. Forest, river . . . and birches here too. Charming, modest birches, I love them better than any other trees. It's nice to live here. The only strange thing is that the railway station is fifteen miles away. . . . And no one knows why it is so.

SOLYONY. I know why it is (*They all look at him.*) Because if the station had been near it would not have been so far, and if it is far, it's because it is not near.

(*An awkward silence.*)

TUSENBACH. He is fond of his joke, Vassily Vassilyevitch.

OLGA. Now I recall you, too. I remember.

VERSHININ. I knew your mother.

TCHEBUTYKIN. She was a fine woman, the kingdom of heaven be hers.

IRINA. Mother is buried in Moscow.

OLGA. In the Novo-Dyevitchy. . . .

MASHA. Would you believe it, I am already beginning to forget her face. So people will not remember us either . . . they will forget us.

VERSHININ. Yes. They will forget us. Such is our fate, there is no help for it. What seems to us serious, significant, very important, will one day be forgotten or will seem unimportant (*a pause*). And it's curious that we can't possibly tell what exactly will be considered great and important, and what will seem paltry and ridiculous. Did not the discoveries of Copernicus or Columbus, let us say, seem useless and ridiculous at first, while the nonsensical writings of some wiseacre seemed true? And it may be that our present life, which we accept so readily, will in time seem queer, uncomfortable, not sensible, not clean enough, perhaps even sinful. . . .

TUSENBACH. Who knows? Perhaps our age will be called a great one and remembered with respect. Now we have no torture-chamber, no executions, no invasions, but at the same time how much unhappiness there is !

SOLYONY (*in a high-pitched voice*). Chook, chook, chook. . . . It's bread and meat to the baron to talk about ideas.

TUSENBACH. Vassily Vassilyevitch, I ask you to let me alone . . . (*moves to another seat*). It gets boring, at last.

SOLYONY (*in a high-pitched voice*). Chook, chook, chook. . . .

TUSENBACH (*to* VERSHININ). The unhappiness which one observes now—there is so much of it—does indicate, however, that society has reached a certain moral level. . . .

VERSHININ. Yes, yes, of course.

TCHEBUTYKIN. You said just now, baron, that our age will be called great ; but people are small all the same . . . (*gets up*). Look how small I am.

(*A violin is played behind the scenes.*)

MASHA. That's Andrey playing, our brother.

IRINA. He is the learned one of the family. We expect him to become a professor. Father was a military man, but his son has gone in for a learned career.

MASHA. It was father's wish.

OLGA. We have been teasing him to-day. We think he is a little in love.

IRINA. With a young lady living here. She will come in to-day most likely.

MASHA. Oh, how she dresses ! It's not that her clothes are merely ugly or out of fashion, they are simply pitiful. A queer gaudy yellowish skirt with some sort of vulgar fringe and a red blouse.

16

And her cheeks scrubbed till they shine! Andrey is not in love with her—I won't admit that, he has some taste anyway—it's simply for fun, he is teasing us, playing the fool. I heard yesterday that she is going to be married to Protopopov, the chairman of our Rural Board. And a very good thing too. . . . (*At the side door*) Andrey, come here, dear, for a minute!

(*Enter* ANDREY.)

OLGA. This is my brother, Andrey Sergeyevitch.

VERSHININ. My name is Vershinin.

ANDREY. And mine is Prozorov (*mops his perspiring face*). You are our new battery commander?

OLGA. Only fancy, Alexandr Ignatyevitch comes from Moscow.

ANDREY. Really? Well, then, I congratulate you. My sisters will let you have no peace.

VERSHININ. I have had time to bore your sisters already.

IRINA. See what a pretty picture-frame Andrey has given me to-day! (*shows the frame*). He made it himself.

VERSHININ (*looking at the frame and not knowing what to say*). Yes . . . it is a thing. . . .

IRINA. And that frame above the piano, he made that too!

(ANDREY *waves his hand in despair and moves away*.)

OLGA. He is learned, and he plays the violin, and he makes all sorts of things with the fretsaw. In fact he is good all round. Andrey, don't go! That's a way he has—he always tries to make off Come here!

(MASHA *and* IRINA *take him by the arms and, laughing, lead him back.*)

MASHA. Come, come !

ANDREY. Leave me alone, please !

MASHA. How absurd he is ! Alexandr Ignatye-vitch used to be called the love-sick major at one time. and he was not a bit offended.

VERSHININ. Not in the least !

MASHA. And I should like to call you the love-sick violinist !

IRINA Or the love-sick professor !

OLGA. He is in love ! Andryusha is in love !

IRINA (*claps her hands*). Bravo, bravo ! En-core ! Andryusha is in love !

TCHEBUTYKIN (*comes up behind* ANDREY *and puts both arms round his waist*). Nature our hearts for love created ! (*laughs, then sits down and reads the newspaper which he takes out of his pocket*).

ANDREY. Come, that's enough, that's enough . . . (*mops his face*). I haven't slept all night and this morning I don't feel quite myself, as they say. I read till four o'clock and then went to bed, but it was no use. I thought of one thing and another, and then it gets light so early ; the sun simply pours into my bedroom. I want while I am here during the summer to translate a book from the English. . . .

VERSHININ. You read English then ?

ANDREY. Yes. Our father, the kingdom of heaven be his, oppressed us with education. It's absurd and silly, but it must be confessed I began to get fatter after his death, and I have grown too fat in one year, as though a weight had been taken off my body. Thanks to our father we all know English, French and German, and Irina knows Italian too. But what it cost us!

MASHA. In this town to know three languages is an unnecessary luxury! Not even a luxury, but an unnecessary encumbrance, like a sixth finger. We know a great deal that is unnecessary.

VERSHININ. What next! (*laughs.*) You know a great deal that is unnecessary! I don't think there can be a town so dull and dismal that intelligent and educated people are unnecessary in it. Let us suppose that of the hundred thousand people living in this town, which is, of course, uncultured and behind the times, there are only three of your sort. It goes without saying that you cannot conquer the mass of darkness round you; little by little, as you go on living, you will be lost in the crowd. You will have to give in to it. Life will get the better of you, but still you will not disappear without a trace. After you there may appear perhaps six like you, then twelve and so on until such as you form a majority. In two or three hundred years life on earth will be unimaginably beautiful, marvellous. Man needs such a life and, though he hasn't it yet, he must have a presentiment of it, expect it, dream of it, prepare for it; for that he must see and know more than his father and grandfather (*laughs*). And you complain of knowing a great deal that's unnecessary.

MASHA (*takes off her hat*). I'll stay to lunch.

IRINA (*with a sigh*). All that really ought to be written down. . . .

(ANDREY *has slipped away unobserved.*)

19

TUSENBACH. You say that after many years life on earth will be beautiful and marvellous. That's true. But in order to have any share, however far off, in it now one must be preparing for it, one must be working. . . .

VERSHININ (*gets up*). Yes. What a lot of flowers you have! (*looking round*). And delightful rooms. I envy you! I've been knocking about all my life from one wretched lodging to another, always with two chairs and a sofa and stoves which smoke. What I have been lacking all my life is just such flowers . . . (*rubs his hands*). But there, it's no use thinking about it!

TUSENBACH. Yes, we must work. I'll be bound you think the German is getting sentimental. But on my honour I am Russian and I can't even speak German. My father belonged to the Orthodox Church . . . (*a pause*).

VERSHININ (*walks about the stage*). I often think, what if one were to begin life over again, knowing what one is about! If one life, which has been already lived, were only a rough sketch so to say, and the second were the fair copy! Then, I fancy, every one of us would try before everything not to repeat himself, anyway he would create a different setting for his life; would have a house like this with plenty of light and masses of flowers. . . . I have a wife and two little girls, my wife is in delicate health and so on and so on, but if I were to begin life over again I would not marry. . . . No, no!

(*Enter* KULIGIN *in the uniform of a school-master.*)

20

KULIGIN (*goes up to* IRINA). Dear sister, allow me to congratulate you on your name-day and with all my heart to wish you good health and everything else that one can desire for a girl of your age. And to offer you as a gift this little book (*gives her a book*). The history of our high-school for fifty years, written by myself. An insignificant little book, written because I had nothing better to do, but still you can read it. Good morning, friends. (*To* VERSHININ) My name is Kuligin, teacher in the high-school here. (*To* IRINA) In that book you will find a list of all who have finished their studies in our high-school during the last fifty years. *Feci quod potui, faciant meliora potentes* (*kisses* MASHA).

IRINA. Why, but you gave me a copy of this book at Easter.

KULIGIN (*laughs*). Impossible! If that's so, give it me back, or better still, give it to the Colonel. Please accept it, Colonel. Some day when you are bored you can read it.

VERSHININ. Thank you (*is about to take leave*). I am extremely glad to have made your acquaintance. . . .

OLGA. You are going? No, no!

IRINA. You must stay to lunch with us. Please do.

OLGA. Pray do!

VERSHININ (*bows*). I believe I have chanced on a name-day. Forgive me, I did not know and have not congratulated you . . . (*walks away with* OLGA *into the dining-room*).

KULIGIN. To-day, gentlemen, is Sunday, a day

of rest. Let us all rest and enjoy ourselves each in accordance with our age and our position. The carpets should be taken up for the summer and put away till the winter. . . . Persian powder or naphthaline. . . . The Romans were healthy because they knew how to work and they knew how to rest, they had *mens sana in corpore sano*. Their life was moulded into a certain framework. Our headmaster says that the most important thing in every life is its framework. . . . What loses its framework, comes to an end—and it's the same in our everyday life. (*Puts his arm round* MASHA'S *waist, laughing*.) Masha loves me. My wife loves me. And the window curtains, too, ought to be put away together with the carpets. . . . To-day I feel cheerful and in the best of spirits. Masha, at four o'clock this afternoon we have to be at the headmaster's. An excursion has been arranged for the teachers and their families.

MASHA. I am not going.

KULIGIN (*grieved*). Dear Masha, why not?

MASHA. We'll talk about it afterwards . . . (*Angrily*) Very well, I will go, only let me alone, please . . . (*walks away*).

KULIGIN. And then we shall spend the evening at the headmaster's. In spite of the delicate state of his health, that man tries before all things to be sociable. He is an excellent, noble personality. A splendid man. Yesterday, after the meeting, he said to me, " I am tired, Fyodor Ilyitch, I am tired." (*Looks at the clock, then at his watch*) Your clock is seven minutes fast. " Yes," he said, " I am tired."

22

(Sounds of a violin behind the scenes.)

OLGA. Come to lunch, please. There's a pie !

KULIGIN. Ah, Olga, my dear Olga ! Yesterday I was working from early morning till eleven o'clock at night and was tired out, and to-day I feel happy *(goes up to the table in the dining-room)*. My dear. . . .

TCHEBUTYKIN *(puts the newspaper in his pocket and combs his beard)*. Pie ? Splendid !

MASHA *(to TCHEBUTYKIN, sternly)*. Only mind you don't drink to-day ! Do you hear ? It's bad for you to drink.

TCHEBUTYKIN. Oh, come, that's a thing of the past. It's two years since I got drunk. *(Impatiently)* But there, my good girl, what does it matter !

MASHA. Anyway, don't you dare to drink. Don't dare. *(Angrily, but so as not to be heard by her husband)* Again, damnation take it, I am to be bored a whole evening at the headmaster's !

TUSENBACH. I wouldn't go if I were you. . . . It's very simple.

TCHEBUTYKIN. Don't go, my love.

MASHA. Oh, yes, don't go ! . . . It's a damnable life, insufferable . . . *(goes to the dining-room)*.

TCHEBUTYKIN *(following her)*. Come, come. . . .

SOLYONY *(going to the dining-room)*. Chook, chook, chook. . . .

TUSENBACH. Enough, Vassily Vassilyevitch ! Leave off !

SOLYONY. Chook, chook, chook. . . .

KULIGIN *(gaily)*. Your health, Colonel ! I am a schoolmaster and one of the family here, Masha's

23

husband. . . . She is very kind really, very kind. . . .

VERSHININ. I'll have some of this dark-coloured vodka . . . (*drinks*). To your health! (*To* OLGA) I feel so happy with all of you!

(*No one is left in the drawing-room but* IRINA *and* TUSENBACH.)

IRINA. Masha is in low spirits to-day. She was married at eighteen, when she thought him the cleverest of men. But now it's not the same. He is the kindest of men, but he is not the cleverest.

OLGA (*impatiently*). Andrey, do come!

ANDREY (*behind the scenes*). I am coming (*comes in and goes to the table*).

TUSENBACH. What are you thinking about?

IRINA. Nothing. I don't like that Solyony of yours, I am afraid of him. He keeps on saying such stupid things. . . .

TUSENBACH. He is a queer man. I am sorry for him and annoyed by him, but more sorry. I think he is shy. . . . When one is alone with him he is very intelligent and friendly, but in company he is rude, a bully. Don't go yet, let them sit down to the table. Let me be by you. What are you thinking of? (*a pause*). You are twenty, I am not yet thirty. How many years have we got before us, a long, long chain of days full of my love for you. . . .

IRINA. Nikolay Lvovitch, don't talk to me about love.

TUSENBACH (*not listening*). I have a passionate craving for life, for struggle, for work, and that craving is mingled in my soul with my love for you,

24

Irina, and just because you are beautiful it seems to me that life too is beautiful! What are you thinking of?

IRINA. You say life is beautiful. . . . Yes, but what if it only seems so! Life for us three sisters has not been beautiful yet, we have been stifled by it as plants are choked by weeds. . . . I am shedding tears. . . . I mustn't do that (*hurriedly wipes her eyes and smiles*). I must work, I must work. The reason we are depressed and take such a gloomy view of life is that we know nothing of work. We come of people who despised work. . . .

(*Enter* NATALYA IVANOVNA; *she is wearing a pink dress with a green sash.*)

NATASHA. They are sitting down to lunch already. . . . I am late . . . (*Steals a glance at herself in the glass and sets herself to rights*) I think my hair is all right. (*Seeing* IRINA) Dear Irina Sergeyevna, I congratulate you! (*gives her a vigorous and prolonged kiss*). You have a lot of visitors, I really feel shy. . . . Good day, Baron!

OLGA (*coming into the drawing-room*). Well, here is Natalya Ivanovna! How are you, my dear? (*kisses her*).

NATASHA. Congratulations on the name-day. You have such a big party and I feel awfully shy. . . .

OLGA. Nonsense, we have only our own people. (*In an undertone, in alarm*) You've got on a green sash! My dear, that's not nice!

NATASHA. Why, is that a bad omen?

25

OLGA. No, it's only that it doesn't go with your dress . . . and it looks queer. . . .

NATASHA (*in a tearful voice*). Really? But you know it's not green exactly, it's more a dead colour (*follows* OLGA *into the dining-room*).

(*In the dining-room they are all sitting down to lunch ; there is no one in the drawing-room.*)

KULIGIN. I wish you a good husband, Irina. It's time for you to think of getting married.

TCHEBUTYKIN. Natalya Ivanovna, I hope we may hear of your engagement, too.

KULIGIN. Natalya Ivanovna has got a suitor already.

MASHA (*strikes her plate with her fork*). Ladies and gentlemen, I want to make a speech !

KULIGIN. You deserve three bad marks for conduct.

VERSHININ. How nice this cordial is ! What is it made of ?

SOLYONY. Beetles.

IRINA (*in a tearful voice*). Ugh, ugh ! How disgusting.

OLGA. We are going to have roast turkey and apple pie for supper. Thank God I am at home all day and shall be at home in the evening. . . . Friends, won't you come this evening ?

VERSHININ. Allow me to come too.

IRINA. Please do.

NATASHA. They don't stand on ceremony.

TCHEBUTYKIN. Nature our hearts for love created ! (*laughs*).

ANDREY (*angrily*). Do leave off, I wonder you are not tired of it !

26

(FEDOTIK *and* RODDEY *come in with a big basket of flowers.*)

FEDOTIK. I say, they are at lunch already.

RODDEY (*speaking loudly, with a lisp*). At lunch ? Yes, they are at lunch already. . . .

FEDOTIK. Wait a minute (*takes a snapshot*). One ! Wait another minute . . . (*takes another snapshot*). Two ! Now it's ready. (*They take the basket and walk into the dining-room, where they are greeted noisily*).

RODDEY (*loudly*). My congratulations ! I wish you everything, everything ! The weather is delightful, perfectly magnificent. I've been out all the morning for a walk with the high-school boys. I teach them gymnastics.

FEDOTIK. You may move, Irina Sergeyevna, you may move (*taking a photograph*). You look charming to-day (*taking a top out of his pocket*). Here is a top, by the way. . . . It has a wonderful note. . . .

IRINA. How lovely !

MASHA. By the sea-shore an oak-tree green. . . . Upon that oak a chain of gold . . . (*Complainingly*) Why do I keep saying that ? That phrase has been haunting me all day. . . .

KULIGIN. Thirteen at table !

RODDEY (*loudly*). Surely you do not attach importance to such superstitions ? (*laughter*).

KULIGIN. If there are thirteen at table, it means that someone present is in love. It's not you, Ivan Romanovitch, by any chance ? (*laughter*).

TCHEBUTYKIN. I am an old sinner, but why Natalya Ivanovna is overcome, I can't imagine . . .

(*Loud laughter*; NATASHA *runs out from the dining-room into the drawing-room, followed by* ANDREY.)

ANDREY. Come, don't take any notice! Wait a minute . . . stop, I entreat you. . . .

NATASHA. I am ashamed. . . . I don't know what's the matter with me and they make fun of me. I know it's improper for me to leave the table like this, but I can't help it. . . . I can't . . . (*covers her face with her hands*).

ANDREY. My dear girl, I entreat you, I implore you, don't be upset. I assure you they are only joking, they do it in all kindness. My dear, my sweet, they are all kind, warm-hearted people and they are fond of me and of you. Come here to the window, here they can't see us . . . (*looks round*).

NATASHA. I am so unaccustomed to society! . . .

ANDREY. Oh youth, lovely, marvellous youth! My dear, my sweet, don't be so distressed! Believe me, believe me. . . . I feel so happy, my soul is full of love and rapture. . . . Oh, they can't see us, they can't see us! Why, why I love you, when I first loved you—oh, I don't know. My dear, my sweet, pure one, be my wife! I love you, I love you . . . as I have never loved anyone . . . (*a kiss*).

(*Two officers come in and, seeing the pair kissing, stop in amazement.*)

CURTAIN

28

ACT II

The same scene as in the First Act. Eight o'clock in the evening. Behind the scenes in the street there is the faintly audible sound of a concertina. There is no light. NATALYA IVANOVNA enters in a dressing-gown, carrying a candle; she comes in and stops at the door leading to ANDREY'S room.

NATASHA. What are you doing, Andryusha? Reading? Never mind, I only just asked . . . *(goes and opens another door and, peeping into it, shuts it again).* Is there a light?

ANDREY *(enters with a book in his hand).* What is it, Natasha?

NATASHA. I was looking to see whether there was a light. . . . It's Carnival, the servants are not themselves; one has always to be on the look-out for fear something goes wrong. Last night at twelve o'clock I passed through the dining-room, and there was a candle left burning. I couldn't find out who had lighted it *(puts down the candle).* What's the time?

ANDREY *(looking at his watch).* A quarter past eight.

NATASHA. And Olga and Irina aren't in yet. They haven't come in. Still at work, poor

29

dears! Olga is at the teachers' council and Irina at the telegraph office . . . (*sighs*). I was saying to your sister this morning, "Take care of yourself, Irina darling," said I. But she won't listen. A quarter past eight, you say? I am afraid our Bobik is not at all well. Why is he so cold? Yesterday he was feverish and to-day he is cold all over. . . . I am so anxious!

ANDREY. It's all right, Natasha. The boy is quite well.

NATASHA. We had better be careful about his food, anyway. I am anxious. And I am told that the mummers are going to be here for the Carnival at nine o'clock this evening. It would be better for them not to come, Andryusha.

ANDREY. I really don't know. They've been invited, you know.

NATASHA. Baby woke up this morning, looked at me, and all at once he gave a smile; so he knew me. "Good morning, Bobik!" said I. "Good morning, darling!" And he laughed. Children understand; they understand very well. So I shall tell them, Andryusha, not to let the carnival party come in.

ANDREY (*irresolutely*). That's for my sisters to say. It's for them to give orders.

NATASHA. Yes, for them too; I will speak to them. They are so kind . . . (*is going*). I've ordered junket for supper. The doctor says you must eat nothing but junket, or you will never get thinner (*stops*). Bobik is cold. I am afraid his room is chilly, perhaps. We ought to put him in a different room till the warm weather comes, anyway. Irina's room, for instance, is just right for a nursery : it's dry and the sun shines there all day. I must tell her ; she might share Olga's room for the time. . . . She is never at home, anyway, except for the night . . . (*a pause*). Andryushantchik, why don't you speak ?

ANDREY. Nothing. I was thinking. . . . Besides, I have nothing to say.

NATASHA. Yes . . . what was it I meant to tell you ? . . . Oh, yes ; Ferapont has come from the Rural Board, and is asking for you.

ANDREY (*yawns*). Send him in.

(NATASHA *goes out ;* ANDREY, *bending down to the candle which she has left behind, reads. Enter* FERAPONT *; he wears an old shabby overcoat, with the collar turned up, and has a scarf over his ears.*)

ANDREY. Good evening, my good man. What is it ?

FERAPONT. The Chairman has sent a book and a paper of some sort here . . . (*gives the book and an envelope*).

ANDREY. Thanks. Very good. But why have you come so late ? It is past eight.

FERAPONT. Eh ?

ANDREY (*louder*). I say, you have come late. It is eight o'clock.

FERAPONT. Just so. I came before it was dark, but they wouldn't let me see you. The master is busy, they told me. Well, of course, if you are busy, I am in no hurry (*thinking that* ANDREY *has asked him a question*). Eh ?

ANDREY. Nothing (*examines the book*). To-

31

morrow is Friday. We haven't a sitting, but I'll come all the same . . . and do my work. It's dull at home . . . (*a pause*). Dear old man, how strangely life changes and deceives one! To-day I was so bored and had nothing to do, so I picked up this book—old university lectures—and I laughed. . . . Good heavens! I am the secretary of the Rural Board of which Protopopov is the chairman. I am the secretary, and the most I can hope for is to become a member of the Board! Me, a member of the local Rural Board, while I dream every night· I am professor of the University of Moscow—a distinguished man, of whom all Russia is proud!

FERAPONT. I can't say, sir. . . . I don't hear well. . . .

ANDREY. If you did hear well, perhaps I should not talk to you. I must talk to somebody, and my wife does not understand me. My sisters I am somehow afraid of—I'm afraid they will laugh at me and make me ashamed. . . . I don't drink, I am not fond of restaurants, but how I should enjoy sitting at Tyestov's in Moscow at this moment, dear old chap!

FERAPONT. A contractor was saying at the Board the other day that there were some merchants in Moscow eating pancakes; one who ate forty, it seems, died. It was either forty or fifty, I don't remember.

ANDREY. In Moscow you sit in a huge room at a restaurant; you know no one and no one knows you, and at the same time you don't feel a stranger. . . . But here you know everyone and everyone

knows you, and yet you are a stranger—a stranger.
. . . A stranger, and lonely. . . .

FERAPONT. Eh? (*a pause*). And the same
contractor says—maybe it's not true—that there's
a rope stretched right across Moscow.

ANDREY. What for?

FERAPONT. I can't say, sir. The contractor
said so.

ANDREY. Nonsense (*reads*). Have you ever
been in Moscow?

FERAPONT (*after a pause*). No, never. It was
not God's will I should (*a pause*). Am I to go?

ANDREY. You can go. Good-bye. (FERA-
PONT *goes out.*) Good-bye (*reading*). Come
to-morrow morning and take some papers here.
. . . Go. . . . (*a pause*). He has gone (*a ring*).
Yes, it is a business . . . (*stretches and goes slowly
into his own room*).

> (*Behind the scenes a Nurse is singing, rocking
> a baby to sleep. Enter* MASHA *and*
> VERSHININ. *While they are talking a
> maidservant is lighting a lamp and candles
> in the dining-room.*)

MASHA. I don't know (*a pause*). I don't know.
Of course habit does a great deal. After father's
death, for instance, it was a long time before we
could get used to having no orderlies in the house.
But apart from habit, I think it's a feeling of
justice makes me say so. Perhaps it is not so in
other places, but in our town the most decent,
honourable, and well-bred people are all in the army.

VERSHININ. I am thirsty. I should like some
tea.

MASHA (*glancing at the clock*). They will soon be bringing it. I was married when I was eighteen, and I was afraid of my husband because he was a teacher, and I had only just left school. In those days I thought him an awfully learned, clever, and important person. And now it is not the same, unfortunately. . . .

VERSHININ. Yes. . . . I see. . . .

MASHA. I am not speaking of my husband—I am used to him ; but among civilians generally there are so many rude, ill-mannered, badly-brought-up people. Rudeness upsets and distresses me : I am unhappy when I see that a man is not refined, not gentle, not polite enough. When I have to be among the teachers, my husband's colleagues, it makes me quite miserable.

VERSHININ. Yes. . . . But, to my mind, it makes no difference whether they are civilians or military men—they are equally uninteresting, in this town anyway. It's all the same ! If one listens to a man of the educated class here, civilian or military, he is worried to death by his wife, worried to death by his house, worried to death by his estate, worried to death by his horses. . . . A Russian is peculiarly given to exalted ideas, but why is it he always falls so short in life ? Why ?

MASHA. Why ?

VERSHININ. Why is he worried to death by his children and by his wife ? And why are his wife and children worried to death by him ?

MASHA. You are rather depressed this evening.

VERSHININ. Perhaps. . . . I've had no dinner to-day, and had nothing to eat since the morning.

My daughter is not quite well, and when my little
girls are ill I am consumed by anxiety ; my
conscience reproaches me for having given them
such a mother. Oh, if you had seen her to-day !
She is a wretched creature ! We began quarrelling
at seven o'clock in the morning, and at nine
I slammed the door and went away (*a pause*).
I never talk about it. Strange, it's only to you
I complain (*kisses her hand*). Don't be angry with
me. . . . Except for you I have no one—no
one . . . (*a pause*).

MASHA. What a noise in the stove ! Before
father died there was howling in the chimney.
There, just like that.

VERSHININ. Are you superstitious ?

MASHA. Yes.

VERSHININ. That's strange (*kisses her hand*).
You are a splendid, wonderful woman. Splendid !
Wonderful ! It's dark, but I see the light in your
eyes.

MASHA (*moves to another chair*). It's lighter here.

VERSHININ. I love you—love, love. . . . I love
your eyes, your movements, I see them in my
dreams. . . . Splendid, wonderful woman !

MASHA (*laughing softly*). When you talk to me
like that, for some reason I laugh, though I am
frightened. . . . Please don't do it again . . .
(*In an undertone*) You may say it, though ;
I don't mind . . . (*covers her face with her hands*).
I don't mind. . . . Someone is coming. Talk of
something else.

(IRINA *and* TUSENBACH *come in through the
dining-room.*)

35

TUSENBACH. I've got a three-barrelled name. My name is Baron Tusenbach-Krone-Altschauer, but I belong to the Orthodox Church and am just as Russian as you. There is very little of the German left in me—nothing, perhaps, but the patience and perseverance with which I bore you. I see you home every evening.

IRINA. How tired I am !

TUSENBACH. And every day I will come to the telegraph office and see you home. I'll do it for ten years, for twenty years, till you drive me away . . . (*Seeing* MASHA *and* VERSHININ, *delightedly*) Oh, it's you ! How are you ?

IRINA. Well, I am home at last. (*To* MASHA) A lady came just now to telegraph to her brother in Saratov that her son died to-day, and she could not think of the address. So she sent it without an address—simply to Saratov. She was crying. And I was rude to her for no sort of reason. Told her I had no time to waste. It was so stupid. Are the Carnival people coming to-night ?

MASHA. Yes.

IRINA (*sits down in an arm-chair*). I must rest. I am tired.

TUSENBACH (*with a smile*). When you come from the office you seem so young, so forlorn . . . (*a pause*).

IRINA. I am tired. No, I don't like telegraph work, I don't like it.

MASHA. You've grown thinner . . . (*whistles*). And you look younger, rather like a boy in the face.

TUSENBACH. That's the way she does her hair.

36

IRINA. I must find some other job, this does not suit me. What I so longed for, what I dreamed of is the very thing that it's lacking in. . . . It is work without poetry, without meaning. . . . (*a knock on the floor*). There's the doctor knocking. . . . (*To* TUSENBACH) Do knock, dear. . . . I can't. . . . I am tired.

(TUSENBACH *knocks on the floor*.)

IRINA. He will come directly. We ought to do something about it. The doctor and our Andrey were at the Club yesterday and they lost again. I am told Andrey lost two hundred roubles.

MASHA (*indifferently*). Well, it can't be helped now.

IRINA. A fortnight ago he lost money, in December he lost money. I wish he'd make haste and lose everything, then perhaps we should go away from this town. My God, every night I dream of Moscow, it's perfect madness (*laughs*). We'll move there in June and there is still left February, March, April, May . . . almost half a year.

MASHA. The only thing is Natasha must not hear of his losses.

IRINA. I don't suppose she cares.

(TCHEBUTYKIN, *who has only just got off his bed—he has been resting after dinner—comes into the dining-room combing his beard, then sits down to the table and takes a newspaper out of his pocket.*)

MASHA. Here he is . . . has he paid his rent?

IRINA (*laughs*). No. Not a kopeck for eight months. Evidently he has forgotten.

MASHA (*laughs*). How gravely he sits. (*They all laugh; a pause.*)

IRINA. Why are you so quiet, Alexandr Ignatyevitch?

VERSHININ. I don't know. I am longing for tea. I'd give half my life for a glass of tea. I have had nothing to eat since the morning.

TCHEBUTYKIN. Irina Sergeyevna!

IRINA. What is it?

TCHEBUTYKIN. Come here. *Venez ici.* (IRINA *goes and sits down at the table*). I can't do without you. (IRINA *lays out the cards for patience.*)

VERSHININ. Well, if they won't bring tea, let us discuss something.

TUSENBACH. By all means. What?

VERSHININ. What? Let us dream . . . for instance of the life that will come after us, in two or three hundred years.

TUSENBACH. Well? When we are dead, men will fly in balloons, change the fashion of their coats, will discover a sixth sense, perhaps, and develop it, but life will remain just the same, difficult, full of mysteries and happiness. In a thousand years man will sigh just the same, " Ah, how hard life is," and yet just as now he will be afraid of death and not want it.

VERSHININ (*after a moment's thought*). Well, I don't know. . . . It seems to me that everything on earth is bound to change by degrees and is already changing before our eyes. In two or three hundred, perhaps in a thousand years— the time does not matter—a new, happy life will come. We shall have no share in that life, of

course, but we are living for it, we are working,
well, yes, and suffering for it, we are creating it
—and that alone is the purpose of our existence,
and is our happiness, if you like.

(MASHA *laughs softly*.)

TUSENBACH. What is it ?

MASHA. I don't know. I've been laughing all day.

VERSHININ. I was at the same school as you
were, I did not go to the Military Academy ; I
read a great deal, but I do not know how to choose
my books, and very likely I read quite the wrong
things, and yet the longer I live the more I want
to know. My hair is turning grey, I am almost
an old man, but I know so little, oh so little !
But all the same I fancy that I do know and
thoroughly grasp what is essential and matters
most. And how I should like to make you see
that there is no happiness for us, that there
ought not to be and will not be. . . . We must
work and work, and happiness is the portion
of our remote descendants (*a pause*). If it is not
for me, at least it is for the descendants of my
descendants. . . .

(FEDOTIK *and* RODDEY *appear in the dining-
room ; they sit down and sing softly, playing
the guitar*.)

TUSENBACH. You think it's no use even
dreaming of happiness ! But what if I am happy ?

VERSHININ. No.

TUSENBACH (*flinging up his hands and laughing*).
It is clear we don't understand each other. Well,
how am I to convince you ?

(MASHA *laughs softly*.)

39

TUSENBACH (*holds up a finger to her*). Laugh! (*To* VERSHININ) Not only in two or three hundred years but in a million years life will be just the same; it does not change, it remains stationary, following its own laws which we have nothing to do with or which, anyway, we shall never find out. Migratory birds, cranes for instance, fly backwards and forwards, and whatever ideas, great or small, stray through their minds, they will still go on flying just the same without knowing where or why. They fly and will continue to fly, however philosophic they may become; and it doesn't matter how philosophical they are so long as they go on flying. . . .

MASHA. But still there is a meaning?

TUSENBACH. Meaning. . . . Here it is snowing. What meaning is there in that? (*a pause*).

MASHA. I think man ought to have faith or ought to seek a faith, or else his life is empty, empty. . . . To live and not to understand why cranes fly; why children are born; why there are stars in the sky. . . . One must know what one is living for or else it is all nonsense and waste (*a pause*).

VERSHININ. And yet one is sorry that youth is over. . . .

MASHA. Gogol says: it's dull living in this world, friends!

TUSENBACH. And I say: it is difficult to argue with you, my friends, God bless you. . . .

TCHEBUTYKIN (*reading the newspaper*). Balzac was married at Berditchev.

(IRINA *hums softly.*)

40

TCHEBUTYKIN. I really must put that down in my book (*writes*) Balzac was married at Berditchev (*reads the paper*).

IRINA (*lays out the cards for patience, dreamily*). Balzac was married at Berditchev.

TUSENBACH. The die is cast. You know, Marya Sergeyevna, I've resigned my commission.

MASHA. So I hear. And I see nothing good in that. I don't like civilians.

TUSENBACH. Never mind . . . (*gets up*). I am not good-looking enough for a soldier. But that does not matter, though . . . I am going to work. If only for one day in my life, to work so that I come home at night tired out and fall asleep as soon as I get into bed . . . (*going into the dining-room*). Workmen must sleep soundly!

FEDOTIK (*to* IRINA). I bought these chalks for you just now as I passed the shop. . . . And this penknife. . . .

IRINA. You've got into the way of treating me as though I were little, but I am grown up, you know . . . (*takes the chalks and the penknife, joyfully*). How lovely!

FEDOTIK. And I bought a knife for myself . . . look . . . one blade, and another blade, a third, and this is for the ears, and here are scissors, and that's for cleaning the nails. . . .

RODDEY (*loudly*). Doctor, how old are you?

TCHEBUTYKIN. I? Thirty-two (*laughter*).

FEDOTIK. I'll show you another patience . . . (*lays out the cards*).

> (*The samovar is brought in;* ANFISA *is at the samovar; a little later* NATASHA *comes*

in and is also busy at the table ; SOLYONY
*comes in, and after greeting the others sits
down at the table.)*

VERSHININ. What a wind there is !

MASHA. Yes. I am sick of the winter. I've
forgotten what summer is like.

IRINA. It's coming out right, I see. We shall
go to Moscow.

FEDOTIK. No, it's not coming out. You see,
the eight is over the two of spades *(laughs).* So
that means you won't go to Moscow.

TCHEBUTYKIN *(reads from the newspaper).* Tsi-
tsi-kar. Smallpox is raging here.

ANFISA *(going up to* MASHA*).* Masha, come
to tea, my dear. *(To* VERSHININ*)* Come, your
honour . . . excuse me, sir, I have forgotten your
name. . . .

MASHA. Bring it here, nurse, I am not going
there.

IRINA. Nurse !

ANFISA. I am coming !

NATASHA *(to* SOLYONY*).* Little babies understand very well. " Good morning, Bobik, good
morning, darling," I said. He looked at me in
quite a special way. You think I say that because
I am a mother, but no, I assure you ! He is an
extraordinary child.

SOLYONY. If that child were mine, I'd fry him
in a frying-pan and eat him *(takes his glass, comes
into the drawing-room and sits down in a corner).*

NATASHA *(covers her face with her hands).* Rude,
ill-bred man !

MASHA. Happy people don't notice whether it

is winter or summer.   I fancy if I lived in Moscow I should not mind what the weather was like. . . .

VERSHININ. The other day I was reading the diary of a French minister written in prison.   The minister was condemned for the Panama affair. With what enthusiasm and delight he describes the birds he sees from the prison window, which he never noticed before when he was a minister. Now that he is released, of course he notices birds no more than he did before.   In the same way, you won't notice Moscow when you live in it. We have no happiness and never do have, we only long for it.

TUSENBACH (*takes a box from the table*).   What has become of the sweets ?

IRINA. Solyony has eaten them.

TUSENBACH. All ?

ANFISA (*handing tea*).   There's a letter for you, sir.

VERSHININ. For me ? (*takes the letter*).   From my daughter (*reads*).   Yes, of course. . . .   Excuse me, Marya Sergeyevna, I'll slip away.   I won't have tea (*gets up in agitation*).   Always these upsets. . . .

MASHA. What is it ?   Not a secret ?

VERSHININ (*in a low voice*).   My wife has taken poison again.   I must go.   I'll slip off unnoticed. Horribly unpleasant it all is. (*Kisses* MASHA'S *hand*) My fine, dear, splendid woman. . . . I'll go this way without being seen. . . . (*goes out*).

ANFISA. Where is he off to ?   I've just given him his tea. . . .   What a man.

MASHA (*getting angry*).   Leave off !   Don't

43

pester, you give one no peace . . . (*goes with her cup to the table*). You bother me, old lady.

ANFISA. Why are you so huffy ? Darling !

(*Andrey's voice :* " ANFISA ! ")

ANFISA (*mimicking*). Anfisa ! he sits there. . . . (*goes out*).

MASHA (*by the table in the dining-room, angrily*). Let me sit down ! (*mixes the cards on the table*). You take up all the table with your cards. Drink your tea !

IRINA. How cross you are, Masha !

MASHA. If I'm cross, don't talk to me. Don't interfere with me.

TCHEBUTYKIN (*laughing*). Don't touch her, don't touch her !

MASHA. You are sixty, but you talk rot like a schoolboy.

NATASHA (*sighs*). Dear Masha, why make use of such expressions in conversation ? With your attractive appearance I tell you straight out, you would be simply fascinating in a well-bred social circle if it were not for the things you say. *Je vous prie, pardonnez-moi, Marie, mais vous avez des manières un peu grossières.*

TUSENBACH (*suppressing a laugh*). Give me . . . give me . . . I think there is some brandy there.

NATASHA. *Il paraît que mon Bobik déjà ne dort pas*, he is awake. He is not well to-day. I must go to him, excuse me. . . . (*goes out*).

IRINA. Where has Alexandr Ignatyevitch gone ?

MASHA. Home. Something queer with his wife again.

TUSENBACH (*goes up to* SOLYONY *with a decanter of brandy in his hand*). You always sit alone, thinking, and there's no making out what you think about. Come, let us make it up. Let us have a drink of brandy. (*They drink.*) I shall have to play the piano all night, I suppose, play all sorts of trash. . . . Here goes !

SOLYONY. Why make it up ? I haven't quarrelled with you.

TUSENBACH. You always make me feel as though something had gone wrong between us. You are a queer character, there's no denying that.

SOLYONY (*declaims*). I am strange, who is not strange ! Be not wrath, Aleko !

TUSENBACH. I don't see what Aleko has got to do with it. . . .

SOLYONY. When I am *tête-à-tête* with somebody, I am all right, just like anyone else, but in company I am depressed, ill at ease and . . . say all sorts of idiotic things, but at the same time I am more conscientious and straightforward than many. And I can prove it. . . .

TUSENBACH. I often feel angry with you, you are always attacking me when we are in company, and yet I somehow like you. Here goes, I am going to drink a lot to-day. Let's drink !

SOLYONY. Let us (*drinks*). I have never had anything against you, Baron. But I have the temperament of Lermontov. (*In a low voice*) In fact I am rather like Lermontov to look at . . . so I am told (*takes out scent-bottle and sprinkles scent on his hands*).

TUSENBACH. I have sent in my papers. I've

had enough of it ! I have been thinking of it for five years and at last I have come up to the scratch. I am going to work.

SOLYONY (*declaims*). Be not wrath, Aleko. . . . Forget, forget thy dreams. . . .

> (*While they are talking* ANDREY *comes in quietly with a book and sits down by a candle.*)

TUSENBACH. I am going to work.

TCHEBUTYKIN (*coming into the drawing-room with* IRINA). And the food too was real Caucasian stuff : onion soup and for the meat course *tchehartma*. . . .

SOLYONY. *Tcheremsha* is not meat at all, it's a plant rather like our onion.

TCHEBUTYKIN. No, my dear soul. It's not onion, but mutton roasted in a special way.

SOLYONY. But I tell you that *tcheremsha* is an onion.

TCHEBUTYKIN. And I tell you that *tchehartma* is mutton.

SOLYONY. And I tell you that *tcheremsha* is an onion.

TCHEBUTYKIN. What's the use of my arguing with you ? You have never been to the Caucasus or eaten *tchehartma*.

SOLYONY. I haven't eaten it because I can't bear it. *Tcheremsha* smells like garlic.

ANDREY (*imploringly*). That's enough ! Please !

TUSENBACH. When are the Carnival party coming ?

IRINA. They promised to come at nine, so they will be here directly.

TUSENBACH (*embraces* ANDREY *and sings*). "Oh my porch, oh my new porch . . . "

ANDREY (*dances and sings*). "With posts of maple wood. . . ."

TCHEBUTYKIN (*dances*). "And lattice work complete. . . ." (*laughter*).

TUSENBACH (*kisses* ANDREY). Hang it all, let us have a drink. Andryusha, let us drink to our everlasting friendship. I'll go to the University when you do, Andryusha.

SOLYONY. Which? There are two universities in Moscow.

ANDREY. There is only one university in Moscow.

SOLYONY. I tell you there are two.

ANDREY. There may be three for aught I care. So much the better.

SOLYONY. There are two universities in Moscow! (*a murmur and hisses*). There are two universities in Moscow : the old one and the new one. And if you don't care to hear, if what I say irritates you, I can keep quiet. I can even go into another room (*goes out at one of the doors*).

TUSENBACH. Bravo, bravo! (*laughs*). Friends, begin, I'll sit down and play! Funny fellow that Solyony. . . . (*sits down to the piano and plays a waltz*).

MASHA (*dances a waltz alone*). The baron is drunk, the baron is drunk, the baron is drunk.

(*Enter* NATASHA.)

NATASHA (*to* TCHEBUTYKIN). Ivan Romanitch! (*Says something to* TCHEBUTYKIN, *then goes out softly.* TCHEBUTYKIN *touches* TUSENBACH *on the shoulder and whispers something to him.*)

IRINA. What is it?

TCHEBUTYKIN. It's time we were going. Good night.

TUSENBACH. Good night. It's time to be going.

IRINA. But I say . . . what about the Carnival party?

ANDREY (*with embarrassment*). They won't be coming. You see, dear, Natasha says Bobik is not well, and so . . . In fact I know nothing about it, and don't care either.

IRINA (*shrugs her shoulders*). Bobik is not well!

MASHA. Well, it's not the first time we've had to lump it! If we are turned out, we must go. (*To* IRINA) It's not Bobik that is ill, but she is a bit . . . (*taps her forehead with her finger*). Petty, vulgar creature!

> (ANDREY *goes by door on right to his own room,*
> TCHEBUTYKIN *following him; they are*
> *saying good-bye in the dining-room.*)

FEDOTIK. What a pity! I was meaning to spend the evening, but of course if the child is ill . .˙. I'll bring him a toy to-morrow.

RODDEY (*loudly*). I had a nap to-day after dinner on purpose, I thought I would be dancing all night. . . . Why, it's only nine o'clock.

MASHA. Let us go into the street; there we can talk. We'll decide what to do.

> (*Sounds of "Good-bye! Good night!" The good-*
> *humoured laugh of* TUSENBACH *is heard.*
> *All go out.* ANFISA *and the maidservant*
> *clear the table and put out the light. There*
> *is the sound of the nurse singing.* ANDREY

in his hat and coat, and TCHEBUTYKIN
come in quietly.)

TCHEBUTYKIN. I never had time to get married,
because life has flashed by like lightning and
because I was passionately in love with your
mother, who was married.

ANDREY. One shouldn't get married. One
shouldn't, because it's boring.

TCHEBUTYKIN. That's all very well, but what
about loneliness ? Say what you like, it's a dreadful thing to be lonely, my dear boy. . . . But no
matter, though !

ANDREY. Let's make haste and go.

TCHEBUTYKIN. What's the hurry ? We have
plenty of time.

ANDREY. I am afraid my wife may stop me.

TCHEBUTYKIN. Oh !

ANDREY. I am not going to play to-day, I shall
just sit and look on. I don't feel well. . . . What
am I to do, Ivan Romanitch, I am so short of
breath ?

TCHEBUTYKIN. It's no use asking me ! I don't
remember, dear boy. . . . I don't know. . . .

ANDREY. Let us go through the kitchen. (*They
go out.*)

(*A ring, then another ring ; there is a sound of
voices and laughter.*)

IRINA (*enters*). What is it ?

ANFISA (*in a whisper*). The mummers, all
dressed up (*a ring*).

IRINA. Nurse, dear, say there is no one at home
They must excuse us.

(ANFISA *goes out.* IRINA *walks about the room*

49

  in hesitation; she is excited. Enter
  SOLYONY.)

SOLYONY (*in perplexity*). No one here. . . .
Where are they all ?

IRINA. They have gone home.

SOLYONY How queer. Are you alone here ?

IRINA. Yes (*a pause*). Good night.

SOLYONY. I behaved tactlessly, without suf-
ficient restraint just now. But you are not like
other people, you are pure and lofty, you see the
truth. You alone can understand me. I love
you, I love you deeply, infinitely.

IRINA. Good night ! You must go.

SOLYONY. I can't live without you (*following
her*). Oh, my bliss ! (*through his tears*). Oh,
happiness ! Those glorious, exquisite, marvellous
eyes such as I have never seen in any other woman.

IRINA (*coldly*). Don't, Vassily Vassilyitch !

SOLYONY. For the first time I am speaking of
love to you, and I feel as though I were not on
earth but on another planet (*rubs his forehead*).
But there, it does not matter. There is no forcing
kindness, of course. . . . But there must be no
happy rivals. . . . There must not. . . . I
swear by all that is sacred I will kill any rival. . . .
O exquisite being !

  (NATASHA *passes with a candle*.)

NATASHA (*peeps in at one door, then at another and
passes by the door that leads to her husband's room*).
Andrey is there. Let him read. Excuse me,
Vassily Vassilyitch, I did not know you were here,
and I am in my dressing-gown. . . .

  SOLYONY. I don't care. Good-bye ! (*goes out*).

NATASHA. You are tired, my poor, dear little girl! (*kisses* IRINA). You ought to go to bed earlier. . . .

IRINA. Is Bobik asleep?

NATASHA. He is asleep, but not sleeping quietly. By the way, dear, I keep meaning to speak to you, but either you are out or else I haven't the time. . . . I think Bobik's nursery is cold and damp. And your room is so nice for a baby. My sweet, my dear, you might move for a time into Olya's room!

IRINA (*not understanding*). Where?

> (*The sound of a three-horse sledge with bells driving up to the door.*)

NATASHA. You would be in the same room with Olya, and Bobik in your room. He is such a poppet. I said to him to-day, " Bobik, you are mine, you are mine! " and he looked at me with his funny little eyes. (*A ring.*) That must be Olya. How late she is!

> (*The maid comes up to* NATASHA *and whispers in her ear.*)

NATASHA. Protopopov? What a queer fellow he is! Protopopov has come, and asks me to go out with him in his sledge (*laughs*). How strange men are! . . . (*a ring*). Somebody has come. I might go for a quarter of an hour. . . . (*To the maid*) Tell him I'll come directly. (*A ring*) You hear . . . it must be Olya (*goes out*).

> (*The maid runs out;* IRINA *sits lost in thought;*
> KULIGIN, OLGA *and* VERSHININ *come in.*)

KULIGIN. Well, this is a surprise! They said they were going to have an evening party.

VERSHININ. Strange! And when I went away half an hour ago they were expecting the Carnival people. . . .

IRINA. They have all gone.

KULIGIN. Has Masha gone too? Where has she gone? And why is Protopopov waiting below with his sledge? Whom is he waiting for?

IRINA. Don't ask questions. . . . I am tired.

KULIGIN. Oh, you little cross-patch. . . .

OLGA. The meeting is only just over. I am tired out. Our headmistress is ill and I have to take her place. Oh, my head, my head does ache; oh, my head! (*sits down*). Andrey lost two hundred roubles yesterday at cards. . . . The whole town is talking about it. . . .

KULIGIN. Yes, I am tired out by the meeting too (*sits down*).

VERSHININ. My wife took it into her head to give me a fright, she nearly poisoned herself. It's all right now, and I am glad, it's a relief. . . . So we are to go away? Very well, then, I will say good-night. Fyodor Ilyitch, let us go somewhere together! I can't stay at home, I absolutely can't. . . . Come along!

KULIGIN. I am tired. I am not coming (*gets up*). I am tired. Has my wife gone home?

IRINA. I expect so.

KULIGIN (*kisses* IRINA'S *hand*). Good-bye! I have all day to-morrow and next day to rest. Good-night! (*going*). I do want some tea. I was reckoning on spending the evening in pleasant company. . . . *O fallacem hominum spem!* . . . Accusative of exclamation

VERSHININ. Well, then, I must go alone (*goes out with* KULIGIN, *whistling*).

OLGA. My head aches, oh, how my head aches. . . . Andrey has lost at cards. . . . The whole town is talking about it. . . . I'll go and lie down (*is going*). To-morrow I shall be free. . . . Oh, goodness, how nice that is! To-morrow I am free, and the day after I am free. . . . My head does ache, oh, my head. . . . (*goes out*).

IRINA (*alone*). They have all gone away. There is no one left.

(*A concertina plays in the street, the nurse sings.*)

NATASHA (*in a fur cap and coat crosses the dining-room, followed by the maid*). I shall be back in half an hour. I shall only go a little way (*goes out*).

IRINA (*left alone, in dejection*). Oh, to go to Moscow, to Moscow!

CURTAIN

ACT III

The Bedroom of OLGA *and* IRINA. *On left and right beds with screens round them. Past two o'clock in the night. Behind the scenes a bell is ringing on account of a fire in the town, which has been going on for some time. It can be seen that no one in the house has gone to bed yet. On the sofa* MASHA *is lying, dressed as usual in black. Enter* OLGA *and* ANFISA.

ANFISA. They are sitting below, under the stairs. . . . I said to them, "Come upstairs; why, you mustn't stay there"—they only cried. "We don't know where father is," they said. "What if he is burnt!" What an idea! And the poor souls in the yard . . . they are all undressed too.

OLGA (*taking clothes out of the cupboard*). Take this grey dress . . . and this one . . . and the blouse too . . . and that skirt, nurse. . . . Oh dear, what a dreadful thing! Kirsanov Street is burnt to the ground, it seems. . . . Take this . . . take this . . . (*throws clothes into her arms*). The Vershinins have had a fright, poor things. . . . Their house was very nearly burnt. Let them stay the night here . . . we can't let them go home. . . . Poor Fedotik has had everything burnt, he has not a thing left. . . .

54

ANFISA. You had better call Ferapont, Olya
darling, I can't carry it all. . . .

OLGA (*rings*). No one will answer the bell (*at the
door*). Come here, whoever is there ! (*Through the
open door can be seen a window red with fire ; the
fire brigade is heard passing the house*). How awful
it is ! And how sickening !

(*Enter* FERAPONT.)

OLGA. Here take these, carry them downstairs.
. . . The Kolotilin young ladies are downstairs
. . . give it to them . . . and give this too.

FERAPONT. Yes, miss. In 1812 Moscow was
burnt too. . . . Mercy on us ! The French
marvelled.

OLGA. You can go now.

FERAPONT. Yes, miss (*goes out*).

OLGA. Nurse darling, give them everything.
We don't want anything, give it all to them. . . .
I am tired, I can hardly stand on my feet. . . .
We mustn't let the Vershinins go home. . . . The
little girls can sleep in the drawing-room, and
Alexandr Ignatyevitch down below at the baron's.
. . . Fedotik can go to the baron's, too, or sleep
in our dining-room. . . . As ill-luck will have it,
the doctor is drunk, frightfully drunk, and no one
can be put in his room. And Vershinin's wife can
be in the drawing-room too.

ANFISA (*wearily*). Olya darling, don't send me
away ; don't send me away !

OLGA. That's nonsense, nurse. No one is
sending you away.

ANFISA (*lays her head on* OLGA'S *shoulder*). My
own, my treasure, I work, I do my best. . . .

I'm getting weak, everyone will say " Be off ! "
And where am I to go ? Where ? I am eighty.
Eighty-one.

OLGA. Sit down, nurse darling. . . . You are
tired, poor thing . . . (*makes her sit down*). Rest,
dear good nurse. . . . How pale you are !

(*Enter* NATASHA.)

NATASHA. They are saying we must form a
committee at once for the assistance of those whose
houses have been burnt. Well, that's a good
idea. Indeed, one ought always to be ready to
help the poor, it's the duty of the rich. Bobik
and baby Sophie are both asleep, sleeping as though
nothing were happening. There are such a lot of
people everywhere, wherever one goes, the house
is full. There is influenza in the town now; I am
so afraid the children may get it.

OLGA (*not listening*). In this room one does not
see the fire, it's quiet here.

NATASHA. Yes . . . my hair must be untidy
(*in front of the looking-glass*) They say I have
grown fatter . . . but it's not true ! Not a bit !
Masha is asleep, she is tired out, poor dear . . .
(*To* ANFISA, *coldly*) Don't dare to sit down in
my presence ! Get up ! Go out of the room !
ANFISA *goes out*; *a pause*). Why you keep that old
woman, I can't understand !

OLGA (*taken aback*). Excuse me, I don't understand either. . . .

NATASHA. She is no use here. She is a peasant;
she ought to be in the country. . . . You spoil
people ! I like order in the house ! There ought
to be no useless servants in the house (*strokes her*

cheek). You are tired, poor darling. Our head-mistress is tired ! When baby Sophie is a big girl and goes to the high-school, I shall be afraid of you.

OLGA. I shan't be headmistress.

NATASHA. You will be elected, Olya. That's a settled thing.

OLGA. I shall refuse. I can't. . . . It's too much for me . . . (*drinks water*). You were so rude to nurse just now. . . . Excuse me, I can't endure it. . . . It makes me feel faint.

NATASHA (*perturbed*). Forgive me, Olya ; for-give me. . . . I did not mean to hurt your feelings.

(MASHA *gets up, takes her pillow, and goes out in a rage.*)

OLGA. You must understand, my dear, it may be that we have been strangely brought up, but I can't endure it. . . . Such an attitude oppresses me, it makes me ill. . . . I feel simply unnerved by it. . . .

NATASHA. Forgive me ; forgive me . . . (*kisses her*).

OLGA. The very slightest rudeness, a tactless word, upsets me . . .

NATASHA. I often say too much, that's true, but you must admit, dear, that she might just as well be in the country.

OLGA. She has been thirty years with us.

NATASHA. But now she can't work ! Either I don't understand, or you won't understand me. She is not fit for work. She does nothing but sleep or sit still.

OLGA. Well, let her sit still.

NATASHA (*surprised*). How, sit still? Why, she is a servant. (*Through tears*) I don't understand you, Olya. I have a nurse to look after the children as well as a wet nurse for baby, and we have a housemaid and a cook, what do we want that old woman for? What's the use of her?

(*The alarm bell rings behind the scenes.*)

OLGA. This night has made me ten years older.

NATASHA. We must come to an understanding, Olya. You are at the high-school, I am at home; you are teaching while I look after the house, and if I say anything about the servants, I know what I'm talking about; I do know what I am talking about. . . . And that old thief, that old hag . . . (*stamps*), that old witch shall clear out of the house to-morrow! . . . I won't have people annoy me! I won't have it! (*feeling that she has gone too far*). Really, if you don't move downstairs, we shall always be quarrelling. It's awful.

(*Enter* KULIGIN.)

KULIGIN. Where is Masha? It's time to be going home. The fire is dying down, so they say (*stretches*). Only one part of the town has been burnt, and yet there was a wind; it seemed at first as though the whole town would be destroyed (*sits down*). I am exhausted. Olya, my dear . . . I often think if it had not been for Masha I should have married you. You are so good. . . . I am tired out (*listens*).

OLGA. What is it?

KULIGIN. It is unfortunate the doctor should have a drinking bout just now; he is helplessly

58

drunk. Most unfortunate (*gets up*). Here he comes, I do believe. . . . Do you hear ? Yes, he is coming this way . . . (*laughs*). What a man he is, really. . . . I shall hide (*goes to the cupboard and stands in the corner*). Isn't he a ruffian !

OLGA. He has not drunk for two years and now he has gone and done it . . . (*walks away with* NATASHA *to the back of the room*).

> (TCHEBUTYKIN *comes in ; walking as though sober without staggering, he walks across the room, stops, looks round ; then goes up to the washing-stand and begins to wash his hands.*)

TCHEBUTYKIN (*morosely*). The devil take them all . . . damn them all. They think I am a doctor, that I can treat all sorts of complaints, and I really know nothing about it, I have forgotten all I did know, I remember nothing, absolutely nothing (OLGA *and* NATASHA *go out unnoticed by him*). The devil take them. Last Wednesday I treated a woman at Zasyp—she died, and it's my fault that she died. Yes . . . I did know something twenty-five years ago, but now I remember nothing, nothing. Perhaps I am not a man at all but only pretend to have arms and legs and head ; perhaps I don't exist at all and only fancy that I walk about, eat and sleep (*weeps*). Oh, if only I did not exist ! (*leaves off weeping, morosely*). I don't care ! I don't care a scrap ! (*a pause*). Goodness knows. . . . The day before yesterday there was a conversation at the club : they talked about Shakespeare, Voltaire. . . . I have read nothing, nothing at all, but I looked as though I had read them. And the others did the same as I did. The vulgarity ! The meanness ! And that woman I killed on Wednesday came back to my mind . . . and it all came back to my mind and everything seemed nasty, disgusting and all awry in my soul. . . . I went and got drunk. . . .

(*Enter* IRINA, VERSHININ *and* TUSENBACH ; TUSENBACH *is wearing a fashionable new civilian suit.*)

IRINA. Let us sit here. No one will come here.

VERSHININ. If it had not been for the soldiers, the whole town would have been burnt down. Splendid fellows ! (*rubs his hands with pleasure*). They are first-rate men ! Splendid fellows !

KULIGIN (*going up to them*). What time is it ?

TUSENBACH. It's past three. It's getting light already.

IRINA. They are all sitting in the dining-room. No one seems to think of going. And that Solyony of yours is sitting there too. . . . (*To* TCHE-BUTYKIN) You had better go to bed, doctor.

TCHEBUTYKIN. It's all right. . . . Thank you ! (*combs his beard*).

KULIGIN (*laughs*). You are a bit fuddled, Ivan Romanitch ! (*slaps him on the shoulder*). Bravo ! *In vino veritas*, the ancients used to say.

TUSENBACH. Everyone is asking me to get up a concert for the benefit of the families whose houses have been burnt down.

IRINA. Why, who is there ? . . .

TUSENBACH. We could get it up, if we wanted to. Marya Sergeyevna plays the piano splendidly, to my thinking.

KULIGIN. Yes, she plays splendidly.

IRINA. She has forgotten. She has not played for three . . . or four years.

TUSENBACH. There is absolutely no one who understands music in this town, not one soul, but I do understand and on my honour I assure you that Marya Sergeyevna plays magnificently, almost with genius.

KULIGIN. You are right, Baron. I am very fond of her ; Masha, I mean. She is a good sort.

TUSENBACH. To be able to play so gloriously and to know that no one understands you !

KULIGIN (*sighs*). Yes. . . . But would it be suitable for her to take part in a concert ? (*a pause*). I know nothing about it, my friends. Perhaps it would be all right. There is no denying that our director is a fine man, indeed a very fine man, very intelligent, but he has such views. . . . Of course it is not his business, still if you like I'll speak to him about it.

(TCHEBUTYKIN *takes up a china clock and examines it.*)

VERSHININ. I got dirty all over at the fire. I am a sight (*a pause*). I heard a word dropped yesterday about our brigade being transferred ever so far away. Some say to Poland, and others to Tchita.

TUSENBACH. I've heard something about it too. Well ! The town will be a wilderness then.

IRINA. We shall go away too.

TCHEBUTYKIN (*drops the clock, which smashes*). To smithereens !

KULIGIN (*picking up the pieces*). To smash such a valuable thing—oh, Ivan Romanitch, Ivan

Romanitch! I should give you minus zero for conduct!

IRINA. That was mother's clock.

TCHEBUTYKIN. Perhaps. . . . Well, if it was hers, it was. Perhaps I did not smash it, but it only seems as though I had. Perhaps it only seems to us that we exist, but really we are not here at all. I don't know anything—nobody knows anything. (*By the door*) What are you staring at? Natasha has got a little affair on with Protopopov, and you don't see it. . . . You sit here and see nothing, while Natasha has a little affair on with Protopopov . . . (*sings*). May I offer you this date? . . . (*goes out*).

VERSHININ. Yes . . . (*laughs*). How very queer it all is, really! (*a pause*). When the fire began I ran home as fast as I could. I went up and saw our house was safe and sound and out of danger, but my little girls were standing in the doorway in their nightgowns; their mother was nowhere to be seen, people were bustling about, horses and dogs were running about, and my children's faces were full of alarm, horror, entreaty, and I don't know what; it wrung my heart to see their faces. My God, I thought, what more have these children to go through in the long years to come! I took their hands and ran along with them, and could think of nothing else but what more they would have to go through in this world! (*a pause*). When I came to your house I found their mother here, screaming, angry.

(MASHA *comes in with the pillow and sits down on the sofa.*)

VERSHININ. And while my little girls were standing in the doorway in their nightgowns and the street was red with the fire, and there was a fearful noise, I thought that something like it used to happen years ago when the enemy would suddenly make a raid and begin plundering and burning. . . . And yet, in reality, what a difference there is between what is now and has been in the past ! And when a little more time has passed—another two or three hundred years—people will look at our present manner of life with horror and derision, and everything of to-day will seem awkward and heavy, and very strange and uncomfortable. Oh, what a wonderful life that will be—what a wonderful life ! (*laughs*). Forgive me, here I am airing my theories again ! Allow me to go on. I have such a desire to talk about the future. I am in the mood (*a pause*). It's as though everyone were asleep. And so, I say, what a wonderful life it wi.l be ! Can you only imagine ? . . . Here there are only three of your sort in the town now, but in generations to come there will be more and more and more; and the time will come when everything will be changed and be as you would have it ; they will live in your way, and later on you too will be out of date—people will be born who will be better than you. . . . (*laughs*). I am in such a strange state of mind to-day. I have a fiendish longing for life. . . . (*sings*). Young and old are bound by love, and precious are its pangs . . . (*laughs*).

MASHA. Tram-tam-tam !

VERSHININ. Tam-tam !

MASHA. Tra-ra-ra ?

VERSHININ. Tra-ta-ta ! *(laughs)*.

(Enter FEDOTIK.)

FEDOTIK *(dances)*. Burnt to ashes ! Burnt to ashes ! Everything I had in the world *(laughter)*.

IRINA. A queer thing to joke about. Is everything burnt ?

FEDOTIK *(laughs)*. Everything I had in the world. Nothing is left. My guitar is burnt, and the camera and all my letters. . . . And the notebook I meant to give you—that's burnt too.

(Enter SOLYONY.)

IRINA. No ; please go, Vassily Vassilyitch. You can't stay here.

SOLYONY. How is it the baron can be here and I can't ?

VERSHININ. We must be going, really. How is the fire ?

SOLYONY. They say it is dying down. No, I really can't understand why the baron may be here and not I *(takes out a bottle of scent and sprinkles himself)*.

VERSHININ. Tram-tam-tam !

MASHA. Tram-tam !

VERSHININ *(laughs, to* SOLYONY). Let us go into the dining-room.

SOLYONY. Very well ; we'll make a note of it. I might explain my meaning further, but fear I may provoke the geese . . . *(looking at* TUSEN-BACH). Chook, chook, chook ! . . . *(goes out with* VERSHININ *and* FEDOTIK).

IRINA. How that horrid Solyony has made

the room smell of tobacco ! . . . (*In surprise*)
The baron is asleep ! Baron, baron !

TUSENBACH (*waking up*). I am tired, though.
. . . The brickyard. I am not talking in my
sleep. I really am going to the brickyard directly,
to begin work. . . . It's nearly settled. (*To
IRINA, tenderly*) You are so pale and lovely and
fascinating. . . . It seems to me as though your
paleness sheds a light through the dark air. . . .
You are melancholy; you are dissatisfied with
life. . . . Ah, come with me; let us go and work
together !

MASHA. Nikolay Lvovitch, do go !

TUSENBACH (*laughing*). Are you here ? I
didn't see you . . . (*kisses IRINA's hand*). Good-
bye, I am going. . . . I look at you now, and I
remember as though it were long ago how on your
name-day you talked of the joy of work, and were
so gay and confident. . . . And what a happy
life I was dreaming of then ! What has become
of it ? (*kisses her hand*). There are tears in your
eyes. Go to bed, it's getting light . . . it is
nearly morning. . . . If it were granted to me
to give my life for you !

MASHA. Nikolay Lvovitch, do go ! Come,
really. . . .

TUSENBACH. I am going (*goes out*).

MASHA (*lying down*). Are you asleep, Fyodor ?

KULIGIN. Eh ?

MASHA. You had better go home.

KULIGIN. My darling Masha, my precious
girl ! . . .

IRINA. She is tired out. Let her rest, Fedya.

KULIGIN. I'll go at once. . . . My dear, charming wife! . . . I love you, my only one! . . .

MASHA (*angrily*). *Amo, amas, amat; amamus, amatis, amant.*

KULIGIN (*laughs*). Yes, really she is wonderful. You have been my wife for seven years, and it seems to me as though we were only married yesterday. Honour bright! Yes, really you are a wonderful woman! I am content, I am content, I am content!

MASHA. I am bored, I am bored, I am bored! . . . (*gets up and speaks, sitting down*). And there's something I can't get out of my head. . . . It's simply revolting. It sticks in my head like a nail; I must speak of it. I mean about Andrey. . . . He has mortgaged this house in the bank and his wife has grabbed all the money, and you know the house does not belong to him alone, but to us four! He ought to know that, if he is a decent man.

KULIGIN. Why do you want to bother about it, Masha? What is it to you? Andryusha is in debt all round, so there it is.

MASHA. It's revolting, anyway (*lies down*).

KULIGIN. We are not poor. I work—I go to the high-school, and then I give private lessons. . . . I do my duty. . . . There's no nonsense about me. *Omnia mea mecum porto,* as the saying is.

MASHA. I want nothing, but it's the injustice that revolts me (*a pause*). Go, Fyodor.

KULIGIN (*kisses her*). You are tired, rest for

half an hour, and I'll sit and wait for you. . . .
Sleep . . . (*goes*). I am content, I am content,
I am content (*goes out*).

IRINA. Yes, how petty our Andrey has grown,
how dull and old he has become beside that
woman! At one time he was working to get
a professorship and yesterday he was boasting of
having succeeded at last in becoming a member
of the Rural Board. He is a member, and Protopopov is chairman. . . . The whole town is
laughing and talking of it and he is the only one
who sees and knows nothing. . . . And here
everyone has been running to the fire while he
sits still in his room and takes no notice. He does
nothing but play his violin . . . (*nervously*). Oh,
it's awful, awful, awful! (*weeps*). I can't bear
it any more, I can't! I can't, I can't!

(OLGA *comes in and begins tidying up her
table.*)

IRINA (*sobs loudly*). Turn me out, turn me
out, I can't bear it any more!

OLGA (*alarmed*). What is it? What is it,
darling?

IRINA (*sobbing*). Where? Where has it all
gone? Where is it? Oh, my God, my God!
I have forgotten everything, everything . . .
everything is in a tangle in my mind. . . . I
don't remember the Italian for window or ceiling. . . . I am forgetting everything; every day
I forget something more and life is slipping away
and will never come back, we shall never, never
go to Moscow. . . . I see that we shan't go. . . .

OLGA. Darling, darling. . . .

IRINA (*restraining herself*). Oh, I am wretched. . . . I can't work, I am not going to work. I have had enough of it, enough of it ! I have been a telegraph clerk and now I have a job in the town council and I hate and despise every bit of the work they give me. . . . I am nearly twenty-four, I have been working for years, my brains are drying up, I am getting thin and old and ugly and there is nothing, nothing, not the slightest satisfaction, and time is passing and one feels that one is moving away from a real, fine life, moving farther and farther away and being drawn into the depths. I am in despair and I don't know how it is I am alive and have not killed myself yet. . . .

OLGA. Don't cry, my child, don't cry. It makes me miserable.

IRINA. I am not crying, I am not crying. . . . It's over. . . . There, I am not crying now. I won't . . . I won't.

OLGA. Darling, I am speaking to you as a sister, as a friend, if you care for my advice, marry the baron !

(IRINA *weeps*.)

OLGA (*softly*). You know you respect him, you think highly of him. . . . It's true he is ugly, but he is such a thoroughly nice man, so good. . . . One doesn't marry for love, but to do one's duty. . . . That's what I think, anyway, and I would marry without love. Whoever proposed to me I would marry him, if only he were a good man. . . . I would even marry an old man. . . .

IRINA. I kept expecting we should move to Moscow and there I should meet my real one. I've been dreaming of him, loving him. . . . But it seems that was all nonsense, nonsense. . . .

OLGA (*puts her arms round her sister*). My darling, lovely sister, I understand it all; when the baron left the army and came to us in a plain coat, I thought he looked so ugly that it positively made me cry. . . . He asked me, "Why are you crying?" How could I tell him! But if God brought you together I should be happy. That's a different thing you know, quite different.

(NATASHA *with a candle in her hand walks across the stage from door on right to door on left without speaking.*)

MASHA (*sits up*). She walks about as though it were she had set fire to the town.

OLGA. Masha, you are silly. The very silliest of the family, that's you. Please forgive me (*a pause*).

MASHA. I want to confess my sins, dear sisters. My soul is yearning. I am going to confess to you and never again to anyone. . . . I'll tell you this minute (*softly*). It's my secret, but you must know everything. . . . I can't be silent . . . (*a pause*). I am in love, I am in love. . . . I love that man. . . . You have just seen him. . . . Well, I may as well say it straight out. I love Vershinin.

OLGA (*going behind her screen*). Leave off. I don't hear anyway.

MASHA. But what am I to do? (*clutches her head*). At first I thought him queer . . . then

I was sorry for him . . . then I came to love him . . . to love him with his voice, his words, his misfortunes, his two little girls. . . .

OLGA (*behind the screen*). I don't hear you anyway. Whatever silly things you say I shan't hear them.

MASHA. Oh, Olya, you are silly. I love him— so that's my fate. It means that that's my lot. . . . And he loves me. . . . It's all dreadful. Yes? Is it wrong? (*takes* IRINA *by the hand and draws her to herself*). Oh, my darling. . . . How are we going to live our lives, what will become of us? . . . When one reads a novel it all seems stale and easy to understand, but when you are in love yourself you see that no one knows anything and we all have to settle things for ourselves. . . . My darling, my sister. . . . I have confessed it to you, now I'll hold my tongue. . . . I'll be like Gogol's madman . . . silence . . . silence. . . .

(*Enter* ANDREY *and after him* FERAPONT.)

ANDREY (*angrily*). What do you want? I can't make it out.

FERAPONT (*in the doorway, impatiently*). I've told you ten times already, Andrey Sergeyevitch.

ANDREY. In the first place I am not Andrey Sergeyevitch, but your honour, to you!

FERAPONT. The firemen ask leave, your honour, to go through the garden on their way to the river. Or else they have to go round and round, an awful nuisance for them.

ANDREY. Very good. Tell them, very good. (FERAPONT *goes out*.) I am sick of them. Where

is Olga? (OLGA *comes from behind the screen*.)
I've come to ask you for the key of the cupboard,
I have lost mine. You've got one, it's a little
key.

(OLGA *gives him the key in silence ;* IRINA
goes behind her screen ; a pause.)

ANDREY. What a tremendous fire ! Now it's
begun to die down. Hang it all, that Ferapont
made me so cross I said something silly to him.
Your honour . . . (*a pause*). Why don't you
speak, Olya? (*a pause*). It's time to drop this
foolishness and sulking all about nothing. . . .
You are here, Masha, and you too, Irina—very
well, then, let us have things out thoroughly, once
for all. What have you against me? What
is it ?

OLGA. Leave off, Andryusha. Let us talk
to-morrow (*nervously*). What an agonising night !

ANDREY (*greatly confused*). Don't excite yourself. I ask you quite coolly, what have you
against me ? Tell me straight out.

(VERSHININ'S *voice : Tram-tam-tam !*)

MASHA (*standing up, loudly*). Tra-ta-ta ! (*To*
OLGA) Good night, Olya, God bless you . . .
(*goes behind the screen and kisses* IRINA). Sleep
well. . . . Good night, Andrey. You'd better
leave them now, they are tired out . . . you can
go into things to-morrow (*goes out*).

OLGA. Yes, really, Andryusha, let us put it
off till to-morrow . . . (*goes behind her screen*).
It's time we were in bed.

ANDREY. I'll say what I have to say and then
go. Directly. . . . First, you have something

71

against Natasha, my wife, and I've noticed that from the very day of my marriage. Natasha is a splendid woman, conscientious, straightforward and honourable—that's my opinion! I love and respect my wife, do you understand? I respect her, and I insist on other people respecting her too. I repeat, she is a conscientious, honourable woman, and all your disagreements are simply caprice, or. rather the whims of old maids. Old maids never like and never have liked their sisters-in-law—that's the rule (*a pause*). Secondly, you seem to be cross with me for not being a professor, not working at something learned. But I am in the service of the Zemstvo, I am a member of the Rural Board, and I consider this service just as sacred and elevated as the service of learning. I am a member of the Rural Board and I am proud of it, if you care to know . . . (*a pause*). Thirdly . . . there's something else I have to say. . . . I have mortgaged the house without asking your permission. . . . For that I am to blame, yes, and I ask your pardon for it. I was driven to it by my debts . . . thirty-five thousand. . . . I am not gambling now—I gave up cards long ago ; but the chief thing I can say in self-defence is that you are, so to say, of the privileged sex—you get a pension . . . while I had not . . . my wages, so to speak . . . (*a pause*).

KULIGIN (*at the door*). Isn't Masha here ? (*Perturbed*) Where is she ? It's strange . . . (*goes out*).

ANDREY. They won't listen. Natasha is an excellent, conscientious woman (*paces up and*

72

down the stage in silence, then stops). When I married her, I thought we should be happy . . . happy, all of us. . . . But, my God ! (*weeps*). Dear sisters, darling sisters, you must not believe what I say, you mustn't believe it . . . (*goes out*).

KULIGIN (*at the door, uneasily*). Where is Masha ? Isn't Masha here ? How strange ! (*goes out*).

(*The firebell rings in the street. The stage is empty.*)

IRINA (*behind the screen*). Olya ! Who is that knocking on the floor ?

OLGA. It's the doctor, Ivan Romanitch. He is drunk.

IRINA. What a troubled night ! (*a pause*). Olya ! (*peeps out from behind the screen*). Have you heard ? The brigade is going to be taken away ; they are being transferred to some place very far off.

OLGA. That's only a rumour.

IRINA. Then we shall be alone. . . . Olya !

OLGA. Well ?

IRINA. My dear, my darling, I respect the baron, I think highly of him, he is a fine man—I will marry him, I consent, only let us go to Moscow ! I entreat you, do let us go ! There's nothing in the world better than Moscow ! Let us go, Olya ! Let us go !

CURTAIN

ACT IV

Old garden of the PROZOROVS' *house. A long avenue of fir trees, at the end of which is a view of the river. On the further side of the river there is a wood. On the right the verandah of the house ; on the table in it are bottles and glasses ; evidently they have just been drinking champagne. It is twelve o'clock in the day. People pass occasionally from the street across the garden to the river ; five soldiers pass rapidly.*

TCHEBUTYKIN, *in an affable mood, which persists throughout the act, is sitting in an easy chair in the garden, waiting to be summoned ; he is wearing a military cap and has a stick.* IRINA, KULIGIN *with a decoration on his breast and with no moustache, and* TUSENBACH, *standing on the verandah, are saying good-bye to* FEDOTIK *and* RODDEY, *who are going down the steps ; both officers are in marching uniform.*

TUSENBACH (*kissing* FEDOTIK). You are a good fellow ; we've got on so happily together. (*Kisses* RODDEY) Once more. . . . Good-bye, my dear boy. . . .

IRINA. Till we meet again !

FEDOTIK. No, it's good-bye for good ; we shall never meet again.

KULIGIN. Who knows! (*wipes his eyes, smiles*). Here I am crying too.

IRINA. We shall meet some day.

FEDOTIK. In ten years, or fifteen perhaps? But then we shall scarcely recognise each other—we shall greet each other coldly . . . (*Takes a snapshot*) Stand still. . . . Once more, for the last time.

RODDEY (*embraces* TUSENBACH). We shall not see each other again . . . (*kisses* IRINA'S *hand*). Thank you for everything, everything. . . .

FEDOTIK (*with vexation*). Oh, do wait!

TUSENBACH. Please God we shall meet again. Write to us. Be sure to write to us.

RODDEY (*taking a long look at the garden*). Good-bye, trees! (*Shouts*) Halloo! (*a pause*). Good-bye, echo!

KULIGIN. I shouldn't wonder if you get married in Poland. . . . Your Polish wife will clasp you in her arms and call you *kochany!* (*laughs*).

FEDOTIK (*looking at his watch*). We have less than an hour. Of our battery only Solyony is going on the barge; we are going with the rank and file. Three divisions of the battery are going to-day and three more to-morrow—and peace and quiet will descend upon the town.

TUSENBACH. And dreadful boredom too.

RODDEY. And where is Marya Sergeyevna?

KULIGIN. Masha is in the garden.

FEDOTIK. We must say good-bye to her.

RODDEY. Good-bye. We must go, or I shall begin to cry . . . (*hurriedly embraces* TUSENBACH *and* KULIGIN *and kisses* IRINA'S *hand*). We've had a splendid time here.

FEDOTIK (*to* KULIGIN). This is a little souvenir for you . . . a notebook with a pencil. . . . We'll go down here to the river . . . (*As they go away both look back.*)

RODDEY (*shouts*). Halloo-oo !

KULIGIN (*shouts*). Good-bye !

>   (RODDEY *and* FEDOTIK *meet* MASHA *in the background and say good-bye to her ; she walks away with them.*)

IRINA. They've gone . . . (*sits down on the bottom step of the verandah*).

TCHEBUTYKIN. They have forgotten to say good-bye to me.

IRINA. And what were you thinking about ?

TCHEBUTYKIN. Why, I somehow forgot, too. But I shall see them again soon, I am setting off to-morrow. Yes . . . I have one day more. In a year I shall be on the retired list. Then I shall come here again and shall spend the rest of my life near you. . . . There is only one year now before I get my pension (*puts a newspaper into his pocket and takes out another*). I shall come here to you and arrange my life quite differently. . . . I shall become such a quiet . . . God-fearing . . . well-behaved person.

IRINA. Well, you do need to arrange your life differently, dear Ivan Romanitch. You certainly ought to somehow.

TCHEBUTYKIN. Yes, I feel it. (*Softly hums*) " Tarara-boom-dee-ay—Tarara-boom-dee-ay."

KULIGIN. Ivan Romanitch is incorrigible ! Incorrigible !

TCHEBUTYKIN. You ought to take me in hand. Then I should reform.

IRINA. Fyodor has shaved off his moustache. I can't bear to look at him !

KULIGIN. Why, what's wrong ?

TCHEBUTYKIN. I might tell you what your countenance looks like now, but I really can't.

KULIGIN. Well ! It's the thing now, *modus vivendi*. Our head-master is clean-shaven and now I am second to him I have taken to shaving too. Nobody likes it, but I don't care. I am content. With moustache or without moustache I am equally content (*sits down*).

(*In the background* ANDREY *is wheeling a baby asleep in a perambulator.*)

IRINA. Ivan Romanitch, darling, I am dreadfully uneasy. You were on the boulevard yesterday, tell me what was it that happened ?

TCHEBUTYKIN. What happened ? Nothing. Nothing much (*reads the newspaper*). It doesn't matter !

KULIGIN. The story is that Solyony and the baron met yesterday on the boulevard near the theatre. . . .

TUSENBACH. Oh, stop it ! Really . . . (*with a wave of his hand walks away into the house*).

KULIGIN. Near the theatre. . . . Solyony began pestering the baron and he couldn't keep his temper and said something offensive. . . .

TCHEBUTYKIN. I don't know. It's all nonsense.

KULIGIN. A teacher at a divinity school wrote "nonsense" at the bottom of an essay and the pupil puzzled over it thinking it was a Latin

word . . . (*laughs*). It was fearfully funny. . . .
They say Solyony is in love with Irina and hates
the baron. . . . That's natural. Irina is a very
nice girl.

(*From the background behind the scenes,
" A a-oo ! Halloo ! "*)

IRINA (*starts*). Everything frightens me somehow to-day (*a pause*). All my things are ready,
after dinner I shall send off my luggage. The
baron and I are to be married to-morrow, to-
morrow we go to the brickyard and the day
after that I shall be in the school. A new life
is beginning. God will help me! How will it
fare with me ? When I passed my exam. as a
teacher I felt so happy, so blissful, that I cried . . .
(*a pause*). The cart will soon be coming for my
things. . . .

KULIGIN. That's all very well, but it does not
seem serious. It's all nothing but ideas and very
little that is serious. However, I wish you success
with all my heart.

TCHEBUTYKIN (*moved to tenderness*). My good,
delightful darling. . . . My heart of gold. . . .

KULIGIN. Well, to-day the officers will be gone
and everything will go on in the old way. Whatever people may say, Masha is a true, good woman.
I love her dearly and am thankful for my lot ! . . .
People have different lots in life. . . . There is
a man called Kozyrev serving in the Excise here.
He was at school with me, but he was expelled
from the fifth form because he could never understand *ut consecutivum*. Now he is frightfully poor
and ill, and when I meet him I say, " How are

78

you, *ut consecutivum* ? " "Yes," he says, " just so—*consecutivum* " . . . and then he coughs. . . . Now I have always been successful, I am fortunate, I have even got the order of the Stanislav of the second degree and I am teaching others that *ut consecutivum*. Of course I am clever, cleverer than very many people, but happiness does not lie in that . . . (*a pause*).

(*In the house the "Maiden's Prayer" is played on the piano*.)

IRINA. To-morrow evening I shall not be hearing that " Maiden's Prayer," I shan't be meeting Protopopov . . . (*a pause*). Protopopov is sitting there in the drawing-room ; he has come again to-day. . . .

KULIGIN. The head-mistress has not come yet ?

IRINA. No. They have sent for her. If only you knew how hard it is for me to live here alone, without Olya. . . . Now that she is head-mistress and lives at the high-school and is busy all day long, I am alone, I am bored, I have nothing to do, and I hate the room I live in. . . . I have made up my mind, since I am not fated to be in Moscow, that so it must be. It must be destiny. There is no help for it. . . . It's all in God's hands, that's the truth. When Nikolay Lvovitch made me an offer again . . . I thought it over and made up my mind. . . . He is a good man, it's wonderful really how good he is. . . . And I suddenly felt as though my soul had grown wings, my heart felt so light and again I longed for work, work. . . . Only something happened yesterday, there is some mystery hanging over me.

79

TCHEBUTYKIN. Nonsense.

NATASHA (*at the window*). Our head-mistress!

KULIGIN. The head-mistress has come. Let us go in (*goes into the house with* IRINA).

TCHEBUTYKIN (*reads the newspaper, humming softly*). " Tarara-boom-dee-ay."

    (MASHA *approaches; in the background* ANDREY *is pushing the perambulator.*)

MASHA. Here he sits, snug and settled.

TCHEBUTYKIN. Well, what then?

MASHA (*sits down*). Nothing . . . (*a pause*). Did you love my mother?

TCHEBUTYKIN. Very much.

MASHA. And did she love you?

TCHEBUTYKIN (*after a pause*). That I don't remember.

MASHA. Is my man here? It's just like our cook Marfa used to say about her policeman: is my man here?

TCHEBUTYKIN. Not yet.

MASHA. When you get happiness by snatches, by little bits, and then lose it, as I am losing it, by degrees one grows coarse and spiteful . . . (*Points to her bosom*) I'm boiling here inside . . . (*Looking at* ANDREY, *who is pushing the perambulator*) Here is our Andrey. . . . All our hopes are shattered. Thousands of people raised the bell, a lot of money and of labour was spent on it, and it suddenly fell and smashed. All at once, for no reason whatever. That's just how it is with Andrey. . . .

ANDREY. When will they be quiet in the house? There is such a noise.

TCHEBUTYKIN. Soon (*looks at his watch*). My watch is an old-fashioned one with a repeater . . . (*winds his watch, it strikes*). The first, the second, and the fifth batteries are going at one o'clock (*a pause*). And I am going to-morrow.

ANDREY. For good?

TCHEBUTYKIN. I don't know. Perhaps I shall come back in a year. Though goodness knows.
. . . It doesn't matter one way or another.

(*There is the sound of a harp and violin being played far away in the street.*)

ANDREY. The town will be empty. It's as though one put an extinguisher over it (*a pause*). Something happened yesterday near the theatre; everyone is talking of it, and I know nothing about it.

TCHEBUTYKIN. It was nothing. Foolishness. Solyony began annoying the baron and he lost his temper and insulted him, and it came in the end to Solyony's having to challenge him (*looks at his watch*). It's time, I fancy. . . . It was to be at half-past twelve in the Crown forest that we can see from here beyond the river . . . Piff-paff! (*laughs*). Solyony imagines he is a Lermontov and even writes verses. Joking apart, this is his third duel.

MASHA. Whose?

TCHEBUTYKIN. Solyony's.

MASHA. And the baron's?

TCHEBUTYKIN. What about the baron? (*a pause*).

MASHA. My thoughts are in a muddle. . . . Anyway, I tell you, you ought not to let them do it. He may wound the baron or even kill him.

81

TCHEBUTYKIN. The baron is a very good fellow, but one baron more or less in the world, what does it matter? Let them! It doesn't matter. (*Beyond the garden a shout of " Aa-oo! Halloo!"*) You can wait. That is Skvortsov, the second, shouting. He is in a boat (*a pause*).

ANDREY. In my opinion to take part in a duel, or to be present at it even in the capacity of a doctor, is simply immoral.

TCHEBUTYKIN. That only seems so. . . . We are not real, nothing in the world is real, we don't exist, but only seem to exist. . . . Nothing matters!

MASHA. How they keep on talking, talking all day long (*goes*). To live in such a climate, it may snow any minute, and then all this talk on the top of it (*stops*). I am not going indoors, I can't go in there. . . . When Vershinin comes, tell me . . . (*goes down the avenue*). And the birds are already flying south . . . (*looks up*). Swans or geese. . . . Darlings, happy things. . . . (*goes out*).

ANDREY. Our house will be empty. The officers are going, you are going, Irina is getting married, and I shall be left in the house alone.

TCHEBUTYKIN. What about your wife?
(*Enter* FERAPONT *with papers.*)

ANDREY. A wife is a wife. She is a straightforward, upright woman, good-natured, perhaps, but for all that there is something in her which makes her no better than some petty, blind, hairy animal. Anyway she is not a human being. I speak to you as to a friend, the one man to whom I can open my soul. I love Natasha, that is so, but sometimes she seems to me wonderfully vulgar, and then I don't know what to think, I can't account for my loving her or, anyway, having loved her.

TCHEBUTYKIN (*gets up*). I am going away to-morrow, my boy, perhaps we shall never meet again, so this is my advice to you. Put on your cap, you know, take your stick and walk off . . . walk off and just go, go without looking back. And the further you go, the better (*a pause*). But do as you like ! It doesn't matter. . . .

(SOLYONY *crosses the stage in the background with two officers; seeing* TCHEBUTYKIN *he turns towards him; the officers walk on.*)

SOLYONY. Doctor, it's time ! It's half-past twelve (*greets* ANDREY).

TCHEBUTYKIN. Directly. I am sick of you all. (*To* ANDREY) If anyone asks for me, Andryusha, say I'll be back directly . . . (*sighs*). Oho-ho-ho !

SOLYONY. He had not time to say alack before the bear was on his back (*walks away with the doctor*). Why are you croaking, old chap ?

TCHEBUTYKIN. Come !

SOLYONY. How do you feel ?

TCHEBUTYKIN (*angrily*). Like a pig in clover.

SOLYONY. The old chap need not excite himself. I won't do anything much, I'll only shoot him like a snipe (*takes out scent and sprinkles his hands*). I've used a whole bottle to-day, and still they smell. My hands smell like a corpse (*a pause*). Yes. . . . Do you remember the poem ? " And, restless, seeks the stormy ocean, as though in tempest there were peace." . . .

TCHEBUTYKIN. Yes. He had not time to say alack before the bear was on his back (*goes out with* SOLYONY. *Shouts are heard:* "*Halloo! Oo-oo!*" ANDREY *and* FERAPONT *come in*).

FERAPONT. Papers for you to sign. . . .

ANDREY (*nervously*). Let me alone! Let me alone! I entreat you! (*walks away with the perambulator*).

FERAPONT. That's what the papers are for—to be signed (*retires into the background*).

(*Enter* IRINA *and* TUSENBACH *wearing a straw hat;* KULIGIN *crosses the stage shouting* "*Aa-oo, Masha, aa-oo!*")

TUSENBACH. I believe that's the only man in the town who is glad that the officers are going away.

IRINA. That's very natural (*a pause*). Our town will be empty now.

TUSENBACH. Dear, I'll be back directly.

IRINA. Where are you going?

TUSENBACH. I must go into the town, and then . . . to see my comrades off.

IRINA. That's not true. . . . Nikolay, why are you so absent-minded to-day? (*a pause*). What happened yesterday near the theatre?

TUSENBACH (*with a gesture of impatience*). I'll be here in an hour and with you again (*kisses her hands*). My beautiful one . . . (*looks into her face*). For five years now I have loved you and still I can't get used to it, and you seem to me more and more lovely. What wonderful, exquisite hair! What eyes! I shall carry you off to-morrow, we will work, we will be rich, my dreams will come true. You shall be happy. There is only one thing, one thing : you don't love me !

IRINA. That's not in my power ! I'll be your wife and be faithful and obedient, but there is no love, I can't help it (*weeps*). I've never been in love in my life ! Oh, I have so dreamed of love, I've been dreaming of it for years, day and night, but my soul is like a wonderful piano of which the key has been lost (*a pause*). You look uneasy.

TUSENBACH. I have not slept all night. There has never been anything in my life so dreadful that it could frighten me, and only that lost key frets at my heart and won't let me sleep. . . . Say something to me . . . (*a pause*). Say something to me. . . .

IRINA. What ? What am I to say to you ? What ?

TUSENBACH. Anything.

IRINA. There, there ! (*a pause*).

TUSENBACH. What trifles, what little things suddenly *à propos* of nothing acquire importance in life ! One laughs at them as before, thinks them nonsense, but still one goes on and feels that one has not the power to stop. Don't let us talk about it ! I am happy. I feel as though I were seeing these pines, these maples, these birch-trees for the first time in my life, and they all seem to be looking at me with curiosity and waiting. What beautiful trees, and, really, how beautiful life ought to be under them ! (*A shout of " Halloo ! Aa-oo ! "*). I must be off ; it's time. . . . See, that tree is dead, but it waves in the wind with the others. And so it seems to me that if I die I shall

85

still have part in life, one way or another. Good-bye, my darling . . . (*kisses her hands*). Those papers of yours you gave me are lying under the calendar on my table.

IRINA. I am coming with you.

TUSENBACH (*in alarm*). No, no! (*goes off quickly, stops in the avenue*). Irina!

IRINA. What is it?

TUSENBACH (*not knowing what to say*). I didn't have any coffee this morning. Ask them to make me some (*goes out quickly*).

(IRINA *stands lost in thought, then walks away into the background of the scene and sits down on the swing. Enter* ANDREY *with the perambulator, and* FERAPONT *comes into sight.*)

FERAPONT. Andrey Sergeyevitch, the papers aren't mine; they are Government papers. I didn't invent them.

ANDREY. Oh, where is it all gone? What has become of my past, when I was young, gay, and clever, when my dreams and thoughts were exquisite, when my present and my past were lighted up by hope? Why on the very threshold of life do we become dull, grey, uninteresting, lazy, indifferent, useless, unhappy? . . . Our town has been going on for two hundred years—there are a hundred thousand people living in it; and there is not one who is not like the rest, not one saint in the past, or the present, not one man of learning, not one artist, not one man in the least remarkable who could inspire envy or a passionate desire to imitate him. . . . They only eat, drink, sleep, and then die . .

others are born, and they also eat and drink and sleep, and not to be bored to stupefaction they vary their lives by nasty gossip, vodka, cards, litigation; and the wives deceive their husbands, and the husbands tell lies and pretend that they see and hear nothing, and an overwhelmingly vulgar influence weighs upon the children, and the divine spark is quenched in them and they become the same sort of pitiful, dead creatures, all exactly alike, as their fathers and mothers . . . (*To* FERAPONT, *angrily*) What do you want?

FERAPONT. Eh? There are papers to sign.

ANDREY. You bother me!

FERAPONT (*handing him the papers*). The porter from the local treasury was saying just now that there was as much as two hundred degrees of frost in Petersburg this winter.

ANDREY. The present is hateful, but when I think of the future, it is so nice! I feel so light-hearted, so free. A light dawns in the distance, I see freedom. I see how I and my children will become free from sloth, from kvass, from goose and cabbage, from sleeping after dinner, from mean, parasitic living. . . .

FERAPONT. He says that two thousand people were frozen to death. The people were terrified. It was either in Petersburg or Moscow, I don't remember.

ANDREY (*in a rush of tender feeling*). My dear sisters, my wonderful sisters! (*through tears*). Masha, my sister!

NATASHA (*in the window*). Who is talking so loud out there? Is that you, Andryusha? You will wake baby Sophie. *Il ne faut pas faire de bruit, la Sophie est dormée déjà. Vous êtes un ours* (*getting angry*). If you want to talk, give the perambulator with the baby to somebody else. Ferapont, take the perambulator from the master !

FERAPONT. Yes, ma'am (*takes the pram*).

ANDREY (*in confusion*). I am talking quietly.

NATASHA (*petting her child, inside the room*). Bobik ! Naughty Bobik ! Little rascal !

ANDREY (*looking through the papers*). Very well, I'll look through them and sign what wants signing, and then you can take them back to the Board . . . (*goes into the house reading the papers ; FERAPONT pushes the pram farther into the garden*).

NATASHA (*speaking indoors*). Bobik, what is mamma's name ? Darling, darling ! And who is this ? This is auntie Olya. Say to auntie, " Good morning, Olya ! "

> (*Two wandering musicians, a man and a girl, enter and play a violin and a harp ; from the house enter VERSHININ with OLGA and ANFISA, and stand for a minute listening in silence ; IRINA comes up.*)

OLGA. Our garden is like a public passage ; they walk and ride through. Nurse, give those people something.

ANFISA (*gives money to the musicians*). Go away, and God bless you, my dear souls ! (*the musicians bow and go away*). Poor things. People don't play if they have plenty to eat. (*To IRINA*) Good morning, Irisha ! (*kisses her*). Aye, aye, my little girl, I am having a time of it ! Living in the high-school, in a government flat, with dear Olya—that's what the Lord has vouchsafed me in my old age! I have never lived so well in my life, sinful woman that I am. . . . It's a big flat, and I have a room to myself and a bedstead. All at the government expense. I wake up in the night and, O Lord, Mother of God, there is no one in the world happier than I!

VERSHININ (*looks at his watch*). We are just going, Olga Sergeyevna. It's time to be off (*a pause*). I wish you everything, everything. . . . Where is Marya Sergeyevna?

IRINA. She is somewhere in the garden. . . . I'll go and look for her.

VERSHININ. Please be so good. I am in a hurry.

ANFISA. I'll go and look for her too. (*Shouts*) Mashenka, aa-oo! (*goes with* IRINA *into the farther part of the garden*). Aa-oo! Aa-oo!

VERSHININ. Everything comes to an end. Here we are parting (*looks at his watch*). The town has given us something like a lunch; we have been drinking champagne, the mayor made a speech. I ate and listened, but my heart was here, with you all . . . (*looks round the garden*). I've grown used to you. . . .

OLGA. Shall we ever see each other again?

VERSHININ. Most likely not (*a pause*). My wife and two little girls will stay here for another two months; please, if anything happens, if they need anything . . .

OLGA. Yes, yes, of course. Set your mind at rest (*a pause*). By to-morrow there won't be a soldier in the town—it will all turn into a memory, and of course for us it will be like beginning a new life . . . (*a pause*). Nothing turns out as we would have it. I did not want to be a head-mistress, and yet I am. It seems we are not to live in Moscow. . . .

VERSHININ. Well. . . . Thank you for everything. . . . Forgive me if anything was amiss. . . . I have talked a great deal : forgive me for that too—don't remember evil against me.

OLGA (*wipes her eyes*). Why doesn't Masha come ?

VERSHININ. What else am I to say to you at parting ? What am I to theorise about ? . . . (*laughs*). Life is hard. It seems to many of us blank and hopeless ; but yet we must admit that it goes on getting clearer and easier, and it looks as though the time were not far off when it will be full of happiness (*looks at his watch*). It's time for me to go ! In old days men were absorbed in wars, filling all their existence with marches, raids, victories, but now all that is a thing of the past, leaving behind it a great void which there is so far nothing to fill : humanity is searching for it passionately, and of course will find it. Ah, if only it could be quickly ! (*a pause*). If, don't you know, industry were united with culture and culture with industry. . . . (*Looks at his watch*) But, I say, it's time for me to go. . . .

OLGA. Here she comes.

(MASHA *comes in*.)

VERSHININ. I have come to say good-bye. . . .

(OLGA *moves a little away to leave them free to say good-bye*.)

90

MASHA (*looking into his face*). Good-bye . . .
(*a prolonged kiss*).

OLGA. Come, come. . . .

(MASHA *sobs violently*.)

VERSHININ. Write to me. . . . Don't forget
me ! Let me go ! . . . . Time is up ! . . . Olga
Sergeyevna, take her, I must . . . go . . . I am
late . . . (*much moved, kisses* OLGA'S *hands ; then
again embraces* MASHA *and quickly goes off*).

OLGA. Come, Masha ! Leave off, darling.

(*Enter* KULIGIN.)

KULIGIN (*embarrassed*). Never mind, let her
cry—let her. . . . My good Masha, my dear
Masha ! . . . You are my wife, and I am happy,
anyway. . . . I don't complain ; I don't say a
word of blame. . . . Here Olya is my witness.
. . . We'll begin the old life again, and I won't
say one word, not a hint. . . .

MASHA (*restraining her sobs*). By the sea-
strand an oak-tree green. . . . Upon that oak a
chain of gold. . . . Upon that oak a chain of
gold. . . . I am going mad. . . . By the sea-
strand . . . an oak-tree green. . . .

OLGA. Calm yourself, Masha. . . . Calm yourself. . . . Give her some water.

MASHA. I am not crying now. . . .

KULIGIN. She is not crying now . . . she is
good. . . .

(*The dim sound of a far-away shot*.) . .

MASHA. By the sea-strand an oak-tree green,
upon that oak a chain of gold. . . . The cat is
green. . . . the oak is green. . . . I am mixing
it up . . . (*drinks water*). My life is a failure. . . .

91

I want nothing now. . . . I shall be calm directly.
. . . It doesn't matter. . . . What does "strand"
mean ? Why do these words haunt me ? My
thoughts are in a tangle.

(*Enter* IRINA.)

OLGA. Calm yourself, Masha. Come, that's a
good girl. Let us go indoors.

MASHA (*angrily*). I am not going in. Let me
alone ! (*sobs, but at once checks herself*). I don't go
into that house now and I won't.

IRINA. Let us sit together, even if we don't
say anything. I am going away to-morrow, you
know . . . (*a pause*).

KULIGIN. I took a false beard and moustache
from a boy in the third form yesterday, just look
. . . (*puts on the beard and moustache*). I look
like the German teacher . . . (*laughs*). Don't I ?
Funny creatures, those boys.

MASHA. You really do look like the German
teacher.

OLGA (*laughs*). Yes.

(MASHA *weeps*.)

IRINA. There, Masha !

KULIGIN. Awfully like. . . .

(*Enter* NATASHA.)

NATASHA (*to the maid*). What ? Mr. Protopopov will sit with Sophie, and let Andrey Sergey-
itch wheel Bobik up and down. What a lot there
is to do with children . . . (*To* IRINA) Irina, you
are going away to-morrow, what a pity. Do stay
just another week (*seeing* KULIGIN *utters a
shriek ; the latter laughs and takes off the beard and
moustache*). Well, what next, you gave me such

melle ivers.

a fright! (*To* IRINA) I am used to you and do you suppose that I don't feel parting with you? I shall put Andrey with his violin into your room— let him saw away there!—and we will put baby Sophie in his room. Adorable, delightful baby! Isn't she a child! To-day she looked at me with such eyes and said " Mamma "!

KULIGIN. A fine child, that's true.

NATASHA. So to-morrow I shall be all alone here (*sighs*). First of all I shall have this avenue of fir-trees cut down, and then that maple. . . . It looks so ugly in the evening. . . . (*To* IRINA) My dear, that sash does not suit you at all. . . . It's in bad taste. You want something light. And then I shall have flowers, flowers planted everywhere, and there will be such a scent. . . . (*Severely*) Why is there a fork lying about on that seat? (*Going into the house, to the maid*) Why is there a fork lying about on this seat, I ask you? (*Shouts*) Hold your tongue!

KULIGIN. She is at it!

(*Behind the scenes the band plays a march; they all listen.*)

OLGA. They are going.

(*Enter* TCHEBUTYKIN.)

MASHA. Our people are going. Well . . . a happy journey to them! (*To her husband*) We must go home. . . . Where are my hat and cape?

KULIGIN. I took them into the house . . . I'll get them directly. . . .

OLGA. Yes, now we can go home, it's time.

TCHEBUTYKIN. Olga Sergeyevna!

OLGA. What is it? (*a pause*) What?

TCHEBUTYKIN. Nothing. . . . I don't know how to tell you (*whispers in her ear*).

OLGA (*in alarm*). It can't be!

TCHEBUTYKIN. Yes . . . such a business. . . . I am so worried and worn out, I don't want to say another word . . . (*with vexation*). But there, it doesn't matter!

MASHA. What has happened?

OLGA (*puts her arms round* IRINA). This is a terrible day. . . . I don't know how to tell you, my precious. . . .

IRINA. What is it? Tell me quickly, what is it? For God's sake! (*cries*).

TCHEBUTYKIN. The baron has just been killed in a duel.

IRINA (*weeping quietly*). I knew, I knew. . . .

TCHEBUTYKIN (*in the background of the scene sits down on a garden seat*). I am worn out . . . (*takes a newspaper out of his pocket*). Let them cry. . . . (*Sings softly*). "Tarara-boom-dee-ay" . . . It doesn't matter.

(*The three sisters stand with their arms round one another.*)

MASHA. Oh, listen to that band! They are going away from us; one has gone altogether, gone forever. We are left alone to begin our life over again. . . . We've got to live . . . we've got to live. . . .

IRINA (*lays her head on* OLGA'S *bosom*). A time will come when everyone will know what all this is for, why there is this misery; there will be no mysteries and, meanwhile, we have got to live . . . we have got to work, only to work! To-morrow

I shall go alone ; I shall teach in the school, and I will give all my life to those to whom it may be of use. Now it's autumn ; soon winter will come and cover us with snow, and I will work, I will work.

OLGA (*embraces both her sisters*). The music is so gay, so confident, and one longs for life ! O my God ! Time will pass, and we shall go away for ever, and we shall be forgotten, our faces will be forgotten, our voices, and how many there were of us; but our sufferings will pass into joy for those who will live after us, happiness and peace will be established upon earth, and they will remember kindly and bless those who have lived before. Oh, dear sisters, our life is not ended yet. We shall live ! The music is so gay, so joyful, and it seems as though a little more and we shall know what we are living for, why we are suffering. . . . If we only knew—if we only knew !

(*The music grows more and more subdued ; KULIGIN, cheerful and smiling, brings the hat and cape ; ANDREY pushes the perambulator in which Bobik is sitting.*)

TCHEBUTYKIN (*humming softly*). " Tararaboom-dee-ay ! " (*reads his paper*). It doesn't matter, it doesn't matter.

OLGA. If we only knew, if we only knew !

CURTAIN

UNCLE VANYA
SCENES FROM COUNTRY LIFE, IN FOUR ACTS
First performed in 1899

CHARACTERS IN THE PLAY

ALEXANDR VLADIMIROVITCH SEREBRYAKOV (*a retired Professor*).

YELENA ANDREYEVNA (*his wife, aged 27*).

SOFYA ALEXANDROVNA (SONYA) (*his daughter by his first wife*).

MARYA VASSILYEVNA VOYNITSKY (*widow of a Privy Councillor and mother of Professor's first wife*).

IVAN PETROVITCH VOYNITSKY (*her son*).

MIHAIL LVOVITCH ASTROV (*a Doctor*).

ILYA ILYITCH TELYEGIN (*a Landowner reduced to poverty*).

MARINA (*an old Nurse*).

A LABOURER.

The action takes place on SEREBRYAKOV'S *estate*

*Garden. Part of the house can be seen with the
verandah. In the avenue under an old poplar
there is a table set for tea. Garden seats and
chairs; on one of the seats lies a guitar. Not
far from the table there is a swing. Between
two and three o'clock on a cloudy afternoon.*

MARINA, *a heavy old woman, slow to move, is sitting
by the samovar, knitting a stocking, and* ASTROV
is walking up and down near her.

MARINA (*pours out a glass of tea*). Here, drink
it, my dear.

ASTROV (*reluctantly takes the glass*). I don't feel
much like it.

MARINA. Perhaps you would have a drop of
vodka?

ASTROV. No. I don't drink vodka every day.
Besides, it's so sultry (*a pause*). Nurse, how many
years have we known each other?

MARINA (*pondering*). How many? The Lord
help my memory. . . . You came into these parts . . .
when? Vera Petrovna, Sonitchka's mother, was
living then. You came to see us two winters before
she died. . . . Well, that must be eleven years ago.
(*After a moment's thought*) Maybe even more. . . .

ASTROV. Have I changed much since then?

99

MARINA. Very much. You were young and handsome in those days, and now you have grown older. And you are not as good-looking. There's another thing too—you take a drop of vodka now.

ASTROV. Yes. . . . In ten years I have become a different man. And what's the reason of it ? I am overworked, nurse. From morning till night I am always on my legs, not a moment of rest, and at night one lies under the bedclothes in continual terror of being dragged out to a patient. All these years that you have known me I have not had one free day. I may well look old ! And the life in itself is tedious, stupid, dirty. . . . This life swallows one up completely. There are none but queer people about one—they are a queer lot, all of them—and when one has lived two or three years among them, by degrees one turns queer too, without noticing it. It's inevitable (*twisting his long moustache*). Ough, what a huge moustache I've grown . . . a stupid moustache. . . . I've turned into a queer fish, nurse. I haven't grown stupid yet, thank God ! My brains are in their place, but my feelings are somehow blunter. There is nothing I want, nothing I care about, no one I am fond of . . . except you, perhaps—I am fond of you (*kisses her on the head*). I had a nurse like you when I was a child.

MARINA. Perhaps you would like something to eat ?

ASTROV. No. In the third week of Lent I went to Malitskoe, where there was an epidemic . . . spotted typhus . . . in the huts the people were lying about in heaps. There was filth, stench, smoke . . . calves on the ground with the sick . . . little pigs about too. I was hard at work all day, did not sit down for a minute, and hadn't a morsel of food, and when I got home they wouldn't let me rest. They brought me a signalman from the line. I laid him on the table to operate upon him, and he went and died under the chloroform. And just when they weren't wanted, my feelings seemed to wake up again, and I was as conscience-stricken as though I had killed him on purpose. I sat down, shut my eyes like this, and thought : those who will live a hundred or two hundred years after us, for whom we are struggling now to beat out a road, will they remember and say a good word for us ? Nurse, they won't, you know !

MARINA. Men will not remember, but God will remember.

ASTROV. Thank you for that. That's a good saying.

(*Enter* VOYNITSKY.)

VOYNITSKY (*comes out of the house ; he has had a nap after lunch and looks rumpled ; he sits down on the garden-seat and straightens his fashionable tie*). Yes . . . (*a pause*). Yes. . . .

ASTROV. Had a good sleep ?

VOYNITSKY. Yes . . . very (*yawns*). Ever since the Professor and his wife have been here our life has been turned topsy-turvy. I sleep at the wrong time, at lunch and dinner I eat all sorts of messes, I drink wine—it's not good for one ! In old days I never had a free moment. Sonya and I used to work in grand style, but now Sonya works alone, while I sleep and eat and drink. It's bad !

MARINA (*shaking her head*). Such goings-on ! The Professor gets up at twelve o'clock, and the samovar is boiling all the morning waiting for him. Before they came we always had dinner about one o'clock, like other people, and now they are here we have it between six and seven. The Professor spends the night reading and writing, and all at once, at two o'clock in the morning, he'll ring his bell. Goodness me ! What is it ? Tea ! People have to be waked out of their sleep to get him the samovar. What goings-on !

ASTROV. And will they be here much longer ?

VOYNITSKY (*whistles*). A hundred years. The Professor has made up his mind to settle here.

MARINA. Look now ! The samovar has been on the table for the last two hours, and they've gone for a walk.

VOYNITSKY. They are coming. They are coming ! Don't worry.

(*There is a sound of voices ; from the farther part of the garden enter* SEREBRYAKOV, YELENA ANDREYEVNA, SONYA *and* TELYEGIN *returning from a walk.*)

SEREBRYAKOV. Lovely, lovely ! . . . Exquisite views !

TELYEGIN. Remarkable, your Excellency.

SONYA. We'll go to the plantation to-morrow, father. Shall we ?

VOYNITSKY. Tea is ready !

SEREBRYAKOV. My friends, be so kind as to send

102

mette ivers.

my tea into the study for me. I have something more I must do to-day.

SONYA. You will be sure to like the plantation.

(YELENA ANDREYEVNA, SEREBRYAKOV, *and* SONYA *go into the house.* TELYEGIN *goes to the table and sits down beside* MARINA.)

VOYNITSKY. It's hot, stifling; but our great man of learning is in his greatcoat and goloshes, with an umbrella and gloves too.

ASTROV. That shows that he takes care of himself.

VOYNITSKY. And how lovely she is! How lovely! I've never seen a more beautiful woman.

TELYEGIN. Whether I drive through the fields, Marina Timofyevna, or walk in the shady garden, or look at this table, I feel unutterably joyful. The weather is enchanting, the birds are singing, we are all living in peace and concord—what more could one wish for? (*taking his glass*). I am truly grateful to you!

VOYNITSKY (*dreamily*). Her eyes . . . an exquisite woman!

ASTROV. Tell us something, Ivan Petrovitch.

VOYNITSKY (*listlessly*). What am I to tell you?

ASTROV. Is there nothing new?

VOYNITSKY. Nothing. Everything is old. I am just as I always was, perhaps worse, for I have grown lazy. I do nothing but just grumble like some old crow. My old magpie *Maman* is still babbling about the rights of women. With one foot in the grave, she is still rummaging in her learned books for the dawn of a new life.

ASTROV. And the Professor?

VOYNITSKY. The Professor, as before, sits in his study writing from morning till dead of night. " With furrowed brow and racking brains, We write and write and write, And ne'er a word of praise we hear, Our labours to requite." Poor paper ! He had much better be writing his autobiography. What a superb subject ! A retired professor, you know—an old dry-as-dust, a learned fish. Gout, rheumatism, migraine, envy and jealousy have affected his liver. The old fish is living on his first wife's estate, living there against his will because he can't afford to live in the town. He is forever complaining of his misfortunes, though, as a matter of fact, he is exceptionally fortunate. (*Nervously*) Just think how fortunate ! The son of a humble sacristan, he has risen to university distinctions and the chair of a professor ; he has become " your Excellency," the son-in-law of a senator, and so on, and so on. All that is no great matter, though. But just take this. The man has been lecturing and writing about art for twenty-five years, though he knows absolutely nothing about art. For twenty-five years he has been chewing over other men's ideas about realism, naturalism, and all sorts of nonsense ; for twenty-five years he has been lecturing and writing on things all intelligent people know about already and stupid ones aren't interested in—so for twenty-five years he has been simply wasting his time. And with all that, what conceit ! What pretensions ! He has retired, and not a living soul knows anything about him ; he is absolutely unknown. So that for twenty-five years all he

104

has done is to keep a better man out of a job!
But just look at him : he struts about like a
demi-god !

ASTROV. Come, I believe you are envious.

VOYNITSKY. Yes, I am. And the success he
has with women ! Don Juan is not in it. His
first wife, my sister, a lovely, gentle creature, pure
as this blue sky, noble, generous, who had more
suitors than he has had pupils, loved him as only
pure angels can love beings as pure and beautiful
as themselves. My mother adores him to this
day, and he still inspires in her a feeling of devout
awe. His second wife, beautiful, intelligent—you
have just seen her—has married him in his old
age, sacrificed her youth, her beauty, her freedom,
her brilliance, to him. What for ? Why ?

ASTROV. Is she faithful to the Professor ?

VOYNITSKY. Unhappily, she is.

ASTROV. Why unhappily ?

VOYNITSKY. Because that fidelity is false from
beginning to end. There is plenty of fine sentiment in it, but no logic. To deceive an old
husband whom one can't endure is immoral ; but
to try and stifle her piteous youth and living feeling
—that's not immoral.

TELYEGIN (*in a tearful voice*). Vanya, I can't
bear to hear you talk like that. Come, really !
Anyone who can betray wife or husband is a
person who can't be trusted and who might betray
his country.

VOYNITSKY (*with vexation*). Dry up, Waffles !

TELYEGIN. Excuse me, Vanya. My wife ran
away from me with the man she loved the day

105

after our wedding, on the ground of my unpre-
possessing appearance. But I have never been
false to my vows. I love her to this day and am
faithful to her. I help her as far as I can, and I
gave all I had for the education of her children by
the man she loved. I have lost my happiness,
but my pride has been left to me. And she?
Her youth is over, her beauty, in accordance with
the laws of nature, has faded, the man she loved
is dead. . . . What has she left?

(*Enter* SONYA *and* YELENA ANDREYEVNA *and
a little later*, MARYA VASSILYEVNA *with a
book; she sits down and reads. They
hand her tea, and she drinks it without
looking at it.*)

SONYA (*hurriedly to the nurse*). Nurse, darling,
some peasants have come. Go and speak to them.
I'll look after the tea.

(*Exit Nurse.* YELENA ANDREYEVNA *takes her
cup and drinks it sitting in the swing.*)

ASTROV (*to* YELENA ANDREYEVNA). I've come
to see your husband. You wrote to me that he
was very ill—rheumatism and something else—
but it appears he is perfectly well.

YELENA. Last night he was poorly, complain-
ing of pains in his legs, but to-day he is all right. . . .

ASTROV. And I have galloped twenty miles at
break-neck speed! But there, it doesn't matter!
it's not the first time. I shall stay with you
till to-morrow to make up for it, and anyway I
shall sleep *quantum satis*.

SONYA. That's splendid! It's not often you stay
the night with us. I expect you've not had dinner?

106

ASTROV. No, I haven't.

SONYA. Oh, well, you will have some dinner, then! We have dinner now between six and seven (*drinks tea*). The tea is cold!

TELYEGIN. The temperature in the samovar has perceptibly dropped.

YELENA. Never mind, Ivan Ivanitch; we will drink it cold.

TELYEGIN. I beg your pardon, I am not Ivan Ivanitch, but Ilya Ilyitch—Ilya Ilyitch Telyegin, or, as some people call me on account of my pockmarked face, Waffles. I stood godfather to Sonetchka, and his Excellency, your husband, knows me very well. I live here now on your estate. If you've been so kind as to observe it, I have dinner with you every day.

SONYA. Ilya Ilyitch is our helper, our right hand. (*Tenderly*) Let me give you another cup, godfather.

MARYA. Ach!

SONYA. What is it, grandmamma?

MARYA. I forgot to tell Alexandr—I am losing my memory—I got a letter to-day from Harkov, from Pavel Alexeyevitch . . . he has sent his new pamphlet.

ASTROV. Is it interesting?

MARYA. It's interesting, but it's rather queer. He is attacking what he himself maintained seven years ago. It's awful.

VOYNITSKY. There's nothing awful in it. Drink your tea, *maman*.

MARYA. But I want to talk.

VOYNITSKY. But we have been talking and

talking for fifty years and reading pamphlets. It's about time to leave off.

MARYA. You don't like listening when I speak ; I don't know why. Forgive my saying so, Jean, but you have so changed in the course of the last year that I hardly know you. You used to be a man of definite principles, of elevating ideas.

VOYNITSKY. Oh, yes ! I was a man of elevating ideas which elevated nobody (*a pause*). . . . A man of elevating ideas . . . you could not have made a more malignant joke ! Now I am forty-seven. Till last year I tried, like you, to blind myself with all your pedantic rubbish on purpose to avoid seeing life as it is—and thought I was doing the right thing. And now, if only you knew ! I can't sleep at night for vexation, for rage that I so stupidly wasted the time when I might have had everything from which my age now shuts me out.

SONYA. Uncle Vanya, it's so dreary !

MARYA (*to her son*). You seem to be blaming your former principles. It is not they that are to blame, but yourself. You forget that principles alone are no use—a dead letter. You ought to have been working.

VOYNITSKY. Working ? It is not everyone who can be a writing machine like your Herr Professor.

MARYA. What do you mean by that ?

SONYA (*in an imploring voice*). Grandmamma ! Uncle Vanya ! I entreat you !

VOYNITSKY. I'll hold my tongue—hold my tongue and apologise.

(A pause.)

108

YELENA. What a fine day ! It's not too hot.
>   (*A pause.*)

VOYNITSKY. A fine day to hang oneself !

>   (TELYEGIN *tunes the guitar.* MARINA *walks to
>   and fro near the house, calling a hen.*)

MARINA. Chook, chook, chook !

SONYA. Nurse, darling, what did the peasants come about ?

MARINA. It's the same thing—about the waste land again. Chook, chook, chook !

SONYA. Which is it you are calling ?

MARINA. Speckly has gone off somewhere with her chickens. . . . The crows might get them (*walks away*).

>   (TELYEGIN *plays a polka ; they all listen to him
>   in silence. Enter a labourer.*)

LABOURER. Is the doctor here ? (*To* ASTROV) If you please, Mihail Lvovitch, they have sent for you.

ASTROV. Where from ?

LABOURER. From the factory.

ASTROV (*with vexation*). Much obliged to you. Well, I suppose I must go (*looks round him for his cap*). What a nuisance, hang it !

SONYA. How annoying it is, really ! Come back from the factory to dinner.

ASTROV. No. It will be too late. " How should I ? . . . How could I ? . . . " (*To the labourer*) Here, my good man, you might get me a glass of vodka, anyway. (*Labourer goes off.*) " How should I ? . . . How could I ? . . . " (*finds his cap*). In one of Ostrovsky's plays there is a man with a big moustache and little wit—that's like me. Well,

I have the honour to wish you all good-bye. (*To* YELENA ANDREYEVNA) If you ever care to look in upon me, with Sofya Alexandrovna, I shall be truly delighted. I have a little estate, only ninety acres, but there is a model garden and nursery such as you wouldn't find for hundreds of miles round—if that interests you. Next to me is the government plantation. The forester there is old and always ill, so that I really look after all the work.

YELENA. I have been told already that you are very fond of forestry. Of course, it may be of the greatest use, but doesn't it interfere with your real work ? You are a doctor.

ASTROV. Only God knows what is one's real work.

YELENA. And is it interesting ?

ASTROV. Yes, it is interesting work.

VOYNITSKY (*ironically*). Very much so !

YELENA (*to* ASTROV). You are still young—you don't look more than thirty-six or thirty-seven . . . and it cannot be so interesting as you say. Nothing but trees and trees. I should think it must be monotonous.

SONYA. No, it's extremely interesting. Mihail Lvovitch plants fresh trees every year, and already they have sent him a bronze medal and a diploma. He tries to prevent the old forests being destroyed. If you listen to him you will agree with him entirely. He says that forests beautify the country, that they teach man to understand what is beautiful and develop a lofty attitude of mind. Forests temper the severity of the climate.

In countries where the climate is mild, less energy is wasted on the struggle with nature, and so man is softer and milder. In such countries people are beautiful, supple and sensitive ; their language is elegant and their movements are graceful. Art and learning flourish among them, their philosophy is not gloomy, and their attitude to women is full of refined courtesy.

VOYNITSKY (*laughing*). Bravo, bravo ! That's all charming but not convincing ; so (*to* ASTROV) allow me, my friend, to go on heating my stoves with logs and building my barns of wood.

ASTROV. You can heat your stoves with peat and build your barns of brick. Well, I am ready to let you cut down wood as you need it, but why destroy the forests ? The Russian forests are going down under the axe. Millions of trees are perishing, the homes of wild animals and birds are being laid waste, the rivers are dwindling and drying up, wonderful scenery is disappearing never to return ; and all because lazy man has not the sense to stoop down and pick up the fuel from the ground. (*To* YELENA ANDREYEVNA) Am I not right, madam ? One must be an unreflecting savage to burn this beauty in one's stove, to destroy what we cannot create. Man is endowed with reason and creative force to increase what has been given him ; but hitherto he has not created but destroyed. There are fewer and fewer forests, the rivers are drying up, the wild creatures are becoming extinct, the climate is ruined, and every day the earth is growing poorer and more hideous. (*To* VOYNITSKY) Here you are looking at me with irony, and all I say seems to you not serious and—perhaps I really am a crank. But when I walk by the peasants' woods which I have saved from cutting down, or when I hear the rustling of the young copse planted by my own hands, I realise that the climate is to some extent in my power, and that if in a thousand years man is to be happy I too shall have had some small hand in it. When I plant a birch tree and see it growing green and swaying in the wind my soul is filled with pride, and I . . . (*seeing the labourer, who has brought a glass of vodka on a tray*). However (*drinks*), it's time for me to go. Probably the truth of the matter is that I am a crank. I have the honour to take my leave ! (*goes towards the house*).

SONYA (*takes his arm and goes with him*). When are you coming to us ?

ASTROV. I don't know.

SONYA. Not for a month again ?

(ASTROV *and* SONYA *go into the house ;* MARYA VASSILYEVNA *and* TELYEGIN *remain at the table ;* YELENA ANDREYEVNA *walks towards the verandah.*)

YELENA. You have been behaving impossibly again, Ivan Petrovitch. Why need you have irritated Marya Vassilyevna and talked about a writing machine ! And at lunch to-day you quarrelled with Alexandr again. How petty it is !

VOYNITSKY. But if I hate him ?

YELENA. There is no reason to hate Alexandr ; he is like everyone else. He is no worse than you are.

VOYNITSKY. If you could see your face, your movements! You are too indolent to live! Ah, how indolent!

YELENA. Ach! indolent and bored! Everyone abuses my husband; everyone looks at me with compassion, thinking, " Poor thing! she has got an old husband." This sympathy for me, oh, how well I understand it! As Astrov said just now, you all recklessly destroy the forests, and soon there will be nothing left on the earth. In just the same way you recklessly destroy human beings, and soon, thanks to you, there will be no fidelity, no purity, no capacity for sacrifice left on earth! Why is it you can never look with indifference at a woman unless she is yours? Because—that doctor is right—there is a devil of destruction in all of you. You have no feeling for the woods, nor the birds, nor for women, nor for one another!

VOYNITSKY. I don't like this moralising.

(A pause.)

YELENA. That doctor has a weary, sensitive face. An interesting face. Sonya is evidently attracted by him; she is in love with him, and I understand her feeling. He has come three times since I have been here, but I am shy and have not once had a proper talk with him, or been nice to him. He thinks I am disagreeable. Most likely that's why we are such friends, Ivan Petrovitch, that we are both such tiresome, tedious people. Tiresome! Don't look at me like that, I don't like it.

VOYNITSKY. How else can I look at you, since

113

I love you ? You are my happiness, my life, my youth ! I know the chances of your returning my feeling are nil, non-existent, but I want nothing, only let me look at you, listen to your voice. . . .

YELENA. Hush, they may hear you ! (*They go into the house.*)

VOYNITSKY (*following her*). Let me speak of my love, don't drive me away—that alone will be the greatest happiness for me. . . .

YELENA. This is agonising.

> (*Both go into the house.* TELYEGIN *strikes the strings and plays a polka.* MARYA VASSILYEVNA *makes a note on the margin of a pamphlet.*)

CURTAIN

ACT II

Dining-room in SEREBRYAKOV'S *house. Night.
A watchman can be heard tapping in the garden.*
SEREBRYAKOV, *sitting in an arm-chair before an
open window, dozing, and* YELENA ANDRE-
YEVNA *sitting beside him, dozing too.*

SEREBRYAKOV (*waking*). Who is it ? Sonya, is
it you ?

YELENA. It's me.

SEREBRYAKOV. You, Lenotchka ! . . . I am in
unbearable pain.

YELENA. Your rug has fallen on the floor
(*wrapping it round his legs*). I'll shut the window,
Alexandr.

SEREBRYAKOV. No, I feel suffocated. . . . I just
dropped asleep and I dreamed that my left leg
did not belong to me. I was awakened by the
agonising pain. No, it's not gout; it's more like
rheumatism. What time is it now ?

YELENA. Twenty minutes past twelve (*a pause*).

SEREBRYAKOV. Look for Batyushkov in the
library in the morning. I believe we have his
works.

YELENA. What ?

SEREBRYAKOV. Look for Batyushkov in the
morning. I remember we did have him. But
why is it so difficult for me to breathe ?

115

YELENA. You are tired. This is the second night you have not slept.

SEREBRYAKOV. I have been told that Turgenev got *angina pectoris* from gout. I am afraid I may have it. Hateful, detestable old age. Damnation take it! Since I have grown old I have grown hateful to myself. And you must all hate the sight of me.

YELENA. You talk of your age as though we were all responsible for it.

SEREBRYAKOV. I am most of all hateful to you.

(YELENA ANDREYEVNA *gets up and sits down farther away*.)

SEREBRYAKOV. Of course, you are right. I am not a fool, and I understand. You are young and strong and good-looking. You want life and I am an old man, almost a corpse. Do you suppose I don't understand? And, of course, it is stupid of me to go on living. But wait a little, I shall soon set you all free. I shan't have to linger on much longer.

YELENA. I am worn out . . . for God's sake be quiet!

SEREBRYAKOV. It seems that, thanks to me, everyone is worn out, depressed, wasting their youth, and I am the only one enjoying life and satisfied. Oh yes, of course!

YELENA. Be quiet! You make me miserable!

SEREBRYAKOV. I make everyone miserable. Of course.

YELENA (*through tears*). It's insufferable! Say, what is it you want of me?

SEREBRYAKOV. Nothing.

YELENA. Well, be quiet then. I implore you!

SEREBRYAKOV. It's a strange thing, Ivan Petrovitch may speak and that old idiot, Marya Vassilyevna, and there is nothing against it, everyone listens—but if I say a word everyone begins to feel miserable. They dislike the very sound of my voice. Well, suppose I am disagreeable, egoistic and tyrannical—haven't I a right, even in my old age, to think of myself? Haven't I earned it? Haven't I the right, I ask you, to be quiet in my old age, to be cared for by other people?

YELENA. No one is disputing your rights. (*The window bangs in the wind.*) The wind has got up; I'll shut the window (*shuts the window*). There will be rain directly. No one disputes your rights.

(*A pause; the watchman in the garden taps and sings.*)

SEREBRYAKOV. After devoting all one's life to learning, after growing used to one's study, to one's lecture-room, to the society of honourable colleagues—all of a sudden to find oneself here in this vault, every day to see stupid people, to hear foolish conversation. I want life, I like success, I like fame, I like distinction, renown, and here—it's like being an exile. Every moment to be grieving for the past, watching the successes of others, dreading death. I can't bear it! It's too much for me! And then they won't forgive me my age!

YELENA. Wait a little, have patience: in five or six years I shall be old too.

(*Enter* SONYA.)

SONYA. Father, you told us to send for Doctor Astrov yourself, and now that he has come you won't see him. It isn't nice. You've troubled him for nothing.

SEREBRYAKOV. What good is your Astrov to me? He knows as much about medicine as I do about astronomy.

SONYA. We can't send for all the great medical authorities here for your gout.

SEREBRYAKOV. I am not going to talk to that crazy crank.

SONYA. That's as you please (*sits down*). It doesn't matter to me.

SEREBRYAKOV. What's the time?

YELENA. Nearly one o'clock.

SEREBRYAKOV. I feel stifled. . . . Sonya, fetch me my drops from the table.

SONYA. In a minute (*gives him the drops*).

SEREBRYAKOV (*irritably*). Oh, not those! It's no use asking for anything!

SONYA. Please don't be peevish. Some people may like it, but please spare me! I don't like it. And I haven't the time. I have to get up early in the morning, we are haymaking to-morrow.

(*Enter* VOYNITSKY *in a dressing-gown with a candle in his hand.*)

VOYNITSKY. There's a storm coming on. (*A flash of lightning.*) There, look! Hélène and Sonya, go to bed. I have come to take your place.

SEREBRYAKOV (*frightened*). No, no! Don't leave me with him No! He will be the death of me with his talking!

VOYNITSKY. But you must let them have some

118

rest ! This is the second night they have had no sleep.

SEREBRYAKOV. Let them go to bed, but you go too. Thank you. I entreat you to go. For the sake of our past friendship, don't make any objections ! We'll talk some other time.

VOYNITSKY (*mockingly*). Our past friendship. . . . Past . . .

SONYA. Be quiet, Uncle Vanya.

SEREBRYAKOV (*to his wife*). My love, don't leave me alone with him ! He will be the death of me with his talking !

VOYNITSKY. This is really getting laughable.

(*Enter* MARINA *with a candle.*)

SONYA. You ought to be in bed, nurse darling ! It's late.

MARINA. The samovar has not been cleared. One can't very well go to bed.

SEREBRYAKOV. Everyone is kept up, everyone is worn out. I am the only one enjoying myself.

MARINA (*going up to* SEREBRYAKOV *tenderly*). Well, master dear, is the pain so bad ? I have a grumbling pain in my legs too, such a pain (*tucks the rug in*). You've had this trouble for years. Vera Petrovna, Sonetchka's mother, used to be up night after night with you, wearing herself out. How fond she was of you ! (*a pause*). The old are like little children, they like someone to be sorry for them ; but no one feels for the old (*kisses* SEREBRYAKOV *on the shoulder*). Come to bed, dear . . . come, my honey. . . . I'll give you some lime-flower tea and warm your legs . . . and say a prayer for you. . . .

119

SEREBRYAKOV (*moved*). Let us go, Marina.

MARINA. I have such a grumbling pain in my legs myself, such a pain (*together with* SONYA *leads him off*). Vera Petrovna used to be crying, and breaking her heart over you. . . . You were only a mite then, Sonetchka, and had no sense. . . . Come along, come along, sir . . .

(SEREBRYAKOV, SONYA *and* MARINA *go out*.)

YELENA. I am quite worn out with him. I can hardly stand on my feet.

VOYNITSKY. You with him, and I with myself. This is the third night I have had no sleep.

YELENA. It's dreadful in this house. Your mother hates everything except her pamphlets and the Professor; the Professor is irritated, he does not trust me, and is afraid of you; Sonya is angry with her father, angry with me and has not spoken to me for a fortnight; you hate my husband and show open contempt for your mother; I am overwrought and have been nearly crying twenty times to-day. . . . It's dreadful in this house.

VOYNITSKY. Let us drop this moralising.

YELENA. You are a well-educated and intelligent man, Ivan Petrovitch, and I should have thought you ought to understand that the world is not being destroyed through fire or robbery, but through hatred, enmity and all this petty wrangling. . . . It ought to be your work to reconcile everyone, and not to grumble.

VOYNITSKY. Reconcile me to myself first! My precious . . . (*bends down and kisses her hand*).

YELENA. Don't! (*draws away her hand*). Go away!

120

VOYNITSKY. The rain will be over directly and everything in nature will be refreshed and sigh with relief. But the storm has brought no relief to me. Day and night the thought that my life has been hopelessly wasted weighs on me like a nightmare. I have no past, it has been stupidly wasted on trifles, and the present is awful in its senselessness. Here you have my life and my love! What use to make of them? What am I to do with them? My passion is wasted in vain like a ray of sunshine that has fallen into a pit, and I am utterly lost, too.

YELENA. When you talk to me about your love, I feel stupid and don't know what to say. Forgive me, there is nothing I can say to you (*is about to go out*). Good-night.

VOYNITSKY (*barring her way*). And if you knew how wretched I am at the thought that by my side, in this same house, another life is being wasted, too—yours! What are you waiting for? What cursed theory holds you back? Understand, do understand . . .

YELENA (*looks at him intently*). Ivan Petrovitch, you are drunk!

VOYNITSKY. I may be, I may be . . .

YELENA. Where is the doctor?

VOYNITSKY. He is in there . . . he is staying the night with me. It may be, it may be . . . anything may be!

YELENA. You have been drinking again to-day. What's that for?

VOYNITSKY. There's a semblance of life in it, anyway. . . . Don't prevent me, Hélène!

YELENA. You never used to drink, and you did not talk so much. . . . Go to bed ! You bore me.

VOYNITSKY (*kisses her hand*). My precious . . . marvellous one !

YELENA (*with vexation*). Don't. This is really hateful (*goes out*).

VOYNITSKY (*alone*). She is gone . . . (*a pause*). Ten years ago I used to meet her at my sister's. Then she was seventeen and I was thirty-seven. Why didn't I fall in love with her then and make her an offer ? It might easily have happened then ! And now she would have been my wife. . . . Yes. . . . Now we should both have been awakened by the storm ; she would have been frightened by the thunder, I should have held her in my arms and whispered, " Don't be frightened, I am here." Oh, wonderful thoughts, what happiness ; it makes me laugh with delight—but, my God, my thoughts are in a tangle. Why am I old ? Why doesn't she understand me ? Her fine phrases, her lazy morality, her nonsensical lazy theories about the ruin of the world—all that is absolutely hateful to me (*a pause*). Oh, how I have been cheated ! I adored that Professor, that pitiful gouty invalid, and worked for him like an ox. Sonya and I squeezed every farthing out of the estate ; we haggled over linseed oil, peas, curds, like greedy peasants ; we grudged ourselves every morsel to save up halfpence and farthings and send him thousands of roubles. I was proud of him and his learning ; he was my life, the breath of my being. All his writings and utterances seemed to me inspired by genius. . . . My God, and now !

Here he is retired, and now one can see the sum total of his life. He leaves not one page of work behind him, he is utterly unknown, he is nothing— a soap bubble! And I have been cheated. . . . I see it—stupidly cheated. . . .

    (*Enter* ASTROV *in his coat, but without waist-coat or tie; he is a little drunk; he is followed by* TELYEGIN *with the guitar*.)

ASTROV. Play something!

TELYEGIN. Everyone is asleep!

ASTROV. Play!

    (TELYEGIN *begins playing softly*.)

ASTROV (*to* VOYNITSKY). Are you alone? No ladies here? (*Putting his arms akimbo sings*) "Dance my hut and dance my stove, the master has no bed to lie on." The storm woke me. Jolly good rain. What time is it?

VOYNITSKY. Goodness knows.

ASTROV. I thought I heard Yelena Andreyevna's voice.

VOYNITSKY. She was here a minute ago.

ASTROV. A fine woman. (*Examines the medicine bottles on the table*) Medicines! What a lot of prescriptions! From Harkov, from Moscow, from Tula. He has bored every town with his gout. Is he really ill or shamming?

VOYNITSKY. He is ill (*a pause*).

ASTROV. Why are you so melancholy to-day? Are you sorry for the Professor, or what?

VOYNITSKY. Let me alone.

ASTROV. Or perhaps you are in love with the Professor's lady?

VOYNITSKY. She is my friend!

ASTROV. Already ?

VOYNITSKY. What do you mean by " already " ?

ASTROV. A woman can become a man's friend only in the following sequence : first agreeable acquaintance, then mistress, then friend

VOYNITSKY. A vulgar theory.

ASTROV. What ? Yes . . . I must own I am growing vulgar. You see, I am drunk too. As a rule I get drunk like this once a month. When I am in this condition I become coarse and insolent in the extreme. I don't stick at anything then ! I undertake the most difficult operations and do them capitally. I make the most extensive plans for the future ; I don't think of myself as a crank at such times, but believe that I am being of immense service to humanity — immense ! And I have my own philosophy of life at such times, and all you, my good friends, seem to me such insects . . . microbes ! (*To* TELYEGIN) Waffles, play !

TELYEGIN. My dear soul, I'd be delighted to do anything for you, but do realise—everyone is asleep !

ASTROV. Play !

(TELYEGIN *begins playing softly.*)

ASTROV. We must have a drink. Come along, I fancy we have still some brandy left. And as soon as it is daylight, we will go to my place. Right ? I have an assistant who never says " right," but " roight." He is an awful scoundrel. So we will go, shall we ? (*Sees* SONYA *entering*) Excuse me, I have no tie on (*goes out hurriedly,* TELYEGIN *following him*).

SONYA. Uncle Vanya, you have been drinking

124

with the doctor again. You **are a** nice pair!
He has always been like that, but why do you do
it? It's so unsuitable at your age.

VOYNITSKY. Age makes no difference. When
one has no real life, one has to live on illusions.
It's better than nothing, anyway.

SONYA. The hay is all cut, it rains every day,
it's all rotting, and you are living in illusions. You
have quite given up looking after things. . . . I
have to work alone, and am quite done up. . . .
(*Alarmed*) Uncle, you have tears in your eyes!

VOYNITSKY. Tears? Not a bit of it . . . nonsense.
. . . You looked at me just now so like your dear
mother. My darling . . . (*eagerly kisses her hands and
face*). My sister . . . my dear sister . . . where is
she now? If she knew! Ah, if she knew!

SONYA. What, uncle? Knew what?

VOYNITSKY. It's painful, useless. . . . Never mind.
. . . Afterwards . . . it's nothing . . . I am going
(*goes out*).

SONYA (*knocks at the door*). Mihail Lvovitch,
you are not asleep, are you? One minute!

ASTROV (*through the door*). I am coming! (*A
minute later he comes out with his waistcoat and tie
on.*) What can I do for you?

SONYA. Drink yourself, if it does not disgust
you, but I implore you, don't let my uncle drink!
It's bad for him.

ASTROV. Very good. We won't drink any
more (*a pause*). I am just going home. That's
settled and signed. It will be daylight by the
time they have put the horses in.

SONYA. It is raining. Wait till morning.

125

ASTROV. The storm is passing over, we shall only come in for the end of it. I'm going. And please don't send for me again to see your father. I tell him it's gout and he tells me it's rheumatism; I ask him to stay in bed and he sits in a chair. And to-day he wouldn't speak to me at all.

SONYA. He is spoiled. (*Looks into the sideboard*) Won't you have something to eat?

ASTROV. Well, perhaps.

SONYA. I like eating at night. I believe there is something in the sideboard. They say he's been a great favourite with the ladies, and women have spoiled him. Here, have some cheese. (*Both stand at the sideboard and eat.*)

ASTROV. I have had nothing to eat all day, only drink. Your father has a difficult temper. (*Takes a bottle from the sideboard*) May I? (*drinks a glass*). There is no one here and one may speak frankly. Do you know, it seems to me that I could not exist in your house for a month, I should be choked by the atmosphere. . . . Your father, who is entirely absorbed in his gout and his books, Uncle Vanya with his melancholy, your grandmother, and your stepmother too. . . .

SONYA. What about my stepmother?

ASTROV. Everything ought to be beautiful in a human being: face, and dress, and soul, and ideas. She is beautiful, there is no denying that, but . . . You know she does nothing but eat, sleep, walk about, fascinate us all by her beauty —nothing more. She has no duties, other people work for her. . . . That's true, isn't it? And an idle life cannot be pure (*a pause*). But perhaps I am

126

too severe. I am dissatisfied with life like your Uncle Vanya, and we are both growing peevish.

SONYA. You are dissatisfied with life, then ?

ASTROV. I love life as such, but our life, our everyday provincial life in Russia, I can't endure. I despise it with every fibre of my being. And as for my own personal life, there is absolutely nothing nice in it, I can assure you. You know when you walk through a forest on a dark night, and a light gleams in the distance, you do not notice your weariness, nor the darkness, nor the sharp twigs that lash you in the face. . . . I work—as you know—harder than anyone in the district, fate is for ever lashing at me ; at times I am un-bearably miserable, but I have no light in the distance. I expect nothing for myself ; I am not fond of my fellow creatures. . . . It's years since I cared for anyone.

SONYA. You care for no one at all ?

ASTROV. No one. I feel a certain affection for your nurse—for the sake of old times. The peasants are too much alike, undeveloped, living in dirt, and it is difficult to get on with the educated people. They are all wearisome. Our good friends are small in their ideas, small in their feelings, and don't see beyond their noses—or, to put it plainly, they are stupid. And those who are bigger and more intelligent are hysterical, morbidly absorbed in introspection and analysis. . . . They are for ever whining ; they are insanely given to hatred and slander ; they steal up to a man sideways, and look at him askance and decide " Oh, he is a neurotic ! " or " he is posing."

And when they don't know what label to stick on my forehead, they say " he is a queer fellow, very queer ! " I am fond of forestry—that's queer; I don't eat meat—that's queer too. There is no direct, genuine, free attitude to people and to nature left among them. . . . None, none ! (*is about to drink*).

SONYA (*prevents him*). No, please, I beg you, don't drink any more !

ASTROV. Why not ?

SONYA. It's so out of keeping with you ! You are so refined, you have such a soft voice. . . . More than that even, you are unlike everyone else I know—you are beautiful. Why, then, do you want to be like ordinary people who drink and play cards ? Oh, don't do it, I entreat you ! You always say that people don't create but only destroy what heaven gives them. Then why do you destroy yourself, why ? You mustn't, you mustn't, I beseech you, I implore you !

ASTROV (*holds out his hand to her*). I won't drink any more !

SONYA. Give me your word.

ASTROV. My word of honour.

SONYA (*presses his hand warmly*). Thank you !

ASTROV. Enough ! I have come to my senses. You see, I am quite sober now and I will be so to the end of my days (*looks at his watch*). And so, as I was saying, my time is over, it's too late for me. . . . I have grown old, I have worked too hard, I have grown vulgar, all my feelings are blunted, and I believe I am not capable of being fond of anyone. I don't love anyone . . . and I don't believe I ever shall. What still affects me is beauty. That does stir me. I fancy if Yelena Andreyevna, for example, wanted to, she could turn my head in one day. . . . But that's not love, that's not affection . . . (*covers his face with his hands and shudders*).

SONYA. What is it ?

ASTROV. Nothing. . . . In Lent one of my patients died under chloroform.

SONYA. You ought to forget that by now (*a pause*). Tell me, Mihail Lvovitch . . . if I had a friend or a younger sister, and if you found out that she . . . well, suppose that she loved you, how would you take that ?

ASTROV (*shrugging his shoulders*). I don't know. Nohow, I expect. I should give her to understand that I could not care for her . . . and my mind is taken up with other things. Anyway, if I am going, it is time to start. Good-bye, my dear girl, or we shall not finish till morning (*presses her hand*). I'll go through the drawing-room if I may, or I am afraid your uncle may detain me (*goes out*).

SONYA (*alone*). He has said nothing to me. . . . His soul and his heart are still shut away from me, but why do I feel so happy ? (*laughs with happiness*). I said to him, you are refined, noble, you have such a soft voice. . . . Was it inappropriate ? His voice trembles and caresses one . . . I still feel it vibrating in the air. And when I spoke to him of a younger sister, he did not understand. . . . (*Wringing her hands*) Oh, how awful it is that I am not beautiful ! How awful it is ! And I

129

know I am not, I know it, I know it ! . . . Last Sunday, as people were coming out of church, I heard them talking about me, and one woman said : " She is a sweet generous nature, but what a pity she is so plain. . . ." Plain. . . .

(*Enter* YELENA ANDREYEVNA.)

YELENA (*opens the window*). The storm is over. What delicious air ! (*a pause*). Where is the doctor ?

SONYA. He is gone (*a pause*).

YELENA. Sophie !

SONYA. What is it ?

YELENA. How long are you going to be sulky with me ? We have done each other no harm. Why should we be enemies ? Let us make it up. . . .

SONYA. I wanted to myself . . . (*embraces her*). Don't let us be cross any more.

YELENA. That's right. (*Both are agitated.*)

SONYA. Has father gone to bed ?

YELENA. No, he is sitting in the drawing-room. . . . We don't speak to each other for weeks, and goodness knows why. . . . (*Seeing that the sideboard is open*) How is this ?

SONYA. Mihail Lvovitch has been having some supper.

YELENA. And there is wine too. . . . Let us drink to our friendship.

SONYA. Yes, let us.

YELENA. Out of the same glass . . . (*fills it*). It's better so. So now we are friends ?

SONYA. Friends. (*They drink and kiss each other.*) I have been wanting to make it up for ever so long, but somehow I felt ashamed . . . (*cries*)

130

YELENA. Why are you crying?

SONYA. It's nothing.

YELENA. Come, there, there . . . (*weeps*). I am a queer creature, I am crying too . . . (*a pause*). You are angry with me because you think I married your father from interested motives. . . . If that will make you believe me, I will swear it—I married him for love. I was attracted by him as a learned, celebrated man. It was not real love, it was all made up; but I fancied at the time that it was real. It's not my fault. And ever since our marriage you have been punishing me with your clever, suspicious eyes.

SONYA. Come, peace! peace! Let us forget.

YELENA. You mustn't look like that—it doesn't suit you. You must believe in everyone—there is no living if you don't (*a pause.*)

SONYA. Tell me honestly, as a friend . . . are you happy?

YELENA. No.

SONYA. I knew that. One more question. Tell me frankly, wouldn't you have liked your husband to be young?

YELENA. What a child you are still! Of course I should! (*laughs*). Well, ask something else, ask away. . . .

SONYA. Do you like the doctor?

YELENA. Yes, very much.

SONYA (*laughs*). Do I look silly . . . yes? He has gone away, but I still hear his voice and his footsteps, and when I look at the dark window I can see his face. Do let me tell you. . . . But I can't speak so loud; I feel ashamed. Come into

my room, we can talk there. You must think me
silly? Own up. . . . Tell me something about him.

YELENA. What am I to tell you?

SONYA. He is clever. . . . He understands everything, he can do anything. . . . He doctors people,
and plants forests too. . . .

YELENA. It is not a question of forests and
medicine. . . . My dear, you must understand he
has a spark of genius! And you know what that
means? Boldness, freedom of mind, width of
outlook. . . . He plants a tree and is already seeing
what will follow from it in a thousand years,
already he has visions of the happiness of
humanity. Such people are rare, one must love
them. . . . He drinks, he is sometimes a little coarse
—but what does that matter? A talented man
cannot keep spotless in Russia. Only think what
sort of life that doctor has! Impassable mud
on the roads, frosts, snow-storms, the immense
distances, the coarse savage peasants, poverty
and disease all around him—it is hard for one who
is working and struggling day after day in such
surroundings to keep spotless and sober till he is
forty (*kisses her*). I wish you happiness with all
my heart; you deserve it . . . (*gets up*). But I
am a tiresome, secondary character. . . : In music
and in my husband's house, and in all the love
affairs, everywhere in fact, I have always
played a secondary part. As a matter of fact, if
you come to think of it, Sonya, I am very, very
unhappy! (*walks up and down the stage in
agitation*). There is no happiness in this world for
me, none! Why do you laugh?

132

SONYA (*laughs, hiding her face*).   I am so happy
. . . so happy !

YELENA. I have a longing for music.   I should
like to play something.

SONYA. Do play something ! (*embraces her*)
I can't sleep. . . . Play something !

YELENA. In a minute.   Your father is not
asleep.   Music irritates him when he is ill.   Go
and ask his leave.   If he doesn't object, I'll play.
Go !

SONYA. Very well (*goes out*).

(*Watchman taps in the garden.*)

YELENA. It's a long time since I have played
the piano.   I shall play and cry, cry like an idiot.
(*In the window*) Is that you tapping, Yefim ?

WATCHMAN'S VOICE. Yes.

YELENA. Don't tap, the master is unwell.

WATCHMAN'S VOICE. I am just going (*whistles*).
Hey there, good dog ! Come, lad ! Good dog !
(*a pause*).

SONYA (*returning*).   We mustn't !

CURTAIN

ACT III

The drawing-room in SEREBRYAKOV'S *house. Three
doors : on the right, on the left and in the middle.
Daytime.*

VOYNITSKY *and* SONYA *seated, and* YELENA
ANDREYEVNA *walking about the stage, thinking.*

VOYNITSKY. The Herr Professor has graciously
expressed a desire that we should all gather
together in this room at one o'clock to-day (*looks
at his watch*). It is a quarter to. He wishes to
make some communication to the world.

YELENA. Probably some business matter.

VOYNITSKY. He has no business. He spends
his time writing twaddle, grumbling and being
jealous.

SONYA (*in a reproachful tone*). Uncle !

VOYNITSKY. Well, well, I am sorry (*motioning
towards* YELENA ANDREYEVNA). Just look at her !
she is so lazy that she almost staggers as she walks.
Very charming ! Very !

YELENA. You keep buzzing and buzzing away
all day—aren't you tired of it ? (*Miserably*) I am
bored to death. I don't know what I'm to do.

SONYA (*shrugging her shoulders*). Isn't there
plenty to do ? If only you cared to do it.

YELENA. For instance ?

SONYA. You could help us with the estate, teach

the children or look after the sick. There's plenty
to do. When father and you were not here, Uncle
Vanya and I used to go to the market ourselves
and sell the flour.

YELENA. I don't know how to do such things.
And they are not interesting. It's only in novels
with a purpose that people teach and doctor the
peasants. How am I, all of a sudden, *à propos*
of nothing, to go and teach them or doctor them ?

SONYA. Well, I don't see how one can help
doing it. Wait a little, and you too will get into
the way of it (*puts her arm round her*). Don't be
depressed, dear (*laughs*). You are bored and don't
know what to do with yourself, and boredom and
idleness are catching. Look at Uncle Vanya—
he does nothing but follow you about like a shadow.
I have left my work and run away to talk to you.
I have grown lazy—I can't help it ! The doctor,
Mihail Lvovitch, used to come and see us very
rarely, once a month ; it was difficult to persuade him to come, and now he drives over every
day. He neglects his forestry and his patients.
You must be a witch.

VOYNITSKY. Why be miserable ? (*Eagerly*)
Come, my precious, my splendid one, be sensible !
You have mermaid blood in your veins—be a
mermaid ! Let yourself go for once in your life !
Make haste and fall head over ears in love with
some water-sprite—and plunge headlong into the
abyss so that the Herr Professor and all of us may
throw up our hands in amazement !

YELENA (*angrily*). Leave me in peace ! How
cruel it is ! (*is about to go out*).

VOYNITSKY (*prevents her*). Come, come, my dearest, forgive me. . . . I apologise (*kisses her hand*). Peace !

YELENA. You would drive an angel out of patience, you know.

VOYNITSKY. As a sign of peace and harmony I'll fetch you a bunch of roses ; I gathered them for you this morning. Autumn roses—exquisite, mournful roses . . . (*goes out*).

SONYA. Autumn roses — exquisite, mournful roses. . . . (*Both look out of window.*)

YELENA. It's September already. However are we to get through the winter here? (*a pause*). Where is the doctor ?

SONYA. In Uncle Vanya's room. He is writing something. I am glad Uncle Vanya is gone. I want to talk to you.

YELENA. What about ?

SONYA. What about ! (*lays her head on* YELENA'S *bosom*).

YELENA. Come, there, there . . . (*strokes her head*).

SONYA. I am not good-looking.

YELENA. You have beautiful hair.

SONYA. No ! (*looks round so as to see herself in the looking-glass*). No ! When a woman is plain, she is always told " You have beautiful eyes, you have beautiful hair." . . . I have loved him for six years. I love him more than my own mother. Every moment I am conscious of him. I feel the touch of his hand and I watch the door. I wait, expecting him every moment to come in. And here you see I keep coming to you simply to talk of him. Now he is here every day, but he doesn't look at me—doesn't see me. . . . That's such agony !

I have no hope at all—none, none! (*In despair*) Oh, my God, give me strength . . . I have been praying all night. . . . I often go up to him, begin talking to him, look into his eyes. I have no pride left, no strength to control myself. I couldn't keep it in and told Uncle Vanya yesterday that I love him. . . . And all the servants know I love him. Everybody knows it.

YELENA. And he?

SONYA. No. He doesn't notice me.

YELENA (*musing*). He is a strange man. . . . Do you know what? Let me speak to him. . . . I'll do it carefully—hint at it . . . (*a pause*). Yes really—how much longer are you to remain in uncertainty? Let me!

(SONYA *nods her head in consent.*)

YELENA. That's right. It won't be difficult to find out whether he loves you or not. Don't you be troubled, darling; don't be uneasy. I'll question him so tactfully that he won't notice it. All we want to find out is yes or no (*a pause*). If it's no, he had better not come here, had he?

(SONYA *nods in agreement.*)

YELENA. It's easier to bear when one doesn't see the man. We won't put things off; we will question him straight away. He was meaning to show me some charts. Go and tell him that I want to see him.

SONYA (*in violent agitation*) You will tell me the whole truth?

YELENA. Yes, of course. It seems to me that the truth, however dreadful it is, is not so dreadful as uncertainty. Rely on me, dear.

SONYA. Yes, yes . . . I shall tell him you want to

137

see his charts (*is going, and stops in the doorway*). No, uncertainty is better. . . . One has hope, at least. . . .

YELENA. What do you say ?

SONYA. Nothing (*goes out*).

YELENA (*alone*). Nothing is worse than knowing somebody else's secret and not being able to help. (*Musing*) He is not in love with her—that's evident ; but why should he not marry her ? She is not good-looking, but she would be a capital wife for a country doctor at his age. She is so sensible, so kind and pure-hearted. . . . No, that's not it . . . (*a pause*). I understand the poor child. In the midst of desperate boredom, with nothing but grey shadows wandering about instead of human beings, with only dull commonplaces to listen to, among people who can do nothing but eat, drink and sleep—he sometimes appears on the scene unlike the rest, handsome, interesting, fascinating, like a bright moon rising in the darkness. . . . To yield to the charm of such a man . . . forget oneself . . . I believe I am a little fascinated myself. Yes, I feel bored when he does not come, and even now I am smiling when I think of him. . . . That Uncle Vanya says I have mermaid's blood in my veins. "Let yourself go for once in your life." Well, perhaps that's what I ought to do. . . . If I could fly, free as a bird, away from all of you—from your sleepy faces, from your talk, forget your existence. . . . But I am cowardly and diffident. . . . My conscience troubles me. . . . He comes here every day. I guess why he comes, and already I have a guilty feeling. I am ready to throw myself on my knees before Sonya, to beg her pardon, to cry. . . .

ASTROV (*comes in with a chart*). Good-day! (*shakes hands*). You wanted to see my handiwork.

YELENA. You promised yesterday to show me. . . . Can you spare the time?

ASTROV. Oh, of course! (*spreads the map on a card table and fixes it with drawing pins*). Where were you born?

YELENA (*helping him*). In Petersburg.

ASTROV. And where did you study?

YELENA. At the School of Music.

ASTROV. I expect this won't be interesting to you.

YELENA. Why not? It's true that I don't know the country, but I have read a great deal.

ASTROV. I have my own table here, in this house . . . in Ivan Petrovitch's room. When I am so exhausted that I feel completely stupefied, I throw everything up and fly here and amuse myself with this for an hour or two. . . . Ivan Petrovitch and Sofya Alexandrovna click their counting beads, and I sit beside them at my table and daub away—and I feel snug and comfortable, and the cricket churrs. But I don't allow myself that indulgence too often—only once a month. . . . (*Pointing to the map*) Now, look here! It's a picture of our district as it was fifty years ago. The dark and light green stands for forest; half of the whole area was covered with forest. Where there is a network of red over the green, elks and wild goats were common. . . . I show both the flora and the fauna here. On this lake there were swans, geese and ducks, and the old people tell us there were " a

139

power " of birds of all sorts, no end of them ; they flew in clouds. Besides the villages and hamlets, you see scattered here and there all sorts of settlements—little farms, monasteries of Old Believers, water-mills. . . . Horned cattle and horses were numerous. That is shown by the blue colour. For instance, the blue colour lies thick on this neighbourhood. Here there were regular droves of horses, and every homestead had three on an average (*a pause*). Now look lower down. That's how it was twenty-five years ago. Already, you see, only a third of the area is under forest. There are no goats left, but there are elks. Both the green and the blue are paler. And so it goes on and on. Let us pass to the third part—a map of the district as it is at present. There is green here and there, but only in patches ; all the elks have vanished, and the swans and the capercailzies too. . . . Of the old settlements and farms and monasteries and mills there is not a trace. In fact, it's a picture of gradual and unmistakable degeneration which will, apparently, in another ten or fifteen years be complete. You will say that it is the influence of civilisation—that the old life must naturally give way to the new. Yes, I understand that. If there were highroads and railways on the site of these ruined forests, if there were works and factories and schools, the peasants would be healthier, better off, more intelligent ; but, you see, there is nothing of the sort ! There are still the same swamps and mosquitoes, the same lack of roads, and poverty, and typhus ana diphtheria and fires in the district. . . .

We have here a degeneration that is the result of too severe a struggle for existence. This degeneration is due to inertia, ignorance, to the complete lack of understanding, when a man, cold, hungry and sick, simply to save what is left of life, to keep his children alive, instinctively, unconsciously clutches at anything to satisfy his hunger and warm himself and destroys everything heedless of the morrow. . . . Almost everything has been destroyed already, but nothing as yet has been created to take its place. (*Coldly*) I see from your face that it doesn't interest you.

YELENA. But I understand so little about all that. . . .

ASTROV. There's nothing to understand in it; it simply doesn't interest you.

YELENA. To speak frankly, I am thinking of something else. Forgive me. I want to put you through a little examination, and I am troubled and don't know how to begin.

ASTROV. An examination?

YELENA. Yes, an examination . . . but not a very formidable one. Let us sit down. (*They sit down.*) It concerns a certain young lady. We will talk like honest people, like friends, without beating about the bush. Let us talk and forget all about it afterwards. Yes?

ASTROV. Yes.

YELENA. It concerns my step-daughter Sonya. You like her, don't you?

ASTROV. Yes, I have a respect for her.

YELENA. Does she attract you as a woman?

ASTROV (*after a pause*). No.

YELENA. A few words more, and I have done. Have you noticed nothing ?

ASTROV. Nothing.

YELENA (*taking him by the hand*). You do not love her . . . I see it from your eyes. . . . She is unhappy. . . . Understand that and . . . give up coming here.

ASTROV (*gets up*). My day is over. Besides, I have too much to do (*shrugging his shoulders*). What time have I for such things ? (*he is confused*).

YELENA. Ough ! What an unpleasant conversation ! I am trembling as though I'd been carrying a ton weight. Well, thank God, that's over ! Let us forget it. Let it be as though we had not spoken at all, and . . . and go away. You are an intelligent man . . . you'll understand (*a pause*). I feel hot all over.

ASTROV. If you had spoken a month or two ago I might, perhaps, have considered it ; but now . . . (*he shrugs his shoulders*). And if she is unhappy, then of course . . . There's only one thing I can't understand : what induced you to go into it ? (*Looks into her eyes and shakes his finger at her*) You are a sly one !

YELENA. What does that mean ?

ASTROV (*laughs*). Sly ! Suppose Sonya is unhappy—I am quite ready to admit it—but why need you go into it ? (*Preventing her from speaking, eagerly*) Please don't try to look astonished. You know perfectly well what brings me here every day. . . . Why, and on whose account, I am here, you know perfectly well. You charming bird of prey, don't look at me like that, I am an old sparrow. . . .

142

YELENA (*perplexed*). Bird of prey! I don't understand.

ASTROV. A beautiful, fluffy weasel. . . . You must have a victim! Here I have been doing nothing for a whole month. I have dropped everything. I seek you greedily—and you are awfully pleased at it, awfully. . . . Well, I am conquered; you knew that before your examination (*folding his arms and bowing his head*). I submit. Come and devour me!

YELENA. You are mad!

ASTROV (*laughs through his teeth*). You—diffident. . . .

YELENA. Oh, I am not so bad and so mean as you think! I swear I'm not! (*tries to go out*).

ASTROV (*barring the way*). I am going away to-day. I won't come here again, but . . . (*takes her hand and looks round*) where shall we see each other? Tell me quickly, where? Someone may come in; tell me quickly. . . . (*Passionately*) How wonderful, how magnificent you are! One kiss. . . . If I could only kiss your fragrant hair. . . .

YELENA. I assure you . . .

ASTROV (*preventing her from speaking*). Why assure me? There's no need. No need of unnecessary words. . . . Oh, how beautiful you are! What hands! (*kisses her hands*).

YELENA. That's enough . . . go away . . . (*withdraws her hands*). You are forgetting yourself.

ASTROV. Speak, speak! Where shall we meet to-morrow? (*puts his arm round her waist*). You see, it is inevitable; we must meet (*kisses her; at that instant* VOYNITSKY *comes in with a bunch of roses and stands still in the doorway*)

YELENA (*not seeing* VOYNITSKY). Spare me . . .
let me go . . . (*lays her head on* ASTROV'S *chest*).
No ! (*tries to go out*).

ASTROV (*holding her by the waist*). Come to the
plantation to-morrow . . . at two o'clock. . . . Yes?
Yes ? You'll come ?

YELENA (*seeing* VOYNITSKY). Let me go ! (*in
extreme confusion goes to the window*). This is
awful !

VOYNITSKY (*lays the roses on a chair ; in
confusion wipes his face and his neck with his
handkerchief*). Never mind . . . no . . . never
mind. . . .

ASTROV (*carrying it off with bravado*). The
weather is not so bad to-day, honoured Ivan
Petrovitch. It was overcast in the morning, as
though we were going to have rain, but now it is
sunny. To tell the truth, the autumn has turned
out lovely . . . and the winter corn is quite
promising (*rolls up the map*). The only thing is
the days are getting shorter . . . (*goes out*).

YELENA (*goes quickly up to* VOYNITSKY). You
will try—you will do your utmost that my husband
and I should leave here to-day ! Do you hear ?
This very day

VOYNITSKY (*mopping his face*). What ? Oh,
yes . . . very well . . . I saw it all, Hélène—all. . . .

YELENA (*nervously*). Do you hear ? I must
get away from here to-day !

(*Enter* SEREBRYAKOV, TELYEGIN *and* MARINA.)

TELYEGIN. I don't feel quite the thing myself,
your Excellency. I have been poorly for the last
two days. My head is rather queer. . . .

SEREBRYAKOV. Where are the others ? I don't like this house. It's a perfect labyrinth. Twenty-six huge rooms, people wander in different directions, and there is no finding anyone (*rings*). Ask Marya Vassilyevna and Yelena Andreyevna to come here.

YELENA. I am here.

SEREBRYAKOV. I beg you to sit down, friends.

SONYA (*going up to* YELENA ANDREYEVNA, *impatiently*). What did he say ?

YELENA. Presently.

SONYA. You are trembling ! You are agitated ! (*Looking searchingly into her face*) I understand. . . . He said that he won't come here again . . . yes ? (*a pause*). Tell me : yes ?

(YELENA ANDREYEVNA *nods.*)

SEREBRYAKOV (*to* TELYEGIN). One can put up with illness, after all ; but what I can't endure is the whole manner of life in the country. I feel as though I had been cast off the earth into some other planet. Sit down, friends, I beg ! Sonya ! (*Sonya does not hear him ; she stands with her head drooping sorrowfully*). Sonya ! (*a pause*). She does not hear. (*To* MARINA) You sit down too, nurse. (*Nurse sits down, knitting a stocking.*) I beg you, my friends, hang your ears on the nail of attention, as the saying is (*laughs*).

VOYNITSKY (*agitated*). Perhaps I am not wanted ? Can I go ?

SEREBRYAKOV. No ; it is you whom we need most.

VOYNITSKY. What do you require of me ?

SEREBRYAKOV. Require of you. . . . Why are you

cross ? (*a pause*) If I have been to blame in any way, pray excuse me.

VOYNITSKY. Drop that tone. Let us come to business. What do you want ?

(*Enter* MARYA VASSILYEVNA.)

SEREBRYAKOV. Here is *maman*. I will begin, friends (*a pause*). I have invited you, gentlemen, to announce that the Inspector-General is coming. But let us lay aside jesting. It is a serious matter. I have called you together to ask for your advice and help, and, knowing your invariable kindness, I hope to receive it. I am a studious, bookish man, and have never had anything to do with practical life. I cannot dispense with the assistance of those who understand it, and I beg you, Ivan Petrovitch, and you, Ilya Ilyitch, and you, *maman*. . . . The point is that *manet omnes una nox* —that is, that we are all mortal. I am old and ill, and so I think it is high time to settle my worldly affairs so far as they concern my family. My life is over. I am not thinking of myself, but I have a young wife and an unmarried daughter (*a pause*). It is impossible for me to go on living in the country. We are not made for country life. But to live in town on the income we derive from this estate is impossible. If we sell the forest, for instance, that's an exceptional measure which we cannot repeat every year. We must take some steps which would guarantee us a permanent and more or less definite income. I have thought of such a measure, and have the honour of submitting it to your consideration. Omitting details I will put it before you in rough outline. Our estate yields on an average not more than two per cent. on its capital value. I propose to sell it. If we invest the money in suitable securities, we should get from four to five per cent., and I think we might even have a few thousand roubles to spare for buying a small villa in Finland.

VOYNITSKY. Excuse me . . . surely my ears are deceiving me ! Repeat what you have said.

SEREBRYAKOV. To put the money in some suitable investment and with the remainder purchase a villa in Finland.

VOYNITSKY. Not Finland. . . . You said something else.

SEREBRYAKOV. I propose to sell the estate.

VOYNITSKY. That's it. You will sell the estate ; superb, a grand idea. . . . And what do you propose to do with me, and your old mother and Sonya here ?

SEREBRYAKOV. We will settle all that in due time. One can't go into everything at once.

VOYNITSKY. Wait a minute. It's evident that up to now I've never had a grain of common sense. Up to now I have always imagined that the estate belongs to Sonya. My father bought this estate as a dowry for my sister. Till now I have been simple ; I did not interpret the law like a Turk, but thought that my sister's estate passed to Sonya.

SEREBRYAKOV. Yes, the estate belongs to Sonya. Who disputes it ? Without Sonya's consent I shall not venture to sell it. Besides, I am proposing to do it for Sonya's benefit.

VOYNITSKY. It's inconceivable, inconceivable ! Either I have gone out of my mind, or . . . or . . .

MARYA. Jean, don't contradict Alexandr. Believe me, he knows better than we do what is for the best.

VOYNITSKY. No; give me some water (*drinks water*). Say what you like—say what you like!

SEREBRYAKOV. I don't understand why you are so upset. I don't say that my plan is ideal. If everyone thinks it unsuitable, I will not insist on it.

(*A pause.*)

TELYEGIN (*in confusion*). I cherish for learning, your Excellency, not simply a feeling of reverence, but a sort of family feeling. My brother Grigory Ilyitch's wife's brother—perhaps you know him? —Konstantin Trofimitch Lakedemonov, was an M.A. . . .

VOYNITSKY. Stop, Waffles; we are talking of business. . . . Wait a little—later. . . . (*To* SEREBRYAKOV) Here, ask him. The estate was bought from his uncle.

SEREBRYAKOV. Oh! why should I ask him? What for?

VOYNITSKY. The estate was bought at the time for ninety-five thousand roubles. My father paid only seventy thousand, and twenty-five thousand remained on mortgage. Now, listen. . . . The estate would never have been bought if I had not renounced my share of the inheritance in favour of my sister, whom I loved dearly. What's more, I worked for ten years like a slave and paid off all the mortgage. . . .

SEREBRYAKOV. I regret that I broached the subject.

Voynitsky. The estate is free from debt and in a good condition only owing to my personal efforts. And now that I am old I am to be kicked out of it !

Serebryakov. I don't understand what you are aiming at.

Voynitsky. I have been managing this estate for twenty-five years. I have worked and sent you money like the most conscientious steward, and you have never thanked me once in all these years. All that time—both when I was young and now—you have given me five hundred roubles a year as salary—a beggarly wage !—and it never occurred to you to add a rouble to it.

Serebryakov. Ivan Petrovitch, how could I tell ? I am not a practical man, and don't understand these things. You could have added as much to it as you chose.

Voynitsky. Why didn't I steal ? How is it you don't all despise me because I didn't steal ? It would have been right and I shouldn't have been a pauper now !

Marya (sternly). Jean !

Telyegin (in agitation). Vanya, my dear soul, don't, don't . . . I am all of a tremble. . . . Why spoil our good relations ? (Kisses him) You mustn't.

Voynitsky. For twenty-five years I have been here within these four walls with mother, buried like a mole. . . . All our thoughts and feelings belonged to you alone. By day we talked of you and your labours. We were proud of you ; with reverence we uttered your name. We wasted our nights reading books and magazines for which now I have the deepest contempt !

TELYEGIN. Don't, Vanya, don't . . . I can't stand it. . . .

SEREBRYAKOV (*wrathfully*). I don't know what it is you want.

VOYNITSKY. To us you were a being of a higher order, and we knew your articles by heart. . . . But now my eyes are opened ! I see it all ! You write of art, but you know nothing about art ! All those works of yours I used to love are not worth a brass farthing ! You have deceived us !

SEREBRYAKOV. Do stop him ! I am going !

YELENA. Ivan Petrovitch, I insist on your being silent ! Do you hear ?

VOYNITSKY. I won't be silent. (*Preventing* SERE-BRYAKOV *from passing*) Stay ! I have not finished. You have destroyed my life ! I have not lived ! I have not lived ! Thanks to you, I have ruined and wasted the best years of my life. You are my bitterest enemy.

TELYEGIN. I can't bear it . . . I can't bear it . . . I must go (*goes out, in violent agitation*).

SEREBRYAKOV. What do you want from me ? And what right have you to speak to me like this ? You nonentity ! If the estate is yours, take it. I don't want it !

YELENA. I am going away from this hell this very minute (*screams*). I can't put up with it any longer !

VOYNITSKY. My life is ruined ! I had talent, I had courage, I had intelligence ! If I had had a normal life I might have been a Schopenhauer, a Dostoevsky. . . . Oh, I am talking like an idiot ! I am going mad. . . . Mother, I am in despair ! Mother !

MARYA (*sternly*). Do as Alexandr tells you.

SONYA (*kneeling down before the nurse and huddling up to her*). Nurse, darling ! Nurse, darling !

VOYNITSKY. Mother ! What am I to do ? Don't speak ; there's no need ! I know what I must do ! (*To* SEREBRYAKOV) You shall remember me ! (*goes out through middle door*).

(MARYA VASSILYEVNA *follows him.*)

SEREBRYAKOV. This is beyond everything ! Take that madman away ! I cannot live under the same roof with him. He is always there (*points to the middle door*)—almost beside me. . . . Let him move into the village, or into the lodge, or I will move ; but remain in the same house with him I cannot. . . .

YELENA (*to her husband*). We will leave this place to-day ! We must pack up this minute !

SEREBRYAKOV. An utterly insignificant creature !

SONYA (*on her knees, turns her head towards her father ; hysterical through her tears*). You must be merciful, father ! Uncle Vanya and I are so unhappy ! (*Mastering her despair*) You must be merciful ! Remember how, when you were younger, Uncle Vanya and grandmamma sat up all night translating books for you, copying your manuscripts . . . all nigh . . . all night . . . Uncle Vanya and I worked without resting—we were afraid to spend a farthing on ourselves and sent it all to you. . . . We did not eat the bread of idleness.

I am saying it all wrong—all wrong; but you ought to understand us, father. You must be merciful!

YELENA (*in agitation, to her husband*). Alexandr, for God's sake make it up with him. . . . I beseech you!

SEREBRYAKOV. Very well, I will talk to him. . . . I am not accusing him of anything, I am not angry with him. But you must admit that his behaviour is strange, to say the least of it. Very well, I'll go to him (*goes out by middle door*).

YELENA. Be gentle with him, soothe him . . . (*follows him out*).

SONYA (*hugging Nurse*). Oh, Nurse, darling! Nurse, darling!

MARINA. Never mind, child. The ganders will cackle a bit and leave off. . . . They will cackle and leave off. . . .

SONYA. Nurse, darling!

MARINA (*stroking her head*). You are shivering as though you were frozen! There, there, little orphan, God is merciful! A cup of lime-flower water, or raspberry tea, and it will pass. . . . Don't grieve, little orphan. (*Looking towards the middle door wrathfully*) What a to-do they make, the ganders! Plague take them!

(*A shot behind the scenes; a shriek from YELENA ANDREYEVNA is heard; SONYA shudders.*)

MARINA. Ough! Botheration take them!

SEREBRYAKOV (*runs in, staggering with terror*). Hold him! hold him! He is out of his mind!

(YELENA ANDREYEVNA *and* VOYNITSKY *struggle in the doorway.*)

YELENA (*trying to take the revolver from him*). Give it up! Give it up, I tell you!

VOYNITSKY. Let me go, Hélène! Let me go! (*Freeing himself from her, he runs in, looking for* SEREBRYAKOV) Where is he? Oh, here he is! (*Fires at him*) Bang! (*a pause*). Missed! Missed again! (*Furiously*) Damnation—damnation take it . . . (*flings revolver on the floor and sinks on to a chair, exhausted.* SEREBRYAKOV *is overwhelmed;* YELENA *leans against the wall, almost fainting*).

YELENA. Take me away! Take me away! Kill me . . . I can't stay here, I can't!

VOYNITSKY (*in despair*). Oh, what am I doing! What am I doing!

SONYA (*softly*). Nurse, darling! Nurse, darling!

CURTAIN

ACT IV

VOYNITSKY'S *room : it is his bedroom and also his office. In the window there is a big table covered with account books and papers of all sorts ; a bureau, bookcases, scales. A smaller table, for* ASTROV ; *on that table there are paints and drawing materials ; beside it a big portfolio. A cage with a starling in it. On the wall a map of Africa, obviously of no use to anyone. A big sofa covered with American leather. To the left a door leading to other apartments. On the right a door into the hall ; near door, on right, there is a doormat, that the peasants may not muddy the floor. An autumn evening. Stillness.*

TELYEGIN *and* MARINA *sitting opposite each other winding wool.*

TELYEGIN. You must make haste, Marina Timofeyevna, they will soon be calling us to say good-bye. They have already ordered the horses.

MARINA (*tries to wind more rapidly*). There is not much left.

TELYEGIN. They are going to Harkov. They'll live there.

MARINA. Much better so.

TELYEGIN. They've had a fright. . . . Yelena

154

Andreyevna keeps saying, " I won't stay here another hour. Let us get away ; let us get away." " We will stay at Harkov," she says ; " we will have a look round and then send for our things. . . ." They are not taking much with them. It seems it is not ordained that they should live here, Marina Timofeyevna. It's not ordained. . . . It's the dispensation of Providence.

MARINA. It's better so. Look at the quarrelling and shooting this morning—a regular disgrace !

TELYEGIN. Yes, a subject worthy of the brush of Aïvazovsky.

MARINA. A shocking sight it was (*a pause*). We shall live again in the old way, as we used to. We shall have breakfast at eight, dinner at one, and sit down to supper in the evening ; everything as it should be, like other people . . . like Christians (*with a sigh*). It's a long while since I have tasted noodles, sinner that I am !

TELYEGIN. Yes, it's a long time since they have given us noodles at dinner (*a pause*). A very long time. . . . As I was walking through the village this morning, Marina Timofeyevna, the man at the shop called after me, " You cadger, living upon other people." And it did hurt me so.

MARINA. You shouldn't take any notice of that, my dear. We all live upon God. Whether it's you or Sonya or Ivan Petrovitch, none of you sit idle, we all work hard ! All of us. . . . Where is Sonya ?

TELYEGIN. In the garden. She is still going round with the doctor looking for Ivan Petrovitch. They are afraid he may lay hands on himself.

MARINA. And where is his pistol ?

155

TELYEGIN (*in a whisper*). I've hidden it in the cellar !

MARINA (*with a smile*). What goings on !

(*Enter* VOYNITSKY *and* ASTROV *from outside*.)

VOYNITSKY. Let me alone. (*To* MARINA *and* TELYEGIN) Go away, leave me alone—if only for an hour ! I won't endure being watched.

TELYEGIN. Certainly, Vanya (*goes out on tiptoe*).

MARINA. The gander says, ga-ga-ga ! (*gathers up her wool and goes out*).

VOYNITSKY. Let me alone !

ASTROV. I should be delighted to. I ought to have gone away ages ago, but I repeat I won't go till you give back what you took from me.

VOYNITSKY. I did not take anything from you.

ASTROV. I am speaking in earnest, don't detain me. I ought to have gone long ago.

VOYNITSKY. I took nothing from you. (*Both sit down.*)

ASTROV. Oh ! I'll wait a little longer and then, excuse me, I must resort to force. We shall have to tie your hands and search you. I am speaking quite seriously.

VOYNITSKY. As you please (*a pause*). To have made such a fool of myself : to have fired twice and missed him ! I shall never forgive myself for that.

ASTROV. If you wanted to be playing with firearms, you would have done better to take a pop at yourself.

VOYNITSKY (*shrugging his shoulders*). It's queer. I made an attempt to commit murder and I have not been arrested ; no one has sent for

the police. So I am looked upon as a madman
(*with a bitter laugh*). I am mad, but people are not
mad who hide their crass stupidity, their flagrant
heartlessness under the mask of a professor, a
learned sage. People are not mad who marry
old men and then deceive them before the eyes of
everyone. I saw you kissing her! I saw!

ASTROV. Yes, I did kiss her, and that's more
than you ever have!

VOYNITSKY (*looking towards the door*). No,
the earth is mad to let you go on living on it!

ASTROV. Come, that's silly.

VOYNITSKY. Well, I am mad. I am not responsible. I have a right to say silly things.

ASTROV. That's a stale trick. You are not a
madman : you are simply a crank. A silly fool.
Once I used to look upon every crank as an invalid
—as abnormal ; but now I think it is the normal
condition of man to be a crank. You are quite
normal.

VOYNITSKY (*covers his face with his hands*).
I am ashamed! If you only knew how ashamed
I am! No pain can be compared with this acute
shame (*miserably*). It's unbearable (*bends over
the table*). What am I to do? What am I to do?

ASTROV. Nothing.

VOYNITSKY. Give me something! Oh, my God!
I am forty-seven. If I live to be sixty, I have
another thirteen years. It's a long time! How
am I to get through those thirteen years? What
shall I do? How am I to fill them up? Oh, you
know . . . (*squeezing* ASTROV'S *hand convulsively*) ;
you know, if only one could live the remnant of

one's life in some new way. Wake up on a still sunny morning and feel that one had begun a new life, that all the past was forgotten and had melted away like smoke (*weeps*). To begin a new life. . . . Tell me how to begin it . . . what to begin. . . .

ASTROV (*with vexation*). Oh, get away with you ! New life, indeed ! Our position—yours and mine—is hopeless.

VOYNITSKY. Yes ?

ASTROV. I am convinced of it.

VOYNITSKY. Give me something. . . . (*Pointing to his heart*) I have a scalding pain here.

ASTROV (*shouts angrily*). Leave off ! (*Softening*) Those who will live a hundred or two hundred years after us, and who will despise us for having lived our lives so stupidly and tastelessly—they will, perhaps, find a means of being happy; but we . . . There is only one hope for you and me. The hope that when we are asleep in our graves we may, perhaps, be visited by pleasant visions (*with a sigh*). Yes, old man, in the whole district there were only two decent, well-educated men : you and I. And in some ten years the common round of the trivial life here has swamped us, and has poisoned our life with its putrid vapours, and made us just as despicable as all the rest. (*Eagerly*) But don't try to put me off : give me what you took away from me.

VOYNITSKY. I took nothing from you.

ASTROV. You took a bottle of morphia out of my travelling medicine-chest (*a pause*). Look here, if you insist on making an end of yourself, go into the forest and shoot yourself. But give me back the morphia or else there will be talk and conjecture. People will think I have given it you. It will be quite enough for me to have to make your post-mortem. Do you think I shall find it interesting?

(*Enter* SONYA.)

VOYNITSKY. Leave me alone.

ASTROV (*to* SONYA). Sofya Alexandrovna, your uncle has taken a bottle of morphia out of my medicine-chest, and won't give it back. Tell him that it's . . . really stupid. And I haven't the time to waste. I ought to be going.

SONYA. Uncle Vanya, did you take the morphia? (*a pause*).

ASTROV. He did. I am certain of it.

SONYA. Give it back. Why do you frighten us? (*Tenderly*) Give it back, Uncle Vanya! I am just as unhappy, perhaps, as you are; but I am not going to give way to despair. I am bearing it, and will bear it, till my life ends of itself. . . . You must be patient too (*a pause*). Give it back! (*kisses his hands*). Dear, good uncle, darling! give it back! (*weeps*). You are kind, you will have pity on us and give it back. Be patient, uncle!—be patient!

VOYNITSKY (*takes the bottle out of the table-drawer and gives it to* ASTROV). There, take it! (*To* SONYA) But we must make haste and work, make haste and do something, or else I can't . . . I can't bear it.

SONYA. Yes, yes, work. As soon as we have seen our people off, we'll sit down to work. . . . (*Nervously turning over the papers on the table*) We have let everything go.

159

ASTROV (*puts the bottle into his case and tightens the straps*). Now I can set off.

(*Enter* YELENA.)

YELENA. Ivan Petrovitch, are you here? We are just starting. Go to Alexandr, he wants to say something to you.

SONYA. Go, Uncle Vanya. (*Takes* VOYNITSKY *by the arm*) Let us go. Father and you must be reconciled. That's essential.

(SONYA *and* VOYNITSKY *go out.*)

YELENA. I am going away. (*Gives* ASTROV *her hand*) Good-bye.

ASTROV. Already?

YELENA. The carriage is waiting.

ASTROV. Good-bye.

YELENA. You promised me to-day that you would go away.

ASTROV. I remember. I am just going (*a pause*). You have taken fright? (*takes her hand*). Is it so terrible?

YELENA. Yes.

ASTROV. You had better stay, after all! What do you say? To-morrow in the plantation——

YELENA. No. It's settled. And I look at you so fearlessly just because it is settled. I have only one favour to ask of you: think better of me. I should like you to have a respect for me.

ASTROV. Ugh! (*makes a gesture of impatience*). Do stay, I ask you to. Do recognise, you have nothing to do in this world, you have no object in life, you have nothing to occupy your mind, and sooner or later you will give way to feeling— it's inevitable. And it had better not be at

160

Harkov, or somewhere in Kursk, but here, in the lap of nature. . . . It's poetical, anyway, even the autumn is beautiful. . . . There is the forest plantation here, half-ruined homesteads in the Turgenev style. . . .

YELENA. How absurd you are. . . . I am angry with you, but yet . . . I shall think of you with pleasure. You are an interesting, original man. We shall never meet again, and so—why conceal it ?—I was really a little bit in love with you. Come, let us shake hands and part friends. Don't remember evil against me.

ASTROV (*pressing her hand*). Yes, you had better go . . . (*musing*). You seem to be a good, warm-hearted creature, and yet there is something strange about your whole personality, as it were. You came here with your husband, and all of us who were at work, toiling and creating something, had to fling aside our work and attend to nothing all the summer but your husband's gout and you. The two of you have infected all of us with your idleness. I was attracted by you and have done nothing for a whole month, and, meanwhile, people have been ill, and the peasants have pastured their cattle in my woods, of young, half-grown trees. . . . And so, wherever you and your husband go, you bring destruction everywhere. . . . I am joking, of course, yet . . . it is strange. And I am convinced that if you had stayed here, the devastation would have been immense. I should have been done for . . . and you wouldn't have fared well either ! Well, go away. *Finita la comedia !*

YELENA (*taking a pencil from his table and*

hurriedly putting it in her pocket). I shall take this pencil as a keepsake.

ASTROV. It is strange. . . . We have been friends and all at once for some reason . . . we shall never meet again. So it is with everything in this world. . . . While there is no one here—before Uncle Vanya comes in with a nosegay—allow me to kiss you at parting. . . . Yes ? (*kisses her on the cheek*). That's right.

YELENA. I wish you all happiness. (*Looks round*) Well, so be it ! For once in my life ! (*embraces him impulsively and both simultaneously draw rapidly apart from each other*). I must go—I must go !

ASTROV. Make haste and go. Since the carriage is there, you had better set off.

YELENA. There's someone coming, I believe. (*Both listen.*)

ASTROV. *Finita !*

(*Enter* SEREBRYAKOV, VOYNITSKY, MARYA VASSILYEVNA, *with a book ;* TELYEGIN *and* SONYA.)

SEREBRYAKOV (*to* VOYNITSKY). Let bygones be bygones. After what has happened, I have gone through and experienced so much in these few hours, that I believe I could write a whole treatise on the art of living for the benefit of posterity. I gladly accept your apologies and apologise myself. Good-bye ! (*He and* VOYNITSKY *kiss each other three times.*)

VOYNITSKY. You shall receive regularly the same sum as hitherto. Everything shall be as before.

(YELENA ANDREYEVNA *embraces* SONYA.)

SEREBRYAKOV (*kisses* MARYA VASSILYEVNA'S *hand*). *Maman.* . . .

MARYA (*kissing him*). Alexandr, have your photograph taken again and send it to me. You know how dear you are to me.

TELYEGIN. Good-bye, your Excellency! Don't forget us!

SEREBRYAKOV (*kissing his daughter*). Good-bye . . . good-bye, everyone. (*Shaking hands with* ASTROV) Thanks for your pleasant company. I respect your way of thinking, your enthusiasms, your impulses, but permit an old man to add one observation to his farewell message: you must work, my friends! you must work! (*He bows to them all.*) I wish you all things good!

(*Goes out, followed by* MARYA VASSILYEVNA *and* SONYA.)

VOYNITSKY (*warmly kisses* YELENA ANDREY-EVNA'S *hand*). Good-bye. . . . Forgive me. . . . We shall never meet again.

YELENA (*moved*). Good-bye, dear Ivan Petro-vitch (*kisses him on the head and goes out*).

ASTROV (*to* TELYEGIN). Waffles, tell them, by the way, to bring my carriage round too.

TELYEGIN. Certainly, my dear soul (*goes out*).

(*Only* ASTROV *and* VOYNITSKY *remain*.)

ASTROV (*clearing his paints from the table and putting them away in his portmanteau*). Why don't you go and see them off?

VOYNITSKY. Let them go, I . . . I can't. My heart is too heavy. I must make haste and occupy myself with something. . . . Work! Work! (*rummages among his papers on the table*).

(*A pause ; there is the sound of bells.*)

ASTROV. They've gone. The Professor is glad, I'll be bound. Nothing will tempt him back.

MARINA (*enters*). They've gone (*sits down in an easy chair and knits her stocking*).

SONYA (*enters*). They've gone (*wipes her eyes*). Good luck to them. (*To her uncle*) Well, Uncle Vanya, let us do something.

VOYNITSKY. Work, work. . . .

SONYA. It's ever so long since we sat at this table together (*lights the lamp on the table*). I believe there is no ink (*takes the inkstand, goes to the cupboard, and fills it with ink*). But I feel sad that they have gone.

(MARYA VASSILYEVNA *comes in slowly.*)

MARYA. They've gone (*sits down and becomes engrossed in reading*).

SONYA (*sits down to the table and turns over the pages of the account book*). First of all, Uncle Vanya, let us make out our accounts. We've neglected it all dreadfully. Someone sent for his account again to-day. Make it out. If you will do one account, I will do another.

VOYNITSKY (*writes*). " Delivered . . . to Mr. . . . " (*Both write in silence.*)

MARINA (*yawning*). I am ready for bye-bye.

ASTROV. How quiet it is ! The pens scratch and the cricket churrs. It's warm and snug. I don't want to go. (*There is the sound of bells.*) There are my horses. . . . There is nothing left for me but to say good-bye to you, my friends—to say good-bye to my table—and be off ! (*packs up his maps in the portfolio*).

mette ivers.

MARINA. Why are you in such a hurry? You might as well stay.

ASTROV. I can't.

VOYNITSKY (*writes*). "Account delivered, two roubles and seventy-five kopecks."

(*Enter a* LABOURER.)

LABOURER. Mihail Lvovitch, the horses are ready.

ASTROV. I heard them. (*Hands him the medicine-chest, the portmanteau and the portfolio*) Here, take these. Mind you don't crush the portfolio.

LABOURER. Yes, sir.

ASTROV. Well? (*goes to say good-bye*).

SONYA. When shall we see you again?

ASTROV. Not before next summer, I expect. Hardly in the winter. . . . Of course, if anything happens, you'll let me know, and I'll come (*shakes hands*). Thank you for your hospitality, for your kindness—for everything, in fact. (*Goes up to nurse and kisses her on the head*) Good-bye, old woman.

MARINA. You are not going without tea?

ASTROV. I don't want any, nurse.

MARINA. Perhaps you'll have a drop of vodka?

ASTROV (*irresolutely*). Perhaps.

(MARINA *goes out.*)

ASTROV (*after a pause*). My trace-horse has gone a little lame. I noticed it yesterday when Petrushka was taking it to water.

VOYNITSKY. You must change his shoes.

ASTROV. I shall have to call in at the blacksmith's in Rozhdestvennoye. It can't be helped. (*Goes up to the map of Africa and looks at it*) I suppose in that Africa there the heat must be something terrific now!

VOYNITSKY. Yes, most likely.

MARINA (*comes back with a tray on which there is a glass of vodka and a piece of bread*). There you are.

(ASTROV *drinks the vodka.*)

MARINA. To your good health, my dear (*makes a low bow*). You should eat some bread with it.

ASTROV. No, I like it as it is. And now, good luck to you all. (*To* MARINA) Don't come out, nurse, there is no need.

(*He goes out;* SONYA *follows with a candle, to see him off;* MARINA *sits in her easy chair.*)

VOYNITSKY (*writes*). " February the second, Lenten oil, twenty pounds. February sixteenth, Lenten oil again, twenty pounds. Buckwheat . . . " (*a pause*).

(*The sound of bells.*)

MARINA. He has gone (*a pause*).

SONYA (*comes back and puts the candle on the table*). He has gone.

VOYNITSKY (*counts on the beads and writes down*). " Total . . . fifteen . . . twenty-five . . ."

(SONYA *sits down and writes.*)

MARINA (*yawns*). Lord have mercy on us !

(TELYEGIN *comes in on tiptoe, sits by the door and softly tunes the guitar.*)

VOYNITSKY (*to* SONYA, *passing his hand over her hair*). My child, how my heart aches ! Oh, if only you knew how my heart aches !

SONYA. There is nothing for it. We must go on living ! (*a pause*). We shall go on living, Uncle Vanya ! We shall live through a long,

166

long chain of days and weary evenings; we shall patiently bear the trials which fate sends us; we shall work for others, both now and in our old age, and have no rest; and when our time comes we shall die without a murmur, and there beyond the grave we shall say that we have suffered, that we have wept, that life has been bitter to us, and God will have pity on us, and you and I, uncle, dear uncle, shall see a life that is bright, lovely, beautiful. We shall rejoice and look back at these troubles of ours with tenderness, with a smile—and we shall rest. I have faith, uncle; I have fervent, passionate faith. (*Slips on her knees before him and lays her head on his hands; in a weary voice*) We shall rest!

(TELYEGIN *softly plays on the guitar.*)

SONYA. We shall rest! We shall hear the angels; we shall see all Heaven lit with radiance; we shall see all earthly evil, all our sufferings, drowned in mercy which will fill the whole world, and our life will be peaceful, gentle and sweet as a caress. I have faith, I have faith (*wipes away his tears with her handkerchief*). Poor Uncle Vanya, you are crying. (*Through her tears*) You have had no joy in your life, but wait, Uncle Vanya, wait. We shall rest (*puts her arms round him*). We shall rest! (*The watchman taps.*)

(TELYEGIN *plays softly;* MARYA VASSILYEVNA *makes notes on the margin of her pamphlet;* MARINA *knits her stocking.*)

SONYA. We shall rest!

CURTAIN DROPS SLOWLY

THE CHERRY ORCHARD

A COMEDY IN FOUR ACTS

First performed at Moscow,
January 17, 1904

CHARACTERS IN THE PLAY

MADAME RANEVSKY (LYUBOV ANDREYEVNA) (*the owner of the Cherry Orchard*).
ANYA *(her daughter, aged 17)*.
VARYA *(her adopted daughter, aged 24)*.
GAEV (LEONID ANDREYEVITCH) *(brother of Madame Ranevsky)*.
LOPAHIN (YERMOLAY ALEXEYEVITCH) *(a Merchant)*.
TROFIMOV (PYOTR SERGEYEVITCH) *(a Student)*.
SEMYONOV-PISHTCHIK *(a Landowner)*.
CHARLOTTA IVANOVNA *(a Governess)*.
EPIHODOV (SEMYON PANTALEYEVITCH) *(a Clerk)*.
DUNYASHA *(a Maid)*.
FIRS *(an old Valet, aged 87)*.
YASHA *(a young Valet)*.
A VAGRANT.
THE STATION MASTER.
A POST-OFFICE CLERK.
VISTORS, SERVANTS.

The action takes place on the estate of
MADAME RANEVSKY.

ACT I

A room, which has always been called the nursery. One of the doors leads into ANYA'S *room. Dawn, sun rises during the scene. May, the cherry trees in flower, but it is cold in the garden with the frost of early morning. Windows closed.*
Enter DUNYASHA *with a candle and* LOPAHIN *with a book in his hand.*

LOPAHIN. The train's in, thank God. What time is it ?

DUNYASHA. Nearly two o'clock (*puts out the candle*). It's daylight already.

LOPAHIN. The train's late ! Two hours, at least (*yawns and stretches*). I'm a pretty one ; what a fool I've been. Came here on purpose to meet them at the station and dropped asleep. . . . Dozed off as I sat in the chair. It's annoying. . . . You might have waked me.

DUNYASHA. I thought you had gone (*listens*). There, I do believe they're coming !

LOPAHIN (*listens*). No, what with the luggage and one thing and another (*a pause*). Lyubov Andreyevna has been abroad five years; I don't know what she is like now. . . . She's a splendid woman. A good-natured, kind-hearted woman. I remember when I was a lad of fifteen, my poor father—he used to keep a little shop here in the village in those days—gave me a punch in the face with his fist and made my nose bleed. We were in the yard here, I forget what we'd come about—he had had a drop. Lyubov Andreyevna—I can see her now—she was a slim young girl then—took me to wash my face, and then brought me into this very room, into the nursery. " Don't cry, little peasant," says she, " it will be well in time for your wedding day" . . . (a pause). Little peasant. . . . My father was a peasant, it's true, but here am I in a white waistcoat and brown shoes, like a pig in a bun shop. Yes, I'm a rich man, but for all my money, come to think, a peasant I was, and a peasant I am (turns over the pages of the book). I've been reading this book and I can't make head or tail of it. I fell asleep over it (a pause).

DUNYASHA. The dogs have been awake all night, they feel that the mistress is coming.

LOPAHIN. Why, what's the matter with you, Dunyasha ?

DUNYASHA. My hands are all of a tremble. I feel as though I should faint.

LOPAHIN. You're a spoilt soft creature, Dunyasha. And dressed like a lady too, and your hair done up. That's not the thing. One must know one's place.

(Enter EPIHODOV with a nosegay ; he wears a pea-jacket and highly polished creaking top-boots ; he drops the nosegay as he comes in.)

EPIHODOV (picking up the nosegay). Here ! the gardener's sent this, says you're to put it in the dining-room (gives DUNYASHA the nosegay).

LOPAHIN. And bring me some kvass.

DUNYASHA. I will (*goes out*).

EPIHODOV. It's chilly this morning, three degrees of frost, though the cherries are all in flower. I can't say much for our climate (*sighs*). I can't. Our climate is not often propitious to the occasion. Yermolay Alexeyevitch, permit me to call your attention to the fact that I purchased myself a pair of boots the day before yesterday, and they creak, I venture to assure you, so that there's no tolerating them. What ought I to grease them with?

LOPAHIN. Oh, shut up! Don't bother me.

EPIHODOV. Every day some misfortune befalls me. I don't complain, I'm used to it, and I wear a smiling face.

(DUNYASHA *comes in, hands* LOPAHIN *the kvass*.)

EPIHODOV. I am going (*stumbles against a chair, which falls over*). There! (*as though triumphant*). There you see now, excuse the expression, an accident like that among others. . . . It's positively remarkable (*goes out*).

DUNYASHA. Do you know, Yermolay Alexeyevitch, I must confess, Epihodov has made me a proposal.

LOPAHIN. Ah!

DUNYASHA. I'm sure I don't know. . . . He's a harmless fellow, but sometimes when he begins talking, there's no making anything of it. It's all very fine and expressive, only there's no understanding it. I've a sort of liking for him too. He loves me to distraction. He's an unfortunate man ; every day there's something. They tease him about it—two and twenty misfortunes they call him.

LOPAHIN (*listening*). There ! I do believe they're coming.

DUNYASHA. They *are* coming ! What's the matter with me ? . . . I'm cold all over.

LOPAHIN. They really are coming. Let's go and meet them. Will she know me ? It's five years since I saw her.

DUNYASHA (*in a flutter*). I shall drop this very minute. . . . Ah, I shall drop.

(*There is a sound of two carriages driving up to the house. LOPAHIN and DUNYASHA go out quickly. The stage is left empty. A noise is heard in the adjoining rooms. FIRS, who has driven to meet MADAME RANEVSKY, crosses the stage hurriedly leaning on a stick. He is wearing old-fashioned livery and a high hat. He says something to himself, but not a word can be distinguished. The noise behind the scenes goes on increasing. A voice: " Come, let's go in here." Enter LYUBOV ANDREYEVNA, ANYA, and CHARLOTTA IVANOVNA with a pet dog on a chain, all in travelling dresses, VARYA in an out-door coat with a kerchief over her head, GAEV, SEMYONOV-PISHTCHIK, LOPAHIN, DUNYASHA with bag and parasol, servants with other articles. All walk across the room.*)

ANYA. Let's come in here Do you remember what room this is, mamma ?

LYUBOV (*joyfully, through her tears*). The nursery!

VARYA. How cold it is, my hands are numb. (*To* LYUBOV ANDREYEVNA) Your rooms, the white room and the lavender one, are just the same as ever, mamma.

LYUBOV. My nursery, dear delightful room. . . . I used to sleep here when I was little . . . (*cries*). And here I am, like a little child . . . (*kisses her brother and* VARYA, *and then her brother again*). Varya's just the same as ever, like a nun. And I knew Dunyasha (*kisses* DUNYASHA).

GAEV. The train was two hours late. What do you think of that? Is that the way to do things?

CHARLOTTA (*to* PISHTCHIK). My dog eats nuts, too.

PISHTCHIK (*wonderingly*). Fancy that!

(*They all go out except* ANYA *and* DUNYASHA.)

DUNYASHA. We've been expecting you so long (*takes* ANYA'S *hat and coat*).

ANYA. I haven't slept for four nights on the journey. I feel dreadfully cold.

DUNYASHA. You set out in Lent, there was snow and frost, and now? My darling! (*laughs and kisses her*). I *have* missed you, my precious, my joy. I must tell you . . . I can't put it off a minute. . . .

ANYA (*wearily*). What now?

DUNYASHA. Epihodov, the clerk, made me a proposal just after Easter.

ANYA. It's always the same thing with you . . . (*straightening her hair*). I've lost all my hairpins . . . (*she is staggering from exhaustion*).

175

DUNYASHA. I don't know what to think, really. He does love me, he does love me so !

ANYA (*looking towards her door, tenderly*). My own room, my windows just as though I had never gone away. I'm home ! To-morrow morning I shall get up and run into the garden. . . . Oh, if I could get to sleep ! I haven't slept all the journey, I was so anxious and worried.

DUNYASHA. Pyotr Sergeyevitch came the day before yesterday.

ANYA (*joyfully*). Petya !

DUNYASHA. He's asleep in the bath house, he has settled in there. I'm afraid of being in their way, says he. (*Glancing at her watch*) I was to have waked him, but Varvara Mihalovna told me not to. Don't you wake him, says she.

(*Enter* VARYA *with a bunch of keys at her waist.*)

VARYA. Dunyasha, coffee and make haste. . . . Mamma's asking for coffee.

DUNYASHA. This very minute (*goes out*).

VARYA. Well, thank God, you've come. You're home again (*petting her*). My little darling has come back ! My precious beauty has come back again !

ANYA. I have had a time of it !

VARYA. I can fancy !

ANYA. We set off in Holy Week—it was so cold then, and all the way Charlotta would talk and show off her tricks. What did you want to burden me with Charlotta for ?

VARYA. You couldn't have travelled all alone, darling. At seventeen !

ANYA. We got to Paris at last, it was cold there

—snow. I speak French shockingly. Mamma lives on the fifth floor, I went up to her, and there were a lot of French people, ladies, an old priest with a book. The place smelt of tobacco and so comfortless. I felt sorry, oh ! so sorry for mamma all at once, I put my arms round her neck, and hugged her and wouldn't let her go. Mamma was as kind as she could be, and she cried. . . .

VARYA (*through her tears*). Don't speak of it, don't speak of it !

ANYA. She had sold her villa at Mentone, she had nothing left, nothing. I hadn't a farthing left either, we only just had enough to get here. And mamma doesn't understand ! When we had dinner at the stations, she always ordered the most expensive things and gave the waiters a whole rouble. Charlotta's just the same. Yasha too must have the same as we do ; it's simply awful. You know Yasha is mamma's valet now, we brought him here with us.

VARYA. Yes, I've seen the young rascal.

ANYA. Well, tell me—have you paid the arrears on the mortgage ?

VARYA. How could we get the money ?

ANYA. Oh, dear ! Oh, dear !

VARYA. In August the place will be sold.

ANYA. My goodness !

LOPAHIN (*peeps in at the door and moo's like a cow*). Moo ! (*disappears*).

VARYA (*weeping*). There, that's what I could do to him (*shakes her fist*).

ANYA (*embracing* VARYA, *softly*). Varya, has he made you an offer ? (VARYA *shakes her head*.)

Why, but he loves you. Why is it you don't come to an understanding? What are you waiting for?

VARYA. I believe that there never will be anything between us. He has a lot to do, he has no time for me . . . and takes no notice of me. Bless the man, it makes me miserable to see him. . . . Everyone's talking of our being married, everyone's congratulating me, and all the while there's really nothing in it; it's all like a dream. (*In another tone*) You have a new brooch like a bee.

ANYA (*mournfully*). Mamma bought it. (*Goes into her own room and in a light-hearted childish tone*) And you know, in Paris I went up in a balloon!

VARYA. My darling's home again! My pretty is home again!

> (DUNYASHA *returns with the coffee-pot and is making the coffee.*)

VARYA (*standing at the door*). All day long, darling, as I go about looking after the house, I keep dreaming all the time. If only we could marry you to a rich man, then I should feel more at rest. Then I would go off by myself on a pilgrimage to Kiev, to Moscow . . . and so I would spend my life going from one holy place to another. . . . I would go on and on. . . . What bliss!

ANYA. The birds are singing in the garden. What time is it?

VARYA. It must be nearly three. It's time you were asleep, darling (*going into* ANYA'S *room*). What bliss!

> (YASHA *enters with a rug and a travelling bag.*)

178

YASHA (*crosses the stage, mincingly*). May one come in here, pray ?

DUNYASHA. I shouldn't have known you, Yasha. How you have changed abroad.

YASHA. H'm ! . . . And who are you ?

DUNYASHA. When you went away, I was that high (*shows distance from floor*). Dunyasha, Fyodor's daughter. . . . You don't remember me !

YASHA. H'm ! . . . You're a peach ! (*looks round and embraces her : she shrieks and drops a saucer* YASHA *goes out hastily*).

VARYA (*in the doorway, in a tone of vexation*). What now ?

DUNYASHA (*through her tears*). I have broken a saucer.

VARYA. Well, that brings good luck.

ANYA (*coming out of her room*). We ought to prepare mamma : Petya is here.

VARYA. I told them not to wake him.

ANYA (*dreamily*). It's six years since father died. Then only a month later little brother Grisha was drowned in the river, such a pretty boy he was, only seven. It was more than mamma could bear, so she went away, went away without looking back (*shuddering*). . . . How well I understand her, if only she knew ! (*a pause*) And Petya Trofimov was Grisha's tutor, he may remind her.

(*Enter* FIRS *: he is wearing a pea-jacket and a white waistcoat.*)

FIRS (*goes up to the coffee-pot, anxiously*). The mistress will be served here (*puts on white gloves*). Is the coffee ready ? (*Sternly to* DUNYASHA) Girl ! Where's the cream ?

DUNYASHA. Ah, mercy on us! (*goes out quickly*).

FIRS (*fussing round the coffee-pot*). Ech! you good-for-nothing! (*muttering to himself*). Come back from Paris. And the old master used to go to Paris too . . . horses all the way (*laughs*).

VARYA. What is it, Firs?

FIRS. What is your pleasure? (*Gleefully*) My lady has come home! I have lived to see her again! Now I can die (*weeps with joy*).

> (*Enter* LYUBOV ANDREYEVNA, GAEV *and* SEMYONOV-PISHTCHIK; *the latter is in a short-waisted full coat of fine cloth, and full trousers.* GAEV, *as he comes in, makes a gesture with his arms and his whole body, as though he were playing billiards.*)

LYUBOV. How does it go? Let me remember. Cannon off the red!

GAEV. That's it—in off the white! Why, once, sister, we used to sleep together in this very room, and now I'm fifty-one, strange as it seems.

LOPAHIN. Yes, time flies.

GAEV. What do you say?

LOPAHIN. Time, I say, flies.

GAEV. What a smell of patchouli!

ANYA. I'm going to bed. Good-night, mamma (*kisses her mother*).

LYUBOV. My precious darling (*kisses her hands*). Are you glad to be home? I can't believe it.

ANYA. Good-night, uncle.

GAEV (*kissing her face and hands*). God bless you! How like you are to your mother! (*To his sister*) At her age you were just the same, Lyuba.

(ANYA *shakes hands with* LOPAHIN *and* PISHTCHIK, *then goes out, shutting the door after her.*)

LYUBOV. She's quite worn out.

PISHTCHIK. Aye, it's a long journey, to be sure.

VARYA (*to* LOPAHIN *and* PISHTCHIK). Well, gentlemen? It's three o'clock and time to say good-bye.

LYUBOV (*laughs*). You're just the same as ever, Varya (*draws her to her and kisses her*). I'll just drink my coffee and then we will all go and rest. (FIRS *puts a cushion under her feet.*) Thanks, friend. I am so fond of coffee, I drink it day and night. Thanks, dear old man (*kisses* FIRS).

VARYA. I'll just see whether all the things have been brought in (*goes out*).

LYUBOV. Can it really be me sitting here? (*laughs*). I want to dance about and clap my hands. (*Covers her face with her hands*) And I could drop asleep in a moment! God knows I love my country, I love it tenderly; I couldn't look out of the window in the train, I kept crying so. (*Through her tears*) But I must drink my coffee, though. Thank you, Firs, thanks, dear old man. I'm so glad to find you still alive.

FIRS. The day before yesterday.

GAEV. He's rather deaf.

LOPAHIN. I have to set off for Harkov directly, at five o'clock. . . . It is annoying! I wanted to have a look at you, and a little talk. . . . You are just as splendid as ever.

PISHTCHIK (*breathing heavily*). Handsomer,

indeed. . . . Dressed in Parisian style . . . completely bowled me over.

LOPAHIN. Your brother, Leonid Andreyevitch here, is always saying that I'm a low-born knave, that I'm a money-grubber, but I don't care one straw for that. Let him talk. Only I do want you to believe in me as you used to. I do want your wonderful tender eyes to look at me as they used to in the old days. Merciful God! My father was a serf of your father and of your grandfather, but you—you—did so much for me once, that I've forgotten all that; I love you as though you were my kin . . . more than my kin.

LYUBOV. I can't sit still, I simply can't . . . (*jumps up and walks about in violent agitation*). This happiness is too much for me. . . . You may laugh at me, I know I'm silly. . . . My own bookcase (*kisses the bookcase*). My little table.

GAEV. Nurse died while you were away.

LYUBOV (*sits down and drinks coffee*). Yes, the Kingdom of Heaven be hers! You wrote me of her death.

GAEV. And Anastasy is dead. Squinting Petrushka has left me and is in service now with the police captain in the town (*takes a box of caramels out of his pocket and sucks one*).

PISHTCHIK. My daughter, Dashenka, wishes to be remembered to you.

LOPAHIN. I want to tell you something very pleasant and cheering (*glancing at his watch*). I'm going directly . . . there's no time to say much . . . well, I can say it in a couple of words. I needn't tell you your cherry orchard is to be sold to pay your debts ; the 22nd of August is the date fixed for the sale ; but don't you worry, dearest lady, you may sleep in peace, there is a way of saving it. . . . This is what I propose. I beg your attention ! Your estate is not twenty miles from the town, the railway runs close by it, and if the cherry orchard and the land along the river bank were cut up into building plots and then let on lease for summer villas, you would make an income of at least 25,000 roubles a year out of it.

GAEV. That's all rot, if you'll excuse me.

LYUBOV. I don't quite understand you, Yermolay Alexeyevitch.

LOPAHIN. You will get a rent of at least 25 roubles a year for a three-acre plot from summer visitors, and if you say the word now, I'll bet you what you like there won't be one square foot of ground vacant by the autumn, all the plots will be taken up. I congratulate you ; in fact, you are saved. It's a perfect situation with that deep river. Only, of course, it must be cleared— all the old buildings, for example, must be removed, this house too, which is really good for nothing and the old cherry orchard must be cut down.

LYUBOV. Cut down ? My dear fellow, forgive me, but you don't know what you are talking about. If there is one thing interesting—remarkable indeed—in the whole province, it's just our cherry orchard.

LOPAHIN. The only thing remarkable about the orchard is that it's a very large one. There's a crop of cherries every alternate year, and then there's nothing to be done with them, no one buys them.

183

GAEV. This orchard is mentioned in the Encyclopædia.'

LOPAHIN (*glancing at his watch*). If we don't decide on something and don't take some steps, on the 22nd of August the cherry orchard and the whole estate too will be sold by auction. Make up your minds ! There is no other way of saving it, I'll take my oath on that. No, no !

FIRS. In old days, forty or fifty years ago, they used to dry the cherries, soak them, pickle them make jam too, and they used——

GAEV. Be quiet, Firs.

FIRS. And they used to send the preserved cherries to Moscow and to Harkov by the waggon-load. That brought the money in ! And the preserved cherries in those days were soft and juicy, sweet and fragrant. . . . They knew the way to do them then. . . .

LYUBOV. And where is the recipe now ?

FIRS. It's forgotten. Nobody remembers it.

PISHTCHIK (*to* LYUBOV ANDREYEVNA). What's it like in Paris ? Did you eat frogs there ?

LYUBOV. Oh, I ate crocodiles.

PISHTCHIK. Fancy that now !

LOPAHIN. There used to be only the gentlefolks and the peasants in the country, but now there are these summer visitors. All the towns, even the small ones, are surrounded nowadays by these summer villas. And one may say for sure, that in another twenty years there'll be many more of these people and that they'll be everywhere. At present the summer visitor only drinks tea in his verandah, but maybe he'll take to working his bit of land too, and then your cherry orchard would become happy, rich and prosperous. . . .

GAEV (*indignant*). What rot !

(*Enter* VARYA *and* YASHA.)

VARYA. There are two telegrams for you, mamma (*takes out keys and opens an old-fashioned bookcase with a loud crack*). Here they are.

LYUBOV. From Paris (*tears the telegrams, without reading them*). I have done with Paris.

GAEV. Do you know, Lyuba, how old that bookcase is ? Last week I pulled out the bottom drawer and there I found the date branded on it. The bookcase was made just a hundred years ago. What do you say to that ? We might have celebrated its jubilee. Though it's an inanimate object, still it is a *book* case.

PISHTCHIK (*amazed*). A hundred years ! Fancy that now.

GAEV. Yes. . . . It is a thing . . . (*feeling the bookcase*). Dear, honoured, bookcase ! Hail to thee who for more than a hundred years hast served the pure ideals of good and justice ; thy silent call to fruitful labour has never flagged in those hundred years, maintaining (*in tears*) in the generations of man, courage and faith in a brighter future and fostering in us ideals of good and social consciousness (*a pause*).

LOPAHIN. Yes. . . .

LYUBOV. You are just the same as ever, Leonid.

GAEV (*a little embarrassed*). Cannon off the right into the pocket !

LOPAHIN (*looking at his watch*). Well, it's time I was off.

YASHA (*handing* LYUBOV ANDREYEVNA *medicine*). Perhaps you will take your pills now.

PISHTCHIK. You shouldn't take medicines, my dear madam . . . they do no harm and no good. Give them here . . . honoured lady (*takes the pill-box, pours the pills into the hollow of his hand, blows on them, puts them in his mouth and drinks off some kvass*). There !

LYUBOV (*in alarm*). Why, you must be out of your mind !

PISHTCHIK. I have taken all the pills.

LOPAHIN. What a glutton ! (*All laugh.*)

FIRS. His honour stayed with us in Easter week, ate a gallon and a half of cucumbers . . . (*mutters*).

LYUBOV. What is he saying ?

VARYA. He has taken to muttering like that for the last three years. We are used to it.

YASHA. His declining years !

(CHARLOTTA IVANOVNA, *a very thin, lanky figure in a white dress with a lorgnette in her belt, walks across the stage.*)

LOPAHIN. I beg your pardon, Charlotta Ivanovna, I have not had time to greet you (*tries to kiss her hand*).

CHARLOTTA (*pulling away her hand*). If I let you kiss my hand, you'll be wanting to kiss my elbow, and then my shoulder.

LOPAHIN. I've no luck to-day ! (*All laugh.*) Charlotta Ivanovna, show us some tricks !

LYUBOV. Charlotta, do show us some tricks !

CHARLOTTA. I don't want to. I'm sleepy (*goes out*).

LOPAHIN. In three weeks' time we shall meet again (*kisses* LYUBOV ANDREYEVNA'S *hand*). Good-bye till then—I must go. (*To* GAEV) Good-bye. (*Kisses* PISHTCHIK) Good-bye. (*Gives his hand to* VARYA, *then to* FIRS *and* YASHA) I don't want to go. (*To* LYUBOV ANDREYEVNA) If you think over my plan for the villas and make up your mind, then let me know; I will lend you 50,000 roubles. Think of it seriously.

VARYA (*angrily*). Well, do go, for goodness sake.

LOPAHIN. I'm going, I'm going (*goes out*).

GAEV. Low-born knave! I beg pardon, though . . . Varya is going to marry him, he's Varya's fiancé.

VARYA. Don't talk nonsense, uncle.

LYUBOV. Well, Varya, I shall be delighted. He's a good man.

PISHTCHIK. He is, one must acknowledge, a most worthy man. And my Dashenka . . . says too that . . . she says . . . various things (*snores, but at once wakes up*). But all the same, honoured lady, could you oblige me . . . with a loan of 240 roubles . . . to pay the interest on my mortgage to-morrow?

VARYA (*dismayed*). No, no.

LYUBOV. I really haven't any money.

PISHTCHIK. It will turn up (*laughs*). I never lose hope. I thought everything was over, I was a ruined man, and lo and behold—the railway passed through my land and . . . they paid me for it. And something else will turn up again, if not to-day, then to-morrow . . . Dashenka'll win two hundred thousand . . . she's got a lottery ticket.

LYUBOV. Well, we've finished our coffee, we can go to bed.

FIRS (*brushes* GAEV, *reprovingly*). You have got on the wrong trousers again ! What am I to do with you ?

VARYA (*softly*). Anya's asleep. (*Softly opens the window*) Now the sun's risen, it's not a bit cold. Look, mamma, what exquisite trees ! My goodness ! And the air ! The starlings are singing !

GAEV (*opens another window*). The orchard is all white. You've not forgotten it, Lyuba ? That long avenue that runs straight, straight as an arrow, how it shines on a moonlight night. You remember ? You've not forgotten ?

LYUBOV (*looking out of the window into the garden*). Oh, my childhood, my innocence ! It was in this nursery I used to sleep, from here I looked out into the orchard, happiness waked with me every morning and in those days the orchard was just the same, nothing has changed (*laughs with delight*). All, all white ! Oh, my orchard ! After the dark gloomy autumn, and the cold winter ; you are young again, and full of happiness, the heavenly angels have never left you. . . . If I could cast off the burden that weighs on my heart, if I could forget the past !

GAEV. H'm ! and the orchard will be sold to pay our debts ; it seems strange. . . .

LYUBOV. See, our mother walking . . . all in white, down the avenue ! (*laughs with delight*). It is she !

GAEV. Where ?

VARYA. Oh, don't, mamma !

LYUBOV. There is no one. It was my fancy. On the right there, by the path to the arbour, there is a white tree bending like a woman. . . .

(*Enter* TROFIMOV *wearing a shabby student's uniform and spectacles.*)

LYUBOV. What a ravishing orchard ! White masses of blossom, blue sky. . . .

TROFIMOV. Lyubov Andreyevna ! (*She looks round at him.*) I will just pay my respects to you and then leave you at once (*kisses her hand warmly*). I was told to wait until morning, but I hadn't the patience to wait any longer. . . .

(LYUBOV ANDREYEVNA *looks at him in perplexity.*)

VARYA (*through her tears*). This is Petya Trofimov.

TROFIMOV. Petya Trofimov, who was your Grisha's tutor. . . . Can I have changed so much ?

(LYUBOV ANDREYEVNA *embraces him and weeps quietly.*)

GAEV (*in confusion*). There, there, Lyuba.

VARYA (*crying*). I told you, Petya, to wait till to-morrow.

LYUBOV. My Grisha . . . my boy . . . Grisha . . . my son !

VARYA. We can't help it, mamma, it is God's will.

TROFIMOV (*softly through his tears*). There . . . there.

LYUBOV (*weeping quietly*). My boy was lost . . . drowned. Why ? Oh, why, dear Petya ? (*More quietly*) Anya is asleep in there, and I'm talking

loudly . . . making this noise. . . . But, Petya?
Why have you grown so ugly? Why do you look
so old?

TROFIMOV. A peasant-woman in the train called
me a mangy-looking gentleman.

LYUBOV. You were quite a boy then, a pretty
little student, and now your hair's thin—and
spectacles. Are you really a student still? (*goes
towards the door*).

TROFIMOV. I seem likely to be a perpetual
student.

LYUBOV (*kisses her brother, then* VARYA). Well,
go to bed. . . . You are older too, Leonid.

PISHTCHIK (*follows her*). I suppose it's time we
were asleep. . . . Ugh! my gout. I'm staying
the night; Lyubov Andreyevna, my dear soul, if
you could . . . to-morrow morning . . . 240
roubles.

GAEV. That's always his story.

PISHTCHIK. 240 roubles . . . to pay the interest
on my mortgage.

LYUBOV. My dear man, I have no money.

PISHTCHIK. I'll pay it back, my dear . . . a
trifling sum.

LYUBOV. Oh, well, Leonid will give it you. . . .
You give him the money, Leonid.

GAEV. Me give it him! Let him wait till he
gets it!

LYUBOV. It can't be helped, give it him. He
needs it. He'll pay it back.

(LYUBOV ANDREYEVNA, TROFIMOV, PISHTCHIK
and FIRS *go out*. GAEV, VARYA *and*
YASHA *remain*.)

GAEV. Sister hasn't got out of the habit of flinging away her money. (*To* YASHA) Get away, my good fellow, you smell of the hen-house.

YASHA (*with a grin*). And you, Leonid Andreyevitch, are just the same as ever.

GAEV. What's that ? (*To* VARYA) What did he say ?

VARYA (*to* YASHA). Your mother has come from the village ; she has been sitting in the servants' room since yesterday, waiting to see you.

YASHA. Oh, bother her !

VARYA. For shame !

YASHA. What's the hurry ? She might just as well have come to-morrow (*goes out*).

VARYA. Mamma's just the same as ever, she hasn't changed a bit. If she had her own way, she'd give away everything.

GAEV. Yes (*a pause*). If a great many remedies are suggested for some disease, it means that the disease is incurable. I keep thinking and racking my brains ; I have many schemes, a great many, and that really means none. If we could only come in for a legacy from somebody, or marry our Anya to a very rich man, or we might go to Yaroslavl and try our luck with our old aunt, the Countess. She's very, very rich, you know.

VARYA (*weeps*). If God would help us.

GAEV. Don't blubber. Aunt's very rich, but she doesn't like us. First, sister married a lawyer instead of a nobleman. . . .

(ANYA *appears in the doorway*.)

GAEV. And then her conduct, one can't call it virtuous. She is good, and kind, and nice, and

191

I love her, but, however one allows for extenuating circumstances, there's no denying that she's an immoral woman. One feels it in her slightest gesture.

VARYA (*in a whisper*). Anya's in the doorway.

GAEV. What do you say ? (*a pause*). It's queer, there seems to be something wrong with my right eye. I don't see as well as I did. And on Thursday when I was in the district Court . . .

(*Enter* ANYA.)

VARYA. Why aren't you asleep, Anya ?

ANYA. I can't get to sleep.

GAEV. My pet (*kisses* ANYA's *face and hands*). My child (*weeps*). You are not my niece, you are my angel, you are everything to me. Believe me, believe . . .

ANYA. I believe you, uncle. Everyone loves you and respects you . . . but, uncle dear, you must be silent . . . simply be silent. What were you saying just now about my mother, about your own sister ? What made you say that ?

GAEV. Yes, yes . . . (*puts his hand over his face*). Really, that was awful ! My God, save me ! And to-day I made a speech to the bookcase . . . so stupid ! And only when I had finished, I saw how stupid it was.

VARYA. It's true, uncle, you ought to keep quiet. Don't talk, that's all.

ANYA. If you could keep from talking, it would make things easier for you, too.

GAEV. I won't speak (*kisses* ANYA's *and* VARYA's *hands*). I'll be silent. Only this is about business. On Thursday I was in the district Court ; well, there was a large party of us there and we began talking of one thing and another, and this and that, and do you know, I believe that it will be possible to raise a loan on an I.O.U. to pay the arrears on the mortgage.

VARYA. If the Lord would help us!

GAEV. I'm going on Tuesday; I'll talk of it again. (*To* VARYA) Don't blubber. (*To* ANYA) Your mamma will talk to Lopahin; of course, he won't refuse her. And as soon as you're rested you shall go to Yaroslavl to the Countess, your great-aunt. So we shall all set to work in three directions at once, and the business is done. We shall pay off arrears, I'm convinced of it (*puts a caramel in his mouth*). I swear on my honour, I swear by anything you like, the estate shan't be sold (*excitedly*). By my own happiness, I swear it! Here's my hand on it, call me the basest, vilest of men, if I let it come to an auction! Upon my soul I swear it!

ANYA (*her equanimity has returned, she is quite happy*). How good you are, uncle, and how clever! (*embraces her uncle*). I'm at peace now! Quite at peace! I'm happy!

(*Enter* FIRS.)

FIRS (*reproachfully*). Leonid Andreyevitch, have you no fear of God? When are you going to bed?

GAEV. Directly, directly. You can go, Firs. I'll . . . yes, I will undress myself. Come, children, bye-bye. We'll go into details to-morrow, but now go to bed (*kisses* ANYA *and* VARYA). I'm a man of the eighties. They run down that period, but still I can say I have had

to suffer not a little for my convictions in my life.
It's not for nothing that the peasant loves me.
One must know the peasant! One must know
how . . .

ANYA. At it again, uncle!

VARYA. Uncle dear, you'd better be quiet!

FIRS (*angrily*). Leonid Andreyevitch!

GAEV. I'm coming. I'm coming. Go to bed.
Potted the shot—there's a shot for you! A
beauty! (*goes out*, FIRS *hobbling after him*).

ANYA. My mind's at rest now. I don't want
to go to Yaroslavl, I don't like my great-aunt,
but still my mind's at rest. Thanks to uncle
(*sits down*).

VARYA. We must go to bed. I'm going. Something unpleasant happened while you were away.
In the old servants' quarters there are only the old
servants, as you know—Efimyushka, Polya and
Yevstigney—and Karp too. They began letting
stray people in to spend the night—I said nothing.
But all at once I heard they had been spreading
a report that I gave them nothing but pease
pudding to eat. Out of stinginess, you know. . . .
And it was all Yevstigney's doing. . . . Very
well, I said to myself. . . . If that's how it is,
I thought, wait a bit. I sent for Yevstigney
. . . (*yawns*). He comes. . . . " How's this,
Yevstigney," I said, " you could be such a
fool as to ? . . ." (*Looking at* ANYA) Anitchka! (*a
pause*). She's asleep (*puts her arm round* ANYA).
Come to bed . . . come along! (*leads her*). My
darling has fallen asleep! Come . . . (*They go.*)

(*Far away beyond the orchard a shepherd plays*

on a pipe. TROFIMOV *crosses the stage
and, seeing* VARYA *and* ANYA, *stands still.*)

VARYA. 'Sh ! She's asleep, asleep. Come, my own.

ANYA (*softly, half asleep*). I'm so tired. Still those bells. Uncle . . . dear . . . mamma and uncle. . . .

VARYA. Come, my own, come along.

(*They go into* ANYA'S *room.*)

TROFIMOV (*tenderly*). My sunshine ! My spring

CURTAIN

ACT II

The open country. An old shrine, long abandoned and fallen out of the perpendicular ; near it a well, large stones that have apparently once been tombstones, and an old garden seat. The road to GAEV'S *house is seen. On one side rise dark poplars ; and there the cherry orchard begins. In the distance a row of telegraph poles and far, far away on the horizon there is faintly outlined a great town, only visible in very fine clear weather. It is near sunset.* CHARLOTTA, YASHA *and* DUNYASHA *are sitting on the seat.* EPIHODOV *is standing near, playing something mournful on a guitar. All sit plunged in thought.* CHARLOTTA *wears an old forage cap ; she has taken a gun from her shoulder and is tightening the buckle on the strap.*

CHARLOTTA (*musingly*). I haven't a real passport of my own, and I don't know how old I am, and I always feel that I'm a young thing. When I was a little girl, my father and mother used to travel about to fairs and give performances—very good ones. And I used to dance *salto-mortale* and all sorts of things. And when papa and mamma died, a German lady took me and had me educated.

And so I grew up and became a governess.
But where I came from, and who I am, I
don't know. . . . Who my parents were, very
likely they weren't married . . . I don't know
(*takes a cucumber out of her pocket and eats*). I
know nothing at all (*a pause*). One wants
to talk and has no one to talk to . . . I have
nobody.

EPIHODOV (*plays on the guitar and sings*).
" What care I for the noisy world! What care
I for friends or foes!" How agreeable it is to
play on the mandoline!

DUNYASHA. That's a guitar, not a mandoline
(*looks in a hand-mirror and powders herself*).

EPIHODOV. To a man mad with love, it's a mandoline. (*Sings*) " Were her heart but aglow with
love's mutual flame." (YASHA *joins in.*)

CHARLOTTA. How shockingly these people sing!
Foo! Like jackals!

DUNYASHA (*to* YASHA). What happiness, though,
to visit foreign lands.

YASHA. Ah, yes! I rather agree with you
there (*yawns, then lights a cigar*).

EPIHODOV. That's comprehensible. In foreign
lands everything has long since reached full
complexion.

YASHA. That's so, of course.

EPIHODOV. I'm a cultivated man, I read remarkable books of all sorts, but I can never make
out the tendency I am myself precisely inclined
for, whether to live or to shoot myself, speaking
precisely, but nevertheless I always carry a
revolver. Here it is . . . (*shows revolver*).

CHARLOTTA. I've had enough, and now I'm going (*puts on the gun*). Epihodov, you're a very clever fellow, and a very terrible one too, all the women must be wild about you. Br-r-r! (*goes*). These clever fellows are all so stupid; there's not a creature for me to speak to. . . . Always alone, alone, nobody belonging to me . . . and who I am, and why I'm on earth, I don't know (*walks away slowly*).

EPIHODOV. Speaking precisely, not touching upon other subjects, I'm bound to admit about myself, that destiny behaves mercilessly to me, as a storm to a little boat. If, let us suppose, I am mistaken, then why did I wake up this morning, to quote an example, and look round, and there on my chest was a spider of fearful magnitude . . . like this (*shows with both hands*). And then I take up a jug of kvass, to quench my thirst, and in it there is something in the highest degree unseemly of the nature of a cockroach (*a pause*). Have you read Buckle? (*a pause*). I am desirous of troubling you, Dunyasha, with a couple of words.

DUNYASHA. Well, speak.

EPIHODOV. I should be desirous to speak with you alone (*sighs*).

DUNYASHA (*embarrassed*). Well—only bring me my mantle first. It's by the cupboard. It's rather damp here.

EPIHODOV. Certainly. I will fetch it. Now I know what I must do with my revolver (*takes guitar and goes off playing on it*).

YASHA. Two and twenty misfortunes! Between ourselves, he's a fool (*yawns*).

DUNYASHA. God grant he doesn't shoot himself !
(*a pause*). I am so nervous, I'm always in a
flutter. I was a little girl when I was taken into
our lady's house, and now I have quite grown out
of peasant ways, and my hands are white, as white
as a lady's. I'm such a delicate, sensitive creature,
I'm afraid of everything. I'm so frightened. And
if you deceive me, Yasha, I don't know what will
become of my nerves.

YASHA (*kisses her*). You're a peach ! Of course
a girl must never forget herself ; what I dislike
more than anything is a girl being flighty in her
behaviour.

DUNYASHA. I'm passionately in love with you,
Yasha ; you are a man of culture—you can give
your opinion about anything (*a pause*).

YASHA (*yawns*). Yes, that's so. My opinion is
this : if a girl loves anyone, that means that she
has no principles (*a pause*). It's pleasant smoking
a cigar in the open air (*listens*). Someone's coming this way . . . it's the gentlefolk (DUNYASHA
embraces him impulsively). Go home, as though
you had been to the river to bathe ; go by that
path, or else they'll meet you and suppose I have
made an appointment with you here. That I can't
endure.

DUNYASHA (*coughing softly*). The cigar has
made my head ache . . . (*goes off*).

(YASHA *remains sitting near the shrine. Enter*
LYUBOV ANDREYEVNA, GAEV *and* LOPAHIN.)

LOPAHIN. You must make up your mind once
for all—there's no time to lose. It's quite a simple
question, you know. Will you consent to letting

the land for building or not ? One word in answer :
Yes or no ? Only one word !

LYUBOV. Who is smoking such horrible cigars
here ? (*sits down*).

GAEV. Now the railway line has been brought
near, it's made things very convenient (*sits down*).
Here we have been over and lunched in town.
Cannon off the white ! I should like to go home
and have a game.

LYUBOV. You have plenty of time.

LOPAHIN. Only one word ! (*Beseechingly*) Give
me an answer !

GAEV (*yawning*). What do you say ?

LYUBOV (*looks in her purse*). I had quite a lot
of money here yesterday, and there's scarcely any
left to-day. My poor Varya feeds us all on milk
soup for the sake of economy ; the old folks in the
kitchen get nothing but pease pudding, while I
waste my money in a senseless way (*drops purse,
scattering gold pieces*). There, they have all fallen
out ! (*annoyed*).

YASHA. Allow me, I'll soon pick them up
(*collects the coins*).

LYUBOV. Pray do, Yasha. And what did I go
off to the town to lunch for ? Your restaurant's
a wretched place with its music and the tablecloth
smelling of soap. . . . Why drink so much,
Leonid ? And eat so much ? And talk so much ?
To-day you talked a great deal again in the restaurant, and all so inappropriately. About the era
of the 'seventies, about the decadents. And to
whom ? Talking to waiters about decadents !

LOPAHIN. Yes.

GAEV (*waving his hand*). I'm incorrigible; that's evident. (*Irritably to* YASHA) Why is it you keep fidgeting about in front of us !

YASHA (*laughs*). I can't help laughing when I hear your voice.

GAEV (*to his sister*). Either I or he . . .

LYUBOV. Get along ! Go away, Yasha.

YASHA (*gives* LYUBOV ANDREYEVNA *her purse*). Directly (*hardly able to suppress his laughter*). This minute . . . (*goes off*).

LOPAHIN. Deriganov, the millionaire, means to buy your estate. They say he is coming to the sale himself.

LYUBOV. Where did you hear that ?

LOPAHIN. That's what they say in town.

GAEV. Our aunt in Yaroslavl has promised to send help ; but when, and how much she will send, we don't know.

LOPAHIN. How much will she send ? A hundred thousand ? Two hundred ?

LYUBOV. Oh, well ! . . . Ten or fifteen thousand, and we must be thankful to get that.

LOPAHIN. Forgive me, but such reckless people as you are—such queer, unbusiness-like people— I never met in my life. One tells you in plain Russian your estate is going to be sold, and you seem not to understand it.

LYUBOV. What are we to do ? Tell us what to do.

LOPAHIN. I do tell you every day. Every day I say the same thing. You absolutely must let the cherry orchard and the land on building leases ; and do it at once, as quick as may be—the auction's close upon us ! Do understand ! Once make up your mind to build villas, and you can raise as much money as you like, and then you are saved.

LYUBOV. Villas and summer visitors—forgive me saying so—it's so vulgar.

GAEV. There I perfectly agree with you.

LOPAHIN. I shall sob, or scream, or fall into a fit. I can't stand it ! You drive me mad ! (*To* GAEV) You're an old woman !

GAEV. What do you say ?

LOPAHIN. An old womán ! (*gets up to go*).

LYUBOV (*in dismay*). No, don't go ! Do stay, my dear friend ! Perhaps we shall think of something.

LOPAHIN. What is there to think of ?

LYUBOV. Don't go, I entreat you ! With you here it's more cheerful, anyway (*a pause*). I keep expecting something, as though the house were going to fall about our ears.

GAEV (*in profound dejection*). Potted the white ! It fails—a kiss.

LYUBOV. We have been great sinners. . . .

LOPAHIN. You have no sins to repent of.

GAEV (*puts a caramel in his mouth*). They say I've eaten up my property in caramels (*laughs*).

LYUBOV. Oh, my sins ! I've always thrown my money away recklessly like a lunatic. I married a man who made nothing but debts. My husband died of champagne—he drank dreadfully. To my misery I loved another man, and immediately—it was my first punishment—the blow fell upon me, here, in the river . . . my boy was drowned and I went abroad—went away for ever, never to return,

202

not to see that river again . . . I shut my eyes, and fled, distracted, and *he* after me . . . pitilessly, brutally. I bought a villa at Mentone, for *he* fell ill there, and for three years I had no rest day or night. His illness wore me out, my soul was dried up. And last year, when my villa was sold to pay my debts, I went to Paris and there he robbed me of everything and abandoned me for another woman ; and I tried to poison myself. . . . So stupid, so shameful ! . . . And suddenly I felt a yearning for Russia, for my country, for my little girl . . . (*dries her tears*). Lord, Lord, be merciful ! Forgive my sins ! Do not chastise me more ! (*Takes a telegram out of her pocket*) I got this to-day from Paris. He implores forgiveness, entreats me to return (*tears up the telegram*). I fancy there is music somewhere (*listens*).

GAEV. That's our famous Jewish orchestra. You remember, four violins, a flute and a double bass.

LYUBOV. That still in existence ? We ought to send for them one evening, and give a dance.

LOPAHIN (*listens*). I can't hear. . . . (*Hums softly*) " For money the Germans will turn a Russian into a Frenchman." (*Laughs*) I did see such a piece at the theatre yesterday ! It was funny !

LYUBOV. And most likely there was nothing funny in it. You shouldn't look at plays, you should look at yourselves a little oftener. How grey your lives are ! How much nonsense you talk.

LOPAHIN. That's true. One may say honestly, we live a fool's life (*pause*). My father was a peasant, an idiot; he knew nothing and taught me nothing, only beat me when he was drunk, and always with his stick. In reality I am just such another blockhead and idiot. I've learnt nothing properly. I write a wretched hand. I write so that I feel ashamed before folks, like a pig.

LYUBOV. You ought to get married, my dear fellow.

LOPAHIN. Yes . . . that's true.

LYUBOV. You should marry our Varya, she's a good girl.

LOPAHIN. Yes.

LYUBOV. She's a good-natured girl, she's busy all day long, and what's more, she loves you. And you have liked her for ever so long.

LOPAHIN. Well? I'm not against it. . . . She's a good girl (*pause*).

GAEV. I've been offered a place in the bank: 6,000 roubles a year. Did you know?

LYUBOV. You would never do for that! You must stay as you are.

(*Enter* FIRS *with overcoat.*)

FIRS. Put it on, sir, it's damp.

GAEV (*putting it on*). You bother me, old fellow.

FIRS. You can't go on like this. You went away in the morning without leaving word (*looks him over*).

LYUBOV. You look older, Firs!

FIRS. What is your pleasure?

LOPAHIN. You look older, she said.

FIRS. I've had a long life. They were arranging

my wedding before your papa was born . . . (*laughs*).
I was the head footman before the emancipation
came. I wouldn't consent to be set free then ;
I stayed on with the old master . . . (*a pause*). I
remember what rejoicings they made and didn't
know themselves what they were rejoicing over.

LOPAHIN. Those were fine old times. There
was flogging anyway.

FIRS (*not hearing*). To be sure ! The peasants
knew their place, and the masters knew theirs ;
but now they're all at sixes and sevens, there's no
making it out.

GAEV. Hold your tongue, Firs. I must go to
town to-morrow. I have been promised an introduction to a general, who might let us have a loan.

LOPAHIN. You won't bring that off. And you
won't pay your arrears, you may rest assured of
that.

LYUBOV. That's all his nonsense. There is no
such general.

(*Enter* TROFIMOV, ANYA *and* VARYA.)

GAEV. Here come our girls.

ANYA. There's mamma on the seat.

LYUBOV (*tenderly*). Come here, come along.
My darlings ! (*embraces* ANYA *and* VARYA). If you
only knew how I love you both. Sit beside me,
there, like that. (*All sit down.*)

LOPAHIN. Our perpetual student is always with
the young ladies.

TROFIMOV. That's not your business.

LOPAHIN. He'll soon be fifty, and he's still a
student.

TROFIMOV. Drop your idiotic jokes.

LOPAHIN. Why are you so cross, you queer fish?

TROFIMOV. Oh, don't persist!

LOPAHIN (*laughs*). Allow me to ask you what's your idea of me?

TROFIMOV. I'll tell you my idea of you, Yermolay Alexeyevitch: you are a rich man, you'll soon be a millionaire. Well, just as in the economy of nature a wild beast is of use, who devours everything that comes in his way, so you too have your use.

(*All laugh.*)

VARYA. Better tell us something about the planets, Petya.

LYUBOV. No, let us go on with the conversation we had yesterday.

TROFIMOV. What was it about?

GAEV. About pride.

TROFIMOV. We had a long conversation yesterday, but we came to no conclusion. In pride, in your sense of it, there is something mystical. Perhaps you are right from your point of view; but if one looks at it simply, without subtlety, what sort of pride can there be, what sense is there in it, if man in his physiological formation is very imperfect, if in the immense majority of cases he is coarse, dull-witted, profoundly unhappy? One must give up glorification of self. One should work, and nothing else.

GAEV. One must die in any case.

TROFIMOV. Who knows? And what does it mean—dying? Perhaps man has a hundred senses, and only the five we know are lost at death, while the other ninety-five remain alive.

206

LYUBOV. How clever you are, Petya!

LOPAHIN (*ironically*). Fearfully clever!

TROFIMOV. Humanity progresses, perfecting its powers. Everything that is beyond its ken now will one day become familiar and comprehensible; only we must work, we must with all our powers aid the seeker after truth. Here among us in Russia the workers are few in number as yet. The vast majority of the intellectual people I know, seek nothing, do nothing, are not fit as yet for work of any kind. They call themselves intellectual, but they treat their servants as inferiors, behave to the peasants as though they were animals, learn little, read nothing seriously, do practically nothing, only talk about science and know very little about art. They are all serious people, they all have severe faces, they all talk of weighty matters and air their theories, and yet the vast majority of us—ninety-nine per cent.—live like savages, at the least thing fly to blows and abuse, eat piggishly, sleep in filth and stuffiness, bugs everywhere, stench and damp and moral impurity. And it's clear all our fine talk is only to divert our attention and other people's. Show me where to find the crèches there's so much talk about, and the reading-rooms? They only exist in novels: in real life there are none of them. There is nothing but filth and vulgarity and Asiatic apathy. I fear and dislike very serious faces. I'm afraid of serious conversations. We should do better to be silent.

LOPAHIN. You know, I get up at five o'clock in the morning, and I work from morning to night;

and I've money, my own and other people's, always passing through my hands, and I see what people are made of all round me. One has only to begin to do anything to see how few honest, decent people there are. Sometimes when I lie awake at night, I think : " Oh ! Lord, thou hast given us immense forests, boundless plains, the widest horizons, and living here we ourselves ought really to be giants."

LYUBOV. You ask for giants ! They are no good except in story-books ; in real life they frighten us.

(EPIHODOV *advances in the background, playing on the guitar.*)

LYUBOV (*dreamily*). There goes Epihodov.

ANYA (*dreamily*). There goes Epihodov.

GAEV. The sun has set, my friends.

TROFIMOV. Yes.

GAEV (*not loudly, but, as it were, declaiming*). O nature, divine nature, thou art bright with eternal lustre, beautiful and indifferent ! Thou, whom we call mother, thou dost unite within thee life and death ! Thou dost give life and dost destroy !

VARYA (*in a tone of supplication*). Uncle !

ANYA. Uncle, you are at it again !

TROFIMOV. You'd much better be cannoning off the red !

GAEV. I'll hold my tongue, I will.

(*All sit plunged in thought. Perfect stillness. The only thing audible is the muttering of* FIRS. *Suddenly there is a sound in the distance, as it were from the sky—the sound of a breaking harp-string, mournfully dying away.*)

LYUBOV. What is that?

LOPAHIN. I don't know. Somewhere far away a bucket fallen and broken in the pits. But somewhere very far away.

GAEV. It might be a bird of some sort—such as a heron.

TROFIMOV. Or an owl.

LYUBOV (*shudders*). I don't know why, but it's horrid (*a pause*).

FIRS. It was the same before the calamity—the owl hooted and the samovar hissed all the time.

GAEV. Before what calamity?

FIRS. Before the emancipation (*a pause*).

LYUBOV. Come, my friends, let us be going; evening is falling. (*To* ANYA) There are tears in your eyes. What is it, darling? (*embraces her*).

ANYA. Nothing, mamma; it's nothing.

TROFIMOV. There is somebody coming.

(*The wayfarer appears in a shabby white forage cap and an overcoat; he is slightly drunk.*)

WAYFARER. Allow me to inquire, can I get to the station this way?

GAEV. Yes. Go along that road.

WAYFARER. I thank you most feelingly (*coughing*). The weather is superb. (*Declaims*) My brother, my suffering brother! . . . Come out to the Volga! Whose groan do you hear? . . . (*To* VARYA) Mademoiselle, vouchsafe a hungry Russian thirty kopecks.

(VARYA *utters a shriek of alarm.*)

LOPAHIN (*angrily*). There's a right and a wrong way of doing everything!

LYUBOV (*hurriedly*). Here, take this (*looks in her purse*). I've no silver. No matter—here's gold for you.

WAYFARER. I thank you most feelingly! (*goes off*). (*Laughter.*)

VARYA (*frightened*). I'm going home—I'm going . . . Oh, mamma, the servants have nothing to eat, and you gave him gold!

LYUBOV. There's no doing anything with me. I'm so silly! When we get home, I'll give you all I possess. Yermolay Alexeyevitch, you will lend me some more . . . !

LOPAHIN. I will.

LYUBOV. Come, friends, it's time to be going. And Varya, we have made a match of it for you. I congratulate you.

VARYA (*through her tears*). Mamma, that's not a joking matter.

LOPAHIN. "Ophelia, get thee to a nunnery!"

GAEV. My hands are trembling; it's a long while since I had a game of billiards.

LOPAHIN. "Ophelia! Nymph, in thy orisons be all my sins remember'd."

LYUBOV. Come, it will soon be supper-time.

VARYA. How he frightened me! My heart's simply throbbing.

LOPAHIN. Let me remind you, ladies and gentlemen : on the 22nd of August the cherry orchard will be sold. Think about that! Think about it!

(*All go off, except* TROFIMOV *and* ANYA.)

ANYA (*laughing*). I'm grateful to the wayfarer! He frightened Varya and we are left alone.

TROFIMOV. Varya's afraid we shall fall in love

mette ivers.

with each other, and for days together she won't leave us. With her narrow brain she can't grasp that we are above love. To eliminate the petty and transitory which hinders us from being free and happy—that is the aim and meaning of our life. Forward! We go forward irresistibly towards the bright star that shines yonder in the distance. Forward! Do not lag behind, friends.

ANYA (*claps her hands*). How well you speak! (*a pause*). It is divine here to-day.

TROFIMOV. Yes, it's glorious weather.

ANYA. Somehow, Petya, you've made me so that I don't love the cherry orchard as I used to. I used to love it so dearly. I used to think that there was no spot on earth like our garden.

TROFIMOV. All Russia is our garden. The earth is great and beautiful—there are many beautiful places in it (*a pause*). Think only, Anya, your grandfather, and great-grandfather, and all your ancestors were slave-owners—the owners of living souls—and from every cherry in the orchard, from every leaf, from every trunk there are human creatures looking at you. Cannot you hear their voices? Oh, it is awful! Your orchard is a fearful thing, and when in the evening or at night one walks about the orchard, the old bark on the trees glimmers dimly in the dusk, and the old cherry trees seem to be dreaming of centuries gone by and tortured by fearful visions. Yes! We are at least two hundred years behind, we have really gained nothing yet, we have no definite attitude to the past, we do nothing but theorise or complain of depression or drink vodka. It is clear that to begin to live in the present we must first expiate our past, we must break with it ; and we can expiate it only by suffering, by extraordinary unceasing labour. Understand that, Anya.

ANYA. The house we live in has long ceased to be our own, and I shall leave it, I give you my word.

TROFIMOV. If you have the house keys, fling them into the well and go away. Be free as the wind.

ANYA (*in ecstasy*). How beautifully you said that !

TROFIMOV. Believe me, Anya, believe me ! I am not thirty yet, I am young, I am still a student, but I have gone through so much already ! As soon as winter comes I am hungry, sick, careworn, poor as a beggar, and what ups and downs of fortune have I not known ! And my soul was always, every minute, day and night, full of inexplicable forebodings. I have a foreboding of happiness, Anya. I see glimpses of it already.

ANYA (*pensively*). The moon is rising.

(EPIHODOV *is heard playing still the same mournful song on the guitar. The moon rises. Somewhere near the poplars* VARYA *is looking for* ANYA *and calling "* Anya ! *where are you ? ")*

TROFIMOV. Yes, the moon is rising (*a pause*). Here is happiness—here it comes ! It is coming nearer and nearer ; already I can hear its footsteps. And if we never see it—if we may never know it—what does it matter ? Others will see it after us.

VARYA'S VOICE. Anya! Where are you?

TROFIMOV. That Varya again! (*Angrily*) It's revolting!

ANYA. Well, let's go down to the river. It's lovely there.

TROFIMOV. Yes, let's go. (*They go.*)

VARYA'S VOICE. Anya! Anya!

CURTAIN

ACT III

A drawing-room divided by an arch from a larger drawing-room. A chandelier burning. The Jewish orchestra, the same that was mentioned in Act II, is heard playing in the ante-room. It is evening. In the larger drawing-room they are dancing the grand chain. The voice of SEMYONOV-PISHTCHIK : " Promenade à une paire ! " *Then enter the drawing-room in couples, first* PISHTCHIK *and* CHARLOTTA IVANOVNA, *then* TROFIMOV *and* LYUBOV ANDREYEVNA, *thirdly* ANYA *with the Post-Office Clerk, fourthly* VARYA *with the Station Master, and other guests.* VARYA *is quietly weeping and wiping away her tears as she dances. In the last couple is* DUNYASHA. *They move across the drawing-room.* PISHTCHIK *shouts :* " Grand rond, balancez ! " *and* " Les Cavaliers à genou et remerciez vos dames."

FIRS *in a swallow-tail coat brings in seltzer water on a tray.* PISHTCHIK *and* TROFIMOV *enter the drawing-room.*

PISHTCHIK. I am a full-blooded man ; I have already had two strokes. Dancing's hard work for me, but as they say, if you're in the pack, you must bark with the rest. I'm as strong, I may

214

say, as a horse. My parent, who would have his
joke—may the Kingdom of Heaven be his !—used
to say about our origin that the ancient stock of
the Semyonov-Pishtchiks was derived from the
very horse that Caligula made a member of the
senate (*sits down*). But I've no money, that's
where the mischief is. A hungry dog believes in
nothing but meat . . . (*snores, but at once wakes up*).
That's like me . . . I can think of nothing but money.

TROFIMOV. There really is something horsy
about your appearance.

PISHTCHIK. Well . . . a horse is a fine beast . . . a
horse can be sold.

> (*There is the sound of billiards being played in
> an adjoining room. VARYA appears in
> the arch leading to the larger drawing-room.*)

TROFIMOV (*teasing*). Madame Lopahin !
Madame Lopahin !

VARYA (*angrily*). Mangy-looking gentleman !

TROFIMOV. Yes, I am a mangy-looking gentleman, and I'm proud of it !

VARYA (*pondering bitterly*). Here we have hired
musicians and nothing to pay them ! (*goes out*).

TROFIMOV (*to PISHTCHIK*). If the energy you
have wasted during your lifetime in trying to find
the money to pay your interest, had gone to something else, you might in the end have turned the
world upside down.

PISHTCHIK. Nietzsche, the philosopher, a very
great and celebrated man . . . of enormous intellect
. . . says in his works, that one can make forged
bank-notes.

TROFIMOV. Why, have you read Nietzsche ?

PISHTCHIK. What next . . . Dashenka told me. . . . And now I am in such a position, I might just as well forge bank-notes. The day after to-morrow I must pay 310 roubles—130 I have procured (*feels in his pockets, in alarm*). The money's gone! I have lost my money! (*Through his tears*) Where's the money? (*Gleefully*) Why here it is behind the lining. . . . It has made me hot all over.

(*Enter* LYUBOV ANDREYEVNA *and* CHARLOTTA IVANOVNA.)

LYUBOV (*hums the Lezginka*). Why is Leonid so long? What can he be doing in town? (*To* DUNYASHA) Offer the musicians some tea.

TROFIMOV. The sale hasn't taken place, most likely.

LYUBOV. It's the wrong time to have the orchestra, and the wrong time to give a dance. Well, never mind (*sits down and hums softly*).

CHARLOTTA (*gives* PISHTCHIK *a pack of cards*). Here's a pack of cards. Think of any card you like.

PISHTCHIK. I've thought of one.

CHARLOTTA. Shuffle the pack now. That's right. Give it here, my dear Mr. Pishtchik. Ein, zwei, drei—now look, it's in your breast pocket.

PISHTCHIK (*taking a card out of his breast pocket*). The eight of spades! Perfectly right! (*Wonderingly*) Fancy that now!

CHARLOTTA (*holding pack of cards in her hands, to* TROFIMOV). Tell me quickly which is the top card.

TROFIMOV. Well, the queen of spades.

216

CHARLOTTA. It is !   (*To* PISHTCHIK) Well, which card is uppermost ?

PISHTCHIK. The ace of hearts.

CHARLOTTA. It is !   (*claps her hands, pack of cards disappears*).   Ah ! what lovely weather it is to-day !

>(*A mysterious feminine voice which seems coming out of the floor answers her. " Oh, yes, it's magnificent weather, madam."*)

CHARLOTTA. You are my perfect ideal.

VOICE. And I greatly admire you too, madam.

STATION MASTER (*applauding*).   The lady ventriloquist—bravo !

PISHTCHIK (*wonderingly*).   Fancy that now ! Most enchanting Charlotta Ivanovna. I'm simply in love with you.

CHARLOTTA. In love ?   (*shrugging shoulders*). What do you know of love, guter Mensch, aber schlechter Musikant.

TROFIMOV (*pats* PISHTCHIK *on the shoulder*). You dear old horse. . . .

CHARLOTTA. Attention, please !   Another trick ! (*takes a travelling rug from a chair*).   Here's a very good rug ; I want to sell it (*shaking it out*). Doesn't anyone want to buy it ?

PISHTCHIK (*wonderingly*).   Fancy that !

CHARLOTTA. Ein, zwei, drei ! (*quickly picks up rug she has dropped ; behind the rug stands* ANYA ; *she makes a curtsey, runs to her mother, embraces her and runs back into the larger drawing-room amidst general enthusiasm.*)

LYUBOV (*applauds*).   Bravo !   Bravo !

CHARLOTTA. Now again !   Ein, zwei, drei ! (*lifts*

217

up the rug ; behind the rug stands VARYA, *bowing*).

PISHTCHIK (*wonderingly*). Fancy that now !

CHARLOTTA. That's the end (*throws the rug at* PISHTCHIK, *makes a curtsey, runs into the larger drawing-room*).

PISHTCHIK (*hurries after her*). Mischievous creature ! Fancy ! (*goes out*).

LYUBOV. And still Leonid doesn't come. I can't understand what he's doing in the town so long ! Why, everything must be over by now. The estate is sold, or the sale has not taken place. Why keep us so long in suspense ?

VARYA (*trying to console her*). Uncle's bought it. I feel sure of that.

TROFIMOV (*ironically*). Oh, yes !

VARYA. Great-aunt sent him an authorisation to buy it in her name, and transfer the debt. She's doing it for Anya's sake, and I'm sure God will be merciful. Uncle will buy it.

LYUBOV. My aunt in Yaroslavl sent fifteen thousand to buy the estate in her name, she doesn't trust us—but that's not enough even to pay the arrears (*hides her face in her hands*). My fate is being sealed to-day, my fate . . .

TROFIMOV (*teasing* VARYA). Madame Lopahin.

VARYA (*angrily*). Perpetual student ! Twice already you've been sent down from the University.

LYUBOV. Why are you angry, Varya ? He's teasing you about Lopahin. Well, what of that ? Marry Lopahin if you like, he's a good man, and interesting ; if you don't want to, don't ! Nobody compels you, darling.

VARYA. I must tell you plainly, mamma, I look at the matter seriously ; he's a good man, I like him.

LYUBOV. Well, marry him. I can't see what you're waiting for.

VARYA. Mamma, I can't make him an offer myself. For the last two years, everyone's been talking to me about him. Everyone talks ; but he says nothing or else makes a joke. I see what it means. He's growing rich, he's absorbed in business, he hàs no thoughts for me. If I had money, were it ever so little, if I had only a hundred roubles, I'd throw everything up and go far away. I would go into a nunnery.

TROFIMOV. What bliss !

VARYA (*to* TROFIMOV). A student ought to have sense ! (*In a soft tone with tears*) How ugly you've grown, Petya ! How old you look ! (*To* LYUBOV ANDREYEVNA, *no longer crying*) But I can't do without work, mamma ; I must have something to do every minute.

(*Enter* YASHA.)

YASHA (*hardly restraining his laughter*). Epihodov has broken a billiard cue ! (*goes out*).

VARYA. What is Epihodov doing here ? Who gave him leave to play billiards ? I can't make these people out (*goes out*).

LYUBOV. Don't tease her, Petya. You see she has grief enough without that.

TROFIMOV. She is so very officious, meddling in what's not her business. All the summer she's given Anya and me no peace. She's afraid of a love affair between us. What's it to do with her ?

219

Besides, I have given no grounds for it. Such triviality is not in my line. We are above love !

LYUBOV. And I suppose I am beneath love. (*Very uneasily*) Why is it Leonid's not here ? If only I could know whether the estate is sold or not ! It seems such an incredible calamity that I really don't know what to think. I am distracted . . . I shall scream in a minute . . . I shall do something stupid. Save me, Petya, tell me something, talk to me !

TROFIMOV. What does it matter whether the estate is sold to-day or not ? That's all done with long ago. There's no turning back, the path is overgrown. Don't worry yourself, dear Lyubov Andreyevna. You mustn't deceive yourself; for once in your life you must face the truth !

LYUBOV. What truth ? You see where the truth lies, but I seem to have lost my sight, I see nothing. You settle every great problem so boldly, but tell me, my dear boy, isn't it because you're young—because you haven't yet understood one of your problems through suffering? You look forward boldly, and isn't it that you don't see and don't expect anything dreadful because life is still hidden from your young eyes ? You're bolder, more honest, deeper than we are, but think, be just a little magnanimous, have pity on me. I was born here, you know, my father and mother lived here, my grandfather lived here, I love this house. I can't conceive of life without the cherry orchard, and if it really must be sold, then sell me with the orchard (*embraces* TROFIMOV, *kisses him on the forehead*).

My boy was drowned here (*weeps*). Pity me, my dear kind fellow.

TROFIMOV. You know I feel for you with all my heart.

LYUBOV. But that should have been said differently, so differently (*takes out her handkerchief, telegram falls on the floor*). My heart is so heavy to-day. It's so noisy here, my soul is quivering at every sound, I'm shuddering all over, but I can't go away ; I'm afraid to be quiet and alone. Don't be hard on me, Petya . . . I love you as though you were one of ourselves. I would gladly let you marry Anya—I swear I would—only, my dear boy, you must take your degree, you do nothing—you're simply tossed by fate from place to place. That's so strange. It is, isn't it ? And you must do something with your beard to make it grow somehow (*laughs*). You look so funny !

TROFIMOV (*picks up the telegram*). I've no wish to be a beauty.

LYUBOV. That's a telegram from Paris. I get one every day. One yesterday and one to-day. That savage creature is ill again, he's in trouble again. He begs forgiveness, beseeches me to go, and really I ought to go to Paris to see him. You look shocked, Petya. What am I to do, my dear boy, what am I to do ? He is ill, he is alone and unhappy, and who'll look after him, who'll keep him from doing the wrong thing, who'll give him his medicine at the right time ? And why hide it or be silent ? I love him, that's clear. I love him ! I love him ! He's a millstone about my neck, I'm going to the bottom with him, but I love that stone and can't live without it (*presses* TROFIMOV's *hand*). Don't think ill of me, Petya, don't tell me anything, don't tell me . . .

TROFIMOV (*through his tears*). For God's sake forgive my frankness : why, he robbed you !

LYUBOV. No! No! No! You mustn't speak like that (*covers her ears*).

TROFIMOV. He is a wretch ! You're the only person that doesn't know it ! He's a worthless creature ! A despicable wretch !

LYUBOV (*getting angry, but speaking with restraint*). You're twenty-six or twenty-seven years old, but you're still a schoolboy.

TROFIMOV. Possibly.

LYUBOV. You should be a man at your age ! You should understand what love means ! And you ought to be in love yourself. You ought to fall in love ! (*angrily*). Yes, yes, and it's not purity in you, you're simply a prude, a comic fool, a freak.

TROFIMOV (*in horror*). The things she's saying !

LYUBOV. I am above love ! You're not above love, but simply as our Firs here says, " You are a good-for-nothing." At your age not to have a mistress !

TROFIMOV (*in horror*). This is awful ! The things she is saying ! (*goes rapidly into the larger drawing-room clutching his head*). This is awful ! I can't stand it ! I'm going ! (*goes off, but at once returns*). All is over between us ! (*goes off into the ante-room*).

LYUBOV (*shouts after him*). Petya ! Wait a

minute! **You funny** creature! I was joking!
Petya! (*There is a sound of somebody running quickly
downstairs and suddenly falling with a crash.
ANYA and VARYA scream, but there is a sound of
laughter at once*).

LYUBOV. What has happened?

(ANYA *runs in.*)

ANYA (*laughing*). Petya's fallen downstairs!
(*runs out*).

LYUBOV. What a queer fellow that Petya is!

(*The Station Master stands in the middle of the
larger room and reads " The Magdalene,"
by Alexey Tolstoy. They listen to him,
but before he has recited many lines strains
of a waltz are heard from the ante-room
and the reading is broken off. All dance.
TROFIMOV, ANYA, VARYA and LYUBOV
ANDREYEVNA come in from the ante-room.*)

LYUBOV. Come, Petya—come, pure heart! I
beg your pardon. Let's have a dance! (*dances
with* PETYA).

(ANYA *and* VARYA *dance.* FIRS *comes in, puts
his stick down near the side door.* YASHA
also comes into the drawing-room and
looks on at the dancing.*)

YASHA. What is it, old man?

FIRS. I don't feel well. In old days we used
to have generals, barons and admirals dancing
at our balls, and now we send for the post-office
clerk and the station master and even they're
not over anxious to come. I am getting feeble.
The old master, the grandfather, used to give
sealing-wax for all complaints. I have been

223

taking sealing-wax for twenty years **or** more. Perhaps that's what's kept me alive.

YASHA. You bore me, old man! (*yawns*). It's time you were done with.

FIRS. Ach, you're a good-for-nothing! (*mutters*).

(TROFIMOV *and* LYUBOV ANDREYEVNA *dance in larger room and then on to the stage*).

LYUBOV. Merci. I'll sit down a little (*sits down*). I'm tired.

(*Enter* ANYA.)

ANYA (*excitedly*). There's a man in the kitchen has been saying that the cherry orchard's been sold to-day.

LYUBOV. Sold to whom?

ANYA. He didn't say to whom. He's gone away.

(*She dances with* TROFIMOV, *and they go off into the larger room.*)

YASHA. There was an old man gossiping there, a stranger.

FIRS. Leonid Andreyevitch isn't here yet, he hasn't come back. He has his light overcoat on, *demi-saison*, he'll catch cold for sure. Ach! Foolish young things!!

LYUBOV. I feel as though I should die. Go, Yasha, find out to whom it has been sold.

YASHA. But he went away long ago, **the** old chap (*laughs*).

LYUBOV (*with slight vexation*). What are you laughing at? What are you pleased at?

YASHA. Epihodov is so funny. He's a silly fellow, two and twenty misfortunes.

LYUBOV. Firs, if the estate is sold, where will you go?

FIRS. Where you bid me, there I'll go.

LYUBOV. Why do you look like that? Are you ill? You ought to be in bed.

FIRS. Yes (*ironically*). Me go to bed and who's to wait here? Who's to see to things without me? I'm the only one in all the house.

YASHA (*to* LYUBOV ANDREYEVNA). Lyubov Andreyevna, permit me to make a request of you; if you go back to Paris again, be so kind as to take me with you. It's positively impossible for me to stay here (*looking about him; in an undertone*) There's no need to say it, you see for yourself— an uncivilised country, the people have no morals, and then the dullness! The food in the kitchen's abominable, and then Firs runs after one muttering all sorts of unsuitable words. Take me with you, please do!

(*Enter* PISHTCHIK.)

PISHTCHIK. Allow me to ask you for a waltz, my dear lady. (LYUBOV ANDREYEVNA *goes with him*.) Enchanting lady, I really must borrow of you just 180 roubles (*dances*), only 180 roubles. (*They pass into the larger room*.)

YASHA (*hums softly*), "Knowest thou my soul's emotion."

> (*In the larger drawing-room, a figure in a grey top hat and in check trousers is gesticulating and jumping about. Shouts of "Bravo, Charlotta Ivanovna."*)

DUNYASHA (*she has stopped to powder herself*). My young lady tells me to dance. There are plenty of gentlemen, and too few ladies, but dancing makes me giddy and makes my heart

225

beat. Firs, the post-office clerk said something to me just now that quite took my breath away.

(*Music becomes more subdued.*)

FIRS. What did he say to you ?

DUNYASHA. He said I was like a flower.

YASHA (*yawns*). What ignorance ! (*goes out*).

DUNYASHA. Like a flower. I am a girl of such delicate feelings, I am awfully fond of soft speeches.

FIRS. Your head's being turned.

(*Enter* EPIHODOV.)

EPIHODOV. You have no desire to see me, Dunyasha. I might be an insect (*sighs*). Ah ! life !

DUNYASHA. What is it you want ?

EPIHODOV. Undoubtedly you may be right (*sighs*) But of course, if one looks at it from that point of view, if I may so express myself, you have, excuse my plain speaking, reduced me to a complete state of mind. I know my destiny. Every day some misfortune befalls me and I have long ago grown accustomed to it, so that I look upon my fate with a smile. You gave me your word, and though I——

DUNYASHA. Let us have a talk later, I entreat you, but now leave me in peace, for I am lost in reverie (*plays with her fan*).

EPIHODOV. I have a misfortune every day, and if I may venture to express myself, I merely smile at it, I even laugh.

(VARYA *enters from the larger drawing-room.*)

VARYA. You still have not gone, Epihodov. What a disrespectful creature you are, really !

(*To* DUNYASHA) Go along, Dunyasha! (*To* EPIHODOV) First you play billiards and break the cue, then you go wandering about the drawing-room like a visitor!

EPIHODOV. You really cannot, if I may so express myself, call me to account like this.

VARYA. I'm not calling you to account, I'm speaking to you. You do nothing but wander from place to place and don't do your work. We keep you as a counting-house clerk, but what use you are I can't say.

EPIHODOV (*offended*). Whether I work or whether I walk, whether I eat or whether I play billiards, is a matter to be judged by persons of understanding and my elders.

VARYA. You dare to tell me that! (*Firing up*) You dare! You mean to say I've no understanding. Begone from here! This minute!

EPIHODOV (*intimidated*). I beg you to express yourself with delicacy.

VARYA (*beside herself with anger*). This moment! get out! away! (*He goes towards the door, she following him*). Two and twenty misfortunes! Take yourself off! Don't let me set eyes on you! (EPIHODOV *has gone out, behind the door his voice,* " I shall lodge a complaint against you "). What! You're coming back? (*snatches up the stick* FIRS *has put down near the door*). Come! Come! Come! I'll show you! What! you're coming? Then take that! (*she swings the stick, at the very moment that* LOPAHIN *comes in*).

LOPAHIN. Very much obliged to you!

VARYA (*angrily and ironically*). I beg your pardon!

LOPAHIN. Not at all! I humbly thank you for your kind reception!

VARYA. No need of thanks for it (*moves away, then looks round and asks softly*) I haven't hurt you?

LOPAHIN. Oh, no! Not at all! There's an immense bump coming up, though!

VOICES FROM LARGER ROOM. Lopahin has come! Yermolay Alexeyevitch!

PISHTCHIK. What do I see and hear? (*kisses* LOPAHIN). There's a whiff of cognac about you, my dear soul, and we're making merry here too!

(*Enter* LYUBOV ANDREYEVNA.)

LYUBOV. Is it you, Yermolay Alexeveyitch? Why have you been so long? Where's Leonid?

LOPAHIN. Leonid Andreyevitch arrived with me. He is coming.

LYUBOV (*in agitation*). Well! Well! Was there a sale? Speak!

LOPAHIN (*embarrassed, afraid of betraying his joy*). The sale was over at four o'clock. We missed our train—had to wait till half-past nine. (*Sighing heavily*) Ugh! I feel a little giddy.

(*Enter* GAEV. *In his right hand he has purchases, with his left hand he is wiping away his tears.*)

LYUBOV. Well, Leonid? What news? (*Impatiently, with tears*) Make haste, for God's sake!

GAEV (*makes her no answer, simply waves his hand. To* FIRS, *weeping*) Here, take them;

there's anchovies, Kertch herrings. I have eaten nothing all day. What I have been through! (*Door into the billiard room is open. There is heard a knocking of balls and the voice of* YASHA *saying* "*Eighty-seven.*" GAEV'S *expression changes, he leaves off weeping*). I am fearfully tired. Firs, come and help me change my things (*goes to his own room across the larger drawing-room*).

PISHTCHIK. How about the sale? Tell us, do!

LYUBOV. Is the cherry orchard sold?

LOPAHIN. It is sold.

LYUBOV. Who has bought it?

LOPAHIN. I have bought it. (*A pause.* LYUBOV *is crushed; she would fall down if she were not standing near a chair and table.*)

> (VARYA *takes keys from her waist-band, flings them on the floor in middle of drawing-room and goes out.*)

LOPAHIN. I have bought it! Wait a bit, ladies and gentlemen, pray. My head's a bit muddled, I can't speak (*laughs*). We came to the auction. Deriganov was there already. Leonid Andreyevitch only had 15,000 and Deriganov bid 30,000, besides the arrears, straight off. I saw how the land lay. I bid against him. I bid 40,000, he bid 45,000, I said 55, and so he went on, adding 5 thousands and I adding 10. Well . . . So it ended. I bid 90, and it was knocked down to me. Now the cherry orchard's mine! Mine! (*chuckles*). My God, the cherry orchard's mine! Tell me that I'm drunk, that I'm out of my mind, that it's all a dream (*stamps with his feet*). Don't laugh at me! If my father and my grandfather could rise from their graves and see all that has happened! How their Yermolay, ignorant, beaten Yermolay, who used to run about barefoot in winter, how that very Yermolay has bought the finest estate in the world! I have bought the estate where my father and grandfather were slaves, where they weren't even admitted into the kitchen. I am asleep, I am dreaming! It is all fancy, it is the work of your imagination plunged in the darkness of ignorance (*picks up keys, smiling fondly*). She threw away the keys ; she means to show she's not the housewife now (*jingles the keys*). Well, no matter. (*The orchestra is heard tuning up.*) Hey, musicians! Play! I want to hear you. Come, all of you, and look how Yermolay Lopahin will take the axe to the cherry orchard, how the trees will fall to the ground! We will build houses on it and our grandsons and great-grandsons will see a new life springing up there. Music! Play up!

(*Music begins to play.* LYUBOV ANDREYEVNA *has sunk into a chair and is weeping bitterly.*)

LOPAHIN (*reproachfully*). Why, why didn't you listen to me? My poor friend! Dear lady, there's no turning back now. (*With tears*) Oh, if all this could be over, oh, if our miserable disjointed life could somehow soon be changed!

PISHTCHIK (*takes him by the arm, in an undertone*). She's weeping, let us go and leave her alone. Come (*takes him by the arm and leads him into the larger drawing-room*).

LOPAHIN. What's that? Musicians, play up! All must be as I wish it. (*With irony*) Here comes the new master, the owner of the cherry orchard!

(*accidentally tips over a little table, almost upsetting the candelabra*). I can pay for everything! (*goes out with* PISHTCHIK. *No one remains on the stage or in the larger drawing-room except* LYUBOV, *who sits huddled up, weeping bitterly. The music plays softly.* ANYA *and* TROFIMOV *come in quickly.* ANYA *goes up to her mother and falls on her knees before her.* TROFIMOV *stands at the entrance to the larger drawing-room*).

ANYA. Mamma! Mamma, you're crying, dear, kind, good mamma! My precious! I love you! I bless you! The cherry orchard is sold, it is gone, that's true, that's true! But don't weep, mamma! Life is still before you, you have still your good, pure heart! Let us go, let us go, darling, away from here! We will make a new garden, more splendid than this one; you will see it, you will understand. And joy, quiet, deep joy, will sink into your soul like the sun at evening! And you will smile, mamma! Come, darling, let us go!

CURTAIN

231

ACT IV

SCENE : *Same as in First Act. There are neither curtains on the windows nor pictures on the walls : only a little furniture remains piled up in a corner as if for sale. There is a sense of desolation ; near the outer door and in the background of the scene are packed trunks, travelling bags, etc. On the left the door is open, and from here the voices of* VARYA *and* ANYA *are audible.* LOPAHIN *is standing waiting.* YASHA *is holding a tray with glasses full of champagne. In front of the stage* EPIHODOV *is tying up a box. In the background behind the scene a hum of talk from the peasants who have come to say goodbye. The voice of* GAEV : " Thanks, brothers, thanks ! "*

YASHA. The peasants have come to say goodbye. In my opinion, Yermolay Alexeyevitch, the peasants are good-natured, but they don't know much about things.

(The hum of talk dies away. Enter across front of stage LYUBOV ANDREYEVNA *and* GAEV. *She is not weeping, but is pale ; her face is quivering—she cannot speak.)*

GAEV. You gave them your purse, Lyuba. That won't do—that won't do !

Lyubov. I couldn't help it ! I couldn't help it !
(*Both go out.*)

Lopahin (*in the doorway, calls after them*). You
will take a glass at parting ? Please do. I didn't
think to bring any from the town, and at the
station I could only get one bottle. Please take
a glass (*a pause*). What ? You don't care for
any ? (*comes away from the door*). If I'd known,
I wouldn't have bought it. Well, and I'm not going
to drink it. (Yasha *carefully sets the tray down
on a chair*.) You have a glass, Yasha, anyway.

Yasha. Good luck to the travellers, and luck to
those that stay behind ! (*drinks*). This champagne
isn't the real thing, I can assure you.

Lopahin. It cost eight roubles the bottle (*a
pause*). It's devilish cold here.

Yasha. They haven't heated the stove to-day—
it's all the same since we're going (*laughs*).

Lopahin. What are you laughing for ?

Yasha. For pleasure.

Lopahin. Though it's October, it's as still and
sunny as though it were summer. It's just right
for building ! (*Looks at his watch ; says in doorway*)
Take note, ladies and gentlemen, the train goes in
forty-seven minutes ; so you ought to start for the
station in twenty minutes. You must hurry up !

(Trofimov *comes in from out of doors wearing
a greatcoat.*)

Trofimov. I think it must be time to start, the
horses are ready. The devil only knows what's
become of my goloshes ; they're lost. (*In the
doorway*) Anya ! My goloshes aren't here. I can't
find them.

LOPAHIN. And I'm getting off to Harkov. I am going in the same train with you. I'm spending all the winter at Harkov. I've been wasting all my time gossiping with you and fretting with no work to do. I can't get on without work. I don't know what to do with my hands, they flap about so queerly, as if they didn't belong to me.

TROFIMOV. Well, we're just going away, and you will take up your profitable labours again.

LOPAHIN. Do take a glass.

TROFIMOV. No, thanks.

LOPAHIN. Then you're going to Moscow now?

TROFIMOV. Yes. I shall see them as far as the town, and to-morrow I shall go on to Moscow.

LOPAHIN. Yes, I daresay, the professors aren't giving any lectures, they're waiting for your arrival.

TROFIMOV. That's not your business.

LOPAHIN. How many years have you been at the University?

TROFIMOV. Do think of something newer than that—that's stale and flat (*hunts for goloshes*). You know we shall most likely never see each other again, so let me give you one piece of advice at parting : don't wave your arms about—get out of the habit. And another thing, building villas, reckoning up that the summer visitors will in time become independent farmers—reckoning like that, that's not the thing to do either. After all, I am fond of you: you have fine delicate fingers like an artist, you've a fine delicate soul.

LOPAHIN (*embraces him*). Good-bye, my dear fellow. Thanks for everything. Let me give you money for the journey, if you need it.

TROFIMOV. What for? I don't need it.

LOPAHIN. Why, you haven't got a halfpenny.

TROFIMOV. Yes, I have, thank you. I got some money for a translation. Here it is in my pocket, (*anxiously*) but where can my goloshes be!

VARYA (*from the next room*). Take the nasty things! (*flings a pair of goloshes on to the stage*).

TROFIMOV. Why are you so cross, Varya? h'm! . . . but those aren't my goloshes.

LOPAHIN. I sowed three thousand acres with poppies in the spring, and now I have cleared forty thousand profit. And when my poppies were in flower, wasn't it a picture! So here, as I say, I made forty thousand, and I'm offering you a loan because I can afford to. Why turn up your nose? I am a peasant—I speak bluntly.

TROFIMOV. Your father was a peasant, mine was a chemist—and that proves absolutely nothing whatever. (LOPAHIN *takes out his pocket-book.*) Stop that—stop that. If you were to offer me two hundred thousand I wouldn't take it. I am an independent man, and everything that all of you, rich and poor alike, prize so highly and hold so dear, hasn't the slightest power over me—it's like so much fluff fluttering in the air. I can get on without you. I can pass by you. I am strong and proud. Humanity is advancing towards the highest truth, the highest happiness, which is possible on earth, and I am in the front ranks.

LOPAHIN. Will you get there?

TROFIMOV. I shall get there (*a pause*). I shall get there, or I shall show others the way to get there.

(*In the distance is heard the stroke of an axe on a tree.*)

LOPAHIN. Good-bye, my dear fellow; it's time to be off. We turn up our noses at one another, but life is passing all the while. When I am working hard without resting, then my mind is more at ease, and it seems to me as though I too know what I exist for; but how many people there are in Russia, my dear boy, who exist, one doesn't know what for. Well, it doesn't matter. That's not what keeps things spinning. They tell me Leonid Andreyevitch has taken a situation. He is going to be a clerk at the bank—6,000 roubles a year. Only, of course, he won't stick to it—he's too lazy.

ANYA (*in the doorway*). Mamma begs you not to let them chop down the orchard until she's gone.

TROFIMOV. Yes, really, you might have the tact (*walks out across the front of the stage*).

LOPAHIN. I'll see to it! I'll see to it! Stupid fellows! (*goes out after him*).

ANYA. Has Firs been taken to the hospital?

YASHA. I told them this morning. No doubt they have taken him.

ANYA (*to* EPIHODOV, *who passes across the drawing-room*). Semyon Pantaleyevitch, inquire, please, if Firs has been taken to the hospital.

YASHA (*in a tone of offence*). I told Yegor this morning—why ask a dozen times?

EPIHODOV. Firs is advanced in years. It's my conclusive opinion no treatment would do him good; it's time he was gathered to his fathers.

And I can only envy him (*puts a trunk down on a cardboard hat-box and crushes it*). There, now, of course—I knew it would be so.

YASHA (*jeeringly*). Two and twenty misfortunes!

VARYA (*through the door*). Has Firs been taken to the hospital?

ANYA. Yes.

VARYA. Why wasn't the note for the doctor taken too?

ANYA. Oh, then, we must send it after them (*goes out*).

VARYA (*from the adjoining room*). Where's Yasha? Tell him his mother's come to say goodbye to him.

YASHA (*waves his hand*). They put me out of all patience! (DUNYASHA *has all this time been busy about the luggage. Now, when* YASHA *is left alone, she goes up to him*).

DUNYASHA. You might just give me one look, Yasha. You're going away. You're leaving me (*weeps and throws herself on his neck*).

YASHA. What are you crying for? (*drinks the champagne*). In six days I shall be in Paris again. To-morrow we shall get into the express train and roll away in a flash. I can scarcely believe it! Vive la France! It doesn't suit me here—it's not the life for me; there's no doing anything. I have seen enough of the ignorance here. I have had enough of it (*drinks champagne*). What are you crying for? Behave yourself properly, and then you won't cry.

DUNYASHA (*powders her face, looking in a pocket-*

mirror). Do send me a letter from Paris. You know how I loved you, Yasha—how I loved you! I am a tender creature, Yasha.

YASHA. Here they are coming!

(*Busies himself about the trunks, humming softly. Enter* LYUBOV ANDREYEVNA, GAEV, ANYA *and* CHARLOTTA IVANOVNA.)

GAEV. We ought to be off. There's not much time now (*looking at* YASHA). What a smell of herrings!

LYUBOV. In ten minutes we must get into the carriage (*casts a look about the room*). Farewell, dear house, dear old home of our fathers! Winter will pass and spring will come, and then you will be no more; they will tear you down! How much those walls have seen! (*kisses her daughter passionately*). My treasure, how bright you look! Your eyes are sparkling like diamonds! Are you glad? Very glad?

ANYA. Very glad! A new life is beginning, mamma.

GAEV. Yes, really, everything is all right now. Before the cherry orchard was sold, we were all worried and wretched, but afterwards, when once the question was settled conclusively, irrevocably, we all felt calm and even cheerful. I am a bank clerk now—I am a financier—cannon off the red. And you, Lyuba, after all, you are looking better; there's no question of that.

LYUBOV. Yes. My nerves are better, that's true. (*Her hat and coat are handed to her*). I'm sleeping well. Carry out my things, Yasha. It's time. (*To* ANYA) My darling, we shall soon see each other again. I am going to Paris. I can live there on the money your Yaroslavl auntie sent us to buy the estate with—hurrah for auntie !—but that money won't last long.

ANYA. You'll come back soon, mamma, won't you ? I'll be working up for my examination in the high school, and when I have passed that, I shall set to work and be a help to you. We will read all sorts of things together, mamma, won't we ? (*kisses her mother's hands*). We will read in the autumn evenings. We'll read lots of books, and a new wonderful world will open out before us (*dreamily*). Mamma, come soon.

LYUBOV. I shall come, my precious treasure (*embraces her*).

(*Enter* LOPAHIN. CHARLOTTA *softly hums a song.*)

GAEV. Charlotta's happy ; she's singing !

CHARLOTTA (*picks up a bundle like a swaddled baby*). Bye, bye, my baby. (*A baby is heard crying : "Ooah ! ooah !"*). Hush, hush, my pretty boy ! (*Ooah ! ooah !*). Poor little thing ! (*throws the bundle back*). You must please find me a situation. I can't go on like this.

LOPAHIN. We'll find you one, Charlotta Ivanovna. Don't you worry yourself.

GAEV. Everyone's leaving us. Varya's going away. We have become of no use all at once.

CHARLOTTA. There's nowhere for me to be in the town. I must go away. (*Hums*) What care I . . .

(*Enter* PISHTCHIK.)

LOPAHIN. The freak of nature !

239

PISHTCHIK (*gasping*). Oh ! . . . let me get my breath. . . . I'm worn out . . . my most honoured . . . Give me some water.

GAEV. Want some money, I suppose ? Your humble servant ! I'll go out of the way of temptation (*goes out*).

PISHTCHIK. It's a long while since I have been to see you . . . dearest lady. (*To* LOPAHIN) You are here . . . glad to see you . . . a man of immense intellect . . . take . . . here (*gives* LOPAHIN *money*) 400 roubles. That leaves me owing 840.

LOPAHIN (*shrugging his shoulders in amazement*). It's like a dream. Where did you get it ?

PISHTCHIK. Wait a bit . . . I'm hot . . . a most extraordinary occurrence ! Some Englishmen came along and found in my land some sort of white clay. (*To* LYUBOV ANDREYEVNA) And 400 for you . . . most lovely . . . wonderful (*gives money*). The rest later (*sips water*). A young man in the train was telling me just now that a great philosopher advises jumping off a house-top. " Jump ! " says he ; " the whole gist of the problem lies in that." (*Wonderingly*) Fancy that, now ! Water, please !

LOPAHIN. What Englishmen ?

PISHTCHIK. I have made over to them the rights to dig the clay for twenty-four years . . . and now, excuse me . . . I can't stay . . . I must be trotting on. I'm going to Znoikovo . . . to Kardamanovo. . . . I'm in debt all round (*sips*). . . . To your very good health ! . . . I'll come in on Thursday.

LYUBOV. We are just off to the town, and to-morrow I start for abroad.

PISHTCHIK. What ! (*in agitation*). Why to the

town ? Oh, I see the furniture . . . the boxes.
No matter . . . (*through his tears*) . . . no matter . . .
men of enormous intellect . . . these Englishmen.
. . . Never mind . . . be happy. God will succour
you . . . no matter . . . everything in this world
must have an end (*kisses* LYUBOV ANDREYEVNA'S
hand). If the rumour reaches you that my end has
come, think of this . . . old horse, and say: " There
once was such a man in the world . . . Semyonov-
Pishtchik . . . the kingdom of heaven be his ! " . . .
most extraordinary weather . . . yes. (*Goes out
in violent agitation, but at once returns and says in
the doorway*) Dashenka wishes to be remembered to
you (*goes out*).

LYUBOV. Now we can start. I leave with two
cares in my heart. The first is leaving Firs ill.
(*Looking at her watch*) We have still five minutes.

ANYA. Mamma, Firs has been taken to the
hospital. Yasha sent him off this morning.

LYUBOV. My other anxiety is Varya. She is used
to getting up early and working ; and now, without
work, she's like a fish out of water. She is thin
and pale, and she's crying, poor dear ! (*a pause*).
You are well aware, Yermolay Alexeyevitch, I
dreamed of marrying her to you, and everything
seemed to show that you would get married
(*whispers to* ANYA *and motions to* CHARLOTTA *and
both go out*). She loves you—she suits you. And I
don't know—I don't know why it is you seem, as it
were, to avoid each other. I can't understand it !

LOPAHIN. I don't understand it myself, I confess. It's queer somehow, altogether. If there's
still time, I'm ready now at once. Let's settle it

241

straight off, and go ahead ; but without you, I feel I shan't make her an offer.

LYUBOV. That's excellent. Why, a single moment's all that's necessary. I'll call her at once.

LOPAHIN. And there's champagne all ready too (*looking into the glasses*). Empty ! Someone's emptied them already. (YASHA *coughs*.) I call that greedy.

LYUBOV (*eagerly*). Capital ! We will go out. Yasha, *allez* ! I'll call her in. (*At the door*) Varya, leave all that; come here. Come along ! (*goes out with* YASHA).

LOPAHIN (*looking at his watch*). Yes.

> (*A pause. Behind the door, smothered laughter and whispering, and, at last, enter* VARYA.)

VARYA (*looking a long while over the things*). It is strange, I can't find it anywhere.

LOPAHIN. What are you looking for ?

VARYA. I packed it myself, and I can't remember (*a pause*).

LOPAHIN. Where are you going now, Varvara Mihailova ?

VARYA. I ? To the Ragulins. I have arranged to go to them to look after the house—as a housekeeper.

LOPAHIN. That's in Yashnovo ? It'll be seventy miles away (*a pause*). So this is the end of life in this house !

VARYA (*looking among the things*). Where is it ? Perhaps I put it in the trunk. Yes, life in this house is over—there will be no more of it.

LOPAHIN. And I'm just off to Harkov—by this next train. I've a lot of business there. I'm leaving Epihodov here, and I've taken him on.

VARYA. Really !

LOPAHIN. This time last year we had snow already, if you remember ; but now it's so fine and sunny. Though it's cold, to be sure—three degrees of frost.

VARYA. I haven't looked (*a pause*). And besides, our thermometer's broken (*a pause*).

(*Voice at the door from the yard :* " Yermolay Alexeyevitch ! ")

LOPAHIN (*as though he had long been expecting this summons*). This minute !

(LOPAHIN *goes out quickly.* VARYA *sitting on the floor and laying her head on a bag full of clothes, sobs quietly. The door opens.* LYUBOV ANDREYEVNA *comes in cautiously.*)

LYUBOV. Well ? (*a pause*). We must be going.

VARYA (*has wiped her eyes and is no longer crying*). Yes, mamma, it's time to start. I shall have time to get to the Ragulins to-day, if only you're not late for the train.

LYUBOV (*in the doorway*). Anya, put your things on.

(*Enter* ANYA, *then* GAEV *and* CHARLOTTA IVANOVNA. GAEV *has on a warm coat with a hood. Servants and cabmen come in.* EPIHODOV *bustles about the luggage.*)

LYUBOV. Now we can start on our travels.

ANYA (*joyfully*). On our travels !

GAEV. My friends — my dear, my precious friends ! Leaving this house for ever, can I be silent ? Can I refrain from giving utterance at leave-taking to those emotions which now flood all my being ?

ANYA (*supplicatingly*). Uncle !

VARYA. Uncle, you mustn't !

GAEV (*dejectedly*). Cannon and into the pocket . . . I'll be quiet. . . .

(*Enter* TROFIMOV *and afterwards* LOPAHIN.)

TROFIMOV. Well, ladies and gentlemen, we must start.

LOPAHIN. Epihodov, my coat !

LYUBOV. I'll stay just one minute. It seems as though I have never seen before what the walls, what the ceilings in this house were like, and now I look at them with greediness, with such tender love.

GAEV. I remember when I was six years old sitting in that window on Trinity Day watching my father going to church.

LYUBOV. Have all the things been taken ?

LOPAHIN. I think all. (*Putting on overcoat, to* EPIHODOV) You, Epihodov, mind you see everything is right.

EPIHODOV (*in a husky voice*). Don't you trouble, Yermolay Alexeyevitch.

LOPAHIN. Why, what's wrong with your voice ?

EPIHODOV. I've just had a drink of water, and I choked over something.

YASHA (*contemptuously*). The ignorance !

LYUBOV. We are going—and not a soul will be left here.

LOPAHIN. Not till the spring.

VARYA (*pulls a parasol out of a bundle, as though about to hit someone with it.* LOPAHIN *makes a gesture as though alarmed*). What is it ? I didn't mean anything.

TROFIMOV. Ladies and gentlemen, let us get

244

into the carriage. It's time. The train will be in directly.

VARYA. Petya, here they are, your goloshes, by that box. (*With tears*) And what dirty old things they are!

TROFIMOV (*putting on his goloshes*). Let us go, friends!

GAEV (*greatly agitated, afraid of weeping*). The train—the station! Double baulk, ah!

LYUBOV. Let us go!

LOPAHIN. Are we all here? (*locks the side-door on left*). The things are all here. We must lock up. Let us go!

ANYA. Good-bye, home! Good-bye to the old life!

TROFIMOV. Welcome to the new life!

(TROFIMOV *goes out with* ANYA. VARYA *looks round the room and goes out slowly.* YASHA *and* CHARLOTTA IVANOVNA, *with her dog, go out.*)

LOPAHIN. Till the spring, then! Come, friends, till we meet! (*goes out*).

(LYUBOV ANDREYEVNA *and* GAEV *remain alone. As though they had been waiting for this, they throw themselves on each other's necks, and break into subdued smothered sobbing, afraid of being overheard.*)

GAEV (*in despair*). Sister, my sister!

LYUBOV. Oh, my orchard!—my sweet, beautiful orchard! My life, my youth, my happiness, good-bye! good-bye!

VOICE OF ANYA (*calling gaily*). Mamma!

VOICE OF TROFIMOV (*gaily, excitedly*). Aa—oo!

LYUBOV. One last look at the walls, at the

windows.   My dear mother loved to walk about this room.

GAEV. Sister, sister !

VOICE OF ANYA. Mamma !

VOICE OF TROFIMOV. Aa—oo !

LYUBOV. We are coming.   (*They go out.*)

>   (*The stage is empty.   There is the sound of the doors being locked up, then of the carriages driving away.   There is silence.   In the stillness there is the dull stroke of an axe in a tree, clanging with a mournful lonely sound.   Footsteps are heard.   FIRS appears in the doorway on the right.   He is dressed as always—in a pea-jacket and white waistcoat, with slippers on his feet.   He is ill.*)

FIRS (*goes up to the doors, and tries the handles*). Locked !   They have gone . . . (*sits down on sofa*). They have forgotten me. . . . Never mind . . . I'll sit here a bit. . . . I'll be bound Leonid Andreyevitch hasn't put his fur coat on and has gone off in his thin overcoat (*sighs anxiously*).   I didn't see after him. . . . These young people . . . (*mutters something that can't be distinguished*).   Life has slipped by as though I hadn't lived. (*Lies down*) I'll lie down a bit. . . . There's no strength in you, nothing left you—all gone !   Ech !   I'm good for nothing (*lies motionless*).

>   (*A sound is heard that seems to come from the sky, like a breaking harp-string, dying away mournfully.   All is still again, and there is heard nothing but the strokes of the axe far away in the orchard.*)

CURTAIN

246

IVANOV

A PLAY IN FOUR ACTS

First performed at Moscow,
November 20, 1887

CHARACTERS IN THE PLAY

NIKOLAY ALEXEYEVITCH IVANOV (*permanent member of the Rural Board*).

ANNA PETROVNA (*his wife, before her baptism and marriage called* SARRA ABRAMSON).

COUNT MATVEY SEMYONITCH SHABELSKY (*his maternal uncle*).

PAVEL KIRILLITCH LEBEDYEV (*Chairman of the District Zemstvo*).

ZINAIDA SAVISHNA (*his wife*).

SASHA (*their daughter, aged twenty*).

YEVGENY KONSTANTINOVITCH LVOV (*a young Zemstvo Doctor*).

MARFA YEGOROVNA BABAKIN (*the young widow of a landowner, daughter of a rich merchant*).

DMITRI NIKITITCH KOSSIH (*Excise officer*).

MIHAIL MIHAILOVITCH BORKIN (*a distant relative of* IVANOV *and Steward of his estate*).

AVDOTYA NAZAROVNA (*an old woman of no definite occupation*).

YEGORUSHKA (*a dependant of the* LEBEDYEVS).

FIRST GUEST.   SECOND GUEST.

THIRD GUEST.   FOURTH GUEST.

PYOTR (IVANOV'S *manservant*).

GAVRIL (LEBEDYEV'S *manservant*).

VISITORS (*of both sexes*).   MENSERVANTS.

The action takes place in one of the provinces of Central Russia.

248

ACT I

The garden on IVANOV'S *estate.   On the left, the front
of the house with the verandah.   One window
is open.   In front of the verandah is a wide
semicircular space, from which an avenue at
right angles to the house, and another to the
right, run into the garden.   On the right side
of the verandah are garden seats and tables.
On one of the latter a lamp is burning.   Evening is coming on.   As the curtain rises there is
the sound of a duet of piano and 'cello being
practised indoors.*

IVANOV *is sitting at a table reading.* BORKIN,
*wearing high boots and carrying a gun, comes
into sight at the further end of the garden—he
is a little drunk ; seeing* IVANOV, *he advances
on tiptoe towards him, and when he reaches
him aims his gun at his face.*

IVANOV (*seeing* BORKIN, *starts and jumps up*).
Misha, what are you about ? . . .   You gave me a
fright. . . .   I am worried as it is, and then you
come with your stupid jokes . . . (*sits down*).   He
has frightened me, and is delighted . . .

BORKIN (*laughs*).   There, there. . . .   I am sorry,
I am sorry (*sits down beside him*).   I won't do it
again, I really won't . . . (*takes off his cap*).   I'm

hot. Would you believe it, my dear soul, I've done nearly twelve miles in three hours ! . . . Just feel how my heart is beating ! . . .

IVANOV (*reading*). All right, presently. . . .

BORKIN. No, feel now (*takes* IVANOV'S *hand and lays it on his chest*). Do you hear ? Too-too-too-too-too-too. . . . It shows I've got heart-disease, you know. I might die suddenly, any minute. I say, will you be sorry if I die ?

IVANOV. I am reading . . . presently. . . .

BORKIN. No, seriously, will you be sorry if I die ? Nikolay Alexeyevitch, will you be sorry if I die ?

IVANOV. Don't pester me !

BORKIN. My dear fellow, do tell me whether you will be sorry.

IVANOV. I am sorry you smell of vodka. Misha, it's disgusting !

BORKIN (*laughs*). Do I smell of it ? How surprising ! . . . Though there is nothing surprising in it, really. At Plesniki I met the examining magistrate, and I must own we put away eight glasses or so each. Drinking is very bad for one, really. I say, it is bad for one, isn't it ? It is, isn't it ?

IVANOV. This is really intolerable. . . . You must see that it's simply maddening. . . .

BORKIN. There, there. . . . I am sorry, I am sorry. . . . God bless you ; sit still . . . (*gets up and walks away*). Queer people ; there's no talking to them ! (*Comes back*) Oh yes, I was almost forgetting. . . . Give me the eighty-two roubles.

IVANOV. What eighty-two roubles ?

mette ivers.

BORKIN. To pay the labourers to-morrow.

IVANOV. I haven't got it.

BORKIN. Very much obliged! (*Mimicking*) I haven't got it. . . . But the labourers must be paid, mustn't they?

IVANOV. I don't know. I haven't the money to-day. Wait till the first of next month, when I get my salary.

BORKIN. Much good it is talking to such a specimen! . . . The labourers won't come for the money on the first; they will come to-morrow morning! . . .

IVANOV. Well, what am I to do? You may cut my throat, hack me to pieces. . . . And what a revolting habit it is of yours to pester me just when I am reading or writing, or . . .

BORKIN. I ask you, must the labourers be paid or not? But what's the use of talking to you! (*waves his hand*). And he is a country gentleman—hang it all, a landowner! . . . Up-to-date agricultural methods. . . . Three thousand acres, and not a penny in his pocket! . . . There is a wine-cellar, and no corkscrew. . . . I'll go and sell the three horses to-morrow! Yes! I have sold the standing oats, and now I'll sell the rye! (*strides about the stage*). Do you suppose I'd hesitate? Eh? No; you've hit on the wrong man for that. . . .

(SHABELSKY'S *voice inside:* " *It is impossible to play with you. . . . You have no more ear than a stuffed pike, and your touch is appalling!* ")

ANNA PETROVNA (*appears at the open window*).

Who was talking here just now? Was it you, Misha? Why are you striding about like that?

BORKIN. Your *Nicolas-voilà* is enough to drive one to anything!

ANNA PETROVNA. I say, Misha, tell them to bring some hay on to the croquet lawn.

BORKIN (*waving her off*). Please let me alone. . . .

ANNA PETROVNA. Goodness! what a way to speak! . . . That tone doesn't suit you at all. If you want women to like you, you must never let them see you cross or standing on your dignity. (*To her husband*) Nikolay, let us roll about on the hay!

IVANOV. It's bad for you to stand at an open window, Anyuta. Please go in . . . (*Calls*) Uncle, shut the window. (*The window is shut.*)

BORKIN. Don't forget that in two days' time you have to pay Lebedyev his interest.

IVANOV. I remember. I shall be at Lebedyev's to-day, and I will ask him to wait (*looks at his watch*).

BORKIN. When are you going?

IVANOV. Directly.

BORKIN (*eagerly*). Wait a minute! I do believe it is Sasha's birthday to-day . . . tut—tut —tut . . . and I forgot it. . . . What a memory! (*skips about*). I am going—I am going (*sings*). I am going. . . . I'll go and have a bathe, chew some paper, take three drops of spirits of ammonia —and I shall be ready to begin all over again. . . . Nikolay Alexeyevitch darling, my precious, angel of my heart, you are always in a state of nerves, complaining, and in the dismal doldrums, and yet the devil only knows what we two might bring off together! I am ready to do anything for you. . . . Would you like me to marry Marfusha Babakin for you? Half her dowry shall be yours . . . no, not half, all, all shall be yours!

IVANOV. Do shut up with your silly rot.

BORKIN. No, seriously! Would you like me to marry Marfusha? We'll go halves over the dowry. . . . But there, why do I talk about it to you? As though you would understand! (*Mimicking*) "Shut up with your silly rot." You are a fine man, an intelligent man, but you've none of that streak in you, you know—none of that go . . . To have a fling to make the devils sick with envy. . . . You are a neurotic, a drooper, but if you were a normal man you would have a million in a year. For instance, if I had at this moment two thousand three hundred roubles, I would have twenty thousand in a fortnight. You don't believe it? You call that silly rot too? No, it's not silly rot. . . . There, give me two thousand three hundred roubles and in a week I'll bring you twenty thousand. On the other side of the river Ovsyanov is selling a strip of land just opposite us for two thousand three hundred roubles. If we were to buy that strip, both sides of the river would be ours, and if both banks were ours, you know, we should have the right to dam up the river, shouldn't we? We'd set about building a mill, and, as soon as we let people know we were going to make a dam, all the people living down the river would make a hullaballoo, and we'd say—*kommen sie hier*, if you don't want to have a dam, buy us off. Do you understand? Zarevsky's factory would give us five thousand, Korolkov three thousand, the monastery five thousand. . . .

IVANOV. That's all stuff and nonsense, Misha. . . . If you don't want to quarrel with me, keep such schemes to yourself.

BORKIN (*sits down to the table*). Of course! . . . I knew it would be so! . . . You won't do anything yourself, and you won't let me.

(*Enter* SHABELSKY *and* LVOV.)

SHABELSKY (*coming out of the house with* LVOV). Doctors are just the same as lawyers; the only difference is that the lawyers rob you, and the doctors rob you and murder you. . . . I am not speaking of present company (*sits down on the garden-seat*). Charlatans, exploiters. . . . Perhaps in Arcadia there may be some exceptions to the general rule, but . . In the course of my life I've spent twenty thousand or so on doctors, and I never met a single one who did not seem to me a licensed swindler.

BORKIN (*to* IVANOV). Yes, you do nothing yourself, and you won't let me do anything. That's why we have no money. . . .

SHABELSKY. I repeat that I am not speaking of present company. . . . Perhaps there are exceptions, though indeed . . . (*yawns*).

IVANOV (*shutting his book*). What do you say, doctor?

LVOV (*looking round towards the window*). What I said to you this morning : she must go to the Crimea at once (*paces about the stage*).

SHABELSKY (*giggles*). Crimea! . . . Why don't you and I go in for being doctors, Misha? It's so simple. . . . As soon as some Madame Angot or Ophelia begins wheezing and coughing because she has nothing better to do, you've to take a sheet of paper and prescribe according to the rules of your science: first, a young doctor, then a trip to the Crimea, a Tatar guide in the Crimea. . . .

IVANOV (*to* SHABELSKY). Oh, do stop it! How you do keep on! (*To* Lvov) To go to the Crimea one must have money. Even if I do manage to get it, she absolutely refuses to go.

LVOV. Yes, she does (*a pause*).

BORKIN. I say, doctor, is Anna Petrovna really so ill that it is necessary for her to go to the Crimea?

LVOV (*looking round towards the window*). Yes, it's consumption.

BORKIN. Ss—ss! . . . That's bad. . . . For some time past I've thought she looked as though she wouldn't last long.

LVOV. But . . . don't talk so loud . . . you will be heard in the house (*a pause*).

BORKIN (*sighing*). Such is life. . . . The life of man is like a flower growing luxuriantly in a field: a goat comes and eats it, and the flower is no more.

SHABELSKY. It's all nonsense, nonsense, nonsense . . . (*yawns*). Nonsense and fraud (*a pause*).

BORKIN. And here, gentlemen, I keep showing Nikolay Alexeyevitch how to make money. I've just given him a glorious idea, but as usual he throws cold water on it. There's no moving him

. . . Just look at him: melancholy, spleen, depression, hypochondria, dejection. . . .

SHABELSKY (*stands up and stretches*). You've got some scheme for everyone, you genius; you teach everyone how to live, you might try it on me for once. . . . Give me a lesson, you brainy person, show me a way of escape. . . .

BORKIN (*getting up*). I'm going to bathe. . . . Good-bye, gentlemen. (*To the* COUNT) There are twenty things you could do. . . . If I were in your place I would have twenty thousand within a week (*is going*).

SHABELSKY (*follows him*). How's that? Come, show me how to do it.

BORKIN. It doesn't need showing. It's very simple (*coming back*). Nikolay Alexeyevitch, give me a rouble!

(IVANOV *gives him the money in silence.*)

BORKIN. *Merci!* (*To the* COUNT) You've still lots of trump cards in your hand.

SHABELSKY (*following him*). Well, what are they?

BORKIN. If I were in your place, within a week I would have thirty thousand, if not more (*goes out with the* COUNT).

IVANOV (*after a pause*). Superfluous people, superfluous words, the necessity of answering foolish questions—all this has so exhausted me that I am quite ill, doctor. I have grown irritable, hasty, harsh, and so petty that I don't know myself. For days together my head aches; I cannot sleep, there's a noise in my ears. . . And there's no getting away from it all . . . simply nothing I can do. . . .

256

Lvov. I want to talk to you seriously, Nikolay Alexeyevitch.

Ivanov. What is it?

Lvov. It's about Anna Petrovna (*sits down*). She won't consent to go to the Crimea, but with you she would go.

Ivanov (*pondering*). To go together we must have the means to do it. Besides, they won't give me a long leave. I've taken my holiday this year already . . .

Lvov. Well, supposing that is so. Now for the next point. The most important condition for the treatment of consumption is absolute peace of mind, and your wife never has a moment's peace of mind. She is in continual agitation over your attitude to her. Forgive me, I am excited and am going to speak frankly to you. Your conduct is killing her (*a pause*). Nikolay Alexeyevitch, allow me to think better of you!

Ivanov. It's all true, quite true. . . . I expect I am terribly to blame, but my thoughts are in a tangle, my soul is paralysed by inertia, and I am incapable of understanding myself. I don't understand others or myself . . . (*looks at the window*). We may be overheard, let us go for a stroll. (*They get up*.) I'd tell you the whole story from the beginning, my dear fellow, but it's a long story and so complicated that I shouldn't be finished by to-morrow morning. (*They are walking away*) Anyuta is a remarkable, exceptional woman. . . . For my sake she has changed her religion, given up her father and mother, abandoned wealth, and if I wanted a hundred more sacrifices she would

257

make them without the quiver of an eyelash. Well, and I am in no way remarkable, and I have made no sacrifices. But it's a long story. . . . The point of it all is, dear doctor (*hesitates*), is that . . . The long and the short of it is that I was passionately in love when I married and vowed I would love her for ever ; but . . . five years have passed, she still loves me, and I . . . (*makes a gesture of despair*). Here you tell me that she is soon going to die, and I feel neither love nor pity, but a sort of emptiness and weariness. . . . If one looks at me from outside it must be horrible. I don't myself understand what is happening in my soul. (*They go out along the avenue.*)

(*Enter* SHABELSKY.)

SHABELSKY (*laughing*). Upon my honour, he is no common rascal, he is a genius, an expert ! We ought to put up a statue to him. He combines in himself every form of modern rottenness : the lawyer's and the doctor's, and the huckster's and the cashier's (*sits down on the lowest step of the verandah*). And yet I believe he has never finished his studies ! That's what is so surprising. . . . What a rascal of genius he would have been if he had absorbed culture and learning ! " You can have twenty thousand in a week," says he. " You've still the ace of trumps in your hands," says he, " your title " (*laughs*). " Any girl with a dowry would marry you. . . ."

(ANNA PETROVNA *opens the window ar.d looks down.*)

SHABELSKY. " Would you like me to make a

match for you with Marfusha ? " says he. *Qui est-ce que c'est Marfusha ?* Ah, it's that Balabalkin . . . Babakalkin . . . who looks like a washerwoman. . . .

ANNA PETROVNA. Is that you, Count ?

SHABELSKY. What is it ?

(ANNA PETROVNA *laughs.*)

SHABELSKY (*with a Jewish accent*). Vot for you laugh ?

ANNA PETROVNA. I thought of something you said. Do you remember you said at dinner : " A thief that is forgiven, a horse . . ." What is it ?

SHABELSKY. A Jew that is christened, a thief that is forgiven, a horse that is doctored—are worth the same price.

ANNA PETROVNA (*laughs*). You can't make even a simple joke without spite in it. You are a spiteful man. (*Earnestly*) Joking apart, Count, you are very spiteful. It's dull and dreadful living with you. You are always snarling and grumbling. You think all men are scoundrels and rascals. Tell me honestly, have you ever said anything good about anyone ?

SHABELSKY. Why this cross-examination ?

ANNA PETROVNA. We've been living under the same roof for five years and I've never once heard you speak of people calmly, without malice and derision. What harm have people done you ? And do you really imagine that you are better than anyone else ?

SHABELSKY. I don't imagine it at all. I am just as great a blackguard and pig in a skull-cap as everyone else, *mauvais ton* and an old rag.

I always abuse myself. Who am I? What am I? I was rich, free and rather happy, but now . . . I am a dependant, a hanger-on, a degraded buffoon. I am indignant, I am contemptuous, and people laugh at me : I laugh and they shake their heads at me mournfully and say the old chap is cracked . . . and most often they don't hear me, don't heed me. . . .

ANNA PETROVNA (*calmly*). It is screeching again.

SHABELSKY. Who is screeching ?

ANNA PETROVNA. The owl. It screeches every evening.

SHABELSKY. Let it screech. Nothing can be worse than what is now (*stretching*). Ah, my dear Sarra, if I were to win a hundred or two hundred thousand I'd show you a thing or two ! You'd see no more of me here. I'd get away from this hole, away from the bread of charity . . . and wouldn't set foot here again till the day of judgment. . . .

ANNA PETROVNA. And what would you do if you did win a lot of money ?

SHABELSKY (*after a moment's thought*). First of all I would go to Moscow to hear the gypsies. Then . . . then I should be off to Paris. I should take a flat there, I should go to the Russian church. . . .

ANNA PETROVNA. And what else ?

SHABELSKY. I should sit for days together on my wife's grave and think. I should sit there till I died. My wife is buried in Paris. . . . (*a pause*).

ANNA PETROVNA. How awfully dull it is ! Shall we play another duet ?

SHABELSKY. Very well, get the music ready.
(ANNA PETROVNA *goes out. Enter* IVANOV *and* LVOV.)

IVANOV (*comes into sight with* LVOV *in the avenue*). You took your degree only last year, my dear friend, you are still young and vigorous while I am five and thirty. I have the right to advise you. Don't marry a Jewess nor a neurotic nor a blue stocking, but choose what is commonplace, grey, with no vivid colours or superfluous flourishes. In fact, build your whole life on the conventional pattern. The greyer and the more monotonous the background the better, my dear boy. Don't fight with thousands single-handed, don't wage war on windmills, don't batter your head against the wall. . . . God preserve you from all sorts of scientific farming, wonderful schools, enthusiastic speeches. . . . Shut yourself up in your shell, do the humble duty God has laid upon you. . . . That's snugger, happier and more honest. But the life that I have led, how tiring it is ! Ah, how tiring ! . . . How many mistakes, how much that was unjust and absurd. . . . (*Seeing the* COUNT, *irritably*) You are always in the way, Uncle, you never let one have a talk in peace !

SHABELSKY (*in a tearful voice*). Oh, the devil take me, there's no refuge for me anywhere ! (*jumps up and goes into the house*).

IVANOV (*calls after him*). Oh, I am sorry ! (*To* LVOV) What made me hurt his feelings ? Yes, I must be out of gear. I must do something with myself, I really must. . . .

LVOV (*in agitation*). Nikolay Alexeyevitch

I have listened to you and . . . and forgive me, I will speak plainly, without beating about the bush. Your voice, your intonation, to say nothing of your words, are full of such soulless egoism, such cold heartlessness. . . . Someone very near to you is dying through her love for you, her days are numbered, and you . . . you can be cold to her, can walk about and give advice, and pose. . . . I cannot tell you, I have no gift for words, but . . . but you are intensely repulsive to me !

IVANOV. Very likely, very likely. . . . You can see it all more clearly from outside. . . . It's very possible that you understand. . . . I daresay I am horribly to blame, horribly . . . (*listens*). I fancy I hear the carriage. I am going to get ready . . . (*goes to the house and stops*). You dislike me, doctor, and don't conceal your dislike. It does credit to your heart . . . (*goes into the house*).

LVOV (*alone*). My cursed weakness ! Again I've missed the chance and haven't said what I ought to have said. . . . I cannot speak to him calmly ! As soon as I open my mouth and say a word I feel such a suffocation, such a heaving here (*points to his chest*), and my tongue sticks to the roof of my mouth. I hate this Tartuffe, this highflown scoundrel, I hate him. . . . Here he is going away. . . . His poor wife's only happiness is to have him near her, she lives in him, she implores him to spend one evening with her, and he . . . he cannot ! He feels stifled and cramped at home, if you please. If he were to spend a single evening at home, he'd be so depressed that he'd blow his brains out. Poor fellow . . . he must have freedom to contrive some new villainy. . . . Oh, I know why you go to these Lebedyevs every evening ! I know !

(*Enter* IVANOV *in his hat and overcoat,* ANNA PETROVNA *and* SHABELSKY.)

SHABELSKY (*as he comes out of the house with* ANNA PETROVNA *and* IVANOV). Really, *Nicolas*, this is positively inhuman ! You go out every evening and we are left alone. We are so bored we go to bed at eight o'clock. It's hideous, it's not life at all ! And why is it that you can go and we mayn't ? Why ?

ANNA PETROVNA. Leave him alone ! Let him go, let him. . . .

IVANOV (*to his wife*). How can you go when you are ill ? You are ill and you mustn't be out after sunset. . . . Ask the doctor. You are not a child, Anyuta, you must be sensible. . . . (*To the* COUNT) And what do you want to go there for ?

SHABELSKY. I'd go to hell, into the jaws of a crocodile, so long as I need not stay here ! I am bored ! I am bored to stupefaction ! Everybody is sick of me. You leave me at home so that she should not be bored alone, but I do nothing but snap and nag at her !

ANNA PETROVNA. Leave him alone, Count, leave him alone ! Let him go if he enjoys it.

IVANOV. Anyuta, why do you speak like that? You know I am not going for pleasure ! I have to speak about the loan.

ANNA PETROVNA. I don't know why you justify yourself! Go! No one is keeping you!

IVANOV. Come, don't let us nag at each other! Surely it isn't necessary?

SHABELSKY (*in a tearful voice*). *Nicolas*, dear boy, I implore you, take me with you! I shall have a look at the knaves and fools there and perhaps it will amuse me! I haven't been anywhere since Easter!

IVANOV (*irritably*). Oh, very well, come along! How sick I am of you all!

SHABELSKY. Yes? Oh, *merci, merci* . . (*cheerfully takes him by the arm and leads him aside*). May I wear your straw hat?

IVANOV. Yes, only make haste!

(*The* COUNT *runs indoors.*)

IVANOV. How sick I am of you all! But, good God, what am I saying? Anyuta, I talk to you in an unpardonable way. I never used to be like this before. Well, good-bye, Anyuta, I shall be back by one.

ANNA PETROVNA. Kolya, darling, stay at home!

IVANOV (*agitated*). My precious, my poor unhappy darling, I entreat you, don't prevent my going out in the evening. It's cruel and unfair of me, but let me be unfair! I feel miserably depressed at home! As soon as the sun sets, I am overcome by acute misery. Such misery! Don't ask why it is. I don't know myself. I swear I don't! Here it is misery; I go to the Lebedyevs and there it is worse still; I come back and here misery again, and it goes on like that all night.
. . It's simply desperate!

ANNA PETROVNA. Kolya . . . but if you stay?
We will talk as we used to. . . . We'll have
supper together; we will read. . . . The old
grumbler and I have learned a lot of duets for
you . . . (*puts her arms round him*). Do stay!
(*a pause*). I don't understand you. This has
been going on for a whole year. Why have you
changed?

IVANOV. I don't know, I don't know. . . .

ANNA PETROVNA. And why don't you want me
to go with you in the evening?

IVANOV. If you will have it, I'll tell you. It's
rather cruel to say it, but it is better to speak out.
. . . When I am depressed I . . . I begin not
to love you. I run away even from you at such
times. In short, I must get away from home.

ANNA PETROVNA. Depression! I understand—I
understand. . . . Do you know what, Kolya?
Try to sing, to laugh, to get cross, as you used to.
. . . Stay, we will laugh, drink home-made wine,
and we'll drive away your depression in an instant.
Shall I sing to you? Or we'll go and sit in your
study in the dark as we used to, and you shall tell
me about your depression. . . . Your eyes are
so full of suffering! I will look into them and
weep, and we shall both feel better . . . (*she
laughs and cries*). Or, Kolya, what is it? The
flowers come again every spring, but joys do not?
Yes? Well, go, go. . . .

IVANOV. Pray for me, Anyuta! (*he moves forward, stops, and ponders*). No, I cannot (*goes out*).

ANNA PETROVNA. Go . . . (*sits down at the
table*).

Lvov (*pacing up and down the stage*). Anna Petrovna, you must make it a rule as soon as the clock strikes six to come indoors and stay there till morning. The damp of the evening is bad for you.

ANNA PETROVNA. Yes, sir!

Lvov. What do you mean by that? I am speaking seriously.

ANNA PETROVNA. And I don't want to be serious (*coughs*).

Lvov. There, you see, you are coughing already.
(*Enter* SHABELSKY).

SHABELSKY (*comes out in a hat and overcoat*). Where is Nikolay? Is the carriage there? (*goes up quickly and kisses* ANNA PETROVNA'S *hand*). Good-night, my charmer! (*grimacing*). *Gewalt!* Vill you pardon me? (*goes out quickly*).

Lvov. The buffoon!
(*A pause; the sound of a concertina far away.*)

ANNA PETROVNA. How dull it is! The coachmen and the cooks have got up a ball, while I . . . I seem to be forsaken. . . . Yevgeny Konstantinitch, why are you striding up and down? Come here, sit down!

Lvov. I can't sit still (*a pause*).

ANNA PETROVNA. They are playing the *Greenfinch* in the kitchen.

(*Sings*) Greenfinch, greenfinch, where have you been?
Drinking vodka under the hill?

(*A pause.*) Doctor, have you got a father and mother?

Lvov. My father is dead, but I have a mother.

ANNA PETROVNA. Do you miss your mother ?

LVOV. I have no time to miss her.

ANNA PETROVNA (*laughs*). The flowers come
again every spring, but joys do not. Who was it
said that to me ? Let me see. . . . I believe
it was Nikolay himself (*listens*). There's the owl
screeching again !

LVOV. Well, let it screech.

ANNA PETROVNA. I begin to think, doctor, that
fate has been unfair to me. Numbers of people
who are perhaps no better than I are happy and
pay nothing for their happiness. I have paid
for everything, absolutely everything ! And what
a price ! Why take from me such terribly high
interest ? . . . My good friend, you are all on your
guard with me—you are so considerate, you are
afraid to tell me the truth ; but do you suppose
I don't know what's the matter with me ? I know
very well. But it's boring to talk about it.
(*In a Jewish accent*) Vill you pardon me, please ?
Can you tell funny stories ?

LVOV. No.

ANNA PETROVNA. Nikolay can. And I begin to
be surprised at people's injustice. Why don't
they return love for love, and why do they repay
truth with falsehood ? Tell me, how long will
my father and mother hate me ? They live forty
miles from here, but day and night, even in my
sleep, I feel their hatred. And what would you
have me make of Nikolay's depression ? He says
that he doesn't love me only in the evenings,
when he is overwhelmed with depression. That I
understand and can allow for. But only imagine

if he should tire of me altogether! Of course it's impossible, but—if he did? No, no, I must not even think about it. (*Sings*) Greenfinch, greenfinch, where have you been? . . . (*starts*). What dreadful ideas come into my mind! You are not married, doctor, and there are many things you can't understand. . . .

Lvov. You are surprised . . . (*sits down beside her*). No, I . . . I am surprised—I am surprised at you! Come, explain, make me understand, how is it that you, intelligent, honest, almost a saint, have allowed yourself to be so shamelessly deceived and dragged into this owl's nest? Why are you here? What have you in common with this cold, soulless . . . but let us leave your husband out! What have you in common with these vulgar, empty surroundings? Oh, good heavens! . . . that everlastingly grumbling, rusty, mad Count, that knave Misha—a scoundrel if ever there was one—with his revolting countenance. . . . Explain to me what you are here for. How did you come here?

Anna Petrovna (*laughs*). That's just how he used once to talk. Word for word. . . . But his eyes are larger, and when he began talking of anything with excitement they glowed like coals. . . . Go on, go on!

Lvov (*gets up with a wave of his hand*). What am I to say? Go indoors!

Anna Petrovna. You say that Nikolay is this and that, one thing and another. How do you know him? Do you suppose that you can get to know a man in six months? He is a remarkable

268

man, doctor, and I am sorry that you did not meet him two or three years ago. Now he is depressed and melancholy, he doesn't talk or do anything ; but in the old days . . . how charming he was ! I loved him at first sight (*laughs*). I looked and the mousetrap went bang ! He said "Come" . . . I cut off everything as, you know, one cuts off dead leaves with scissors, and followed him (*a pause*). But now it is different. Now he goes to the Lebedyevs to distract his mind with other women, while I . . . sit in the garden and listen to the owl screeching . . . (*A watchman's tap.*) And have you any brothers, doctor ?

Lvov. No.

(ANNA PETROVNA *breaks into sobs.*)

Lvov. Well, what now ? What's the matter ?

ANNA PETROVNA (*gets up*). I can't bear it, doctor . . . I am going. . . .

Lvov. Where ?

ANNA PETROVNA. Where he is . . . I am going. Tell them to put the horses in (*runs into the house*).

Lvov. No, I must absolutely decline to treat a patient under such conditions ! It's not enough that they don't pay me a farthing, but they turn my soul inside out as well ! . . . No, I decline ! It's too much . . . (*goes into the house*).

CURTAIN

A drawing-room in LEBEDYEV'S house; facing the
    stage a door into the garden; doors on right and
    left. Old-fashioned expensive furniture. A
    chandelier, candelabras, and pictures—all under
    covers.
ZINAIDA SAVISHNA, KOSSIH, AVDOTYA NAZAROVNA,
    YEGORUSHKA, GAVRIL, a MAIDSERVANT, OLD
    LADY VISITORS, YOUNG PEOPLE, and MADAME
    BABAKIN.
ZINAIDA SAVISHNA is sitting on the sofa. OLD
    LADIES are sitting in arm-chairs on either side
    of her, and YOUNG PEOPLE on ordinary chairs.
    In the background, near the way out into the
    garden, they are playing cards; among the
    players are KOSSIH, AVDOTYA NAZAROVNA and
    YEGORUSHKA. GAVRIL is standing by the door
    on right; a MAIDSERVANT carries round a tray
    full of sweets. Throughout the act GUESTS
    pass across the stage from the garden to door on
    right and back again. MADAME BABAKIN
    comes in from door on right and goes up to
    ZINAIDA SAVISHNA.

ZINAIDA (joyfully). My darling Marfa
Yegorovna !
    MADAME BABAKIN. How are you, Zinaida

Savishna ? I have the honour to congratulate you on your daughter's birthday. (*They kiss.*) God grant that . . .

ZINAIDA. Thank you, darling, I am so glad. . . . Well, how are you ?

MADAME BABAKIN. Thank you very much indeed (*sits down beside her on the sofa*). How do you do, young people ?

(*The* GUESTS *get up and bow.*)

FIRST GUEST (*laughs*). Young people ! . . . Why, are you old, then ?

MADAME BABAKIN (*with a sigh*). Well, I am sure I don't claim to be young. . . .

FIRST GUEST (*laughing respectfully*). Upon my word, what next ! You don't look like a widow ; you can give points to any young girl.

(GAVRIL *hands* MADAME BABAKIN *tea.*)

ZINAIDA (*to* GAVRIL). Why do you bring it like that ? Fetch some jam. Gooseberry or something.

MADAME BABAKIN. Please don't trouble. Thanks ever so much. . . .

(*A pause.*)

FIRST GUEST. Did you drive through Mushkino, Marfa Yegorovna ?

MADAME BABAKIN. No, through Zaimishtche. The road is better that way.

FIRST GUEST. To be sure.

KOSSIH. Two spades.

YEGORUSHKA. Pass.

AVDOTYA. Pass.

SECOND GUEST. Pass.

MADAME BABAKIN. Lottery tickets have gone

271

up shockingly, Zinaida Savishna, darling. It's unheard of : the first drawings are worth two hundred and seventy and the second nearly two hundred and fifty. It has never been so much before. . . .

ZINAIDA (*sighs*).   It's a good thing for those who have plenty of them.

MADAME BABAKIN. Don't say that, darling. Though the price is so high, it does not pay to put one's money into them.   The insurance alone is enough to drive you crazy.

ZINAIDA. That may be so ; but still, my dear, one has hopes . . . (*she sighs*).   God is merciful.

THIRD GUEST. From my point of view, *mesdames*, I maintain that it does not pay to have capital at all nowadays.   Investments yield a very small dividend and to put money into business is extremely risky.   The way I look at it, *mesdames*, is that the man who has capital in the present day is in a much more critical position than a man who . . .

MADAME BABAKIN (*sighing*).   That's true !

(FIRST GUEST *yawns*.)

MADAME BABAKIN. Is that the way to behave before ladies ?

FIRST GUEST. Pardon, *mesdames*, it was an accident.

(ZINAIDA SAVISHNA *gets up and goes out at the door on right.   Prolonged silence.*)

YEGORUSHKA. Two of diamonds.

AVDOTYA. Pass.

SECOND GUEST. Pass.

KOSSIH. Pass.

MADAME BABAKIN (*aside*). O Lord, how deadly dull it is !

(*Enter* ZINAIDA SAVISHNA *and* LEBEDYEV.)

ZINAIDA (*coming out of door on right with* LEBEDYEV, *quietly*). What do you want to stick there for all alone ! As though you were a prima-donna ! Sit with your visitors (*sits down in the same place as before*).

LEBEDYEV (*yawns*). Oh dear, oh dear ! (*Seeing* MADAME BABAKIN) Saints alive, here is strawberry cream ! Turkish delight ! (*shakes hands*). How is your precious self ?

MADAME BABAKIN. All right, thanks ever so much.

LEBEDYEV. Well, thank God for that ! (*sits down*). Yes, yes. . . . Gavril !

(GAVRIL *brings him a wineglass of vodka and a tumbler of water ; he drinks up the vodka and sips the water.*)

FIRST GUEST. To your very good health !

LEBEDYEV. Very good health indeed ! . . . I must be thankful I've not snuffed it altogether. (*To his wife*) Zyuzushka, where is the queen of the day ?

KOSSIH (*plaintively*). I should like to know why it is we have taken no tricks (*jumps up*). Why have we lost every game ? May the devil flay me entirely !

AVDOTYA (*jumps up and says angrily*). Why, because if you can't play, my good man, you had better not take a hand. Whatever business had you to lead your opponent's suit ? That's why you were left with your ace in pickle ! (*They both run forward from the table.*)

273

KOSSIH (*in a tearful voice*). Listen. . . . I had the ace, king, queen and eight more diamonds, the ace of spades and one little heart, you know. . . . And she could not declare a little slam—the devil knows why ! I said no trumps . . .

AVDOTYA. It was I who said no trumps ! You said two and no trumps. . . .

KOSSIH. It's revolting ! . . . Excuse me . . . you had . . . I had . . . you had . . . (*To* LEBEDYEV) Just think, Pavel Kirillitch . . . I had the ace, king, queen and eight more diamonds. . . .

LEBEDYEV (*putting his fingers in his ears*). Let me alone, if you don't mind . . .

AVDOTYA (*shouts*). It was I said no trumps !

KOSSIH (*ferociously*). May I be damned and disgraced if I ever sit down again to play with that cross old crab ! (*goes quickly into the garden.* SECOND GUEST *goes after him.* YEGORUSHKA *is left at the table*).

AVDOTYA. Ugh ! I am hot all over. . . . A crab ! . . . You are a crab yourself !

MADAME BABAKIN. You are a hasty one, too, Granny. . . .

AVDOTYA (*seeing* MADAME BABAKIN, *flings up her hands*). My joy, my beauty ! She is here, and me so blind as not to see her ! . . . My darling . . . (*kisses her on the shoulder and sits down beside her*). How delightful ! Let me have a look at you, my white swan ! . . . I'll knock on the wood !

LEBEDYEV. Now you are off. . . . You'd much better be finding her a husband. . . .

AVDOTYA. I will find her one ! I won't lay my

sinful old bones in my coffin till I have married her off, and Sasha too ! . . . I won't ! . . . (*a sigh*). Only where are they to be found nowadays, these husbands ? Here they sit ruffling up their feathers like cocks in the rain, our young men !

THIRD GUEST. A very unhappy comparison. In my opinion, *mesdames*, if young men nowadays prefer a bachelor existence, the reason is to be found in social conditions, so to say. . . .

LEBEDYEV. Come, come, no moralising ! . . . I don't care for it . . .

(*Enter* SASHA.)

SASHA (*goes up to her father*). Such glorious weather, and you all sit here in this stuffy room.

ZINAIDA. Sashenka, don't you see that Marfa Yegorovna is here ?

SASHA. I am sorry (*goes up to* MADAME BABAKIN *and shakes hands*).

MADAME BABAKIN. You are growing proud, Sasha. You have not been to see me once (*kisses her*). I congratulate you, darling. . . .

SASHA. Thank you (*sits down beside her father*).

LEBEDYEV. Yes, Avdotya Nazarovna, it is a difficult job with the young men nowadays. One can't get a decent best man for a wedding, let alone a husband. Nowadays young people (no offence to present company) are so limp and flabby, God help them ! . . . They can't talk, they can't dance, they can't drink. . . .

AVDOTYA. Oh, they are all equal to drinking if they have the chance.

LEBEDYEV. There's no great art in drinking —even a horse can drink. . . . The thing is to

275

drink like a gentleman. In our time we used to be struggling all day with lectures, and as soon as evening came on we would go off anywhere and be twirling like a top till morning . . . and we danced and amused the young ladies and had a good drink too. We talked nonsense or talked philosophy till our tongues were tired. . . . But the young men nowadays . . . (*waves his hand*). I can't make them out. . . . Neither a candle to God nor a poker to the devil. There's only one sensible fellow in the district, and he is married (*sighs*), and I fancy he is beginning to go off his head too. . . .

MADAME BABAKIN. Who is that?

LEBEDYEV. Nikolasha Ivanov.

MADAME BABAKIN. Yes, he is a nice gentleman (*makes a grimace*). Only unfortunate! . . .

ZINAIDA. How could he be fortunate, my dear? (*sighs*). What a mistake he made, poor fellow! He married his Jewess and reckoned, poor fellow! that her father and mother would give mountains of gold with her; but it has turned out quite the other way. . . . Ever since she changed her religion her father and mother have cast her off— they cursed her. . . . So he hasn't got a farthing. Now he is sorry, but it is too late. . . .

SASHA. Mother, that's not true.

MADAME BABAKIN (*hotly*). Sasha! not true? Why, everybody knows it. If it weren't for money why ever should he have married a Jewess? There are plenty of Russian girls, aren't there? He made a mistake, darling, he made a mistake . . . (*Eagerly*) And, I say, how she catches it

276

anette ivers.

from him now ! It is simply too funny. As soon as he comes home he is at her at once : " Your father and mother have cheated me ! Get out of my house ! " And where is she to go ? Her father and mother won't take her ; she would go for a housemaid, but she has never been trained to do anything . . . And he goes on from one thing to another till the Count takes her part. If it were not for the Count he would have been the death of her long ago. . . .

AVDOTYA. And sometimes he will shut her in the cellar and make her eat garlic. . . . She will eat it and eat it till she is sick (*laughter*).

SASHA. Father, that's a lie, you know !

LEBEDYEV. Well, what of it ? Let them babble as they like . . . (*Shouts*) Gavril !

(GAVRIL *hands him vodka and water*.)

ZINAIDA. That's how it is he has come to ruin, poor fellow ! His affairs are in a bad way, my dear. . . . If Borkin did not look after the estate he and his Jewess would have nothing to eat (*sighs*). And what we have had to put up with on his account, my dear. . . . God only knows what we have had to put up with ! Would you believe it, dear, he has been owing us nine thousand for these three years !

MADAME BABAKIN (*with horror*). Nine thousand !

ZINAIDA. Yes. . . . It was my precious Pashenka's idea to give it to him. He never knows whom one can lend to and whom one can't. I say nothing of the capital—it's no good worrying about that—but he might at least pay the interest regularly.

SASHA (*hotly*).   Mother, you have talked of that thousands of times already !

ZINAIDA. What is it to you ?   Why do you defend him ?

SASHA (*getting up*).   But how can you have the face to talk like that about a man who has done you no sort of harm ?   Why, what has he done to you ?

THIRD GUEST. Alexandra Pavlovna, allow me to say a couple of words.   I respect Nikolay Alexeyevitch, and always considered it an honour . . . but, speaking *entre nous*, my opinion is that he is an adventurer.

SASHA. Well, I congratulate you on your opinion.

THIRD GUEST. In support of it I beg to mention the following fact which was reported to me by his *attaché* or, so to speak, *cicerone*, Borkin.   Two years ago at the time of the cattle plague he bought cattle, insured them . . .

ZINAIDA. Yes, yes, yes !   I remember the incident.   I was told of it too.

THIRD GUEST. Insured them—mark that—then infected them with the cattle plague and got the insurance money.

SASHA. Ugh, that's all such rubbish !   No one bought cattle or infected them !   That was all Borkin's invention, and he boasted of the plan everywhere.   When Ivanov heard of it, Borkin was begging his pardon for a fortnight before he would forgive him.   Ivanov is only to blame for being weak and not having the heart to kick that Borkin out, and he is to blame for putting too

much trust in people too ! He has been robbed
and plundered on all sides : everyone who could
made money out of his generous schemes.

LEBEDYEV. Sasha, you little spitfire, shut up !

SASHA. Why do they talk such nonsense ? It's
so dull—so boring ! Ivanov, Ivanov, Ivanov—you
talk of nothing else (*goes to the door and turns back*).
I wonder ! (*to the young men*). I positively wonder
at your patience, gentlemen ! Aren't you tired of
sitting still like this ? The very air is heavy with
boredom ! Do say something ; entertain the
young ladies ; move about a little ! Come, if
you have no other subject but Ivanov, laugh, sing,
dance or something. . . .

LEBEDYEV (*laughing*). Give it to them, give it
to them well !

SASHA. Come, I say, do something for me ! If
you don't care to dance, to laugh, to sing, if all
that bores you, I beg you, I entreat you, just for
once in your life—as a curiosity—to surprise or
amuse us : make a great effort and all together
think of something witty and brilliant ; say something, even if it is rude or vulgar, so long as it is
amusing and new ! Or all together do some little
thing, however inconspicuous, so long as it is just
conceivably worth doing, so that for once in their
lives the young ladies may cry " Oh ! " as they
look at you. You do want to please, don't you ?
So why don't you try to be pleasing ? Ah ! my
friends, you are not up to much—not up to much,
any of you. . . . The very flies die of boredom
and the lamps begin smoking when they look at
you. . . . You are not up to much, any of you.

. . . I have told you so a thousand times already, and I shall always say so.

(*Enter* IVANOV *and* SHABELSKY.)

SHABELSKY (*entering with* IVANOV *by door on right*). Who is preaching here? You, Sasha? (*laughs and shakes hands with her*). Happy returns, my angel. God grant that you die as late as possible and are not born again. . . .

ZINAIDA (*delightedly*). Nikolay Alexeyevitch! Count!

LEBEDYEV. Bah! Whom do I see? . . . The Count! (*goes to meet him*).

SHABELSKY (*seeing* ZINAIDA SAVISHNA *and* MADAME BABAKIN, *stretches out his hands to them*). Two gold mines on one sofa! . . . Delightful spectacle! (*shakes hands. To* ZINAIDA SAVISHNA) How do you do, Zyuzushka! (*To* MADAME BABAKIN) How do you do, dumpling!

ZINAIDA. I am glad. You are such a rare visitor, Count! (*Shouts*) Gavril, tea! Please sit down (*gets up, goes out of door on right and at once returns; she looks extremely preoccupied.* SASHA *sits down in the same place as before.* IVANOV *greets everyone in silence*).

LEBEDYEV (*to* SHABELSKY). Where have you dropped from? What brought you here? It is a surprise! (*kisses him*). Count, you are a rascal! Is that the way for decent people to behave? (*leads him by the hand to the footlights*). Why do you never come and see us? Are you cross, or what?

SHABELSKY. How can I come and see you? Astride a stick? I have no horses, and Nikolay won't bring me with him : he tells me to stay with Sarra, to keep her company. Send your horses for me, and then I will come. . . .

LEBEDYEV (*with a wave of his hand*). Oh, well ! Zyuzushka would burst before she'd let me have the horses. You dear creature, you darling, you know you are nearer and dearer to me than anyone ! Of all the old set there is no one left but you and me ! In you I love my sorrows of past years, and my fair youth so idly flung away. . . . Joking apart, I feel ready to cry ! (*kisses the* COUNT).

SHABELSKY. Let go—let go ! You smell like a wine-cellar. . . .

LEBEDYEV. My dear soul, you can't think how I miss my old friends ! I could hang myself, I am so miserable (*softly*). Zyuzushka, with her money-grubbing, has driven all decent people away, and as you see we have none but Zulus left . . . these Dudkins and Budkins. . . . Come, drink your tea !

(GAVRIL *brings* SHABELSKY *tea.*)

ZINAIDA (*anxiously to* GAVRIL). What are you doing ? Bring some jam . . . gooseberry, or something . . .

SHABELSKY (*laughs ; to* IVANOV). There ; did I not tell you ? (*To* LEBEDYEV) I bet him on the way that as soon as we got here Zyuzushka would regale us with gooseberry jam. . . .

ZINAIDA. You are just as fond of your joke as ever, Count (*sits down*).

LEBEDYEV. She has made two barrels of gooseberry jam, so what is she to do with it ?

SHABELSKY (*sitting down near the table*). You are saving money, Zyuzushka, aren't you? I suppose you are a millionaire by now, eh?

ZINAIDA (*with a sigh*). Yes, to outsiders it seems as though we are richer than anyone, but where could we get money from? That's all gossip. . . .

SHABELSKY. Come, come! We know all about that! . . . We know what a poor hand you are at the game . . . (*To* LEBEDYEV) Pasha, tell the truth, have you saved a million?

LEBEDYEV. I don't know. Ask Zyuzushka. . . .

SHABELSKY (*to* MADAME BABAKIN). And our fat little dumpling will soon have a million too! She gets plumper and prettier, not every day, but every hour! That's what it is to have plenty of money. . . .

MADAME BABAKIN. I am very much obliged to your Excellency, but I am not fond of being jeered at.

SHABELSKY. My dear gold-mine, do you suppose it was a jeer? It was simply a cry from the heart. Out of the fullness of the heart the mouth speaketh. . . . There is no limit to my affection for you and Zyuzushka (*gaily*). It's rapture, ecstasy! I can't look at either of you unmoved!

ZINAIDA. You are just the same as ever. (*To* YEGORUSHKA) Yegorushka, put out the candles! Why let them burn for nothing when you are not playing? (YEGORUSHKA *starts; puts out the candles and sits down. To* IVANOV) Nikolay Alexeyevitch, how is your wife?

IVANOV. She is very ill. The doctor told us to-day that it is certainly consumption.

ZINAIDA. Really? What a pity ! (*a sigh*). We are all so fond of her.

SHABELSKY. Nonsense, nonsense, nonsense ! . . . There is no consumption at all : it's all quackery—doctors' tricks. The learned gentleman likes to hang about the house, so he makes out it's consumption. Luckily for him the husband is not jealous. (IVANOV *makes a gesture of impatience*.) As for Sarra herself, I don't trust a word she says or a thing she does. All my life I've never trusted doctors, lawyers, or women. It's all nonsense and nonsense, quackery and tricks !

LEBEDYEV (*to* SHABELSKY). You are a strange individual, Matvey! . . . You've taken up this affectation of misanthropy and play about with it like a fool with a new hat. You are a man like anyone else, but you are as peevish in your talk as though you had a blister on your tongue, or indigestion. . . .

SHABELSKY. Why, would you have me kiss rogues and scoundrels, or what?

LEBEDYEV. Where do you see rogues and scoundrels?

SHABELSKY. I don't refer to present company, of course, but . . .

LEBEDYEV. There you are with your buts. . . . It's all affectation.

SHABELSKY. Affectation? . . . It's a good thing you've no philosophy of life.

LEBEDYEV. What philosophy could I have? I sit every minute expecting to kick the bucket. That's my philosophy of life. It's too late for you and me, old man, to talk of philosophies of life. Yes, indeed ! (*Shouts*) Gavril !

283

SHABELSKY. You have had too much of Gavril as it is. . . . Your nose is like beetroot already.

LEBEDYEV (*drinks*). Never mind, my dear soul . . . it's not my wedding day.

ZINAIDA. It is a long while since Dr. Lvov has been to see us. He has quite deserted us.

SASHA. My pet aversion. The walking image of honesty. He can't ask for a glass of water or smoke a cigarette without displaying his extraordinary honesty. If he walks about or talks, his face is always labelled " I am an honest man." He bores me.

SHABELSKY. He is a stiff-necked, narrow-minded individual ! (*Mimicking*) " Make way for honest labour ! " He shouts like a cockatoo at every step, and he fancies he is really a second Dobrolyubov. If a man does not shout as he does, he is a scoundrel. His views are wonderfully profound. If a peasant is well off and lives like a human being, he is a scoundrel and a blood-sucker. I put on a velvet jacket and am dressed by a valet, so I am a scoundrel and a slave-owner. He is simply bursting with honesty. Nothing is good enough for him. I am positively afraid of him. . . . Yes, indeed ! any minute he may slap you in the face or call you a scoundrel from a sense of duty.

IVANOV. He wearies me dreadfully, but at the same time I like him ; he is so sincere.

SHABELSKY. Nice sort of sincerity ! He came up to me yesterday evening, and *apropos* of nothing at all : " You are deeply repulsive to me, Count ! " I am very much obliged ! And all that not simply, but from principle : his voice shakes, his eyes flash, and he is all of a tremor. . . . Damnation take his wooden sincerity ! He may find me hateful and disgusting ; it's natural enough. . . . I can see that, but why tell me so to my face ? I am a wretched creature, but anyway my hair is grey. . . . A stupid, pitiless honesty !

LEBEDYEV. Come, come, come ! . . . You've been young yourself, and can make allowances.

SHABELSKY. Yes, I've been young and foolish : I've played the Tchatsky in my day. I've denounced rascals and blackguards, but never in my life have I called a man a thief to his face, or talked of the gallows in the house of a man who has been hanged. I was decently brought up. But your dull-witted doctor would be in the seventh heaven and feel that he was fulfilling his mission, if fate would grant him the opportunity of publicly slapping me in the face and punching me in the pit of the stomach for the sake of principle and the great ideals of humanity.

LEBEDYEV. Young people are always self-assertive. I had an uncle, a Hegelian . . . he would invite a houseful of visitors, drink with them, stand up on a chair like this and begin : " You are ignorant ! You are the powers of darkness ! The dawn of a new life," etc., etc., etc. . . . He would go on and on at them.

SASHA. And what did the visitors do ?

LEBEDYEV. Oh, nothing . . . they just listened and went on drinking. Once, though, I challenged him to a duel . . . my own uncle. It was about Bacon. I remember, if I am right, I was sitting where Matvey is now, and my uncle and Gerassim Nilitch were standing as it might be here, where Nikolay is. . . . And Gerassim Nilitch, if you please, puts the question . . .

(BORKIN, *foppishly dressed, with a parcel in his hand, comes in at door on right, humming and skipping about. A murmur of approval.*)

YOUNG LADIES. Mihail Mihailitch!

LEBEDYEV. Mihail Mihailitch! My ears tell me . . .

SHABELSKY. The soul of the party!

BORKIN. Here I am! (*runs up to* SASHA). Noble lady! I venture to make so bold as to congratulate the universe on the birth of so marvellous a flower as you. . . . As the tribute of my enthusiasm may I dare to offer you (*gives her the parcel*) some fireworks and Bengal fires of my own manufacture? May they illuminate the night as you lighten the gloom of the kingdom of darkness (*makes a theatrical bow*).

SASHA. Thank you. . . .

LEBEDYEV (*laughing, to* IVANOV). Why don't you get rid of that Judas?

BORKIN (*to* LEBEDYEV). My respects to Pavel Kirillitch! (*To* IVANOV) To my patron! (*Sings.*) *Nicolas, voilà, ho-hi-ho.* (*Makes the round of the whole party*) To the most honoured Zinaida Savishna! Divine Marfa Yegorovna . . . most ancient Avdotya Nazarovna . . . most illustrious Count. . . .

SHABELSKY (*laughs*). The soul of the party. . . . As soon as he comes in the atmosphere grows lighter. Have you noticed it?

BORKIN. Ough, I am tired. . . . I believe I have greeted everybody now. Well, what's the news, ladies and gentlemen? Is there nothing special to wake us up? (*Briskly to* ZINAIDA SAVISHNA) I say, mamma . . . as I was on the way here . . . (*To* GAVRIL) Give me some tea, Gavril, but no gooseberry jam! (*To* ZINAIDA SAVISHNA) As I was on the way here I saw the peasants stripping the bark of your osiers on the river. Why don't you let a dealer have them?

LEBEDYEV (*to* IVANOV). Why don't you get rid of that Judas?

ZINAIDA (*aghast*). I might, that's true, the idea never struck me!

BORKIN (*does drill exercises with his arms*). I can't get on without exercise. . . . What can I do that's extra special, mamma? Marfa Yegorovna, I *am* in form to-night . . . wild with excitement! (*Sings.*) "Once more I stand before thee. . . ."

ZINAIDA. Get up something, for we are all bored.

BORKIN. Really! Why are you all so down in the mouth? You sit like jurymen! . . . Let us do something. What would you like? Forfeits? Hide the ring? Touch third? Dancing? Fireworks?

YOUNG LADIES (*clap their hands*). Fireworks! Fireworks! (*they run into the garden*).

SASHA (*to* IVANOV). Why are you so depressed this evening?

IVANOV. My head aches, Sasha, and I am bored. . . .

SASHA. Come into the drawing-room. (*They go towards door on right ; everyone goes into the garden except* ZINAIDA SAVISHNA *and* LEBEDYEV.)

ZINAIDA. Well, that's something like a young man—before he has been here a minute he has cheered them all up (*turns down the big lamp*). While they are all out in the garden it is no use wasting the candles (*puts out the candles*).

LEBEDYEV (*following her*). Zyuzushka, we ought to give our visitors something to eat. . . .

ZINAIDA. There, what a lot of candles . . . no wonder people think we are rich (*puts out the candles*).

LEBEDYEV (*following her*). Zyuzushka, you ought to give the people something to eat. . . . They are young people, I bet they are hungry, poor things. . . . Zyuzushka. . . .

ZINAIDA. The Count has not finished his glass. Simply wasting sugar ! (*goes towards door on left*).

LEBEDYEV. Tfoo ! (*goes out into the garden*).

(*Enter* IVANOV *and* SASHA.)

SASHA (*comes in with* IVANOV *from door on right*). They have all gone into the garden.

IVANOV. That's how it is, Sasha. In old days I did a lot of work and a lot of thinking and never got tired ; now I do nothing and think of nothing, and I am weary body and soul. My conscience aches night and day, I feel that I am terribly to blame, but exactly in what way I am to blame I don't know. And then my wife's illness, no money, the everlasting nagging and gossip, un-necessary talk, that fool Borkin. . . . My home has grown hateful to me, and living in it is worse than torture. I tell you openly, Sasha, even to be with my wife who loves me has become unbearable. You are my old friend, and won't be angry with me for speaking the truth. I have come to you to distract my mind, but I am bored here too, and I am longing to get home again. Forgive me, I will just slip away.

SASHA. Nikolay Alexeyevitch, I understand you. Your misfortune is that you are all alone. You ought to have someone by you whom you love and who understands you. Nothing can renew you but love.

IVANOV. What next, Sasha! That would be the last straw for a wretched bedraggled old creature like me to start a new love affair! God preserve me from such a calamity! No, my wise little friend, it is not a case for love affairs. I tell you in all solemnity, I can put up with everything —misery and neurasthenia and bankruptcy and the loss of my wife and my premature old age and my loneliness—but I cannot endure my contempt for myself. I could die with shame at the thought that I, a strong healthy man, have turned into a sort of Hamlet or a Manfred or a superfluous man . . . the devil knows what. There are pitiful creatures who are flattered at being called Hamlets or superfluous men, but to me it is a disgrace! It wounds my pride, I am crushed by shame, and I am miserable. . . .

SASHA (*jestingly through tears*). Nikolay Alexeyevitch, let us run off to America.

IVANOV. I am too lazy to move to this door, and you talk of America . . . (*They go to the door*

289

into the garden.) Of course, Sasha, you don't have an easy time of it here. When I look at the people that surround you, I feel horrified at the thought of whom you can marry. The only hope is that some lieutenant or student will pass this way and carry you off. . . .

(ZINAIDA SAVISHNA *comes in from door on left with a jar of jam.*)

IVANOV. Excuse me, Sasha, I will come after you. . . .

(SASHA *goes out into the garden.*)

IVANOV. Zinaida Savishna, I've come to ask you a favour.

ZINAIDA. What is it, Nikolay Alexeyevitch ?

IVANOV (*hesitates*). Well, you see, the fact is that the day after to-morrow the interest on your loan is due. You would very greatly oblige me if you would give me a little longer, or would let me add the interest on to the principal. I have no money at all at the moment. . . .

ZINAIDA (*alarmed*). Nikolay Alexeyevitch, how is that possible ? That's not the way to do things ! No, don't think of such a thing. For God's sake don't worry me, I have troubles enough. . . .

IVANOV. I am sorry, I am sorry . . . (*goes out into the garden*).

ZINAIDA. Ough, he has upset me ! I am all of a shake . . . all of a shake . . . (*goes out at door on right*).

(*Enter* KOSSIH.)

KOSSIH (*enters from left door and crosses the stage*). I had the ace, king, queen, and eight more diamonds, the ace of spades and just one . . . one

little heart, and she could not declare a little slam,
the devil take her entirely. . . . (*goes out at door
on right*).

(*Enter* AVDOTYA NAZAROVNA *and* FIRST GUEST.)

AVDOTYA (*coming from the garden with* FIRST
GUEST). I could tear her to pieces, I could tear
her to pieces, the old skinflint ! It's no joke. I've
been sitting here since five o'clock and she has not
offered us as much as a stale herring ! . . . It
is a house ! . . . It is a way to manage !

FIRST GUEST. I am so bored that I could run
and bash my head against the wall ! They are
people, Lord have mercy upon us ! One is so
hungry and so bored; it's enough to make one
howl like a wolf and begin snapping at people.

AVDOTYA. Couldn't I tear her to pieces, sinful
woman that I am !

FIRST GUEST. I'll have a drink, old lady, and
get home ! I don't want your eligible young
ladies. How the devil is one to think of love when
one has not had one glass of wine since dinner ?

AVDOTYA. Let's go and look for something. . . .

FIRST GUEST. Sh-sh ! Quietly ! I believe there
is vodka in the sideboard in the dining-room.
We'll get hold of Yegorushka. . . . Sh-sh ! (*They
go out by door on left.*)

(ANNA PETROVNA *and* LVOV *come out of door
on right.*)

ANNA PETROVNA. It's all right, they will be
pleased to see us. Nobody here. They must be
in the garden.

LVOV. I wonder why you have brought me here
into this nest of vultures ? This is no place for

IVANOV

you or me. Honest people ought to keep out of
this atmosphere!

ANNA PETROVNA. Listen, Mr. honest man!
It is not polite to take a lady out and to talk to
her of nothing but your honesty all the way!
It may be honest, but to say the least of it, it is
wearisome. You should never talk to women
about your virtues. Let them see those for themselves. When my Nikolay was your age he did
nothing but sing songs and tell stories in the
company of ladies, but they could all see what
sort of man he was.

LVOV. Oh, don't talk to me about your Nikolay.
I understand him perfectly!

ANNA PETROVNA. You are a good man, but you
don't understand anything. Let us go into the
garden. He never used such expressions as " I am
honest! I am stifled in this atmosphere! Vultures! Owl's nest! Crocodiles! " He used to
leave the menagerie alone, and when he had been
indignant all I heard from him was, " Ah, how
unjust I was to-day! " or " Anyuta, I am sorry
for that man! " That's what he was like, while
you . . . (*They go out*).

(*Enter* AVDOTYA NAZAROVNA *and* FIRST GUEST.)

FIRST GUEST (*coming in from door on left*). It's
not in the dining-room, so it must be somewhere
in the larder. We must try Yegorushka. Let
us go through the drawing-room.

AVDOTYA. Couldn't I tear her to pieces! (*They
go out at door on right*).

(MADAME BABAKIN *and* BORKIN *run out of the
garden, laughing ;* SHABELSKY *comes trip-*

ping after them, laughing, and rubbing his hands.)

MADAME BABAKIN. How dull it is! (*laughs*). It is dull! They all sit and walk about as though they had swallowed a poker. I am stiff with boredom (*skips about*). I must stretch my legs! (BORKIN *puts his arm round her waist and kisses her on the cheek.*)

SHABELSKY (*laughs and snaps his fingers*). Dash it all! (*clears his throat*). After all . . .

MADAME BABAKIN. Let go, take away your arm, you shameless fellow, or goodness knows what the Count will think! Leave off! . . .

BORKIN. Angel of my soul, jewel of my heart! . . . (*kisses her*). Do lend me two thousand three hundred roubles! . . .

MADAME BABAKIN. N-no, n-no, n-no. . . . You may say what you like, but as regards money, no thank you. . . . No, no, no! Oh, take your arms away!

SHABELSKY (*prances round them*). The little dumpling. . . . She has her charm. . . .

BORKIN (*gravely*). Come, that's enough. Let us come to the point. Let us discuss things straightforwardly, in a businesslike way. Give me a direct answer, without any tricks or subtleties: yes or no? Listen (*points to the* COUNT). He wants money, at least three thousand roubles a year. You want a husband. Would you like to be a Countess?

SHABELSKY (*laughs*). A wonderful cynic!

BORKIN. Would you like to be a Countess? Yes or no?

MADAME BABAKIN (*agitated*). Do think what you are saying, Misha, really! And such things aren't done in this slap-dash way. . . . If the Count wishes it he can himself . . . and I don't know really how, all of a minute. . . .

BORKIN. Come, come, that's enough airs and graces! It's a business matter. . . . Yes or no?

SHABELSKY (*laughing and rubbing his hands*). Yes, really, eh? Dash it all, why not play this dirty trick? What? The dumpling! (*kisses* MADAME BABAKIN *on the cheek*). Charmer! Peach!

MADAME BABAKIN. Wait a minute, wait a minute. . . . You've quite upset me. . . . Go away, go away! No, don't go! . . .

BORKIN. Make haste! Yes or no? We've no time to waste. . . .

MADAME BABAKIN. I tell you what, Count. You come and stay with me for two or three days. . . . You'll find it jolly, it's not like this house. Come to-morrow. . . . (*To* BORKIN) No, you are joking, aren't you?

BORKIN (*angrily*). As though one would joke about serious things!

MADAME BABAKIN. Wait a minute, wait a minute. . . . Oh, I feel faint! I feel faint! Countess . . . I am fainting . . . I shall drop. . . . (BORKIN *and the* COUNT, *laughing, take her arm-in-arm and, kissing her on the cheek, lead her out by door on right.*)

(IVANOV *and* SASHA *run in from the garden.*)

IVANOV (*clutching his head in despair*). It cannot be! Don't, don't, Sasha! . . . Oh, don't!

SASHA (*carried away*). I love you madly. . . . There is no meaning in life, no joy, no happiness without you ! You are everything to me ! . . .

IVANOV. What's the use, what's the use ? My God ! I don't understand it ! Sasha, don't ! . . .

SASHA. In my childhood you were my only joy ; I loved you and your soul like myself, but now . . . I love you, Nikolay Alexeyevitch ! . . . I'll go with you to the ends of the earth, where you like, to the grave, if you will, but for God's sake let it be soon or I shall be stifled. . . .

IVANOV (*breaks into a happy laugh*). What is it ? Beginning life again then, Sasha, yes ? . . . My happiness ! (*draws her to him*). My youth, my freshness ! . . .

> (ANNA PETROVNA *comes in from the garden and, seeing her husband and* SASHA, *stands rooted to the spot.*)

IVANOV. I am to live then ? Yes ? To get to work again ? (*A kiss. After the kiss* IVANOV *and* SASHA *look round and see* ANNA PETROVNA.)

IVANOV (*in horror*). Sarra !

CURTAIN

ACT III

IVANOV'S *study.* *A writing-table on which papers,
books, official envelopes, knick-knacks and
revolvers are lying in disorder ; near the papers
a lamp, a decanter of vodka, a plate of herring,
pieces of bread and cucumber. On the walls
maps, pictures, guns, pistols, sickles, whips,
etc. It is midday.*

SHABELSKY, LEBEDYEV, BORKIN *and* PYOTR.
SHABELSKY *and* LEBEDYEV *are sitting by
the writing-table,* BORKIN *in the middle of the
stage astride a chair.* PYOTR *is standing at
the door.*

LEBEDYEV. The policy of France is clear and
definite. . . . The French know what they want.
All they want is to flay the sausage-eaters, while
it is quite a different story with Germany.
Germany has plenty of specks in her eye besides
France. . . .

SHABELSKY. Nonsense ! . . . What I think is
that the Germans are cowards and the French are
cowards too. They are simply putting out their
tongues at each other on the sly. Believe me,
things won't go further than that. They won't
come to fighting.

BORKIN. And to my mind, there is no need to

fight. What is the use of all these armaments, congresses, expenditure? I tell you what I should do. I should collect dogs from all over the country, innoculate them with a good dose of Pasteur's virus and let them loose in the enemy's country. All the enemy would run mad with hydrophobia in a month.

LEBEDYEV (*laughs*). His head is small to look at, but there are as many great ideas in it as fish in the sea.

SHABELSKY. He is a specialist in them!

LEBEDYEV. God bless you, you do amuse me, Mihail Mihailovitch. (*Stops laughing*) We keep chattering away, but what about vodka? *Repetatur!* (*fills three wine-glasses*). To our good health! (*They drink and eat a little.*) Good old red herring is the best sort of snack one can have.

SHABELSKY. No, cucumber is better. . . . The learned men have been busy thinking since the creation of the world, but they have thought of nothing better than salted cucumber. (*To* PYOTR) Pyotr, go and get some more cucumbers and tell the cook to fry us four onion turnovers, and send them hot.

(PYOTR *goes out.*)

LEBEDYEV. Caviare is not bad with vodka either. But you want to use it properly. . . . You want to take a quarter of a pound of pressed caviare, two spring onions, olive oil, mix it all together . . . and just a little wee drop of lemon on the top of it, you know. Gorgeous! The very smell of it is stunning.

BORKIN. A dish of fried gudgeon is good after vodka too. Only one must know how to fry them. They must be cleaned, then dipped in sifted breadcrumbs and fried till they are dry, so that they crunch in the teeth. . . . Kroo-kroo-kroo. . . .

SHABELSKY. We had a good dish at Madame Babakin's yesterday—mushrooms.

LEBEDYEV. I daresay. . . .

SHABELSKY. Only it was prepared in some special way. You know, with onion and bay leaves and all sorts of condiments. As soon as the cover was taken off there was a steam, a smell . . . delicious!

LEBEDYEV. Well, what do you say? *Repetatur*, gentlemen. (*They drink.*) To our good health! (*Looks at his watch*) I am afraid I can't wait for Nikolay. It's time I was off. You say you had mushrooms at Madame Babakin's, and we have not seen a mushroom yet. And just tell me, if you please, why the devil are you so often at Marfa's?

SHABELSKY (*nods towards* BORKIN). Why, he wants to marry me to her.

LEBEDYEV. Marry? Why, how old are you?

SHABELSKY. Sixty-two.

LEBEDYEV. The very time to get married. And Marfa is just the match for you.

BORKIN. It is not a question of Marfa, but of Marfa's roubles.

LEBEDYEV. Anything else! Marfa's roubles! You will be crying for the moon next!

BORKIN. When the man is married and has

stuffed his pockets, you will see whether it's crying for the moon ! You will envy his luck.

SHABELSKY. And you know he is in earnest. This genius is convinced that I'll do what he tells me and marry her.

BORKIN. Why, of course ! Aren't you convinced of it too ?

SHABELSKY. You are crazy. . . . When was I convinced ? Phew !

BORKIN. Thank you. . . . Thank you very much ! So you want to make a fool of me ? First, it's I'll marry and then I won't marry. . . . Who the devil is to make you out ? And I have given my word of honour ! So you won't marry her ?

SHABELSKY (*shrugging his shoulders*). He is in earnest ! Amazing person !

BORKIN (*indignant*). In that case what do you want to upset a respectable woman for ? She is mad on being a countess, can't sleep or eat. . . . Is it a subject to joke about ? Is it honest ?

SHABELSKY (*snapping his fingers*). Well, and how if I do play this dirty trick after all ? What ? Just for mischief ? I'll go and do it ! On my word. . . . It will be fun !

(*Enter* LVOV.)

LEBEDYEV. Doctor, our humble respects ! (*gives* LVOV *his hand and sings*). Doctor, save me kindly, sir, I am in deadly fear of death !

LVOV. Nikolay Alexeyevitch has not come in yet ?

LEBEDYEV. Why no, I have been waiting for

299

him for more than an hour. (Lvov *strides impatiently up and down the stage*.) Well, my dear fellow, how is Anna Petrovna ?

Lvov. Very ill.

LEBEDYEV (*sighs*). Can I go and pay her my respects ?

Lvov. No, please don't go. I believe she is asleep . . . (*a pause*).

LEBEDYEV. She is a nice, sweet woman (*sighs*). On Sasha's birthday, when she fainted at our house, I looked at her face and I saw she had not long to live, poor dear. I don't know why she was taken ill then. I ran up, I looked at her and she was lying pale as death, with Nikolay on his knees beside her as pale as she, and Sasha in tears. Sasha and I went about as though we were dazed for a week after.

SHABELSKY (*to* Lvov). Tell me, honoured votary of science, what learned sage was it discovered that ladies with delicate chests are benefited by the frequent visits of a young doctor ? It's a great discovery, great ! To which is it to be ascribed : to the allopaths or the homeopaths ?

(Lvov *is on the point of answering, but with a contemptuous gesture walks away*.)

SHABELSKY. What a withering glance. . . .

LEBEDYEV. And what devil sets your tongue wagging ? Why did you insult him ?

SHABELSKY (*irritably*). And what does he tell lies for ? Consumption, no hope, she is dying. . . . It's all lies ! I can't endure it !

LEBEDYEV. What makes you think he is lying ?

SHABELSKY (*gets up and walks about*). I can't

admit the idea that a living creature should suddenly, *à propos* of nothing, go and die. Let us drop the subject !

(*Enter* KOSSIH.)

KOSSIH (*runs in, breathless*). Is Nikolay Alexeyevitch at home ? Good morning ! (*rapidly shakes hands with everyone*). Is he at home ?

BORKIN. No ; he is out.

KOSSIH (*sits down and leaps up*). If that's so, good-bye ! (*drinks a glass of vodka and hurriedly eats something*). I'll go on . . . I am busy . . . I am worn out . . . I can hardly stand up. . . .

LEBEDYEV. Where have you dropped from ?

KOSSIH. From Barabanov's. . . . We were playing vint all night, and have only just finished. . . . I am cleaned out. . . . That Barabanov plays like a cobbler ! (*In a weeping voice*) Just listen : all the time I was playing hearts. . . . (*Addresses* BORKIN, *who skips away from him*) He leads diamonds, but I play hearts again ; he diamonds. . . . Well, I made no tricks. (*To* LEBEDYEV) We play four clubs. I had the ace, the queen, and five more clubs in my hand, the ace, the ten, and two more spades. . . .

LEBEDYEV (*putting his fingers in his ears*). Spare me, for mercy's sake, spare me !

KOSSIH (*to the Count*). Do you see : the ace, the queen, and five more clubs, the ace, the ten, and two more spades. . . .

SHABELSKY (*waving him off*). Go away ; I don't want to hear you !

KOSSIH. And all at once such ill-luck : my ace of spades was trumped in the first round.

SHABELSKY (*picking up a revolver from the table*).
Go away, I'll shoot ! . . .

KOSSIH (*waves his hand*). Damnation take
it. . . . Is there nobody one can say a word to ?
One might be in Australia : no common interests,
no sympathy. . . . They are all absorbed in
themselves. . . . I must go, though . . . it's
time (*snatches up his cap*). Time is precious
(*shakes hands with* LEBEDYEV). Pass ! (*laughter*).

(KOSSIH *goes out, and in the doorway stumbles
against* AVDOTYA NAZAROVNA.)

AVDOTYA (*screams*). Plague take you ! Knocking me off my feet !

ALL. A-ah ! she is everywhere at once !

AVDOTYA. So this is where they are, and I have
been looking all over the house. Good morning !
my bright falcons, enjoying your meal ? (*greets
them*).

LEBEDYEV. What have you come about ?

AVDOTYA. Business, my good sir. (*To the
Count*) Business that concerns you, your
Excellency (*bows*). I was told to greet you and
inquire after your health. . . . And my pretty
poppet bid me say that if you don't come and see
her this evening, she will cry her eyes out. Take
him aside, my dear, she said, and whisper it into
his ear in secret. But what's the need of secrets ?
We are old friends here. Besides, it's not as if
we were robbing a hen-roost, but aiming at lawful
wedlock with the love and mutual consent of both
parties. Sinful woman that I am, I never touch
a drop, but on such an occasion, I will have a
glass !

LEBEDYEV. And I'll have one too (*fills the glasses*). And you, old crow, seem none the worse for wear. You were an old woman when I met you first, thirty years ago.

AVDOTYA. I've lost count of the years. . . . I've buried two husbands, and would marry a third, but no one cares to take me without a dowry. I had eight children . . . (*takes the glass*). Well, please God, we've begun a good work and God grant we finish it ! They will live and prosper and we shall look at them and rejoice. God give them love and good counsel ! (*drinks*). It's stiff vodka !

SHABELSKY (*laughing, to* LEBEDYEV). But what's the oddest thing of all, you know, is that they seriously think that I . . . It's amazing ! (*gets up*). What do you think, Pasha—shall I really play this dirty trick ? For mischief. . . . Why should not the old dog snap up his bone, Pasha, eh ?

LEBEDYEV. You are talking nonsense, Count. It's time for you and me to think of kicking the bucket ; the time for Marfas and roubles has passed long ago. . . . Our day is over.

SHABELSKY. No, I will do it—on my honour, I will !

(*Enter* IVANOV *and* LVOV.)

LVOV. I beg you to spare me only five minutes.

LEBEDYEV. Nikolasha ! (*goes up to* IVANOV *and kisses him*). Good morning, my dear boy. I have been waiting for you for a good hour.

AVDOTYA (*bows*). Good morning, sir.

IVANOV (*bitterly*). Gentlemen, again you've

turned my study into a drinking bar !. . . A thousand times I have asked each and all of you not to do it . . . (*goes up to the table*). There, now . . . you've spilt vodka over my papers . . . here are crumbs and bits of cucumber. . . . It's disgusting !

LEBEDYEV. I am sorry, Nikolasha, I am sorry. . . . Forgive us. I want to talk to you, dear boy, about something very important. . . .

BORKIN. And I, too.

LVOV. Nikolay Alexeyevitch, can I have a word with you ?

IVANOV (*pointing to* LEBEDYEV). You see he wants me too. Wait a little ; you can come afterwards. . . . (*To* LEBEDYEV) What is it ?

LEBEDYEV. Gentlemen, I want to have a confidential talk. Please. . . .

(*The* COUNT *goes out with* AVDOTYA NAZAR-OVNA, BORKIN *follows them, then* LVOV.)

IVANOV. Pasha, you may drink as much as you like—it's an illness with you ; but I beg you not to lead Uncle into it. He never used to drink before. It's bad for him.

LEBEDYEV (*alarmed*). My dear, I did not know. . . . I did not even notice. . . .

IVANOV. If, which God forbid, the old baby should die, it wouldn't matter to you, but it would to me. . . . What is it you want ? (*a pause*).

LEBEDYEV. You see, my dear friend. . . . I don't know how to begin to make it sound less shameless. . . . Nikolasha, I am ashamed, I blush, I can't bring myself to say it, but, my dear boy, put yourself in my position—realise that I

304

am a man in bondage, a nigger, a rag. . . .
Forgive me. . . .

IVANOV. What is it ?

LEBEDYEV. My wife has sent me. . . . Do
me a favour—be a friend, pay her your interest !
You wouldn't believe how she nags at me, drives
me, wears me out ! Do get rid of her, for goodness' sake ! . . .

IVANOV. Pasha, you know I have no money
just now.

LEBEDYEV. I know, I know ; but what am I to
do ? She won't wait. If she summons you, how
can Sasha and I ever look you in the face again ?

IVANOV. I am ashamed myself, Pasha—I should
like to sink into the earth ; but . . . but where
am I to get it ? Tell me, where ? The only
thing is to wait till the autumn, when I sell the
corn.

LEBEDYEV (*shouts*). She won't wait ! (*a pause*).

IVANOV. Your position is unpleasant and difficult, and mine is worse still (*walks up and down
thinking*). And there is no plan one can think
of. . . . There's nothing to sell. . . .

LEBEDYEV. You might go to Milbach and ask
him ; he owes you sixteen thousand, you know.

(IVANOV *waves his hand hopelessly*.)

LEBEDYEV. I tell you what, Nikolasha. . . .
I know you will begin scolding, but . . . do a
favour to an old drunkard. Between friends. . . .
Look upon me as a friend. . . . We have both
been students, liberals. . . . We have common
ideas and interests. . . . We both studied in
Moscow. . . . *Alma mater* . . . (*takes out his*

305

pocket-book). Here I've got a secret hoard; no one at home knows of it. Let me lend it to you . . . (*takes out money and lays it on the table*). Drop your pride and look at it as a friend. . . . I would take it from you—on my honour, I would (*a pause*). Here it is, on the table, eleven hundred. You go to her to-day and give it with your own hands. . . . Take it, Zinaida Savishna, and may it choke you! Only mind you don't make a sign that it comes from me, God preserve you! or I shall get it hot from old Gooseberry Jam (*looks into* IVANOV's *face*). Oh, all right, never mind! (*hastily takes the money from the table and puts it into his pocket*). Never mind! I was joking. . . . Forgive me, for Christ's sake! (*a pause*). You are sick at heart?

(IVANOV *makes a gesture of despair.*)

LEBEDYEV. Yes, it is a business . . . (*sighs*). A time of woe and tribulation has come for you. A man is like a samovar, old boy. It is not always in the cool on the shelf—there are times when they put hot coals into it. . . . The comparison is not worth much, but I can't think of anything better . . . (*sighs*). Troubles strengthen the spirit. I am not sorry for you, Nikolasha—you'll get out of your difficulties, things will come right; but I feel vexed and offended with people. . . . I should like to know where these scandals come from! There are such stories going about you all over the district that you might get a call from the public prosecutor any day. . . . You are a murderer and a blood-sucker and a robber. . . .

306

IVANOV. That doesn't matter; what does matter is that my head aches.

LEBEDYEV. That's all from thinking too much.

IVANOV. I don't think at all.

LEBEDYEV. You just snap your fingers at everything, Nikolasha, and come over to us. Sasha is fond of you; she understands you and appreciates you. She is a good, fine creature, Nikolasha. She takes neither after father nor mother, but after some passing stranger. . . . Sometimes I look at her and can't believe that a bottle-nosed old drunkard like me can have such a treasure. Come over; you can talk about intellectual subjects with her, and it will be a change for you. She has a faithful, sincere nature . . . (*a pause*).

IVANOV. Pasha, my dear soul, leave me alone.

LEBEDYEV. I understand, I understand . . . (*looks hurriedly at his watch*). I understand (*kisses* IVANOV). Good-bye. I've got to go to the dedication of a school (*goes to the door and stops*). She is a clever girl. . . . Yesterday she and I were talking about gossip (*laughs*). And she made an epigram: "Father," she said, "glow-worms shine at night simply so that the night birds may see and devour them more easily; and good people exist to provide food for gossip and slander." What do you say to that? A genius! A George Sand!

IVANOV. Pasha! (*stops him*). What is the matter with me?

LEBEDYEV. I wanted to ask you that myself, but, to tell you the truth, I did not like to. I

don't know, dear boy! On the one hand, it
seemed to me that you were crushed by misfortunes
of all sorts, and on the other hand, I know you
are not the sort to . . . You are not the one
to be mastered by trouble. There is something
else in it, Nikolasha, but what it is I don't know.

IVANOV. I don't know myself. I fancy it is
either . . . but no! (*a pause*). You see, what
I meant to say was this. I had a workman called
Semyon—you remember him. One day at thresh-
ing time he wanted to show the girls how strong
he was, put two sacks of rye on his back, and
ruptured himself. He died soon after. It seems
to me that I have ruptured myself, too. The
high-school, university, then managing my estate,
plans, schools. . . . My beliefs were not like
other people's, my marriage was not like other
people's. I was enthusiastic, I took risks, threw
away my money right and left, as you know. I
have had more happiness and more misery than
anyone in the whole district. All this was like
those sacks for me, Pasha. . . . I took a burden
on my back, and my back was broken. At
twenty we are heroes—we tackle anything, we can
do anything ; and at thirty we are already
exhausted and good for nothing. How do you
explain that liability to exhaustion, tell me ?
But perhaps it's not that, though. . . . That's
not it, that's not it! . . . Go along, Pasha,
God bless you ; I have been boring you.

LEBEDYEV (*eagerly*). You know what it is,
old boy ? It's your environment has destroyed
you.

IVANOV. Oh, that's stupid, Pasha, and stale. Run along !

LEBEDYEV. Yes, it is certainly stupid. I can see for myself now it is stupid. I am going ! I am going ! (goes out).

IVANOV (alone). I am a bad, abject, worthless man. One has to be as abject, broken and shattered as Pasha to like and respect me. How I despise myself, my God ! How I hate my voice, my step, my hands, these clothes, my thoughts ! Isn't it absurd, isn't it mortifying ? It's not a year since I was strong and well, I was inexhaustible, full of warmth and confidence, I worked with these same hands, I could speak so as to move even the ignorant to tears, I could weep at the sight of sorrow, was moved to wrath at the sight of wrong-doing. I knew the meaning of inspiration, I felt the charm and poetry of still nights when from sunset to sunrise one sits at one's writing-table or gladdens one's soul with dreams. I had faith, I could look into the future as into my mother's eyes. . . . But now, oh, my God ! I am worn out, I have no faith, I spend days and nights doing nothing. My brains do not obey me, nor my hands nor my feet. My property is going to ruin, the forest is falling under the axe (weeps). My land looks at me like a deserted child. I expect nothing, I regret nothing; my soul shudders with fear of the morrow. . . . And the way I have treated Sarra ! I swore to love her for ever, I promised her happiness, I displayed before her a future she had not imagined in her dreams. She believed me. For

309

five years I've seen her pining away under the weight of her sacrifice, and worn out by the struggle with her conscience, but, as God is above, there has not been one doubtful glance, not one word of reproach! And here I've ceased to love her. . . . How? Why? What for? I don't understand it. Here she is suffering; her days are numbered, and I, like the meanest sneak, run away from her pale face, her sunken chest, her supplicating eyes. It's shameful, shameful! (a pause). Sasha, a child, is touched by my misery. She tells me, at my age, that she loves me, and I am intoxicated, forget everything in the world, enchanted as though by music, and shout "A new life! happiness!" And next day I believe as little in that new life and happiness as in goblins. . . . What's the matter with me? To what depths am I making myself sink? What has brought this weakness on me? What has happened to my nerves? If my sick wife wounds my vanity or a servant does not please me, or my gun misses fire, I become brutal, angry and unlike myself (a pause). I don't understand, I don't understand! I might as well shoot myself and have done with it!

Lvov (enters). I must have things out with you, Nikolay Alexeyevitch.

IVANOV. If we are to have things out every day, Doctor, it's more than anyone could stand.

Lvov. Will you hear me out?

IVANOV. I hear you out every day, and I still can't make out what it is you want of me.

Lvov. I speak clearly and definitely, and no

one but a heartless man could fail to understand
me.

IVANOV. That my wife is dying—I know; that
I am hopelessly to blame in regard to her, I know
also. That you are an honest, upright man, I
know too! What more do you want?

LVOV. I am revolted by human cruelty. . . .
A woman is dying. She has a father and mother
whom she loves and would like to see before her
death; they know quite well that she will soon
die and that she still loves them, but, damnable
cruelty! they seem to want to impress people
by their religious hardness—they still persist
in cursing her! You are the man to whom she
has sacrificed everything—her home and her
peace of conscience; yet in the most undisguised
way, with the most undisguised objects, you go
off every day to those Lebedyevs! . . .

IVANOV. Oh, I have not been there for a fortnight. . . .

LVOV (not heeding him). With people like you
one must speak plainly without beating about
the bush, and if you don't care to listen to me, then
don't listen! I am accustomed to call a spade
a spade. . . . Her death will suit you and pave
the way for your new adventures; so be it, but
surely you might wait? If you would let her die
naturally without persistently worrying her by
your open cynicism, surely you would not lose
the Lebedyev girl and her dowry? If not now,
then in a year or two you would succeed, you
marvellous hypocrite, in turning the girl's head
and getting her money just as easily. . . . Why

311

are you in such a hurry ?   Why do you want your wife to die now, and not in a month or in a year ? . . .

IVANOV. This is simply agony. . . .   You can't be a very good doctor if you imagine that a man can restrain himself indefinitely.   It's a fearful effort to me not to answer your insults.

LVOV. Come, whom do you think you are taking in ?   Throw off your mask !

IVANOV. You clever person, think a little !   You suppose there is nothing easier than understanding me, yes ?   I married Anna for the sake of her fortune . . . they did not let me have it.   I made a blunder, and now I am getting rid of her so as to marry another girl and get her money, yes ? How simple and straightforward !   Man is such a simple, uncomplicated machine. . . .   No, doctor, there are too many wheels and screws and levers in any one of us for us to be able to judge each other from the first impression or from two or three external signs.   I don't understand you, you don't understand me, and we don't understand ourselves.   One may be a good doctor and at the same time utterly ignorant of human nature. Don't be too self-confident, and do see that.

LVOV. Can you really imagine that you are so difficult to see through, and that I am so brainless that I can't see the difference between a rogue and an honest man ?

IVANOV. It is evident that we shall never come to an understanding.   For the last time I ask you the question, and please answer it without any preliminary words : what exactly do you want of me ? What are you trying to get at ? (*Irritably*) And to whom have I the honour of speaking— my judge or my wife's doctor ?

Lvov. I am a doctor, and as a doctor I insist on your behaving differently. Your behaviour is killing Anna Petrovna.

IVANOV. But what am I to do ? What ? Since you understand me better than I understand myself, tell me definitely, what am I to do?

Lvov. At least you might keep up appearances.

IVANOV. Oh, my God ! Do you suppose you understand what you are saying ? (*drinks water*). Leave me alone. I am infinitely to blame : I must answer for it to God ; but no one has authorised you to torment me every day. . . .

Lvov. And who has authorised you to outrage my sense of justice ? You torture and poison my soul. Before I came into this district I admitted that silly, mad, impulsive people did exist, but I never believed that there were people so criminal as intentionally, consciously, wilfully to choose the path of evil. . . . I loved and respected man-kind, but since I have known you . . .

IVANOV. I have heard about that already.

(*Enter* SASHA.)

Lvov. Oh, have you ? (*seeing* SASHA; *she is in a riding habit*). Now I trust we quite understand each other ! (*shrugs his shoulders and goes out*).

IVANOV (*with alarm*). Sasha, is it you ?

SASHA. Yes, it is me. How are you ? You did not expect me ? Why haven't you been to see us for so long ?

IVANOV. Sasha, for goodness' sake, this is un-

313

wise ! Your coming may have a terrible effect on my wife.

SASHA. She won't see me. I came by the back way. I am just going. I am uneasy : are you well ? Why is it you haven't come all this time ?

IVANOV. My wife is distressed as it is ; she is almost dying, and you come here. Sasha, Sasha, it's thoughtless and inhuman !

SASHA. I couldn't help it. You haven't been to see us for a fortnight, you haven't answered my letters. I was worried to death. I fancied that you were unbearably miserable here, ill, dying. I haven't had one good night's sleep. I am just going. . . . Tell me, anyway, are you well ?

IVANOV. No. I torment myself, and people torment me endlessly. . . . It's simply more than I can bear ! And now you on the top of it all ! How morbid, how abnormal it all is ! How guilty I feel, Sasha—how guilty ! . . .

SASHA. How fond you are of saying dreadful and tragic things ! So you are guilty. . . . Yes ? Guilty ? Tell me then, what of ?

IVANOV. I don't know, I don't know. . . .

SASHA. That's not an answer. Every sinner ought to know what his sins are. Have you forged notes, or what ?

IVANOV. That's stupid.

SASHA. Are you guilty because you have changed to your wife ? Perhaps, but man is not master of his feelings, you didn't want your feelings to change. Are you guilty because she saw me telling you that I love you ? No, you did not want her to see. . . .

314

IVANOV (*interrupting*). And so on, so on. . . .
In love, out of love, not master of his feelings—
these are commonplaces, stock phrases, which
don't help. . . .

SASHA. It's wearisome talking to you (*looks at a
picture*). How well that dog is drawn. Is that
from life ?

IVANOV. Yes. And all our love story is
commonplace and hackneyed : he has lost heart
and is plunged in despair, she appears on the scene,
full of strength and courage—holds out a helping
hand. That's fine and sounds all right in novels,
but in real life . . .

SASHA. In real life it's the same.

IVANOV. I see, you've such a subtle understanding of life ! My whining excites your reverent
awe, you fancy you have discovered a second
Hamlet in me, but to my mind my morbid state
with all accessories provides good material for
ridicule and nothing else ! You ought to laugh
at my antics while you cry " Help ! " To save
me, to do something heroic ! Oh, how cross I am
with myself to-day ! I feel this nervous strain
will make me do something. . . . Either I shall
smash something, or . . .

SASHA. That's it, that's it, just what you ought
to do. Break something, smash things, or scream.
You are angry with me ; it was silly of me to think
of coming here. Well, be angry, shout at me,
stamp ! Well ? Begin to rage ! (*a pause*). Well ?

IVANOV. Ridiculous girl !

SASHA. Excellent ! I believe you are smiling !
Be kind and graciously smile again !

IVANOV (*laughs*). I've noticed when you begin saving me and giving me good advice your face becomes very, very naïve and your eyes as big as though you were looking at a comet. Wait a minute, your shoulder is dusty (*brushes some dust off her shoulder*). A naïve man is a fool, but you women have the art of being naïve so that it is sweet and natural and warm and not so silly as it seems. But isn't it a queer trick in all of you—so long as a man is strong and well and cheerful, you take no notice of him, but as soon as he begins running rapidly downhill and sets up a whine, you throw yourselves upon his neck! Is it worse to be the wife of a strong, brave man than to be the nurse of some lachrymose failure?

SASHA. Yes, it is.

IVANOV. Why is it? (*laughs*). Darwin knows nothing about it, or he would give it to you! You are ruining the race. Thanks to you there will soon be none but snivellers and neurotics born into the world!

SASHA. There is a great deal men don't understand. Any girl will prefer a man who is a failure to one who is a success, because every woman longs to love actively. . . . Do you understand, actively? A man is absorbed in his work and so love with him is in the background. To talk to his wife, to walk in the garden and spend the time pleasantly with her and weep on her grave—that's all he wants. While with us love is life. I love you, that means that I am dreaming how I shall heal you of your misery, how I shall go to the ends of the earth with you. If you go uphill, I go uphill too ; if you go down into a pit, I go down into the pit too. To me, for instance, it would be a great happiness to spend a whole night copying your papers, or the whole night watching that no one should wake you, or walking a hundred miles with you ! I remember once three years ago at thresh-ing time you came to see us, all covered with dust, sunburnt and exhausted and asked for water. By the time I brought you a glass, you were lying on the sofa, sleeping like the dead. You slept for twelve hours, and all the time I stood on guard at the door that no one should come in. And how happy I was ! The harder the work, the better the love, that is, the more strongly it's felt, you understand.

IVANOV. Active love. . . . Hm. Decadence, a young girl's philosophy or perhaps that's how it should be . . . (*shrugs his shoulders*). Devil only knows ! (*gaily*). Sasha, on my honour I am a decent man ! . . . Think of this : I have always been fond of generalising, but I have never in my life said that " our women were demoralised " or that " woman was on the wrong track." I have only been grateful to them and nothing else ! Nothing else ! My good little girl, how amusing you are ! And what an absurd duffer I am ! I shock good people and do nothing but whine for days together (*laughs*). Oo-oo ! Oo-oo ! (*walks quickly away*). But do go, Sasha ! we are forgetting . . .

SASHA. Yes, I must go. Good-bye ! I am afraid your honest doctor's sense of duty may make him tell Anna Petrovna that I am here. Listen to me :

go to your wife at once and sit by her, sit by her.
. . . If you have to sit by her for a year, sit by
her for a year. . . . If it is ten years—sit ten
years. Do your duty. Grieve and beg her forgiveness and weep—all that is only right. And,
above all, don't neglect your work.

IVANOV. Again I have that feeling as though I
were poisoned. Again !

SASHA. Well, God bless you ! You need not
think about me at all. If you send me a line once
a fortnight, that will do for me. I will write to
you. . . .

(BORKIN *peeps in at the door*.)

BORKIN. Nikolay Alexeyevitch, may I come in ?
(*Seeing* SASHA) I beg your pardon, I did not see
you . . . (*comes in*). Bong jour ! (*bows*).

SASHA (*in confusion*). How do you do ?

BORKIN. You have grown plumper and prettier.

SASHA (*to* IVANOV). I am just going, Nikolay
Alexeyevitch. . . . I am going (*goes out*).

BORKIN. Lovely vision ! I came for prose and
stumbled on poetry. . . . (*Sings*) " Thou dids't
appear like a bird at dawn." . . .

(IVANOV *walks up and down the stage in agitation*.)

BORKIN (*sits down*). There is a certain something about her, you know, *Nicolas*, unlike other
girls. Isn't there ? Something special . . . phan-
tasmagoric . . . (*sighs*). As a matter of fact she
is the wealthiest match in the countryside, but
the mother is such a bitter radish that no one cares
to be mixed up with her. When she is dead everything will be left to Sasha, but till then she will

give nothing but a miserable ten thousand, with flat irons and gophering tongs, and one will have to go down on one's knees to her for that too (*fumbles in his pockets*). I'll smoke *De-los-mahoros.* Wouldn't you like one? (*offers his cigar-case*). They are good. . . . They are worth smoking.

IVANOV (*goes up to* BORKIN, *breathless with anger*). Clear out of my house this minute and do not set foot in it again! This minute!

(BORKIN *gets up and drops his cigar.*)

IVANOV. Get out! This minute!

BORKIN. *Nicolas*, what's the matter? Why are you angry?

IVANOV. What for? Where did you get those cigars? And do you suppose I don't know where you are taking the old man every day and what your object is?

BORKIN (*shrugging his shoulders*). But what has that to do with you?

IVANOV. You blackguard! The vile projects which you scatter all over the district have disgraced my name in the eyes of everyone! We have nothing in common, and I beg you to leave my house this minute! (*strides rapidly up and down*).

BORKIN. I know you are saying all this because you are irritated and so I am not angry with you. You can insult me as much as you like (*picks up his cigar*). But it's time to shake off your melancholy. You are not a schoolboy. . . .

IVANOV. What did I say to you? (*trembling*). Are you playing with me?

(*Enter* ANNA PETROVNA.)

319

BORKIN. Well, here is Anna Petrovna. . . . I will go (*goes out*).

(IVANOV *stops at the table and stands with bowed head.*)

ANNA PETROVNA (*after a pause*). What did she come for just now? (*a pause*). I ask you, what did she come for?

IVANOV. Don't ask me, Anyuta . . . (*a pause*). I am terribly to blame. You can think of anything you like to punish me, I'll bear anything, but . . . don't question me. . . . I am not equal to talking.

ANNA PETROVNA (*angrily*). What has she been here for? (*a pause*). Ah, so that's what you are like! Now I understand you. At last I see what sort of man you are. Dishonourable, mean. . . . Do you remember you came and told a lie, saying that you loved me. . . . I believed you; I gave up my father and mother and my religion and followed you. . . . You told me lies about truth and goodness and your noble plans. I believed every word. . . .

IVANOV. Anyuta, I've never told you a lie.

ANNA PETROVNA. I have lived with you five years. I have been depressed and ill, but I have loved you, and have never left you for a moment. . . . You have been my idol. . . . And all the while you have been deceiving me in the most shameless way. . . .

IVANOV. Anyuta, don't say what is untrue. I have made mistakes, yes, but I have never told a lie in my life. . . . You dare not reproach me with that . . .

ANNA PETROVNA. I see it all now. . . . You married me thinking my father and mother would forgive me and give me money . . . that was what you expected. . . .

IVANOV. Oh, my God! Anyuta, to try my patience like this . . . (*weeps*).

ANNA PETROVNA. Hold your tongue! When you saw the money was not coming, you started a fresh game. . . . Now I remember it all and understand (*weeps*). You never loved me, and were never faithful to me. . . . Never!

IVANOV. Sarra, that's a lie! Say what you like, but don't insult me with lies. . . .

ANNA PETROVNA. Mean, dishonourable man! . . . You are in debt to Lebedyev, and now to wriggle out of your debt you are trying to turn his daughter's head, to deceive her as you did me. Isn't that true?

IVANOV (*gasping*). For God's sake, hold your tongue! I can't answer for myself. . . . I am choking with rage, and I . . . I may say something to hurt you. . . .

ANNA PETROVNA. You have always shamelessly deceived people, not only me. You put down everything discreditable to Borkin, but now I know who is responsible.

IVANOV. Sarra, be quiet! Go away, or I may say something! I feel tempted to say to you something horrible, insulting. . . . (*Shouts*) Hold your tongue, Jewess!

ANNA PETROVNA. I won't be silent. . . . You've deceived me too long, and I must speak. . . .

IVANOV. So you won't hold your tongue (*struggling with himself*). For God's sake . . .

ANNA PETROVNA. Now you can go and deceive the Lebedyev girl. . . .

IVANOV. Well, let me tell you that you . . . are going to die. . . . The doctor told me that you can't last long. . . .

ANNA PETROVNA (*sits down; in a sinking voice*). When did he say that ? (*a pause*).

IVANOV (*clutches his head*). What a brute I am ! My God, what a brute ! (*sobs*).

CURTAIN

(*Between the Third and the Fourth Acts about a year elapses.*)

ACT IV

A drawing-room in LEBEDYEV'S *house. In fore-ground an arch dividing the front drawing-room from the back drawing-room ; doors to right and to left. Old bronzes, family portraits. Every-thing has a festive look. A piano ; lying on it a violin ; near it stands a 'cello. Throughout the act* GUESTS *cross the stage dressed as for a ball.*

LVOV (*comes in, looking at his watch*). It's past four. I suppose it is just time for the blessing. . . . They will bless her, and take her to church to be married. Here is the triumph of virtue and justice ! He did not succeed in robbing Sarra ; he worried her into her grave, and now he has found another. He will play a part to her too until he has plundered her, and then he will lay her in her grave like poor Sarra. It's the old money-grubbing story . . . (*a pause*). He is in the seventh heaven of bliss: will live happily to old age, and will die with an easy conscience. No, I'll expose you ! When I tear off your damn-able mask and all learn what sort of a creature you are, you will fall headlong from the seventh heaven into depths such as the very devil cannot pull you out of ! I am an honest man : it's my duty to interfere and open their blind eyes. I will do my duty, and to-morrow leave this cursed district for ever ! (*Muses*) But how am I to do it ? Talking to the Lebedyevs is waste of time. Challenge him to a duel ? Make a row ? My God, I am as nervous as a schoolboy and have quite lost all power of reflection ! What am I to do ? A duel ?

KOSSIH (*coming in, joyfully to* Lvov). Yesterday I declared a little slam in clubs and took a grand slam. Only that Barabanov spoiled it all again ! We were playing. I said "No trumps." He said "Pass." I played the two of clubs. He said "Pass." I played the two of diamonds . . . the three of clubs . . . and would you believe it — can you imagine it !—I declared a slam, and he did not show his ace ! If he had shown his ace—the blackguard !—I could have declared a grand slam on no trumps. . . .

Lvov. Excuse me, I don't play cards, and so I cannot share your enthusiasm. Will the blessing be soon ?

KOSSIH. It must be soon. They are bringing Zyuzushka to her senses. . . . She is howling like a calf : she is sorry to lose the dowry.

Lvov. And not her daughter ?

KOSSIH. It's the dowry. Besides, it's galling for her. If he marries into the family, he won't pay what he owes her. You cannot summon your own son-in-law.

MADAME BABAKIN (*grandly dressed, with a dignified air, walks across the stage past* LVOV *and* KOSSIH ; *the latter guffaws into his fist ; she looks round*). How stupid !

(KOSSIH *touches her waist with his finger and laughs.*)

MADAME BABAKIN. You lout! (*goes out*).

KOSSIH (*laughs*). The silly woman has gone right off her head! Before she set her cap at a title she was a woman like any other, and now there is no approaching her. (*Mimicking her*) " You lout! "

Lvov (*agitated*). I say, tell me honestly, what is your opinion of Ivanov?

KOSSIH. He is no good. He plays like a cobbler. I'll tell you what happened last year in Lent. We were all sitting down to cards—the Count, Borkin, he and I—and I was dealing . . .

Lvov (*interrupting*). Is he a good man?

KOSSIH. He? He is a shark! He is a tricky fellow; he has seen some ups and downs. . . . The Count and he—they are a pair of them. They have a keen scent for what they can lay their hands on. He put his foot in it with the Jewess, came a cropper, and now he has got his eye on Zyuzushka's money-bags. I'll bet anything, damn my soul, if he does not bring Zyuzushka to beggary within a year. He'll do for Zyuzushka and the Count for the widow. They'll grab the money and live happy ever afterwards. Doctor, why are you so pale to-day? You don't look like yourself.

Lvov. Oh, it's nothing! I drank a little too much yesterday.

(*Enter* LEBEDYEV *and* SASHA.)

LEBEDYEV (*coming in with* SASHA). We can talk here (*to* LVOV *and* KOSSIH). You can go and join the ladies, you Zulus. We want to talk secrets.

325

Kossih (*snaps his fingers enthusiastically as he passes* Sasha). A picture ! A queen of trumps.

Lebedyev. Run along, you cave-man—run along !

(Lvov *and* Kossih *go out.*)

Lebedyev. Sit down, Sasha ; that's right . . . (*sits down and looks round*). Listen attentively and with befitting reverence. It's like this : your mother has told me to make this communication. . . . You understand, I am not going to say this from myself : it's your mother's orders.

Sasha. Father, do be brief !

Lebedyev. You are to have fifteen thousand roubles at your marriage. There. . . . Mind that there is no talk about it afterwards ! Wait a minute , be quiet ! There are more treats to come. Your portion is fifteen thousand, but, since Nikolay Alexeyevitch owes your mother nine thousand, that is to be deducted from your dowry. . . . Well, besides that . . .

Sasha. What are you telling me this for ?

Lebedyev. Your mother told me to.

Sasha. Do leave me alone ! If you had the slightest respect for me or for yourself, you could not bring yourself to speak to me in this way. I don't want your dowry ! I did not ask for it, and do not ask for it !

Lebedyev. Why do you fly out at me ? In Gogol the two rats first sniffed, then went away, but you are so advanced you fly at me without sniffing.

Sasha. Leave me alone ! Don't insult my ears with your reckonings of halfpence !

LEBEDYEV (*firing up*). Tfoo! The way you all go on will drive me to murder someone or stick a knife into myself! One is howling from morning to night, nagging and jawing away, counting her farthings, while the other's so clever, and humane and emancipated—dash it all!—she can't understand her own father! I insult her ears! Why, before coming here to insult your ears, out there (*points to the door*) I was torn to pieces, hacked into bits. She cannot understand! Her head is turned, and she has lost all sense. . . . Confound you all! (*goes to the door and stops*). I dislike it—I dislike everything in you!

SASHA. What do you dislike?

LEBEDYEV. I dislike everything—everything!

SASHA. What everything?

LEBEDYEV. Do you suppose I am going to sit down and begin telling you? There is nothing I like about it, and I can't bear to see your wedding! (*Goes up to* SASHA *and says caressingly*) Forgive me, Sasha, perhaps your marriage is all very clever, honourable, elevated, full of high principles, but there is something all wrong in it— all wrong! It's not like other marriages. You are young and fresh and clear as a bit of glass, and beautiful, while he is a widower, rather frayed and shabby, and I don't understand him, God bless the man! (*kisses his daughter*). Sasha, forgive me, but there is something not quite straight. People are saying all sorts of things. The way his Sarra died, and then the way he was set on marrying you all at once . . . (*briskly*). But there, I am an old woman—an old woman!

I am as womanish as an old crinoline. Don't listen to me. Listen to no one but yourself.

SASHA. Father, I feel myself that there is something wrong. . . . There is—there is! If only you knew how heavy my heart is! It's unbearable! I am ashamed and frightened to admit it. Father darling, do help me to be brave, for God's sake . . . tell me what to do.

LEBEDYEV. What is it? What is it?

SASHA. I am frightened as I have never been before (*looks round*). It seems as though I don't understand him and never shall. All the while I have been engaged to him he has never once smiled, has never looked me straight in the face. He is full of complaints, remorse for something, shudderings, hints at some wrong he has done. . . . I am exhausted. There are minutes when I even fancy that I . . . that I don't love him as I ought. And when he comes to us or talks to me I am bored. What does it all mean, father? I am frightened.

LEBEDYEV. My darling, my only one, listen to your old father. Break it off.

SASHA (*in alarm*). What are you saying?

LEBEDYEV. Yes, really, Sasha. There will be a scandal, all the countryside will be wagging their tongues, but it is better to face a scandal than to ruin your whole life.

SASHA. Don't speak of it, father. I won't listen. I must struggle against gloomy thoughts. He is a fine man, unhappy and misunderstood. I will love him; I will understand him; I will set him on his feet; I will carry out my task. That's settled!

LEBEDYEV. It's not a task—it's neurosis.

SASHA. That's enough. I have confessed to you what I would not admit to myself. Don't tell anyone. Let us forget it.

LEBEDYEV. I can't make head or tail of it. Either I've gone dotty with old age, or you have all grown too clever. Anyway, I can make nothing of it ; I'll be hanged if I can.

SHABELSKY (*entering*). The devil take them all and me into the bargain. It's revolting.

LEBEDYEV. What's wrong with you ?

SHABELSKY. No, seriously, come what may. I must play some dirty, shabby trick so that other people may be as sick as I am. And I will too. Honour bright ! I've told Borkin to announce my engagement to-day (*laughs*). Everyone is a scoundrel, and I'll be a scoundrel too.

LEBEDYEV. Oh, you bore me ! Do you know what, Matvey ?—you will talk yourself into such a state that, excuse my saying so, they will clap you into a madhouse.

SHABELSKY. And is a madhouse worse than any other house ? You can take me there to-day if you like ; I don't care. Everyone is mean, petty, trivial and dull. I am disgusting to myself ; I don't believe a word I say. . . .

LEBEDYEV. I tell you what, Matvey—you should take some tow in your mouth, put a match to it, and breathe out fire and flame. Or, better still, take your cap and go home. This is a wedding ; everyone is making merry, while you croak like a crow. Yes, really. . . .

(SHABELSKY *bends over the piano and sobs.*)

LEBEDYEV. Holy saints! Matvey! Count! What is the matter with you? Matyusha, my dear . . . my angel . . . I have offended you? Come, you must forgive an old dog like me. . . . Forgive a drunkard . . . have some water.

SHABELSKY. I don't want it (*raises his head*).

LEBEDYEV. Why are you crying?

SHABELSKY. Oh, it's nothing! . . .

LEBEDYEV. Come, Matyusha, don't tell stories. What's the reason?

SHABELSKY. I happened to look at that 'cello . . . and thought of the poor little Jewess. . . .

LEBEDYEV. Phew! you've pitched on the right minute to think of her! The kingdom of heaven and eternal peace be hers! But this is not the time to remember her.

SHABELSKY. We used to play duets together. . . . She was a wonderful, splendid woman!

(SASHA *sobs*.)

LEBEDYEV. What's the matter with you now? Give over! Lord, they are both howling! And I—I . . . You might at least go somewhere else; people may see you.

SHABELSKY. Pasha, when the sun shines it's merry in the churchyard. If one has hope one may be happy in old age. But I have no hopes left, not one!

LEBEDYEV. Yes, things really aren't very bright for you. . . . You've no children, no money, no work. . . . Well, it can't be helped. (*To* SASHA) And what's the matter with you?

SHABELSKY. Pasha, give me some money. We'll settle accounts in the next world. I'll go to

Paris and look at my wife's grave. I've given away a lot in my day: I gave away half my property, and so I have a right to ask. Besides, I am asking a friend. . . .

LEBEDYEV (*in a fluster*). My dear boy I haven't a penny! But all right, all right! That is, I don't promise anything, but you understand . . . very good, very good! . . . (*Aside*) They worry the life out of me.

MADAME BABAKIN (*coming in*). Where is my partner? Count, how dare you leave me alone? Ah, horrid man! (*taps the* COUNT *on the hand with her fan*).

SHABELSKY (*shrinking away*). Leave me alone! I hate you!

MADAME BABAKIN (*aghast*). What? . . . Eh? . . .

SHABELSKY. Go away!

MADAME BABAKIN (*sinks into a chair*). Oh! (*weeps*).

ZINAIDA SAVISHNA (*enters, weeping*). Somebody has arrived. . . . I believe it's the best man. It's time for the blessing (*sobs*).

SASHA (*in a voice of entreaty*). Mother!

LEBEDYEV. Well, they are all howling! It's a quartet! Oh, leave off, you are making the place so damp! Matvey . . . Marfa Yegorovna! . . . Why, I shall cry myself in a minute . . . (*weeps*). My goodness!

ZINAIDA. Well, since you don't care for your mother, since you are disobedient . . . I'll comply with your wishes and give you my blessing.

(IVANOV *comes in; he is in a dress-suit and gloves.*)

LEBEDYEV. This is the last straw! What is it?

SASHA. Why have you come?

IVANOV. I am sorry. May I speak to Sasha alone?

LEBEDYEV. That's not at all the thing for you to come to the bride before the wedding! You ought to be on your way to the church!

IVANOV. Pasha, I beg you . . .

(LEBEDYEV *shrugs his shoulders*; *he*, ZINAIDA SAVISHNA, SHABELSKY *and* MADAME BABAKIN *go out*.)

SASHA (*severely*). What do you want?

IVANOV. I am choking with fury, but I can speak coolly. Listen! Just now I was dressing for the wedding. I looked in the glass and saw that I had grey hairs on my temples. . . . Sasha, it's not right! While there is still time we ought to break off this senseless farce. . . . You are young and pure, your life is before you, while I...

SASHA. That's all stale. I have heard it a thousand times and I am sick of it! Go to the church! Don't keep people waiting.

IVANOV. I am going home at once, and you tell your people that there will be no wedding. Give them some explanation. We have been foolish long enough. I've played the Hamlet and you the noble maiden, and that will do.

SASHA (*flaring up*). What do you mean by speaking like that? I won't listen.

IVANOV. But I am speaking, and I will speak.

SASHA. What have you come for? Your whining is turning into jeering.

IVANOV. No, I am not whining now. Jeering?
Yes, I am jeering. And if I could jeer at myself
a thousand times more bitterly and set the whole
world laughing, I would do it. I looked at myself
in the looking-glass and it was as though a shell
exploded in my conscience! I laughed at myself
and almost went out of my mind with shame
(*laughs*). Melancholy! Noble sorrow! Mysterious sadness! To crown it all I ought to write
verses. . . . To whine, to lament, to make people
miserable, to recognise that vital energy is lost
for ever, that I have gone to seed, outlived my
day, that I have given in to weakness and sunk
over my ears in this loathsome apathy—to feel all
this when the sun is shining brightly, when even
the ant is dragging his little load and is satisfied
with himself—no, thanks! To see some people
thinking you a fraud, others sorry for you, others
holding out a helping hand, while some—worst of
all—listen with reverence to your sighs, look upon
you as a prophet, and are all agog for you to reveal
some new religion. . . . No, thank God I have
still some pride and conscience! As I came here,
I laughed at myself and felt as though the very
birds, the trees, were laughing at me. . . .

SASHA. This is not anger, it's madness.

IVANOV. Do you think so? No, I am not mad.
Now I see things in their true light and my mind
is as clear as your conscience. We love each
other, but we shall never be married! I can rave
and be melancholy as much as I like, but I have no
right to ruin other people. I poisoned the last
year of my wife's life with my whining. While

333

you have been engaged to me, you have forgotten how to laugh and have grown five years older. Your father, to whom everything in life was clear, is at a loss to understand people, thanks to me. Whether I go to a meeting, or on a visit, or shooting, wherever I am, I bring boredom, depression, and dissatisfaction with me. Wait, don't interrupt me ! I am harsh and savage, but forgive me, I am choked with fury and cannot speak in any other way. I used never to tell lies about life or abuse it, but now that I have become an old grumbler I unconsciously abuse life falsely, repine against destiny and complain, and everyone who hears me is affected by the distaste for life and begins abusing it too. And what an attitude ! As though I were doing a favour to nature by living ! Damnation take me !

SASHA. Wait a minute. . . . From what you said just now it follows that you are weary of re-pining and that it's time to begin a new life ! . . . And a good thing too. . . .

IVANOV. I see nothing good, and what's the use of talking about a new life ? I am lost beyond all hope ! It is time for us both to realise it. A new life !

SASHA. Nikolay, pull yourself together ! What makes you think that you are lost ? Why this cynicism ? No, I won't speak or listen. . . . Go to the church !

IVANOV. I am lost !

SASHA. Don't shout like that, the visitors will hear you !

IVANOV. If an educated, healthy man who is

not a fool begins, for no apparent reason, lamenting and rolling downhill, he will roll down without stopping, and nothing can save him! Come, where can I look for help? In what? I can't drink—wine makes my head ache; I can't write bad verse; I can't worship my spiritual sloth and see something lofty in it. Sloth is sloth, weakness is weakness—I have no other names for them. I am done for, done for—and it's no good talking about it! (*looks round*). We may be interrupted. Listen! If you love me, help me. This very minute, at once, break it off with me. Make haste! . . .

SASHA. Oh, Nikolay, if you knew how you exhaust me! How you weary my soul! You are a good, clever man: judge for yourself, how can you set me such tasks? Every day there is some fresh problem, each harder than the one before. . . . I wanted active love, but this is martyrdom!

IVANOV. And when you are my wife the problems will be more complicated still. Break it off! You must understand; it is not love but the obstinacy of an honest nature that is working in you. You've made it your aim at all costs to make a man of me again, to save me. It flattered you to think you were doing something heroic. . . . Now you are ready to draw back but are hindered by a false sentiment. Do understand that!

SASHA. What queer, mad logic! Why, can I break it off with you? How can I break it off? You have neither mother, nor sister, nor friends.

. . . You are ruined, you have been robbed right and left, everyone is telling lies about you. . . .

IVANOV. It was stupid of me to have come here . . . I ought to have done as I meant. . . .

(*Enter* LEBEDYEV.)

SASHA (*runs to her father*). Father, for mercy's sake! He has rushed here as though he were frantic and is torturing me! He insists on my breaking it off; he doesn't want to spoil my life. Tell him that I won't accept his generosity. I know what I am doing.

LEBEDYEV. I can't make head or tail of it. . . . What generosity?

IVANOV. There will be no marriage!

SASHA. There shall be! Father, tell him that there shall be!

LEBEDYEV. Wait a minute, wait a minute! . . . Why don't you want to marry her?

IVANOV. I told her why, but she refuses to understand.

LEBEDYEV. No, don't explain to her, but to me, and explain it so that I can understand! Ah, Nikolay Alexeyevitch, God be your judge! You've brought such a lot of muddle into our life that I feel as though I were living in a museum of curiosities: I look about and I can make nothing of it. . . . It is an infliction. . . . What is an old man to do with you? Challenge you to a duel or what?

IVANOV. There's no need of a duel. All that is needed is to have a head on your shoulders and to understand Russian.

SASHA (*walks up and down the stage in agitation*). This is awful, awful! Simply like a child. . . .

LEBEDYEV. One can only throw up one's hands in amazement, that's all. Listen, Nikolay! To you all this seems clever, subtle, and according to all the rules of psychology, but to me it seems a scandal and a misfortune. Listen to an old man for the last time! This is what I advise you: give your mind a rest! Look at things simply, like everyone else! Everything is simple in this world. The ceiling is white, the boots are black, sugar is sweet. You love Sasha, she loves you. If you love her—stay; if you don't love her—go; we won't make a fuss. Why, it's so simple! You are both healthy, clever, moral, and you have food to eat and clothes to wear, thank God. . . . What more do you want? You've no money? As though that mattered. . . . Money does not give happiness. . . . Of course I understand . . . your estate is mortgaged, you have no money to pay the interest, but I am a father, I understand. . . . Her mother can do as she likes, bless the woman; if she won't give the money, she need not. Sasha says she does not want a dowry. Principles, Schopenhauer. . . . That's all tosh . . . I have a private ten thousand in the bank (*looks round*). Not a dog in the house knows of it. . . . Granny's money . . . that is for you too. . . . Take it, only on one condition: give Matvey two thousand. . . .

(GUESTS *assemble in the back drawing-room*).

IVANOV. Pasha, it's no use talking. I shall act as my conscience tells me.

337

SASHA. And I shall act as my conscience tells me. You can say what you like, I won't give you up. I'll go and call mother (*goes out*).

LEBEDYEV. I can't make head or tail of it.

IVANOV. Listen, poor fellow. . . . I am not going to tell you what I am—honest or a fraud, healthy or a neurotic. There is no making you understand. I used to be young, ardent, earnest, and not a fool : I loved, I hated, and I believed not as others do ; I hoped and did the work of ten ; I fought with windmills, I knocked my head against the wall ; not measuring my strength, not considering, knowing nothing of life, I took up a burden which broke my back and strained my muscles ; I made haste to spend all of myself in my youth ; I was intoxicated, I worked myself up, I toiled, I knew no moderation. And tell me, could I have done otherwise ? We are few, you know, and there is so much to do, so much ! My God ! how much ! And see how cruelly the life with which I struggled has paid me out ! I have overstrained myself. At thirty came the awakening, I was already old and slothful. Exhausted, overstrained, broken, with my head heavy and my soul indolent, without faith, without love, without an object in life, I linger like a shadow among men and don't know what I am, what I am living for, what I want. . . . And I fancy that love is nonsense and tenderness, mawkish, that there is no sense in work, that songs and words of enthusiasm are vulgar and stale, and everywhere I bring with me misery, chilly boredom, dissatisfaction, distaste for life. . . . I am lost beyond all

hope! Before you stands a man worn out at thirty-five; disillusioned, crushed by his own paltry efforts; he is burning with shame, mocking at his own feebleness. . . . Oh, how my pride revolts, how I choke with rage! (*staggering*). There, what I have brought myself to! I am simply reeling. . . . I feel ill. Where is Matvey? Let him take me home.

(VOICES *in the back room:* "*The best man has come!*")

SHABELSKY (*entering*). In a shabby, borrowed coat . . . with no gloves . . . and how many jeering looks, silly jokes, vulgar grins on account of it! . . . Disgusting cads!

BORKIN (*enters hurriedly, with a bouquet; he is in evening dress and wearing a flower as the badge of the best man*). Ough! Where is he? (*To* IVANOV) They have been waiting for you at the church for ever so long and here you are airing your views. He is a funny chap! He really is a funny chap! You mustn't go to church with your bride, but separately, with me, and I will come back from the church and fetch the bride. Do you mean to say you don't even know that? He really is a funny chap!

LVOV (*entering, to* IVANOV). Ah, you are here? (*Loudly*) Nikolay Alexeyevitch Ivanov, I proclaim in the hearing of all that you are a scoundrel!

IVANOV (*coldly*). I am very much obliged to you.
(*General perturbation.*)

BORKIN (*to* LVOV). Sir, this is contemptible! I challenge you to a duel!

LVOV. Mr. Borkin, I regard it as degrading not

339

only to fight, but even to speak with you! But Mr. Ivanov may receive satisfaction whenever he chooses.

SHABELSKY. Sir, I shall fight you!

SASHA (*to* Lvov). What have you insulted him for? What is it for? Gentlemen, please, let him tel me what made him do it.

LVOV. Alexandra Pavlovna, I did not insult him without grounds. I came here as an honest man to open your eyes, and I beg you to hear me.

SASHA. What can you say? That you are an honest man? The whole world knows that! You had better tell me on your conscience whether you understand yourself or not! You have come in here just now as an honest man and flung at him a terrible insult which has almost killed me; in old days, when you used to follow him about like a shadow and poisoned his life, you were convinced that you were doing your duty, that you were an honest man. You have meddled in his private life, you have blackened his name and condemned him; whenever you could you pelted me and all his friends with anonymous letters— and all the time you thought you were a conscientious man. You, a doctor, thought it honourable and did not spare even his sick wife; you gave her no peace with your suspicions. And whatever outrage, whatever cruel meanness you may commit, you will always believe that you are a conscientious and advanced man!

IVANOV (*laughing*). This is not a wedding, but a debate! Bravo, bravo!

SASHA (*to* Lvov). So now think a little: do you

understand yourself or not ? Dull-witted, heart-less people ! (*Takes* IVANOV *by the hand*) Come away, Nikolay ! Father, come !

IVANOV. Come where ? Wait a minute, I will make an end of it all ! My youth is awakened in me, my old self is roused ! (*takes out his revolver*).

SASHA (*screams*). I know what he means to do ! Nikolay, for God's sake !

IVANOV. I've been rolling down hill long enough, now a halt ! It's time to know when to take leave ! Stand back ! Thanks, Sasha !

SASHA (*screams*). Nikolay, for God's sake ! Hold him !

IVANOV Let me alone ! (*runs aside and shoots himself*).

CURTAIN

THE SEA-GULL

A COMEDY IN FOUR ACTS

First performed at St. Petersburg,
October 17, 1896

CHARACTERS IN THE PLAY

IRINA NIKOLAYEVNA ARKADIN (MADAME TREPLEV)
   (*an Actress*).
KONSTANTIN GAVRILOVITCH TREPLEV (*her son, a
   young man*).
PYOTR NIKOLAYEVITCH SORIN (*her brother*).
NINA MIHAILOVNA ZARETCHNY (*a young girl, the
   daughter of a wealthy Landowner*).
ILYA AFANASYEVITCH SHAMRAEV (*a retired Lieu-
   tenant*, SORIN'S *Steward*).
POLINA ANDREYEVNA (*his wife*).
MASHA (*his daughter*).
BORIS ALEXEYEVITCH TRIGORIN (*a literary man*).
YEVGENY SERGEYEVITCH DORN (*a Doctor*).
SEMYON SEMYONOVITCH MEDVEDENKO (*a School-
   master*).
YAKOV (*a Labourer*).
A MAN COOK.
A HOUSEMAID.

The action takes place in SORIN'S *house and garden.
   Between the Third and the Fourth Acts there is
   an interval of two years.*

ACT I

Part of the park on SORIN'S *estate. Wide avenue leading away from the spectators into the depths of the park towards the lake is blocked up by a platform roughly put together for private theatricals, so that the lake is not visible. To right and left of the platform, bushes. A few chairs, a little table.*

The sun has just set. YAKOV *and other labourers are at work on the platform behind the curtain; there is the sound of coughing and hammering.* MASHA *and* MEDVEDENKO *enter on the left, returning from a walk.*

MEDVEDENKO. Why do you always wear black ?

MASHA. I am in mourning for my life. I am unhappy.

MEDVEDENKO. Why ? (*Pondering*) I don't understand. . . . You are in good health ; though your father is not very well off, he has got enough. My life is much harder than yours. I only get twenty-three roubles a month, and from that they deduct something for the pension fund, and yet I don't wear mourning. (*They sit down.*)

MASHA. It isn't money that matters. A poor man may be happy.

MEDVEDENKO. Theoretically, yes ; but in practice it's like this : there are my two sisters and my mother and my little brother and I, and my salary is only twenty-three roubles. We must eat and drink, mustn't we? One must have tea and sugar. One must have tobacco. It's a tight fit.

MASHA (*looking round at the platform*). The play will soon begin.

MEDVEDENKO. Yes. Miss Zaretchny will act: it is Konstantin Gavrilitch's play. They are in love with each other and to-day their souls will be united in the effort to realise the same artistic effect. But your soul and mine have not a common point of contact. I love you. I am so wretched I can't stay at home. Every day I walk four miles here and four miles back and I meet with nothing but indifference from you. I can quite understand it. I am without means and have a big family to keep. . . . Who would care to marry a man who hasn't a penny to bless himself with?

MASHA. Oh, nonsense! (*takes a pinch of snuff*). Your love touches me, but I can't reciprocate it— that's all. (*Holding out the snuff-box to him*) Help yourself.

MEDVEDENKO. I don't feel like it (*a pause*).

MASHA. How stifling it is! There must be a storm coming. . . . You're always discussing theories or talking about money. You think there is no greater misfortune than poverty, but to my mind it is a thousand times better to go in rags and be a beggar than . . . But you wouldn't understand that, though. . . .

(SORIN *and* TREPLEV *enter on the right.*)

SORIN (*leaning on his walking-stick*). I am never

quite myself in the country, my boy, and, naturally enough, I shall never get used to it. Last night I went to bed at ten and woke up this morning at nine feeling as though my brain were glued to my skull, through sleeping so long (*laughs*). And after dinner I accidentally dropped off again, and now I am utterly shattered and feel as though I were in a nightmare, in fact. . . .

TREPLEV. Yes, you really ought to live in town. (*Catches sight of* MASHA *and* MEDVEDENKO) When the show begins, my friends, you will be summoned, but you mustn't be here now. You must please go away.

SORIN (*to* MASHA). Marya Ilyinishna, will you be so good as to ask your papa to tell them to take the dog off the chain ?—it howls. My sister could not sleep again last night.

MASHA. Speak to my father yourself ; I am not going to. Please don't ask me. (*To* MEDVEDENKO) Come along !

MEDVEDENKO (*to* TREPLEV). So you will send and let us know before it begins. (*Both go out.*)

SORIN. So I suppose the dog will be howling all night again. What a business it is ! I have never done as I liked in the country. In old days I used to get leave for twenty-eight days and come here for a rest and so on, but they worried me so with all sorts of trifles that before I had been here two days I was longing to be off again (*laughs*). I've always been glad to get away from here. . . . But now I am on the retired list, and I have nowhere else to go, as a matter of fact. I've got to live here whether I like it or not. . . .

YAKOV (*to* TREPLEV). We are going to have a bathe, Konstantin Gavrilitch.

TREPLEV. Very well; but don't be more than ten minutes (*looks at his watch*). It will soon begin.

YAKOV. Yes, sir (*goes out*).

TREPLEV (*looking round the stage*). Here is our theatre. The curtain, then the first wing, then the second, and beyond that—open space. No scenery of any sort. There is an open view of the lake and the horizon. We shall raise the curtain at exactly half-past eight, when the moon rises.

SORIN. Magnificent.

TREPLEV. If Nina is late it will spoil the whole effect. It is time she was here. Her father and her stepmother keep a sharp eye on her, and it is as hard for her to get out of the house as to escape from prison (*puts his uncle's cravat straight*). Your hair and your beard are very untidy. They want clipping or something. . . .

SORIN (*combing out his beard*). It's the tragedy of my life. Even as a young man I looked as though I had been drinking for days or something of the sort. I was never a favourite with the ladies (*sitting down*). Why is your mother out of humour ?

TREPLEV. Why ? Because she is bored (*sitting down beside him*). She is jealous. She is set against me, and against the performance, and against my play because Nina is acting in it, and she is not. She does not know my play, but she hates it.

SORIN (*laughs*). What an idea !

TREPLEV. She is annoyed to think that even on this little stage Nina will have a triumph and not she (*looks at his watch*). My mother is a psychological freak. Unmistakably talented, intelligent, capable of sobbing over a book, she will reel off all Nekrassov by heart ; as a sick nurse she is an angel ; but just try praising Duse in her presence ! O-ho ! You must praise no one but herself, you must write about her, make a fuss over her, be in raptures over her extraordinary acting in " La Dame aux Camélias " or the " Ferment of Life " ; but she has none of this narcotic in the country, she is bored and cross, and we are all her enemies—we are all in fault. Then she is superstitious—she is afraid of three candles, of the number thirteen. She is stingy. She has got seventy thousand roubles in a bank at Odessa—I know that for a fact—but ask her to lend you some money, and she will burst into tears.

SORIN. You imagine your mother does not like your play, and you are already upset and all that. Don't worry ; your mother adores you.

TREPLEV (*pulling the petals off a flower*). Loves me, loves me not ; loves me, loves me not ; loves me, loves me not (*laughs*). You see, my mother does not love me. I should think not ! She wants to live, to love, to wear light blouses ; and I am twenty-five, and I am a continual reminder that she is no longer young. When I am not there she is only thirty-two, but when I am there she is forty-three, and for that she hates me. She knows, too, that I have no belief in the theatre. She loves the stage, she fancies she is working for humanity, for the holy cause of art, while to my mind the modern theatre is nothing but tradition and conventionality. When the curtain goes up, and by artificial light, in a room with three walls, these great geniuses, the devotees of holy art, represent how people eat, drink, love, move about, and wear their jackets ; when from these commonplace sentences and pictures they try to draw a moral—a petty moral, easy of comprehension and convenient for domestic use ; when in a thousand variations I am offered the same thing over and over again—I run away as Maupassant ran away from the Eiffel Tower which weighed upon his brain with its vulgarity.

SORIN. You can't do without the stage.

TREPLEV. We need new forms of expression. We need new forms, and if we can't have them we had better have nothing (*looks at his watch*). I love my mother—I love her very much—but she leads a senseless sort of life, always taken up with this literary gentleman, her name is always trotted out in the papers—and that wearies me. And sometimes the simple egoism of an ordinary mortal makes me feel sorry that my mother is a celebrated actress, and I fancy that if she were an ordinary woman I should be happier. Uncle, what could be more hopeless and stupid than my position ? She used to have visitors, all celebrities —artists and authors—and among them all I was the only one who was nothing, and they only put up with me because I was her son. Who am I ? What am I ? I left the University in my third year—owing to circumstances " for which

350

we accept no responsibility," as the editors say; I have no talents, I haven't a penny of my own, and on my passport I am described as an artisan of Kiev. You know my father was an artisan of Kiev, though he too was a well-known actor. So, when in her drawing-room all these artists and authors graciously noticed me, I always fancied from their faces that they were taking the measure of my insignificance—I guessed their thoughts and suffered from the humiliation. . . .

SORIN. And, by the way, can you tell me, please, what sort of man this literary gentleman is? There's no making him out. He never says anything.

TREPLEV. He is an intelligent man, good-natured and rather melancholy, you know. A very decent fellow. He is still a good distance off forty, but he is already celebrated and has enough and to spare of everything. As for his writings . . . what shall I say? They are charming, full of talent, but . . . after Tolstoy or Zola you do not care to read Trigorin.

SORIN. Well, I am fond of authors, my boy. At one time I had a passionate desire for two things: I wanted to get married, and I wanted to become an author; but I did not succeed in doing either. Yes, it is pleasant to be even a small author, as a matter of fact.

TREPLEV (*listens*). I hear steps . . . (*embraces his uncle*). I cannot live without her. . . . The very sound of her footsteps is lovely. . . . I am wildly happy (*goes quickly to meet* NINA ZARETCHNY *as she enters*). My enchantress—my dream. . . .

NINA (*in agitation*). I am not late. . . . Of course I am not late. . . .

TREPLEV (*kissing her hands*). No, no, no!

NINA. I have been uneasy all day. I was so frightened. I was afraid father would not let me come. . . . But he has just gone out with my stepmother. The sky is red, the moon is just rising, and I kept urging on the horse (*laughs*). But I am glad (*shakes* SORIN's *hand warmly*).

SORIN (*laughs*). Your eyes look as though you have been crying. . . . Fie, fie! That's not right!

NINA. Oh, it was nothing. . . . You see how out of breath I am. I have to go in half an hour. We must make haste. I can't stay, I can't! For God's sake don't keep me! My father doesn't know I am here.

TREPLEV. It really is time to begin. We must go and call the others.

SORIN. I'll go this minute (*goes to the right, singing* "To France two grenadiers." *Looks round*) Once I sang like that, and a deputy prosecutor said to me, "You have a powerful voice, your Excellency"; then he thought a little and added, "but not a pleasant one" (*laughs and goes off*).

NINA. My father and his wife won't let me come here. They say it is so Bohemian here . . . they are afraid I shall go on the stage. . . . But I feel drawn to the lake here like a sea-gull. . . . My heart is full of you (*looks round*).

TREPLEV. We are alone.

NINA. I fancy there is someone there.

352

TREPLEV. There's nobody. (*They kiss.*)

NINA. What tree is this ?

TREPLEV. An elm.

NINA. Why is it so dark ?

TREPLEV. It's evening ; everything is getting dark. Don't go away early, I entreat you !

NINA. I must.

TREPLEV. And if I come to you, Nina, I'll stand in the garden all night, watching your window.

NINA. You can't ; the watchman would notice you. Trésor is not used to you, and he would bark.

TREPLEV. I love you !

NINA. Sh-h. . . .

TREPLEV (*hearing footsteps*). Who is there ? You, Yakov ?

YAKOV (*behind the stage*). Yes, sir.

TREPLEV. Take your places. It's time to begin. Is the moon rising ?

YAKOV. Yes, sir.

TREPLEV. Have you got the methylated spirit ? Have you got the sulphur ? When the red eyes appear there must be a smell of sulphur. (*To NINA*) Go, it's all ready. Are you nervous ?

NINA. Yes, awfully ! Your mother is all right —I am not afraid of her—but there's Trigorin . . . I feel frightened and ashamed of acting before him . . . a celebrated author. . . . Is he young ?

TREPLEV. Yes.

NINA. How wonderful his stories are.

TREPLEV (*coldly*). I don't know. I haven't read them.

NINA. It is difficult to act in your play. There are no living characters in it.

TREPLEV. Living characters! One must depict life not as it is, and not as it ought to be, but as we see it in our dreams.

NINA. There is very little action in your play—nothing but speeches. And to my mind there ought to be love in a play. (*Both go behind the stage.*)

(*Enter* POLINA ANDREYEVNA *and* DORN.)

POLINA. It is getting damp. Go back and put on your goloshes.

DORN. I am hot.

POLINA. You don't take care of yourself. It's obstinacy. You are a doctor, and you know perfectly well that damp air is bad for you, but you want to make me miserable; you sat out on the verandah all yesterday evening on purpose. . . .

DORN (*hums*). " Do not say that youth is ruined."

POLINA. You were so absorbed in conversation with Irina Nikolayevna . . . you did not notice the cold. Own up . . . you are attracted by her.

DORN. I am fifty-five.

POLINA. Nonsense! That's not old for a man. You look very young for your age, and are still attractive to women.

DORN. Well, what would you have?

POLINA. All you men are ready to fall down and worship an actress, all of you!

DORN (*hums*). " Before thee once again I stand." If artists are liked in society and treated differently from merchants, for example, that's only in the nature of things. It's idealism.

354

POLINA. Women have always fallen in love with you and thrown themselves on your neck. Is that idealism too ?

DORN (*shrugs his shoulders*). Well, in the attitude of women to me there has been a great deal that was good. What they principally loved in me was a first-rate doctor. You remember that ten or fifteen years ago I was the only decent accoucheur in the district. Then, too, I have always been an honest man.

POLINA (*seizes him by the hand*). Dearest !

DORN. Sh-h ! They are coming.

(*Enter* MADAME ARKADIN *arm in arm with* SORIN, TRIGORIN, SHAMRAEV, MEDVEDENKO *and* MASHA.)

SHAMRAEV. In the year 1873 she acted marvellously at the fair at Poltava. It was a delight ! She acted exquisitely ! Do you happen to know, madam, where Pavel Semyonitch Tchadin, a comic actor, is now ? His Rasplyuev was inimitable, even finer than Sadovsky's, I assure you, honoured lady. Where is he now ?

MADAME ARKADIN. You keep asking me about antediluvians. How should I know ? (*sits down*).

SHAMRAEV (*with a sigh*). Pashka Tchadin ! There are no such actors now. The stage has gone down, Irina Nikolayevna ! In old days there were mighty oaks, but now we see nothing but stumps.

DORN. There are few actors of brilliant talents nowadays, that's true ; but the average level of acting is far higher than it was.

SHAMRAEV. I can't agree with you. But, of

course, it's a matter of taste. *De gustibus aut bene aut nihil.*

(TREPLEV *comes out from behind the stage.*)

MADAME ARKADIN (*to her son*). My dear son, when is it going to begin ?

TREPLEV. In a minute. I beg you to be patient.

MADAME ARKADIN (*recites from* " Hamlet ").

" Oh, Hamlet, speak no more !
Thou turn'st mine eyes into my very soul ;
And there I see such black and grained spots
As will not leave their tinct."

TREPLEV (*from* " Hamlet ").

" And let me wring your heart, for so I shall,
If it be made of penetrable stuff."

(*A horn is sounded behind the stage.*)

TREPLEV. Ladies and gentlemen, we begin ! I beg you to attend (*a pause*). I begin (*taps with a stick and recites aloud*). Oh, you venerable old shadows that float at night-time over this lake, lull us to sleep and let us dream of what will be in two hundred thousand years !

SORIN. There will be nothing in two hundred thousand years.

TREPLEV. Then let them present that nothing to us.

MADAME ARKADIN. Let them. We are asleep.

(*The curtain rises ; the view of the lake is revealed ; the moon is above the horizon, its reflection in the water ;* NINA ZARETCHNY, *all in white, is sitting on a big stone.*)

NINA. Men, lions, eagles and partridges, horned

356

deer, geese, spiders, silent fish that dwell in the water, starfishes and creatures which cannot be seen by the eye—all living things, all living things, all living things, having completed their cycle of sorrow, are extinct. . . . For thousands of years the earth has borne no living creature on its surface, and this poor moon lights its lamp in vain. On the meadow the cranes no longer waken with a cry, and there is no sound of the May beetles in the lime trees. It is cold, cold, cold ! Empty, empty, empty ! Dreadful, dreadful, dreadful ! (*a pause*). The bodies of living creatures have vanished into dust, and eternal matter has transformed them into rocks, into water, into clouds, while the souls of all have melted into one. That world-soul I am—I. . . . In me is the soul of Alexander the Great, of Cæsar, of Shakespeare and of Napoleon, and of the lowest leech. In me the consciousness of men is blended with the instincts of the animals, and I remember all, all, all ! And I live through every life over again in myself ! (*Will-of-the-wisps appear.*)

MADAME ARKADIN (*softly*). It's something decadent.

TREPLEV (*in an imploring and reproachful voice*). Mother !

NINA. I am alone. Once in a hundred years I open my lips to speak, and my voice echoes mournfully in the void, and no one hears. . . . You too, pale lights, hear me not. . . . The stagnant marsh begets you before daybreak and you wander until dawn, but without thought, without will, without the tremor of life. For fear that life

357

should spring up in you the father of eternal
matter, the devil, keeps the atoms in you, as in
the stones and in the water, in continual flux, and
you are changing perpetually. For in all the
universe nothing remains permanent and un-
changed but the spirit (*a pause*). Like a prisoner
cast into a deep, empty well I know not where
I am and what awaits me. All is hidden from me
but that in the cruel, persistent struggle with the
devil—the principle of the forces of matter—I am
destined to conquer, and, after that, matter and
spirit will be blended in glorious harmony and the
Kingdom of the Cosmic Will will come. But that
will come only little by little, through long, long
thousands of years when the moon and the
bright Sirius and the earth are changed to dust. . . .
Till then—terror, terror . . . (*a pause ; two red spots
appear upon the background of the lake*). Here
my powerful foe, the devil, is approaching. I see
his dreadful crimson eyes. . . .

MADAME ARKADIN. There's a smell of sulphur.
Is that as it should be ?

TREPLEV. Yes.

MADAME ARKADIN (*laughs*). Oh, it's a stage
effect !

TREPLEV. Mother !

NINA. He is dreary without man——

POLINA (*to* DORN). You have taken your hat off.
Put it on or you will catch cold.

MADAME ARKADIN. The doctor has taken his
hat off to the devil, the father of eternal matter.

TREPLEV (*firing up, aloud*). The play is over !
Enough ! Curtain !

358

MADAME ARKADIN. What are you cross about ?

TREPLEV. Enough ! The curtain ! Let down
the curtain ! (*stamping*). Curtain ! (*The curtain
falls.*) I am sorry ! I lost sight of the fact that
only a few of the elect may write plays and act in
them. I have infringed the monopoly. I . . . I . . .
(*tries to say something more, but with a wave of his
hand goes out on left*).

MADAME ARKADIN. What's the matter with him ?

SORIN. Irina, you really must have more consideration for youthful vanity, my dear.

MADAME ARKADIN. What did I say to him ?

SORIN. You hurt his feelings.

MADAME ARKADIN. He told us beforehand that
it was a joke, and I regarded his play as a joke.

SORIN. All the same . . .

MADAME ARKADIN. Now it appears that he has
written a great work. What next ! So he has
got up this performance and smothered us with sulphur not as a joke but as a protest. . . . He wanted
to show us how to write and what to act. This is
getting tiresome ! These continual sallies at my
expense—these continual pin-pricks would put
anyone out of patience, say what you like. He
is a vain, whimsical boy !

SORIN. He meant to give you pleasure.

MADAME ARKADIN. Really ? He did not choose
an ordinary play, however, but made us listen to
this decadent delirium. For the sake of a joke I am
ready to listen to delirium, but here we have pretensions to new forms and a new view of art.
To my thinking it's no question of new forms at
all, but simply bad temper.

TRIGORIN. Everyone writes as he likes and as he can.

MADAME ARKADIN. Let him write as he likes and as he can, only let him leave me in peace.

DORN. Jupiter ! you are angry. . . .

MADAME ARKADIN. I am not Jupiter—I am a woman (*lights a cigarette*). I am not angry—I am only vexed that a young man should spend his time so drearily. I did not mean to hurt his feelings.

MEDVEDENKO. No one has any grounds to separate spirit from matter, seeing that spirit itself may be a combination of material atoms. (*With animation, to* TRIGORIN) But you know someone ought to write a play on how we poor teachers live, and get it acted. We have a hard, hard life.

MADAME ARKADIN. That's true, but don't let us talk either of plays or of atoms. It is such a glorious evening ! Do you hear ? There is singing ! (*listens*). How nice it is !

POLINA. It's on the other side of the lake (*a pause*).

MADAME ARKADIN (*to* TRIGORIN). Sit down beside me. Ten or fifteen years ago there were sounds of music and singing on that lake continually almost every night. There are six country houses on the shores of the lake. I remember laughter, noise, shooting, and love affairs without end. . . . The *jeune premier* and the idol of all those six households was in those days our friend here, the doctor (*motions with her head towards* DORN), Yevgeny Sergeitch. He is fascinating still, but in those days he was irresistible. But my conscience is beginning to trouble me. Why did I hurt my poor boy's feelings? I feel worried. (*Aloud*) Kostya! Son! Kostya!

MASHA. I'll go and look for him.

MADAME ARKADIN. Please do, my dear.

MASHA (*going to the left*). Aa-oo! Konstantin Gavrilitch! Aa-oo! (*goes off*).

NINA (*coming out from behind the stage*). Apparently there will be no going on, and I may come out. Good evening! (*kisses* MADAME ARKADIN *and* POLINA ANDREYEVNA).

SORIN. Bravo! Bravo!

MADAME ARKADIN. Bravo! Bravo! We admired you. With such an appearance, with such a lovely voice, you really cannot stay in the country; it is a sin. You must have talent. Do you hear? It's your duty to go on the stage.

NINA. Oh, that's my dream! (*sighing*). But it will never be realised.

MADAME ARKADIN. Who knows? Here, let me introduce Boris Alexeyevitch Trigorin.

NINA. Oh, I am so glad . . . (*overcome with embarrassment*). I am always reading your . . .

MADAME ARKADIN (*making her sit down beside them*). Don't be shy, my dear. He is a celebrity, but he has a simple heart. You see, he is shy himself.

DORN. I suppose we may raise the curtain; it's rather uncanny.

SHAMRAEV (*aloud*). Yakov, pull up the curtain, my lad. (*The curtain goes up.*)

NINA (*to* TRIGORIN). It is a queer play, isn't it?

TRIGORIN. I did not understand it at all. But I enjoyed it. You acted so genuinely. And the scenery was delightful (*a pause*). There must be a lot of fish in that lake.

NINA. Yes.

TRIGORIN. I love angling. There is nothing I enjoy so much as sitting on the bank of a river in the evening and watching the float.

NINA. But I should have thought that for any-one who has known the enjoyment of creation, no other enjoyment can exist.

MADAME ARKADIN (*laughing*). Don't talk like that. When people say nice things to him he is utterly floored.

SHAMRAEV. I remember one evening in the opera theatre in Moscow the celebrated Silva took the lower *C* ! As it happened, there was sitting in the gallery the bass of our church choir, and all at once—imagine our intense astonishment—we heard from the gallery " Bravo, Silva ! " a whole octave lower—like this : (*in a deep bass*) " Bravo, Silva ! " The audience sat spellbound (*a pause*).

DORN. The angel of silence has flown over us.

NINA. It's time for me to go. Good-bye.

MADAME ARKADIN. Where are you off to ? Why so early ? We won't let you go.

NINA. My father expects me.

MADAME ARKADIN. What a man, really ... (*kisses her*). Well, there is no help for it. I am sorry— I am sorry to let you go.

NINA. If you knew how grieved I am to go.

MADAME ARKADIN. Someone ought to see you home, my little dear.

NINA (*frightened*). Oh, no, no !

SORIN (*to her, in an imploring voice*). Do stay !

NINA. I can't, Pyotr Nikolayevitch.

SORIN. Stay for an hour. What is there in that ?

NINA (*thinking a minute, tearfully*). I can't ! (*shakes hands and hurriedly goes off*).

MADAME ARKADIN. Unfortunate girl she is, really. They say her mother left her father all her immense property—every farthing of it—and now the girl has got nothing, as her father has already made a will leaving everything to his second wife. It's monstrous !

DORN. Yes, her father is a pretty thorough scoundrel, one must do him the justice to say so.

SORIN (*rubbing his cold hands*). Let us go too, it's getting damp. My legs ache.

MADAME ARKADIN. They seem like wooden legs, you can hardly walk. Let us go, unlucky old man ! (*takes his arm*).

SHAMRAEV (*offering his arm to his wife*). Madame ?

SORIN. I hear that dog howling again. (*To* SHAMRAEV) Be so kind, Ilya Afanasyitch, as to tell them to let it off the chain.

SHAMRAEV. It's impossible, Pyotr Nikolayevitch, I am afraid of thieves getting into the barn. Our millet is there. (*To* MEDVEDENKO *who is walking beside him*) Yes, a whole octave lower : " Bravo, Silva ! " And he not a singer—simply a church chorister !

MEDVEDENKO. And what salary does a chorister get ? (*All go out except* DORN.)

DORN (*alone*). I don't know, perhaps I know nothing about it, or have gone off my head, but

I liked the play. There is something in it. When that girl talked about loneliness and afterwards when the devil's eyes appeared, I was so excited that my hands trembled. It is fresh, naïve. . . . Here he comes, I believe. I want to say all the nice things I can to him.

TREPLEV (*enters*). They have all gone.

DORN. I am here.

TREPLEV. Mashenka is looking for me all over the park. Insufferable creature she is !

DORN. Konstantin Gavrilitch, I liked your play extremely. It's a strange thing, and I haven't heard the end, and yet it made a strong impression ! You are a gifted man—you must persevere.

(TREPLEV *presses his hand warmly and embraces him impulsively*.)

DORN. Fie, what an hysterical fellow ! There are tears in his eyes ! What I mean is this. You have taken a subject from the realm of abstract ideas. So it should be, for a work of art ought to express a great idea. A thing is only fine when it is serious. How pale you are !

TREPLEV. So you tell me to persevere ?

DORN. Yes. . . . But write only of what is important and eternal. You know, I have had varied experiences of life, and have enjoyed it ; I am satisfied, but if it had been my lot to know the spiritual heights which artists reach at the moment of creation, I should, I believe, have despised my bodily self and all that appertains to it and left all things earthly as far behind as possible.

TREPLEV. Excuse me, where is Nina ?

DORN. And another thing. In a work of art

there ought to be a clear definite idea. You ought to know what is your aim in writing, for if you go along that picturesque route without a definite goal you will be lost and your talent will be your ruin.

TREPLEV (*impatiently*). Where is Nina?

DORN. She has gone home.

TREPLEV (*in despair*). What am I to do? I want to see her . . . I must see her. . . . I must go. . . .

(*Enter* MASHA.)

DORN (*to* TREPLEV). Calm yourself, my boy.

TREPLEV. But I am going all the same. I must go.

MASHA. Come indoors, Konstantin Gavrilitch. Your mother wants you. She is worried.

TREPLEV. Tell her that I have gone away. And I beg you—all of you—leave me in peace! Let me alone! Don't follow me about!

DORN. Come, come, come, dear boy. . . . You can't go on like that. . . . That's not the thing.

TREPLEV (*in tears*). Good-bye, doctor. Thank you . . . (*goes off*).

DORN (*with a sigh*). Youth! youth!

MASHA. When people have nothing better to say, they say, "Youth! youth!" . . . (*takes a pinch of snuff*).

DORN (*takes her snuff-box from her and flings it into the bushes*). That's disgusting! (*a pause*). I believe they are playing the piano indoors. We must go in.

MASHA. Wait a little.

DORN. What is it?

MASHA. I want to tell you once more. I have a longing to talk . . . (*growing agitated*). I don't care for my father . . . but I feel drawn to you. For some reason I feel with all my heart that you are very near me. . . . Help me. Help me, or I shall do something silly, I shall make a mock of my life and ruin it. . . . I can't go on. . . .

DORN. What is it? Help you in what?

MASHA. I am miserable. No one, no one knows how miserable I am! (*Laying her head on his breast, softly*) I love Konstantin!

DORN. How hysterical they all are! How hysterical! And what a lot of love. . . . Oh, the sorcery of the lake! (*Tenderly*) But what can I do, my child? What? What?

CURTAIN

*A croquet lawn. The house with a big verandah
    in the background on the right, on the left is
    seen the lake with the blazing sun reflected in it.*
Flower beds. Midday. Hot. MADAME ARKADIN,
    DORN *and* MASHA *are sitting on a garden seat
    in the shade of an old lime tree on one side of
    the croquet lawn.* DORN *has an open book on
    his knee.*

MADAME ARKADIN (*to* MASHA). Come, let us
stand up. (*They both get up.*) Let us stand side
by side. You are twenty-two and I am nearly
twice as old. Yevgeny Sergeitch, which of us
looks the younger ?

DORN. You, of course.

MADAME ARKADIN. There ! And why is it ?
Because I work, I feel I am always on the go,
while you stay always in the same place and
have no life at all. . . . And it is my rule never to
look into the future. I never think about old age
or death. What is to be, will be.

MASHA. And I feel as though I had been born long,
long ago ; I trail my life along like an endless
train. . . . And often I have not the slightest desire
to go on living (*sits down*). Of course, that's all
nonsense. I must shake myself and throw it all
off.

367

DORN (*hums quietly*). " Tell her, my flowers."

MADAME ARKADIN. Then I am as particular as an Englishman. I keep myself in hand, as they say, my dear, and am always dressed and have my hair done *comme il faut*. Do I allow myself to go out of the house even into the garden in a dressing-gown, or without my hair being done ? Never ! What has preserved me, is that I have never been a dowdy, I have never let myself go, as some women do . . . (*walks about the lawn with her arms akimbo*). Here I am, as brisk as a bird. I could take the part of a girl of fifteen.

DORN. Nevertheless, I shall go on (*takes up the book*). We stopped at the corn merchant and the rats. . . .

MADAME ARKADIN. And the rats. Read (*sits down*). But give it to me, I'll read. It is my turn (*takes the book and looks in it*). And rats. . . . Here it is. . . . (*Reads*) " And of course for society people to spoil novelists and to attract them to themselves is as dangerous as for a corn merchant to rear rats in his granaries. And yet they love them. And so, when a woman has picked out an author whom she desires to captivate, she lays siege to him by means of compliments, flattery and favours . . . " Well, that may be so with the French, but there is nothing like that with us, we have no set rules. Among us, before a woman sets to work to captivate an author, she is generally head over ears in love herself, if you please. To go no further, take Trigorin and me. . . .

368

(*Enter* SORIN, *leaning on his stick and with
    him* NINA ; MEDVEDENKO *wheels an
    empty bath-chair in after them.*)

SORIN (*in a caressing tone, as to a child*).   Yes ?
We are delighted, aren't we ?   We are happy
to-day at last ?   (*To his sister*) We are delighted !
Our father and stepmother have gone off to Tver,
and we are free now for three whole days.

NINA (*sits down beside* MADAME ARKADIN *and
embraces her*).   I am happy !   Now I belong to you.

SORIN (*sits down in his bath-chair*).   She looks
quite a beauty to-day.

MADAME ARKADIN.   Nicely dressed and interesting. . . . That's a good girl (*kisses* NINA).   But we
mustn't praise you too much for fear of ill-luck.
Where is Boris Alexeyevitch ?

NINA.   He is in the bathing-house, fishing.

MADAME ARKADIN.   I wonder he doesn't get
sick of it !   (*is about to go on reading*).

NINA.   What is that ?

MADAME ARKADIN.   Maupassant's " Sur l'eau,"
my dear (*reads a few lines to herself*).   Well, the
rest isn't interesting or true (*shuts the book*).
I feel uneasy.   Tell me, what's wrong with my
son ?   Why is he so depressed and ill-humoured ?
He spends whole days on the lake and I hardly
ever see him.

MASHA.   His heart is troubled.   (*To* NINA,
timidly) Please, do read us something out of his
play !

NINA (*shrugging her shoulders*).   Would you
like it ?   It's so uninteresting.

MASHA (*restraining her enthusiasm*).   When he

reads anything himself his eyes glow and his face turns pale. He has a fine mournful voice, and the gestures of a poet.

(*There is a sound of* SORIN *snoring.*)

DORN. Good-night !

MADAME ARKADIN. Petrusha !

SORIN. Ah ?

MADAME ARKADIN. Are you asleep ?

SORIN. Not a bit of it (*a pause*).

MADAME ARKADIN. You do nothing for your health, brother, and that's not right.

SORIN. I should like to take something, but the doctor won't give me anything.

DORN. Take medicine at sixty !

SORIN. Even at sixty one wants to live !

DORN (*with vexation*). Oh, very well, take valerian drops !

MADAME ARKADIN. It seems to me it would do him good to go to some mineral springs.

DORN. Well, he might go. And he might not.

MADAME ARKADIN. What is one to make of that ?

DORN. There's nothing to make of it. It's quite clear (*a pause*).

MEDVEDENKO. Pyotr Nikolayevitch ought to give up smoking.

SORIN. Nonsense !

DORN. No, it's not nonsense. Wine and tobacco destroy the personality. After a cigar or a glass of vodka, you are not Pyotr Nikolayevitch any more but Pyotr Nikolayevitch plus somebody else ; your ego is diffused and you feel towards yourself as to a third person.

SORIN (*laughs*). It's all very well for you to argue! You've lived your life, but what about me? I have served in the Department of Justice for twenty-eight years, but I haven't lived yet, I've seen and done nothing as a matter of fact, and very naturally I want to live very much. You've had enough and you don't care, and so you are inclined to be philosophical, but I want to live, and so I drink sherry at dinner and smoke cigars and so on. That's all it comes to.

DORN. One must look at life seriously, but to go in for cures at sixty and to regret that one hasn't enjoyed oneself enough in one's youth is frivolous, if you will forgive my saying so.

MASHA (*gets up*). It must be lunch-time (*walks with a lazy, lagging step*). My leg is gone to sleep (*goes off*).

DORN. She will go and have a couple of glasses before lunch.

SORIN. She has no personal happiness, poor thing.

DORN. Nonsense, your Excellency.

SORIN. You argue like a man who has had all he wants.

MADAME ARKADIN. Oh, what can be more boring than this sweet country boredom! Hot, still, no one ever doing anything, everyone airing their theories. . . . It's nice being with you, my friends, charming to listen to you, but . . . to sit in a hotel room somewhere and learn one's part is ever so much better.

NINA (*enthusiastically*). Delightful! I understand you.

SORIN. Of course, it's better in town. You sit in your study, the footman lets no one in unannounced, there's a telephone . . . in the streets there are cabs and everything. . . .

DORN (*hums*). " Tell her, my flowers."

(*Enter* SHAMRAEV, *and after him* POLINA ANDREYEVNA.)

SHAMRAEV. Here they are ! Good morning ! (*kisses* MADAME ARKADIN'S *hand and then* NINA'S). Delighted to see you in good health. (*To* MADAME ARKADIN) My wife tells me that you are proposing to drive into town with her to-day. Is that so ?

MADAME ARKADIN. Yes, we are thinking of it

SHAMRAEV. Hm ! that's splendid, but how are you going, honoured lady ? They are carting the rye to-day ; all the men are at work. What horses are you to have, allow me to ask ?

MADAME ARKADIN. What horses ? How can I tell which ?

SORIN. We've got carriage horses.

SHAMRAEV (*growing excited*). Carriage horses ! But where am I to get collars for them ? Where am I to get collars ? It's a strange thing ! It passes my understanding ! Honoured lady ! forgive me, I am full of reverence for your talent. I 'would give ten years of my life for you, but I cannot let you have the horses !

MADAME ARKADIN. But if I have to go ! It's a queer thing !

SHAMRAEV. Honoured lady ! you don't know what farming means.

MADAME ARKADIN (*flaring up*). That's the old story ! If that's so, I go back to Moscow to-day.

372

Give orders for horses to be hired for me at the village, or I'll walk to the station.

SHAMRAEV (*flaring up*). In that case I resign my position ! You must look for another steward (*goes off*).

MADAME ARKADIN. It's like this every summer; every summer I am insulted here ! I won't set my foot in the place again (*goes off at left where the bathing shed is supposed to be ; a minute later she can be seen entering the house.* TRIGORIN *follows her, carrying fishing rods and tackle, and a pail*).

SORIN (*flaring up*). This is insolence ! It's beyond everything. I am thoroughly sick of it. Send all the horses here this minute !

NINA (*to* POLINA ANDREYEVNA). To refuse Irina Nikolayevna, the famous actress ! Any wish of hers, any whim even, is of more consequence than all your farming. It's positively incredible !

POLINA (*in despair*). What can I do? Put yourself in my position : what can I do ?

SORIN (*to* NINA). Let us go to my sister. We will all entreat her not to go away. Won't we ? (*Looking in the direction in which* SHAMRAEV *has gone*) Insufferable man ! Despot !

NINA (*preventing him from getting up*). Sit still, sit still. We will wheel you in. (*She and* MED-VEDENKO *push the bath-chair.*) Oh, how awful it is !

SORIN. Yes, yes, it's awful. But he won't leave, I'll speak to him directly. (*They go out ;* DORN *and* POLINA ANDREYEVNA *are left alone on the stage.*)

DORN. People are tiresome. Your husband ought to be simply kicked out, but it will end in that old woman Pyotr Nikolayevitch and his sister begging the man's pardon. You will see !

POLINA. He has sent the carriage horses into the fields too ! And there are misunderstandings like this every day. If you only knew how it upsets me ! It makes me ill ; see how I am trembling . . . . I can't endure his rudeness. (*In an imploring voice*) Yevgeny, dearest, light of my eyes, my darling, let me come to you. . . . Our time is passing, we are no longer young, and if only we could lay aside concealment and lying for the end of our lives, anyway . . . (*a pause*).

DORN. I am fifty-five ; it's too late to change my life.

POLINA. I know you refuse me because there are other women too who are as near to you. You can't take them all to live with you. I understand. Forgive me, you are tired of me.

(NINA *appears near the house ; she is picking flowers.*)

DORN. No, it's all right.

POLINA. I am wretched from jealousy. Of course you are a doctor, you can't avoid women. I understand.

DORN (*to* NINA, *who comes up to them*). How are things going ?

NINA. Irina Nikolayevna is crying and Pyotr Nikolayevitch has an attack of asthma.

DORN (*gets up*). I'd better go and give them both valerian drops.

NINA (*gives him the flowers*). Please take these

DORN. *Merci bien* (*goes towards the house*).

POLINA (*going with him*). What charming flowers! (*Near the house, in a smothered voice*) Give me those flowers! Give me those flowers! (*on receiving them tears the flowers to pieces and throws them away; both go into the house*).

NINA (*alone*). How strange it is to see a famous actress cry, and about such a trivial thing! And isn't it strange? A famous author, adored by the public, written about in all the papers, his photographs for sale, his works translated into foreign languages—and he spends the whole day fishing and is delighted that he has caught two gudgeon. I thought famous people were proud, unapproachable, that they despised the crowd, and by their fame and the glory of their name, as it were, revenged themselves on the vulgar herd for putting rank and wealth above everything. But here they cry and fish, play cards, laugh and get cross like everyone else!

TREPLEV (*comes in without a hat on, with a gun and a dead sea-gull*). Are you alone here?

NINA. Yes.

(TREPLEV *lays the sea-gull at her feet.*)

NINA. What does that mean?

TREPLEV. I was so mean as to kill this bird to-day. I lay it at your feet.

NINA. What is the matter with you? (*picks up the bird and looks at it*).

TREPLEV (*after a pause*). Soon I shall kill myself in the same way.

NINA. You have so changed, I hardly know you.

TREPLEV. Yes, ever since the day when I hardly

375

knew you. You have changed to me, your eyes are cold, you feel me in the way.

NINA. You have become irritable of late, you express yourself so incomprehensibly, as it were in symbols. This bird is a symbol too, I suppose, but forgive me, I don't understand it (*lays the sea-gull on the seat*). I am too simple to understand you.

TREPLEV. This began from that evening when my play came to grief so stupidly. Women never forgive failure. I have burnt it all; every scrap of it. If only you knew how miserable I am! Your growing cold to me is awful, incredible, as though I had woken up and found this lake had suddenly dried up or sunk into the earth. You have just said that you are too simple to understand me. Oh, what is there to understand? My play was not liked, you despise my inspiration, you already consider me commonplace, insignificant, like so many others . . . (*stamping*). How well I understand it all, how I understand it! I feel as though I had a nail in my brain, damnation take it together with my vanity which is sucking away my life, sucking it like a snake . . . (*sees* TRIGORIN, *who comes in reading a book*). Here comes the real genius, walking like Hamlet and with a book too. (*Mimics*) " Words, words, words." . . . The sun has scarcely reached you and you are smiling already, your eyes are melting in its rays. I won't be in your way (*goes off quickly*).

TRIGORIN (*making notes in his book*). Takes snuff and drinks vodka. Always in black. The schoolmaster is in love with her. . . .

mitte ivers

NINA. Good morning, Boris Alexeyevitch !

TRIGORIN. Good morning. Circumstances have turned out so unexpectedly that it seems we are setting off to-day. We are hardly likely to meet again. I am sorry. I don't often have the chance of meeting young girls, youthful and charming ; I have forgotten how one feels at eighteen or nineteen and can't picture it to myself, and so the young girls in my stories and novels are usually false. I should like to be in your shoes just for one hour to find out how you think, and altogether what sort of person you are.

NINA. And I should like to be in your shoes.

TRIGORIN. What for ?

NINA. To know what it feels like to be a famous, gifted author. What does it feel like to be famous ? How does it affect you, being famous ?

TRIGORIN. How ? Nohow, I believe. I have never thought about it. (*After a moment's thought*) It's one of two things : either you exaggerate my fame, or it never is felt at all.

NINA. But if you read about yourself in the newspapers ?

TRIGORIN. When they praise me I am pleased, and when they abuse me I feel out of humour for a day or two.

NINA. What a wonderful world ! If only you knew how I envy you ! How different people's lots in life are ! Some can scarcely get through their dull, obscure existence, they are all just like one another, they are all unhappy ; while others —you, for instance—you are one out of a million,

377

have an interesting life full of brightness and significance. You are happy.

TRIGORIN. I ? (*shrugging his shoulders*). Hm. . . . You talk of fame and happiness, of bright interesting life, but to me all those fine words, if you will forgive my saying so, are just like a sweetmeat which I never taste. You are very young and very good-natured.

NINA. Your life is splendid !

TRIGORIN. What is there particularly nice in it ? (*Looks at his watch*) I must go and write directly. Excuse me, I mustn't stay . . . (*laughs*). You have stepped on my favourite corn, as the saying is, and here I am beginning to get excited and a little cross. Let us talk though. We will talk about my splendid bright life. . . . Well, where shall we begin ? (*After thinking a little*) There are such things as fixed ideas, when a man thinks day and night for instance, of nothing but the moon. And I have just such a moon. I am haunted day and night by one persistent thought : I ought to be writing, I ought to be writing, I ought . . . I have scarcely finished one novel when, for some reason, I must begin writing another, then a third, after the third a fourth. I write incessantly, post haste, and I can't write in any other way. What is there splendid and bright in that, I ask you ? Oh, it's an absurd life ! Here I am with you ; I am excited, yet every moment I remember that my unfinished novel is waiting for me. Here I see a cloud that looks like a grand piano. I think that I must put into a story somewhere that a cloud sailed

by that looked like a grand piano. There is a
scent of heliotrope. I hurriedly make a note :
a sickly smell, a widow's flower, to be mentioned
in the description of a summer evening. I catch
up myself and you at every sentence, every word,
and make haste to put those sentences and words
away into my literary treasure-house—it may
come in useful ! When I finish work I race off
to the theatre or to fishing ; if only I could rest
in that and forget myself. But no, there's a new
subject rolling about in my head like a heavy
iron cannon ball, and I am drawn to my writing
table and must make haste again to go on writing
and writing. And it's always like that, always.
And I have no rest from myself, and I feel that
I am eating up my own life, and that for the sake
of the honey I give to someone in space I am
stripping the pollen from my best flowers, tearing
up the flowers themselves and trampling on their
roots. Don't you think I am mad ? Do my
friends and acquaintances treat me as though I
were sane ? " What are you writing ? What
are you giving us ? " It's the same thing again
and again, and it seems to me as though my
friends' notice, their praises, their enthusiasm—
that it's all a sham, that they are deceiving me
as an invalid and I am somehow afraid that they
will steal up to me from behind, snatch me and
carry me off and put me in a mad-house. And
in those years, the best years of my youth, when
I was beginning, my writing was unmixed torture.
A small writer, particularly when he is not
successful, seems to himself clumsy, awkward,

unnecessary; his nerves are strained and over-wrought. He can't resist hanging about people connected with literature and art, unrecognised and unnoticed by anyone, afraid to look anyone boldly in the face, like a passionate gambler without any money. I hadn't seen my reader, but for some reason I always imagined him hostile, and mistrustful. I was afraid of the public, it alarmed me, and when I had to produce my first play it always seemed to me that all the dark people felt hostile and all the fair ones were coldly indifferent. Oh, how awful it was! What agony it was!

NINA. But surely inspiration and the very process of creation give you moments of exalted happiness?

TRIGORIN. Yes. While I am writing I enjoy it. And I like reading my proofs, but . . . as soon as it is published I can't endure it, and I see that it is all wrong, a mistake, that it ought not to have been written at all, and I feel vexed and sick about it . . . (*laughing*). And the public reads it and says: "Yes, charming, clever. Charming, but very inferior to Tolstoy," or, "It's a fine thing, but Turgenev's ' Fathers and Children ' is finer." And it will be the same to my dying day, only charming and clever, charming and clever—and nothing more. And when I die my friends, passing by my tomb, will say, "Here lies Trigorin. He was a good writer, but inferior to Turgenev."

NINA. Forgive me, but I refuse to understand you. You are simply spoiled by success.

TRIGORIN. What success? I have never liked

myself; I dislike my own work. The worst of it is that I am in a sort of delirium, and often don't understand what I am writing. I love this water here, the trees, the sky. I feel nature, it arouses in me a passionate, irresistible desire to write. But I am not simply a landscape painter; I am also a citizen. I love my native country, my people; I feel that if I am a writer I am in duty bound to write of the people, of their sufferings, of their future, to talk about science and the rights of man and so on, and so on, and I write about everything. I am hurried and flustered, and on all sides they whip me up and are angry with me; I dash about from side to side like a fox beset by hounds. I see life and culture continually getting farther and farther away while I fall farther and farther behind like a peasant too late for the train; and what it comes to is that I feel I can only describe scenes and in everything else I am false to the marrow of my bones.

NINA. You are overworked and have not the leisure nor the desire to appreciate your own significance. You may be dissatisfied with yourself, but for others you are great and splendid! If I were a writer like you, I should give up my whole life to the common herd, but I should know that there could be no greater happiness for them than to rise to my level, and they would harness themselves to my chariot.

TRIGORIN. My chariot, what next! Am I an Agamemnon, or what? (*Both smile.*)

NINA. For such happiness as being a writer or an artist I would be ready to endure poverty,

381

disappointment, the dislike of those around me ; I would live in a garret and eat nothing but rye bread, I would suffer from being dissatisfied with myself, from recognising my own imperfections, but I should ask in return for fame . . . real, resounding fame. . . . (*covers her face with her hands*). It makes me dizzy. . . . Ough !

(*The voice of* MADAME ARKADIN *from the house.*)

MADAME ARKADIN. Boris Alexeyevitch !

TRIGORIN. They are calling for me. I suppose it's to pack. But I don't want to leave here. (*Looks round at the lake*) Just look how glorious it is ! It's splendid !

NINA. Do you see the house and garden on the other side of the lake ?

TRIGORIN. Yes.

NINA. That house was my dear mother's. I was born there. I have spent all my life beside this lake and I know every little islet on it.

TRIGORIN. It's very delightful here ! (*Seeing the sea-gull*) And what's this ?

NINA. A sea-gull. Konstantin Gavrilitch shot it.

TRIGORIN. A beautiful bird. Really, I don't want to go away. Try and persuade Irina Nikolayevna to stay (*makes a note in his book*).

NINA. What are you writing ?

TRIGORIN. Oh, I am only making a note. A subject struck me (*putting away the note-book*). A subject for a short story : a young girl, such as you, has lived all her life beside a lake ; she loves the lake like a sea-gull, and is as free and happy as a sea-gull. But a man comes by chance, sees her, and having nothing better to do, destroys her like that sea-gull here (*a pause*).

(MADAME ARKADIN *appears at the window.*)

MADAME ARKADIN. Boris Alexeyevitch, where are you?

TRIGORIN. I am coming (*goes and looks back at* NINA. *To* MADAME ARKADIN *at the window*) What is it?

MADAME ARKADIN. We are staying.

(TRIGORIN *goes into the house.*)

NINA (*advances to the footlights; after a few moments' meditation*) It's a dream!

CURTAIN

ACT III

The dining-room in SORIN'S *house. Doors on right and on left. A sideboard. A medicine cupboard. A table in the middle of the room. A portmanteau and hat-boxes ; signs of preparation for departure.* TRIGORIN *is having lunch ;* MASHA *stands by the table.*

MASHA. I tell all this to you as a writer. You may make use of it. I am telling you the truth : if he had hurt himself seriously I would not have gone on living another minute. But I have pluck enough all the same. I just made up my mind that I would tear this love out of my heart, tear it out by the roots.

TRIGORIN. How are you going to do that ?

MASHA. I am going to be married. To Medvedenko.

TRIGORIN. That's the schoolmaster ?

MASHA. Yes.

TRIGORIN. I don't understand what's the object of it.

MASHA. To love without hope, to spend whole years waiting for something. . . . But when I marry, there will be no time left for love, new cares will smother all the old feelings. And, anyway, it will be a change, you know. Shall we have another ?

TRIGORIN. Won't that be too much ?

MASHA. Oh, come ! (*fills two glasses*). Don't look at me like that ! Women drink much oftener than you imagine. Only a small proportion drink openly as I do, the majority drink in secret. Yes. And it's always vodka or brandy. (*Clinks glasses*) My best wishes ! You are a good-hearted man ; I am sorry to be parting from you. (*They drink.*)

TRIGORIN. I don't want to go myself.

MASHA. You should beg her to stay.

TRIGORIN. No, she won't stay now. Her son is behaving very tactlessly. First he shoots himself, and now they say he is going to challenge me to a duel. And whatever for ? He sulks, and snorts, and preaches new forms of art. . . . But there is room for all—new and old—why quarrel about it ?

MASHA. Well, there's jealousy too. But it is nothing to do with me.

> (*A pause.* YAKOV *crosses from right to left with a portmanteau.* NINA *enters and stands by the window.*)

MASHA. My schoolmaster is not very brilliant, but he is a good-natured man, and poor, and he is very much in love with me. I am sorry for him. And I am sorry for his old mother. Well, let me wish you all happiness. Don't remember evil against me (*shakes hands with him warmly*). I am very grateful for your friendly interest. Send me your books and be sure to put in an inscription. Only don't write, " To my honoured friend," but write simply, " To Marya who belongs

nowhere and has no object in life." Good-bye !
(*goes out*).

NINA (*stretching out her arm towards* TRIGORIN,
with her fist clenched). Odd or even ?

TRIGORIN. Even.

NINA (*with a sigh*). Wrong. I had only one
pea in my hand. I was trying my fortune whether
to go on the stage or not. I wish someone would
advise me.

TRIGORIN. It's impossible to advise in such a
matter (*a pause*).

NINA. We are parting and . . . perhaps we
shall never meet again. Won't you please take
this little medallion as a parting gift ? I had
your initials engraved on one side of it . . . and
on the other the title of your book, " Days
and Nights."

TRIGORIN. How exquisite ! (*kisses the medallion*).
A charming present !

NINA. Think of me sometimes.

TRIGORIN. I shall think of you. I shall think
of you as you were on that sunny day—do you
remember ?—a week ago, when you were wearing
a light dress . . . we were talking . . . there was
a white sea-gull lying on the seat.

NINA (*pensively*). Yes, a sea-gull . . . (*a pause*).
We can't talk any more, there's someone coming.
. . . Let me have two minutes before you go,
I entreat you . . . (*goes out on the left*).

(*At the same instant* MADAME ARKADIN,
SORIN *in a dress coat with a star of some
order on it, then* YAKOV, *occupied with
the luggage, enter on the right.*)

386

MADAME ARKADIN. Stay at home, old man. With your rheumatism you ought not to go gadding about. (*To* TRIGORIN) Who was that went out ? Nina ?

TRIGORIN. Yes.

MADAME ARKADIN. *Pardon*, we interrupted you (*sits down*). I believe I have packed everything. I am worn out.

TRIGORIN (*reads on the medallion*). " ' Days and Nights,' page 121, lines 11 and 12."

YAKOV (*clearing the table*). Am I to pack your fishing things too, sir ?

TRIGORIN. Yes, I shall want them again. You can give away the hooks.

YAKOV. Yes, sir.

TRIGORIN (*to himself*). Page 121, lines 11 and 12. What is there in those lines ? (*To* MADAME ARKADIN) Are there copies of my books in the house ?

MADAME ARKADIN. Yes, in my brother's study, in the corner bookcase.

TRIGORIN. Page 121 . . . (*goes out*).

MADAME ARKADIN. Really, Petrusha, you had better stay at home.

SORIN. You are going away ; it will be dreary for me at home without you.

MADAME ARKADIN. And what is there in the town ?

SORIN. Nothing particular, but still . . . (*laughs*). There will be the laying of the foundation-stone of the Zemstvo hall, and all that sort of thing. One longs to shake oneself free from this stagnant existence, if only for an hour or two. I've been too long on the shelf like some old cigarette-holder. I have ordered the horses for one o'clock; we'll set off at the same time.

MADAME ARKADIN (*after a pause*). Come, stay here, don't be bored and don't catch cold. Look after my son. Take care of him. Give him good advice (*a pause*). Here I am going away and I shall never know why Konstantin tried to shoot himself. I fancy jealousy was the chief cause, and the sooner I get Trigorin away from here, the better.

SORIN. What can I say? There were other reasons too. It's easy to understand; he is young, intelligent, living in the country, in the wilds, with no money, no position and no future. He has nothing to do. He is ashamed of his idleness and afraid of it. I am very fond of him indeed, and he is attached to me, yet in spite of it all he feels he is superfluous in the house, that he is a dependant, a poor relation. It's easy to understand, it's *amour propre*. . . .

MADAME ARKADIN. He is a great anxiety to me! (*Pondering*) He might go into the service, perhaps.

SORIN (*begins to whistle, then irresolutely*). I think that quite the best thing would be if you were to . . . let him have a little money. In the first place he ought to be able to be dressed like other people and all that. Just look at him, he's been going about in the same wretched jacket for the last three years and he has no overcoat . . . (*laughs*). It would do him no harm to have a

388

little fun . . . to go abroad or something. . . . It wouldn't cost much.

MADAME ARKADIN. But all the same . . . I might manage the suit, perhaps, but as for going abroad . . . No, just at the moment I can't even manage the suit. (*Resolutely*) I have no money!
(SORIN *laughs*.)

MADAME ARKADIN. No!

SORIN (*begins to whistle*). Quite so. Forgive me, my dear, don't be cross. I believe you. . . . You are a generous, noble-hearted woman.

MADAME ARKADIN (*weeping*). I have no money.

SORIN. If I had money, of course I would give him some myself, but I have nothing, not a halfpenny (*laughs*). My steward takes all my pension and spends it all on the land and the cattle and the bees, and my money is all wasted. The bees die, and the cows die, they never let me have horses. . . .

MADAME ARKADIN. Yes, I have money, but you see I am an actress; my dresses alone are enough to ruin me.

SORIN. You are a kind, good creature . . . I respect you. . . . Yes . . . but there, I got a touch of it again . . . (*staggers*). I feel dizzy (*clutches at the table*). I feel ill and all that.

MADAME ARKADIN (*alarmed*). Petrusha! (*trying to support him*). Petrusha, my dear! (*Calling*) Help! help!

    (*Enter* TREPLEV *with a bandage round his head and* MEDVEDENKO.)

MADAME ARKADIN. He feels faint!

SORIN. It's all right, it's all right ! (*smiles and drinks some water*). It's passed off . . . and all that.

TREPLEV (*to his mother*). Don't be frightened, mother, it's not serious. Uncle often has these attacks now. (*To his uncle*) You must lie down, uncle.

SORIN. For a little while, yes. . . . But I am going to the town all the same. . . . I'll lie down a little and then set off. . . . It's quite natural (*goes out leaning on his stick*).

MEDVEDENKO (*gives him his arm*). There's a riddle : in the morning on four legs, at noon on two, in the evening on three. . . .

SORIN (*laughs*). Just so. And at night on the back. Thank you, I can manage alone. . . .

MEDVEDENKO. Oh come, why stand on ceremony ! (*goes out with* SORIN).

MADAME ARKADIN. How he frightened me !

TREPLEV. It is not good for him to live in the country. He gets depressed. If you would be generous for once, mother, and lend him fifteen hundred or two thousand roubles, he could spend a whole year in town.

MADAME ARKADIN. I have no money. I am an actress, not a banker (*a pause*).

TREPLEV. Mother, change my bandage. You do it so well.

MADAME ARKADIN (*takes out of the medicine cupboard some iodoform and a box with bandaging material*). The doctor is late.

TREPLEV. He promised to be here at ten, and it is midday already.

MADAME ARKADIN. Sit down (*takes the band-*

390

age off his head). It's like a turban. Yesterday
a stranger asked in the kitchen what nationality
you were. But you have almost completely healed.
There is the merest trifle left (*kisses him on the
head*). You won't do anything naughty again
while I am away, will you ?

TREPLEV. No, mother. It was a moment of
mad despair when I could not control myself.
It won't happen again. (*Kisses her hand*) You
have such clever hands. I remember, long ago,
when you were still acting at the Imperial Theatre
—I was little then—there was a fight in our yard
and a washerwoman, one of the tenants, was
badly beaten. Do you remember ? She was
picked up senseless . . . you looked after her, took
her remedies and washed her children in a tub.
Don't you remember ?

MADAME ARKADIN. No (*puts on a fresh
bandage*).

TREPLEV. Two ballet dancers lived in the same
house as we did at the time. . . . They used to
come to you and have coffee. . . .

MADAME ARKADIN. I remember that.

TREPLEV. They were very pious (*a pause*).
Just lately, these last days, I have loved you as
tenderly and completely as when I was a child.
I have no one left now but you. Only why, why
do you give yourself up to the influence of that
man ?

MADAME ARKADIN. You don't understand him,
Konstantin. He is a very noble character. . . .

TREPLEV. And yet when he was told I was
going to challenge him, the nobility of his character

did not prevent him from funking it. He is going away. Ignominious flight!

MADAME ARKADIN. What nonsense! It is I who am asking him to go.

TREPLEV. A very noble character! Here you and I are almost quarrelling over him, and at this very moment he is somewhere in the drawing-room or the garden laughing at us . . . developing Nina, trying to convince her finally that he is a genius.

MADAME ARKADIN. You take a pleasure in saying unpleasant things to me. I respect that man and beg you not to speak ill of him before me,

TREPLEV. And I don't respect him. You want me to think him a genius too, but forgive me, I can't tell lies, his books make me sick.

MADAME ARKADIN. That's envy. There's nothing left for people who have pretension without talent but to attack real talent. Much comfort in that, I must say!

TREPLEV (*ironically*). Real talent! (*Wrathfully*) I have more talent than all of you put together if it comes to that! (*tears the bandage off his head*). You, with your hackneyed conventions, have usurped the supremacy in art and consider nothing real and legitimate but what you do yourselves; everything else you stifle and suppress. I don't believe in you! I don't believe in you or in him!

MADAME ARKADIN. Decadent!

TREPLEV. Get away to your charming theatre and act there in your paltry, stupid plays!

MADAME ARKADIN. I have never acted in such

plays. Let me alone ! You are not capable of writing even a wretched burlesque ! You are nothing but a Kiev shopman ! living on other people !

TREPLEV. You miser !

MADAME ARKADIN. You ragged beggar !

(TREPLEV *sits down and weeps quietly*.)

MADAME ARKADIN. Nonentity ! (*walking up and down in agitation*). Don't, cry. . . . You mustn't cry (*weeps*). Don't . . . (*kisses him on the forehead, on the cheeks and on the head*). My dear child, forgive me. . . . Forgive your sinful mother. Forgive me, you know I am wretched.

TREPLEV (*puts his arms round her*). If only you knew ! I have lost everything ! She does not love me, and now I cannot write . . . all my hopes are gone. . . .

MADAME ARKADIN. Don't despair . . . Everything will come right. He is going away directly, she will love you again (*wipes away his tears*). Give over. We have made it up now.

TREPLEV (*kisses her hands*). Yes, mother.

MADAME ARKADIN (*tenderly*). Make it up with him too. You don't want a duel, do you ?

TREPLEV. Very well. Only, mother, do allow me not to meet him. It's painful to me—it's more than I can bear. (*Enter* TRIGORIN.) Here he is . . . I am going . . . (*rapidly puts away the dressings in the cupboard*). The doctor will do the bandaging now.

TRIGORIN (*looking in a book*). Page 121 . . . lines 11 and 12. Here it is. (*Reads*) " If ever my life can be of use to you, come and take it."

(TREPLEV *picks up the bandage from the floor and goes out*.)

MADAME ARKADIN (*looking at her watch*). The horses will soon be here.

TRIGORIN (*to himself*). "If ever my life can be of use to you, come and take it."

MADAME ARKADIN. I hope all your things are packed?

TRIGORIN (*impatiently*). Yes, yes. (*Musing*) Why is it that I feel so much sorrow in that appeal from a pure soul and that it wrings my heart so painfully? "If ever my life can be of use to you, come and take it." (*To* MADAME ARKADIN) Let us stay one day longer.

(MADAME ARKADIN *shakes her head.*)

TRIGORIN. Let us stay!

MADAME ARKADIN. Darling, I know what keeps you here. But have control over yourself. You are a little intoxicated, try to be sober.

TRIGORIN. You be sober too, be sensible and reasonable, I implore you ; look at it all as a true friend should. (*Presses her hand*) You are capable of sacrifice. Be a friend to me, let me be free !

MADAME ARKADIN (*in violent agitation*). Are you so enthralled?

TRIGORIN. I am drawn to her ! Perhaps it is just what I need.

MADAME ARKADIN. The love of a provincial girl? Oh, how little you know yourself !

TRIGORIN. Sometimes people sleep as they walk—that's how it is with me, I am talking to you and yet I am asleep and dreaming of her. . . . I am possessed by sweet, marvellous dreams. . . . Let me be free. . . .

MADAME ARKADIN (*trembling*). No, no ! I am

an ordinary woman, you can't talk like that to me.
Don't torture me, Boris. It terrifies me.

TRIGORIN. If you cared to, you could be not
ordinary. Love—youthful, charming, poetical,
lifting one into a world of dreams—that's the only
thing in life that can give happiness ! I have never
yet known a love like that. . . . In my youth
I never had time, I was always hanging about
the editors' offices, struggling with want. Now
it is here, that love, it has come, it beckons to me.
What sense is there in running away from it ?

MADAME ARKADIN (*wrathfully*). You have gone
mad !

TRIGORIN. Well, let me ?

MADAME ARKADIN. You are all in a conspiracy
together to torment me to-day ! (*weeps*).

TRIGORIN (*clutching at his heart*). She does not
understand ! She won't understand !·

MADAME ARKADIN. Am I so old and ugly that
you don't mind talking of other women to me ?
(*puts her arms round him and kisses him*). Oh,
you are mad ! My wonderful, splendid darling.
. . . You are the last page of my life ! (*falls on her
knees*). My joy, my pride, my bliss ! . . . (*embraces
his knees*). If you forsake me even for one hour I
shall not survive it, I shall go mad, my marvellous,
magnificent one, my master. . . .

TRIGORIN. Someone may come in (*helps her to
get up*).

MADAME ARKADIN. Let them, I am not ashamed
of my love for you (*kisses his hands*). My
treasure, you desperate boy, you want to be mad,
but I won't have it, I won't let you . . . (*laughs*).

395

You are mine . . . mine. . . . This forehead is mine, and these eyes, and this lovely silky hair is mine too . . . you are mine all over. You are so gifted, so clever, the best of all modern writers, you are the one hope of Russia. . . . You have so much truthfulness, simplicity, freshness, healthy humour. . . . In one touch you can give all the essential characteristics of a person or a landscape, your characters are living. One can't read you without delight ! You think this is exaggerated ? That I am flattering you? But look into my eyes . . . look. . . . Do I look like a liar ? You see, I am the only one who can appreciate you ; I am the only one who tells you the truth, my precious, wonderful darling. . . . Are you coming ? Yes ? You won't abandon me ? . . .

TRIGORIN. I have no will of my own . . . I have never had a will of my own. . . . Flabby, feeble, always submissive—how can a woman care for such a man ? Take me, carry me off, but don't let me move a step away from you. . . .

MADAME ARKADIN (*to herself*). Now he is mine ! (*In an easy tone as though nothing had happened*) But, of course, if you like, you can stay. I'll go by myself and you can come afterwards, a week later. After all, why should you be in a hurry ?

TRIGORIN. No, we may as well go together.

MADAME ARKADIN. As you please. Let us go together then (*a pause*).

(TRIGORIN *makes a note.*)

MADAME ARKADIN. What are you writing ?

TRIGORIN. I heard a good name this morning,

" The Maiden's Forest." It may be of use (*stretches*). So we are to go then ? Again there will be railway carriages, stations, refreshment bars, mutton chops, conversations. . . .

SHAMRAEV (*enters*). I have the honour to announce, with regret, that the horses are ready. It's time, honoured lady, to set off for the station ; the train comes in at five minutes past two. So please do me a favour, Irina Nikolaevna, do not forget to inquire what has become of the actor Suzdaltsev. Is he alive and well ? We used to drink together at one time. . . . In " The Plundered Mail " he used to play incomparably . . . I remember the tragedian Izmaïlov, also a remarkable personality, acted with him in Elisavetograd. . . . Don't be in a hurry, honoured lady, you need not start for five minutes. Once they were acting conspirators in a melodrama and when they were suddenly discovered Izmaïlov had to say, " We are caught in a trap," but he said, " We are caught in a tap ! " (*Laughs*) A tap !

> (*While he is speaking* YAKOV *is busy looking after the luggage. The maid brings* MADAME ARKADIN *her hat, her coat, her umbrella and her gloves ; they all help* MADAME ARKADIN *to put on her things. The man-cook looks in at the door on left and after some hesitation comes in. Enter* POLINA ANDREYEVNA, *then* SORIN *and* MEDVEDENKO.)

POLINA (*with a basket*). Here are some plums for the journey. . . . Very sweet ones. You may be glad to have something nice. . . .

MADAME ARKADIN. You are very kind, Polina Andreyevna.

POLINA. Good-bye, my dear ! If anything has not been to your liking, forgive it (*weeps*).

MADAME ARKADIN (*embraces her*). Everything has been nice, everything ! But you mustn't cry.

POLINA. The time flies so fast !

MADAME ARKADIN. There's no help for it.

SORIN (*in a great-coat with a cape to it, with his hat on and a stick in his hand, enters from door on left, crossing the stage*). Sister, it's time to start, or you may be too late after all. I am going to get into the carriage (*goes out*).

MEDVEDENKO. And I shall walk to the station . . . to see you off. I'll be there in no time . . . (*goes out*).

MADAME ARKADIN. Good-bye, dear friends. . . . If we are all alive and well, we shall meet again next summer. (*The maid, the cook and* YAKOV *kiss her hand.*) Don't forget me. (*Gives the cook a rouble*) Here's a rouble for the three of you.

THE COOK. We humbly thank you, madam ! Good journey to you ! We are very grateful for your kindness !

YAKOV. May God give you good luck !

SHAMRAEV. You might rejoice our hearts with a letter ! Good-bye, Boris Alexeyevitch !

MADAME ARKADIN. Where is Konstantin ? Tell him that I am starting ; I must say good-bye. Well, don't remember evil against me. (*To* YAKOV) I gave the cook a rouble. It's for the three of you.

(*All go out on right. The stage is empty.*

398

Behind the scenes the noise that is usual when people are being seen off. The maid comes back to fetch the basket of plums from the table and goes out again.)

TRIGORIN (*coming back*). I have forgotten my stick. I believe it is out there, on the verandah (*goes and, at door on left, meets* NINA *who is coming in*). Is that you? We are going. . . .

NINA. I felt that we should see each other once more. (*Excitedly*) Boris Alexeyevitch, I have come to a decision, the die is cast, I am going on the stage. I shall be gone from here to-morrow; I am leaving my father, I am abandoning everything, I am beginning a new life. Like you, I am going . . . to Moscow. We shall meet there.

TRIGORIN (*looking round*). Stay at the " Slavyansky Bazaar " . . . Let me know at once . . . Molchanovka, Groholsky House. . . . I am in a hurry . . . (*a pause*).

NINA. One minute more. . . .

TRIGORIN (*in an undertone*). You are so lovely. . . . Oh, what happiness to think that we shall see each other soon! (*She sinks on his breast.*) I shall see again those wonderful eyes, that inexpressibly beautiful tender smile . . . those soft features, the expression of angelic purity. . . . My darling . . . (*a prolonged kiss*).

CURTAIN

(Between the Third and Fourth Acts there is an interval of two years.)

ACT IV

One of the drawing-rooms in SORIN'S *house, which
has been turned into a study for* KONSTANTIN
TREPLEV. *On the right and left, doors leading
to inner apartments. In the middle, glass
door leading on to the verandah. Besides the
usual drawing-room furniture there is, in
corner on right, a writing-table, near door on
left, a sofa, a bookcase and books in windows
and on the chairs. Evening. There is a single
lamp alight with a shade on it. It is half
dark. There is the sound of the trees rustling,
and the wind howling in the chimney. A
watchman is tapping. Enter* MEDVEDENKO
and MASHA.

MASHA (*calling*). Konstantin Gavrilitch!
Konstantin Gavrilitch! (*Looking round*) No,
there is no one here. The old man keeps asking
every minute, where is Kostya, where is Kostya?
He cannot live without him. . . .

MEDVEDENKO. He is afraid of being alone.
(*Listening*) What awful weather! This is the
second day of it.

MASHA (*turns up the lamp*). There are waves
on the lake. Great big ones.

MEDVEDENKO. How dark it is in the garden!
We ought to have told them to break up that stage

400

in the garden. It stands as bare and ugly as a skeleton, and the curtain flaps in the wind. When I passed it yesterday evening, it seemed as though someone were crying in it.

MASHA. What next . . . (*a pause*).

MEDVEDENKO. Let us go home, Masha.

MASHA (*shakes her head*). I shall stay here for the night.

MEDVEDENKO (*in an imploring voice*). Masha, do come ! Our baby must be hungry.

MASHA. Nonsense. Matryona will feed him (*a pause*).

MEDVEDENKO. I am sorry for him. He has been three nights now without his mother.

MASHA. You are a bore. In old days you used at least to discuss general subjects, but now it is only home, baby, home, baby—that's all one can get out of you.

MEDVEDENKO. Come along, Masha !

MASHA. Go by yourself.

MEDVEDENKO. Your father won't let me have a horse.

MASHA. Yes, he will. You ask, and he will.

MEDVEDENKO. Very well, I'll ask. Then you will come to-morrow ?

MASHA (*taking a pinch of snuff*). Very well, to-morrow. How you pester me.

> (*Enter* TREPLEV *and* POLINA ANDREYEVNA ; TREPLEV *brings in pillows and a quilt, and* POLINA ANDREYEVNA *sheets and pillow-cases ; they lay them on the sofa, then* TREPLEV *goes to his table and sits down.*)

MASHA. What's this for, mother ?

POLINA. Pyotr Nikolayevitch asked us to make a bed for him in Kostya's room.

MASHA. Let me do it (*makes the bed*).

POLINA (*sighing*).   Old people are like children (*goes up to the writing-table, and leaning on her elbow, looks at the manuscript ; a pause*).

MEDVEDENKO. Well, I am going then.   Good-bye, Masha (*kisses his wife's hand*).   Good-bye, mother (*tries to kiss his mother-in-law's hand*).

POLINA (*with vexation*).   Come, if you are going, go.

MEDVEDENKO. Good-bye, Konstantin Gavrilitch.

(TREPLEV *gives him his hand without speaking ;*
MEDVEDENKO *goes out.*)

POLINA (*looking at the MS.*).   No one would have guessed or thought that you would have become a real author, Kostya.   And now, thank God, they send you money from the magazines. (*Passes her hand over his hair.*) And you have grown good-looking too. . . . Dear, good Kostya, do be a little kinder to my Mashenka !

MASHA (*as she makes the bed*).   Leave him alone, mother.

POLINA (*to* TREPLEV).   She is a nice little thing (*a pause*).   A woman wants nothing, you know, Kostya, so long as you give her a kind look.   I know from myself.

(TREPLEV *gets up from the table and walks
away without speaking.*)

MASHA. Now you have made him angry.   What induced you to pester him ?

POLINA. I feel so sorry for you, Mashenka.

MASHA. Much use that is !

POLINA. My heart aches for you. I see it all, you know, I understand it all.

MASHA. It's all foolishness. There is no such thing as hopeless love except in novels. It's of no consequence. The only thing is one mustn't let oneself go and keep expecting something, waiting for the tide to turn. . . . When love gets into the heart there is nothing to be done but to clear it out. Here they promised to transfer my husband to another district. As soon as I am there, I shall forget it all . . . I shall tear it out of my heart.

(*Two rooms away a melancholy waltz is played.*)

POLINA. That's Kostya playing. He must be depressed.

MASHA (*noiselessly dances a few waltz steps*). The great thing, mother, is not to have him before one's eyes. If they only give my Semyon his transfer, trust me, I shall get over it in a month. It's all nonsense.

(*Door on left opens.* DORN *and* MEDVEDENKO *wheel in* SORIN *in his chair.*)

MEDVEDENKO. I have six of them at home now. And flour is two kopeks per pound.

DORN. You've got to look sharp to make both ends meet.

MEDVEDENKO. It's all very well for you to laugh. You've got more money than you know what to do with.

DORN. Money ? After thirty years of practice, my boy, troublesome work during which I could not call my soul my own by day or by night, I only succeeded in saving two thousand roubles, and that I spent not long ago abroad. I have nothing.

MASHA (*to her husband*). You have not gone?

MEDVEDENKO (*guiltily*). Well, how can I when they won't let me have a horse?

MASHA (*with bitter vexation in an undertone*). I can't bear the sight of you.

> (*The wheel-chair remains in the left half of the room;* POLINA ANDREYEVNA, MASHA *and* DORN *sit down beside it,* MEDVEDENKO *moves mournfully to one side.*)

DORN. What changes there have been here! The drawing-room has been turned into a study.

MASHA. It is more convenient for Konstantin Gavrilitch to work here. Whenever he likes, he can walk out into the garden and think there.

> (*A watchman taps.*)

SORIN. Where is my sister?

DORN. She has gone to the station to meet Trigorin. She will be back directly.

SORIN. Since you thought it necessary to send for my sister, I must be dangerously ill. (*After a silence*) It's a queer thing, I am dangerously ill and here they don't give me any medicines.

DORN. Well, what would you like to have? Valerian drops? Soda? Quinine?

SORIN. Ah, he is at his moralising again! What an infliction it is! (*With a motion of his head towards the sofa*) Is that bed for me?

POLINA. Yes, it's for you, Pyotr Nikolayevitch.

SORIN. Thank you.

DORN (*hums*). " The moon is floating in the midnight sky."

SORIN. I want to give Kostya a subject for a story. It ought to be called " The Man who Wished "—*L'homme qui a voulu*. In my youth I wanted to become a literary man—and didn't ; I wanted to speak well—and I spoke horribly badly, (*mimicking himself*) " and all the rest of it, and all that, and so on, and so forth " . . . and I would go plodding on and on, trying to sum up till I was in a regular perspiration ; I wanted to get married—and I didn't ; I always wanted to live in town and here I am ending my life in the country—and so on.

DORN. I wanted to become an actual civil councillor—and I have.

SORIN (*laughs*). That I had no hankerings after. That happened of itself.

DORN. To be expressing dissatisfaction with life at sixty-two is really ungracious, you know.

SORIN. What a persistent fellow he is ! You might understand that one wants to live !

DORN. That's just frivolity. It's the law of nature that every life must have an end.

SORIN. You argue like a man who has had enough. You are satisfied and so you are indifferent to life, nothing matters to you. But even you will be afraid to die.

DORN. The dread of death is an animal fear. One must overcome it. A rational fear of death is only possible for those who believe in eternal life and are conscious of their sins. And you, in the first place, don't believe, and, in the second, what sins have you to worry about? You have served in the courts of justice for twenty-five years—that's all.

SORIN (*laughs*). Twenty-eight. . . .

(TREPLEV *comes in and sits down on a stool at* SORIN'S *feet.* MASHA *never takes her eyes off him.*)

DORN. We are hindering Konstantin Gavrilitch from working.

TREPLEV. Oh no, it doesn't matter (*a pause*).

MEDVEDENKO. Allow me to ask you, doctor, what town did you like best abroad?

DORN. Genoa.

TREPLEV. Why Genoa?

DORN. The life in the streets is so wonderful there. When you go out of the hotel in the evening, the whole street is packed with people. You wander aimlessly zigzagging about among the crowd, backwards and forwards; you live with it, are psychologically at one with it and begin almost to believe that a world-soul is really possible, such as was acted by Nina Zaretchny in your play. And, by the way, where is she now? How is she getting on?

TREPLEV. I expect she is quite well.

DORN. I was told that she was leading a rather peculiar life. How was that?

TREPLEV. That's a long story, doctor.

DORN. Well, tell it us shortly (*a pause*).

TREPLEV. She ran away from home and had an affair with Trigorin. You know that?

DORN. I know.

TREPLEV. She had a child. The child died.

Trigorin got tired of her and went back to his old ties, as might have been expected. Though, indeed, he had never abandoned them, but in his weak-willed way contrived to keep both going. As far as I can make out from what I have heard, Nina's private life was a complete failure.

DORN. And the stage ?

TREPLEV. I fancy that was worse still. She made her début at some holiday place near Moscow, then went to the provinces. All that time I did not lose sight of her, and wherever she went I followed her. She always took big parts, but she acted crudely, without taste, screamingly, with violent gestures. There were moments when she uttered a cry successfully or died successfully, but they were only moments.

DORN. Then she really has some talent ?

TREPLEV. It was difficult to make it out. I suppose she has. I saw her but she would not see me, and the servants would not admit me at the hotel. I understood her state of mind and did not insist on seeing her (*a pause*). What more can I tell you ? Afterwards, when I was back at home, I had some letters from her— warm, intelligent, interesting letters. She did not complain, but I felt that she was profoundly unhappy ; every line betrayed sick overstrained nerves. And her imagination is a little unhinged. She signed herself the Sea-gull. In Pushkin's " Mermaid " the miller says that he is a raven, and in the same way in her letters she kept repeating that she was a sea-gull. Now she is here.

DORN. Here ? How do you mean ?

TREPLEV. In the town, staying at an inn. She has been there for five days. I did go to see her, and Marya Ilyinishna here went too, but she won't see anyone. Semyon Semyonitch declares he saw her yesterday afternoon in the fields a mile and a half from here.

MEDVEDENKO. Yes, I saw her. She went in that direction, towards the town. I bowed to her and asked her why she did not come to see us. She said she would come.

TREPLEV. She won't come (*a pause*). Her father and stepmother refuse to recognise her. They have put watchmen about so that she may not even go near the house (*walks away with the doctor towards the writing table*). How easy it is to be a philosopher on paper, doctor, and how difficult it is in life !

SORIN. She was a charming girl.

DORN. What ?

SORIN. She was a charming girl, I say. Actual Civil Councillor Sorin was positively in love with her for a time.

DORN. The old Lovelace.

(SHAMRAEV'S *laugh is heard.*)

POLINA. I fancy our people have come back from the station. . . .

TREPLEV. Yes, I hear mother.

(*Enter* MADAME ARKADIN, TRIGORIN *and with them* SHAMRAEV.)

SHAMRAEV (*as he enters*). We all grow old and dilapidated under the influence of the elements, while you, honoured lady, are still young . . . a light blouse, sprightliness, grace. . . .

MADAME ARKADIN. You want to bring me ill-luck again, you tiresome man !

TRIGORIN. How do you do, Pyotr Nikolayevitch ! So you are still poorly ? That's bad ! (*Seeing* MASHA, *joyfully*) Marya Ilyinishna !

MASHA. You know me, do you ? (*shakes hands*).

TRIGORIN. Married ?

MASHA. Long ago.

TRIGORIN. Are you happy ? (*Bows to* DORN *and* MEDVEDENKO, *then hesitatingly approaches* TREPLEV) Irina Nikolayevna has told me that you have forgotten the past and are no longer angry.

(TREPLEV *holds out his hand.*)

MADAME ARKADIN (*to her son*). Boris Alexeyevitch has brought the magazine with your new story in it.

TREPLEV (*taking the magazine, to* TRIGORIN). Thank you, you are very kind. (*They sit down.*)

TRIGORIN. Your admirers send their greetings to you. . . . In Petersburg and Moscow there is great interest in your work and I am continually being asked questions about you. People ask what you are like, how old you are, whether you are dark or fair. Everyone imagines, for some reason, that you are no longer young. And no one knows your real name, as you always publish under a pseudonym. You are as mysterious as the Iron Mask.

TREPLEV. Will you be able to make a long stay ?

TRIGORIN. No, I think I must go back to Moscow to-morrow. I am obliged to. I am in a hurry to finish my novel, and besides, I have promised something for a collection of tales that is being published. It's the old story, in fact.

> (*While they are talking* MADAME ARKADIN *and* POLINA ANDREYEVNA *put a card-table in the middle of the room and open it out.* SHAMRAEV *lights candles and sets chairs.* A game of loto is brought out of the cupboard.)

TRIGORIN. The weather has not given me a friendly welcome. There is a cruel wind. If it has dropped by to-morrow morning I shall go to the lake to fish. And I must have a look at the garden and that place where—you remember?—your play was acted. I've got a subject for a story, I only want to revive my recollections of the scene in which it is laid.

MASHA (*to her father*). Father, let my husband have a horse! He must get home.

SHAMRAEV (*mimicking*). Must get home—a horse! (*Sternly*) You can see for yourself: they have just been to the station. I can't send them out again.

MASHA. But there are other horses. (*Seeing that her father says nothing, waves her hand*) There's no doing anything with you.

MEDVEDENKO. I can walk, Masha. Really. . . .

POLINA (*with a sigh*). Walk in such weather . . . (*sits down to the card-table*). Come, friends.

MEDVEDENKO. It is only four miles. Good-bye (*kisses his wife's hand*). Good-bye, mother. (*His mother-in-law reluctantly holds out her hand for him to kiss.*) I wouldn't trouble anyone, but

410

the baby . . . (*bows to the company*).   Good-bye
. . . (*goes out with a guilty step*).

SHAMRAEV. He can walk right enough.   He's
not a general.

POLINA (*tapping on the table*).   Come, friends.
Don't let us waste time, we shall soon be called
to supper.

(SHAMRAEV, MASHA *and* DORN *sit down at
the table.*)

MADAME ARKADIN (*to* TRIGORIN).   When the
long autumn evenings come on, they play loto
here.   Look, it's the same old loto that we had
when our mother used to play with us, when we
were children.   Won't you have a game before
supper ? (*sits down to the table with* TRIGORIN).
It's a dull game, but it is not so bad when you are
used to it (*deals three cards to everyone*).

TREPLEV (*turning the pages of the magazine*).
He has read his own story, but he has not even
cut mine (*puts the magazine down on the writing-
table, then goes towards door on left ; as he passes
his mother he kisses her on the head*).

MADAME ARKADIN. And you, Kostya ?

TREPLEV. Excuse me, I would rather not . . .
I am going out (*goes out*).

MADAME ARKADIN. The stake is ten kopeks.
Put it down for me, doctor, will you ?

DORN. Right.

MASHA. Has everyone put down their stakes ?
I begin . . . Twenty-two.

MADAME ARKADIN. Yes.

MASHA. Three !

DORN. Right !

MASHA. Did you play three ?   Eight !   Eighty-one !   Ten !

SHAMRAEV. Don't be in a hurry !

MADAME ARKADIN. What a reception I had in Harkov ! My goodness ! I feel dizzy with it still.

MASHA. Thirty-four !

(*A melancholy waltz is played behind the scenes.*)

MADAME ARKADIN. The students gave me an ovation. . . . Three baskets of flowers . . . two wreaths and this, see (*unfastens a brooch on her throat and lays it on the table*).

SHAMRAEV. Yes, that is a thing. . . .

MASHA. Fifty !

DORN. Exactly fifty ?

MADAME ARKADIN. I had a wonderful dress. . . . Whatever I don't know, I do know how to dress.

POLINA. Kostya is playing the piano ; he is depressed, poor fellow.

SHAMRAEV. He is awfully abused in the news-papers.

MASHA. Seventy-seven !

MADAME ARKADIN. As though that mattered !

TRIGORIN. He never quite comes off.   He has not yet hit upon his own medium.   There is always something queer and vague, at times almost like delirium.   Not a single living character.

MASHA. Eleven !

MADAME ARKADIN (*looking round at* SORIN). Petrusha, are you bored ? (*a pause*).   He is asleep.

DORN. The actual civil councillor is asleep.

MASHA. Seven !   Ninety !

TRIGORIN. If I lived in such a place, beside a

412

lake, do you suppose I should write ? I should overcome this passion and should do nothing but fish.

MASHA. Twenty-eight !

TRIGORIN. Catching perch is so delightful !

DORN. Well, I believe in Konstantin Gavrilitch. There is something in him ! There is something in him ! He thinks in images ; his stories are vivid, full of colour and they affect me strongly. The only pity is that he has not got definite aims. He produces an impression and that's all, but you can't get far with nothing but an impression. Irina Nikolayevna, are you glad that your son is a writer ?

MADAME ARKADIN. Only fancy, I have not read anything of his yet. I never have time.

MASHA. Twenty-six !

(TREPLEV *comes in quietly and sits down at his table.*)

SHAMRAEV (*to* TRIGORIN). We have still got something here belonging to you, Boris Alexeyevitch.

TRIGORIN. What's that ?

SHAMRAEV. Konstantin Gavrilitch shot a seagull and you asked me to get it stuffed for you.

TRIGORIN. I don't remember ! (*Pondering*) I don't remember !

MASHA. Sixty-six ! One !

TREPLEV (*flinging open the window, listens*). How dark it is ! I don't know why I feel so uneasy.

MADAME ARKADIN. Kostya, shut the window, there's a draught.

(TREPLEV *shuts the window.*)

MASHA. Eighty-eight !

TRIGORIN. The game is mine !

MADAME ARKADIN (*gaily*). Bravo, bravo !

SHAMRAEV. Bravo !

MADAME ARKADIN. That man always has luck in everything (*gets up*). And now let us go and have something to eat. Our great man has not dined to-day. We will go on again after supper. (*To her son*) Kostya, leave your manuscripts and come to supper.

TREPLEV. I don't want any, mother, I am not hungry.

MADAME ARKADIN. As you like. (*Wakes* SORIN) Petrusha, supper ! (*Takes* SHAMRAEV'S *arm*) I'll tell you about my reception in Harkov.

(POLINA ANDREYEVNA *puts out the candles on the table. Then she and* DORN *wheel the chair. All go out by door on left; only* TREPLEV, *sitting at the writing-table, is left on the stage.*)

TREPLEV (*settling himself to write; runs through what he has written already*). I have talked so much about new forms and now I feel that little by little I am falling into a convention myself. (*Reads*) " The placard on the wall proclaimed. . . . The pale face in its setting of dark hair." Proclaimed, setting. That's stupid (*scratches out*). I will begin where the hero is awakened by the patter of the rain, and throw out all the rest. The description of the moonlight evening is long and over elaborate. Trigorin has worked out methods for himself, it's easy for him now. . . . With him

the broken bottle neck glitters on the dam and
the mill-wheel casts a black shadow—and there
you have the moonlight night, while I have the
tremulous light, and the soft twinkling of the
stars, and the far-away strains of the piano dying
away in the still fragrant air. . . . It's agonising
(*a pause*). I come more and more to the con-
viction that it is not a question of new and old
forms, but that what matters is that a man should
write without thinking about forms at all, write
because it springs freely from his soul. (*There
is a tap at the window nearest to the table*) What is
that ? (*looks out of window*). There is nothing to
be seen . . . (*opens the glass door and looks out
into the garden*). Someone ran down the steps.
(*Calls*) Who is there ? (*Goes out and can be heard
walking rapidly along the verandah ; returns half a
minute later with* NINA ZARETCHNY). Nina, Nina !
    (NINA *lays her head on his breast and weeps
with subdued sobs.*)

TREPLEV (*moved*). Nina ! Nina ! It's you . . .
you. . . . It's as though I had foreseen it, all day
long my heart has been aching and restless (*takes
off her hat and cape*). Oh, my sweet, my precious,
she has come at last ! Don't let us cry, don't let
us !

NINA. There is someone here.

TREPLEV. No one.

NINA. Lock the doors, someone may come in.

TREPLEV. No one will come in.

NINA. I know Irina Nikolayevna is here. Lock
the doors.

TREPLEV (*locks the door on right, goes to door*

on left). There is no lock on this one, I'll put a chair against it (*puts an armchair against the door*). Don't be afraid, no one will come.

NINA (*looking intently into his face*). Let me look at you. (*Looking round*) It's warm, it's nice. . . . In old days this was the drawing-room. Am I very much changed ?

TREPLEV. Yes. . . . You are thinner and your eyes are bigger. Nina, how strange it is that I should be seeing you. Why would not you let me see you ? Why haven't you come all this time ? I know you have been here almost a week. . . . I have been to you several times every day ; I stood under your window like a beggar.

NINA. I was afraid that you might hate me. I dream every night that you look at me and don't know me. If only you knew ! Ever since I came I have been walking here . . . by the lake. I have been near your house many times and could not bring myself to enter it. Let us sit down. (*They sit down.*) Let us sit down and talk and talk. It's nice here, it's warm and snug. Do you hear the wind ? There's a passage in Turgenev, " Well for the man on such a night who sits under the shelter of home, who has a warm corner in safety." I am a sea-gull. . . . No, that's not it (*rubs her forehead*). What was I saying ? Yes . . . Turgenev . . . " And the Lord help all homeless wanderers ! " . . . It doesn't matter (*sobs*).

TREPLEV. Nina, you are crying again. . . . Nina !

NINA. Never mind, it does me good . . . I haven't cried for two years. Yesterday, late in the evening, I came into the garden to see whether

416

our stage was still there. It is still standing.
I cried for the first time after two years and it
eased the weight on my heart and made it lighter.
You see, I am not crying now (*takes him by the
hand*). And so now you are an author. . . . You
are an author, I am an actress. . . . We too have
been drawn into the whirlpool. I lived joyously,
like a child—I woke up singing in the morning ;
I loved you and dreamed of fame, and now ?
Early to-morrow morning I must go to Yelets
third-class . . . with peasants, and at Yelets the
cultured tradesmen will pester me with attentions.
Life is a coarse business !

TREPLEV. Why to Yelets ?

NINA. I have taken an engagement for the whole
winter. It is time to go.

TREPLEV. Nina, I cursed you, I hated you,
I tore up your letters and photographs, but I was
conscious every minute that my soul is bound to
yours for ever. It's not in my power to leave off
loving you, Nina. Ever since I lost you and began
to get my work published my life has been unbearable—I am wretched. . . . My youth was, as
it were, torn away all at once and it seems to me
as though I have lived for ninety years already.
I call upon you, I kiss the earth on which you
have walked ; wherever I look I see your face,
that tender smile that lighted up the best days
of my life. . . .

NINA (*distractedly*). Why does he talk like this,
why does he talk like this ?

TREPLEV. I am alone in the world, warmed
by no affection. I am as cold as though I were

in a cellar, and everything I write is dry, hard and gloomy. Stay here, Nina, I entreat you, or let me go with you !

(NINA *rapidly puts on her hat and cape.*)

TREPLEV. Nina, why is this ? For God's sake, Nina ! (*looks at her as she puts her things on ; a pause*).

NINA. My horses are waiting at the gate. Don't see me off, I'll go alone. . . . (*Through her tears*) Give me some water. . . .

TREPLEV (*gives her some water*). Where are you going now ?

NINA. To the town (*a pause*). Is Irina Nikolayevna here ?

TREPLEV. Yes. . . . Uncle was taken worse on Thursday and we telegraphed for her.

NINA. Why do you say that you kissed the earth on which I walked ? I ought to be killed. (*Bends over the table*) I am so tired ! If I could rest . . . if I could rest ! (*Raising her head*) I am a sea-gull. . . . No, that's not it. I am an actress. Oh, well ! (*Hearing* MADAME ARKADIN *and* TRIGORIN *laughing, she listens, then runs to door on left and looks through the keyhole*). He is here too. . . . (*Turning back to* TREPLEV) Oh, well . . . it doesn't matter . . . no. . . . He did not believe in the stage, he always laughed at my dreams and little by little I left off believing in it too, and lost heart. . . . And then I was fretted by love and jealousy, and continually anxious over my little one. . . . I grew petty and trivial, I acted stupidly. . . . I did not know what to do with my arms, I did not know how to stand on the stage, could not control

418

ιny voice.   You can't understand what it feels like when one knows one is acting disgracefully.   I am a sea-gull.   No, that's not it. . . .   Do you remember you shot a sea-gull ?   A man came by chance, saw it and, just to pass the time, destroyed it. . . .   A subject for a short story. . . .   That's not it, though (*rubs her forehead*).   What was I saying ? . . .   I am talking of the stage.   Now I am not like that. I am a real actress, I act with enjoyment, with enthusiasm, I am intoxicated when I am on the stage and feel that I am splendid.   And since I have been here, I keep walking about and thinking, thinking and feeling that my soul is getting stronger every day.   Now I know, I understand, Kostya, that in our work—in acting or writing—what matters is not fame, not glory, not what I dreamed of, but knowing how to be patient.   To bear one's cross and have faith.   I have faith and it all doesn't hurt so much, and when I think of my vocation I am not afraid of life.

TREPLEV (*mournfully*).   You have found your path, you know which way you are going, but I am still floating in a chaos of dreams and images, not knowing what use it is to anyone.   I have no faith and don't know what my vocation is.

NINA (*listening*).   'Sh-sh . . . I am going.   Goodbye.   When I become a great actress, come and look at me.   Will you promise ?   But now . . . (*presses his hand*) it's late.   I can hardly stand on my feet. . . .   I am worn out and hungry. . . .

TREPLEV.   Stay, I'll give you some supper.

NINA.   No, no. . . .   Don't see me off, I will go by

myself. My horses are close by. . . . So she brought him with her? Well, it doesn't matter. When you see Trigorin, don't say anything to him. . . . I love him! I love him even more than before. . . . A subject for a short story . . . I love him, I love him passionately, I love him to despair. It was nice in old days, Kostya! Do you remember? How clear, warm, joyous and pure life was, what feelings we had—feelings like tender, exquisite flowers. . . . Do you remember? (*Recites*) " Men, lions, eagles, and partridges, horned deer, geese, spiders, silent fish that dwell in the water, star-fishes, and creatures which cannot be seen by the eye—all living things, all living things, all living things, have completed their cycle of sorrow, are extinct. . . . For thousands of years the earth has borne no living creature on its surface, and this poor moon lights its lamp in vain. On the meadow the cranes no longer waken with a cry and there is no sound of the May beetles in the lime trees . . ." (*impulsively embraces* TREPLEV *and runs out of the glass door*).

TREPLEV (*after a pause*). It will be a pity if someone meets her in the garden and tells mother. It may upset mother. . . .

(*He spends two minutes in tearing up all his manuscripts and throwing them under the table ; then unlocks the door on right and goes out.*)

DORN (*trying to open the door on left*). Strange. The door seems to be locked . . . (*comes in and puts the armchair in its place*). An obstacle race.

420

(*Enter* MADAME ARKADIN *and* POLINA ANDREYEVNA, *behind them* YAKOV *carrying a tray with bottles;* MASHA; *then* SHAMRAEV *and* TRIGORIN.)

MADAME ARKADIN. Put the claret and the beer for Boris Alexeyevitch here on the table. We will play as we drink it. Let us sit down, friends.

POLINA (*to* YAKOV). Bring tea too at the same time (*lights the candles and sits down to the card table*).

SHAMRAEV (*leads* TRIGORIN *to the cupboard*). Here's the thing I was speaking about just now (*takes the stuffed sea-gull from the cupboard*). This is what you ordered.

TRIGORIN (*looking at the sea-gull*). I don't remember it. (*Musing*) I don't remember.

(*The sound of a shot coming from right of stage; everyone starts.*)

MADAME ARKADIN (*frightened*). What's that?

DORN. That's nothing. It must be something in my medicine-chest that has gone off. Don't be anxious (*goes out at door on right, comes back in half a minute*). That's what it is. A bottle of ether has exploded. (*Hums*) "I stand before thee enchanted again. . . ."

MADAME ARKADIN (*sitting down to the table*). Ough, how frightened I was. It reminded me of how . . . (*hides her face in her hands*). It made me quite dizzy. . . .

DORN (*turning over the leaves of the magazine, to* TRIGORIN). There was an article in this two months ago—a letter from America—and I wanted to ask you, among other things (*puts his arm round*

TRIGORIN'S *waist and leads him to the footlights*) as I am very much interested in the question. . . . (*In a lower tone, dropping his voice*) Get Irina Nikolayevna away somehow. The fact is, Konstantin Gavrilitch has shot himself. . . .

CURTAIN

APPRECIATION

by

ARNOLD B. McMILLIN

Chekhov began his literary career, whilst still at school, with short humorous sketches and stories under various pen-names like Antosha Chekhonte, and he continued to use and develop the short prose narrative form throughout his life, even when, towards the end, drama and work with the Moscow Art Theatre were consuming the greater part of his time and energy. He was fond of comparing short story writing to a reliable and faithful wife, with the theatre as a cunning, albeit beautiful lover; and, indeed, if we study the development of his drama and the fate of his plays on the stages of St. Petersburg and Moscow we will see a strong contrast between the easily won success and popularity of the master of the short story, and the incomprehension and indignation that greeted the revolutionary and uncompromising dramatist. Even today Chekhov is best known in his own country as a short story writer, although in the West it is his contribution to the theatre that has established him as a major figure in European culture—possibly because the plays deal with less specific and more universal moods than the stories.

The first productions of his early plays were traumatic experiences for Chekhov, thanks to the incompetence of the actors, confused by the unfamiliar demands made on them, and the "atmosphere of incomprehension and ill-will" that prevailed in the theatres. Critics (whom Chekhov compared to gad-flies hindering the work of a plough-horse) were reluctant to see the plays as anything more than the aberration of a talented *raconteur,* whilst the audiences were perplexed by the undramatic "scenes from life," particularly as the actors themselves seem to have had little idea about how such plays should be approached. It was not until the formation of the Moscow Art Theatre by Stanislavsky and Nemirovich-Danchenko in 1898 that Chekhov had for the first time the opportunity of seeing the plays performed more or less according to his own ideas, rather than according to the prejudices of producers accustomed to "melodrama and meaningless histrionics"; in his letters Chekhov again and again praises the education, culture and sensibility of the Art Theatre actors.

But if we are fully to understand this enthusiasm for the Moscow Art Theatre we must look back to his earlier comments on the theatre and the state of the acting profession. In a letter of 1888, critising Leontyev's suggestion that the theatre ought to be a "school" in which to enlighten the public, he declared the public to be more elevated than the theatre which was supposed to be instructing it—"a world of senselessness and empty sounds." Of actors he writes: "They know neither landowners, priests, merchants nor civil servants. On the other hand, they are excellent when portraying billiard-scorers, kept women, hollow-cheeked card sharpers, and in general all those individuals that they can observe by chance as they totter between public houses and stag parties. Their ignorance is appalling . . ."

Against this background it is not difficult to see why Chekhov resolved to abandon the theatre after the first performance of *Ivanov,* a resolution that was repeated after the failure of *The Wood Demon* (later to become *Uncle Vanya*) and the catastrophic première of *The Seagull.* As late as 1900, when he had already estab-

426

lished a fruitful relationship with the Moscow Art Theatre, Chekhov wrote to Olga Knipper, the actress whom he was to marry in the following year: "I am abandoning the theatre . . . It is possible to write for the theatre in Germany, Switzerland, or even in Spain; anywhere except Russia, where actors are not respected, are kicked and trampled on and are forgiven neither success nor failure."

The "beautiful lover's" attraction was too strong, however, and it is largely thanks to Chekhov and Stanislavsky that this situation was changed, and the theatre raised from the lowly position into which it had been allowed to sink.

The relationship between Chekhov's stories and plays is a complicated one, and in both themes and construction they have several features in common; but whereas prose came to him very easily and his narrative talent was recognised almost immediately, the plays (apart from a few short vaudeville sketches at the end of the 1880s) were written slowly and with great difficulty. After successive fiascos Chekhov lamented the waste of subjects that could have been used for stories, and he did, actually, attempt to incorporate the themes of *The Wood Demon* in *Uncle Vanya*, which was originally envisaged as a story. In their apparently simple but actually highly polyphonic construction Chekhov's plays, particularly *The Seagull* and *The Three Sisters*, do in fact by their complexity remind one of a novelist's technique, although the characters' inner relationships are for the most part subtly masked by the seemingly prosaic and inconsequent nature of the dialogue.

The problem of creating a new dramatic form when the instruments of its presentation, the actors, were so ill-prepared discouraged but did not defeat Chekhov.

427

Unlike Ibsen, who, once his plays were written, abandoned them to the interpretation of producers and actors without further concerning himself, and unlike Turgenev, who made little effort even to get his plays performed, Chekhov took a vital interest in the theatre as such, both in its history and in its present-day problems and possibilities. Whilst Ibsen boasted that he did not need to read the work of other people to be fully in touch with the times, Chekhov was a voracious reader with an immense knowledge of classical and modern literature, especially drama in all its aspects. His interest extended from the broadest questions of historical development to the smallest details of staging, scenery and props.

Chekhov's interest in the theatre began at an early age, when as a boy he made friends with the actors of a local theatre, himself taking part in various humorous sketches and charades, and by the time he left school he had even completed three plays, which, however, have been lost. Not that his family upbringing was one calculated to foster an interest in the theatre, or, indeed, anything cultural. He was born on January 16th, 1860, in Taganrog, a small town near Rostov in Southern Russia. His father, Pavel, was the son of a freed serf who had been established in a grocery shop by his father, but whose interests lay elsewhere, principally in the church, where as choirmaster he could revel in the pomp and ceremony that meant so much to him and at the same time enjoy a modicum of kudos not offered by the grocery shop—particularly when his children performed as soloists after long hours of forced practice.

Described by Chekhov as "a mediocrity, a man of little ability," Pavel was as tyrannical at home as he was hypocritical and fawning in public, and his purely formal but fanatical attitude to religion was enough to turn Chekhov away from the church for the rest of his life.

Bringing his children up in an atmosphere of "despotism and lies," Pavel drove his two eldest sons to drink, and his wife to near despair; Anton himself seems to have come through these early experiences unscathed, but with a highly developed sensitivity to the feelings of other people. Thanks to being forced to work in the shop at night, he twice failed his exams and took two extra years over the school course, but in any case derived little pleasure from the rigorous formal rote-learning offered by most of his teachers.

We can perhaps draw some conclusions about his attitude to academic studies from the figures of Kuligin in *The Three Sisters* and of Serebryakov in *Uncle Vanya*, two of the most selfish characters of all that he created. When he still had three years to go at school his father's shop, after a period of ailing fortunes, thanks mainly to its proprietor's other, more glamorous interests, finally went bankrupt. The swift departure of Pavel, soon followed by his wife with the youngest children, to Moscow where they settled in a miserable slum left Anton penniless but free, at least, and it was during this period that his contacts with the Taganrog actors were formed, no doubt stimulating some of the ideas he was to develop in the future.

Thus left to support himself he engaged in various activities, including birdcatching, coaching younger school children, and editing a small humorous magazine for which he also wrote a few sketches and short stories, following the example of his elder brother Alexander, who had demonstrated this as a potential source of income. At this stage he had no thought of a literary career, and on leaving school in 1879 came to Moscow to enter the medical faculty at the university and to join his family, who, incidentally, had been enjoying some support from his humble earnings in Taganrog. Whilst studying there he continued to contribute to various comic papers of the time like Leykin's *Splinters,* or *The Dragon Fly,* and by the time he finally qualified as a doctor he had already acquired an enthusiastic public for his squibs and short farcical sketches. And so, encouraged by the millionaire publisher Suvorin, he resolved to devote all his energies to literature.

Chekhov wrote his first serious play, *Platonov,* at the age of about twenty, but it was rejected, being long and unwieldy, and the manuscript was duly destroyed. Almost a decade passed, during which time he became well-established as a short story writer, before he again attempted the dramatic form with *Ivanov.* The play, which already contains many of the features, both technically and thematically, of Chekhov's later work, was greeted with cheers and boos at its first performance. This was the first of many theatrical scandals and disappointments for Chekhov—not so much disappointment at the lack of immediate popularity and success as at the lack of understanding shown in press reviews and even in the letters and comments of personal friends like Suvorin.

We are fortunate that Chekhov wrote extensively in private correspondance about his aims and ideas in creating *Ivanov,* a thing that with subsequent plays time increasingly prevented him from doing; and, indeed, two years later the play enjoyed far greater success in the Alexandrinsky theatre in St. Petersburg, although there were still many misunderstandings between author, actors and audience. The play was originally to have been called *Ivan Ivanovich Ivanov* to stress the central character's absolute typicality and lack of unusual or heroic qualities, and Chekhov admits that he "cherished the bold idea of summing up all that has hitherto been written about moaning, pining people, and with *Ivanov* putting an end to all these writings." Certainly Ivanov does seem to belong to the line of nineteenth century Russian literature's weak, "superfluous" heroes, as portrayed by Pushkin, Turgenev and Goncharov, but instead of putting an end to them with his first play, Chekhov provided a fuller and more sympathetic gallery of dissatisfied, "superfluous" people than any of his predecessors had done.

Although weaker and more uneven in construction than the later plays, *Ivanov* contains many of the themes that characterise Chekhov's drama as a whole: exhaustion, boredom, loneliness and the typically Russian feeling of guilt are all strongly felt, whilst the play is also typical in that all the basic elements of the conflict and tragedy are evident from the very start, so that as the play progresses we simply go deeper into the fibre of the relationships and the basic situation. There are no surprises or external clashes, for even without the pharisaical Lvov, who is "not content that all men are sinners, but also wants saints and villains," Ivanov is doomed. The tragedy is not of conflict between individuals but of attrition: the hero is destroyed from within.

Chekhov himself fully understood the originality of his work in relation to the plays that were currently dominating the stages of St. Petersburg and Moscow; it lay basically in his apparently directionless, purely realistic approach to life, without artificially generated excitement and without moralising: the type of inner drama described by Maeterlinck when he wrote that a motionless old man seated in his arm-chair but sensing the world around him seemed to him to be living "a deeper, more human and more general life than the lover who strangles his mistress ... or the husband who avenges his honour." Chekhov had, even in his first play, almost completely removed the element of melodrama so characteristic of the Russian theatre at the end of the nineteenth century. Later this element, principally found in the various shootings (but already weakened, for the violence in Chekhov's plays comes as a psychological rather than physical or dramatic climax), gradually recedes, until in *The Cherry Orchard* it disappears completely.

Ivanov is a play about Russian life and Russian problems—we may notice the number of times Ivanov himself lets fall the word "Russian"—and accordingly many critics addressed themselves as much to its message as to its artistic merits. Chekhov believed that to involve his reader or spectator an author must remain completely cold and objective, but many prominent critics, like Shestov, called Chekhov's work "a creation out of nothing" and accused him of "destroying everything: art, science, love, inspiration." His objectivity was taken for indifference to good and evil, a lack of ideas and ideals, and he was blamed for not making clear his own sympathies and the moral message of his plays; for, as he put it ironically in a letter to a friend, "describing horse-thieves without saying: 'horse stealing is wrong'."

Chekhov did not, in fact, believe in art for art's sake, but felt that writers should have a goal and lead their readers towards it; in his story, *The House with a Mezzanine,* the artist says: "The sciences and the arts, if they are genuine, strive not for temporary or private aims, but towards what is eternal and all-embracing—they seek truth and the meaning of existence." Chekhov's goal was the simplest and, at the same time, least accessible of all: to open his audience's eyes to the kind of life around them, to the quality of life they were living. The press reacted almost unanimously, declaring the playwright to be a cold cynic, lacking in moral ideas and, moreover, a gloomy pessimist, capable only of throwing his audience into despondency. But if Chekhov was a pessimist, then it was

432

1
Chekhov with his brother in Moscow in 1880. The twenty-year-old Anton was studying medicine and writing on the side to support his family.

2-3
Chekhov's Russia: removing snow from the streets, and (above) Moscow in 1880.

4
The Chekhov family and friends in Moscow in the 1880's, Anton at the center and his tyrannical father, Pavel, at the rear.

5

Chekhov's modest house at Melikhovo, outside Moscow. Here he wrote *The Seagull* and *Uncle Vanya*.

surely in the Galsworthian sense of a realist: one "who can not only bear the world as it is, but loves it well enough to draw it faithfully." Chekhov, in his faith in human nature and belief in the future, was in many ways a deeply optimistic man, but not in such a way as to lead him from the almost clinical accuracy and realism that resulted in part from his medical training. If the theatre was to be a "school," then it must be as a guide to self-knowledge rather than the instrument for didacticism and moralising that it becomes in Tolstoy's problem plays, or later in the work of Brecht.

His next play, *The Wood Demon,* staged at Abramova's private theatre, was a great failure, something foreseen by the author after he had attended a few rehearsals. As he wrote to Suvorin, *"The Wood Demon* would be suitable for a novel, but I have not the strength for a novel. I could make a short story of it"; indeed, he did attempt to incorporate the idea of the unsuccessful play in a new story, *Uncle Vanya,* which, however, developed into a play before it saw the light of day in 1899. In the meantime, despite his renewed vows to abandon the theatre, Chekhov had produced a number of highly successful one-act vaudevilles like *The Bear, The Proposal* and *The Jubilee,* and another full-length play, *The Seagull.* Written for the Maly theatre in Moscow, but instead staged at the Alexandrinsky, *The Seagull* seems to have proved even less comprehensible to the actors than *Ivanov,* with the result that the première was a complete fiasco. "The theatre literally breathed ill-will," wrote Chekhov later, "and there was a heavy atmosphere of bewilderment and shame: it was as if literary Moscow had deliberately arranged a scandal."

Subsequent performances of the play were much more successful, particularly when it was taken up by the newly formed Moscow Art Theatre, who, as a tribute to Chekhov, adopted the now famous seagull motif as their emblem. In that *The Seagull* dramatises a group rather than an individual, it is a step away from *Ivanov* towards *The Three Sisters,* although we are still a long way from the collective heroes of Gorky or Hauptmann *(The Weavers),* for example. Indeed it may be said of Chekhov in general that he was more interested in humanity as a whole than in individuals, a fact evident in the plays, but especially clear in the stories, where, in their relatively uniform speech and lack of distinguishing features, the characters often seem to be representing moods, feelings or certain types of behaviour rather than leading individual existences.

Although *The Seagull* enjoyed considerable success at the Moscow Art Theatre it was not immediately understood by either Stanislavsky or Nemirovich-Danchenko, whose general ideas of what a play should be were seriously upset. Indeed, it does raise problems of interpretation which are common to all the later plays, especially *The Cherry Orchard,* for like the latter it is described by Chekhov as a comedy despite the apparently tragic nature of much of the content. Perhaps Chekhov's reputation as a cold cynic simply stemmed from the critics' difficulties in classifying the plays and their inability to readily determine the author's sympathies. We may laugh in the opening scene when Masha declares that she is wearing black in mourning for her life, but are we to laugh at the failure of Treplev's play, Trigorin's deception of Nina, the symbolism of the seagull, Treplev's suicide ? When considering the question of Chekhov's sympathies and intentions we should not forget the innate penchant for the incongruous and odd that found rich expression in early stories like *A Letter to a Learned Neighbour, The Daughter of Albion* or *The Malefactor.*

Tragic though many of the themes in his plays are, some of the bizarre and potentially comic characters and situations clearly look back to Antosha Chekhonte and should not be ignored or allowed to submerge in an overall atmosphere of melancholy. Chekhov used to complain that it was Stanislavsky who had made his plays so tearful: "I had other intentions ... I simply wanted to say to people: 'Look at yourselves. Look how badly and boringly you all live!'" It is, indeed, a typical feature of Russian comedy that it is closely attached to the Russians' constant preoccupation with everyday reality, and we may recall in this connection the comedies of Griboyedov and Gogol, and the latter's theme of "laughter through tears"; but nonetheless this ambiguity in merging the genres of comedy and tragedy was one of the main reasons for the confusion of producers and actors, and a cause of subsequent conflict between Stanislavsky and the author.

Today one still sees widely contrasting productions of Chekhov's plays, particularly the comedies, *The Seagull* and *The Cherry Orchard*. This duality may be the reason why, unlike Ibsen, he was reluctant to leave a play to its fate, once written, but always tried to advise and assist the actors on how best to interpret their roles. "A play," he would say, "belongs to the author, not the actors."

The Seagull is rich in literary associations. On the one hand we have echoes of *Hamlet,* one of Chekhov's favourite plays, whilst on the other there is an obvious parallel with Ibsen's *The Wild Duck,* where the symbolism is also very strong, although Chekhov condemned the earlier play as "sluggish, uninteresting and weak." In general, he had little use for Ibsen, whom he considered too schematic and intellectual, and, although Chekhov's characters may seem to bear out Ibsen's dictum that "to be a man at all is to be neurotic, self-destructive and unhappy," Chekhov himself believed firmly in the possibility of genuine happiness and self-fulfilment.

Nor does the atmosphere of *The Seagull* bear much resemblance to that of *The Wild Duck;* it is far closer to that of Turgenev's *A Month in the Country,* or, particularly with its enchanted lake, Maeterlinck's *Pelléas et Mélisande.* The lyrical symbolism is very strong in this play, looking forward to *The Three Sisters* where it is almost overpowering, and to *The Cherry Orchard* where it is transformed into something lighter and less ominous. When, in the first act, Nina says: "Like the seagull I am drawn towards this lake," we can already feel that the seagull and Nina are both doomed, and it is no surprise later when Treplev shoots it and is at the end presented with the stuffed bird. Similarly in *The Three Sisters* Natasha announces her plans to cut down the trees of which Tusenbach had said: "What beautiful trees, and, in reality, how beautiful life should be near them"; and Chebutykin breaks the clock that used to belong to the sisters' mother, whom he once loved.

The Seagull is a highly charged and emotional play, despite its background of rustic boredom: using pauses with great dramatic effect Chekhov creates a dual atmosphere of tension and impending doom on the one hand, and of vulgar indifference and self-satisfaction on the other. Here, as elsewhere, selfish vulgarity, represented by Irina Nikolayevna and Trigorin, triumphs over sensitivity, just as it does in *Uncle Vanya* and *The Three Sisters* where, in the victory of Natasha over the Prozorov sisters, it has become one of the principal themes of the play. Almost all the characters are unhappy and lonely, thanks mainly to their inability to communicate with one another, and none seems able to break out of the melancholy, which according to Dorn the doctor makes them so utterly boring. But the overall impression of *The Seagull*

436

is not one of gloom and disillusionment so much as of lyrical melancholy; even more than in his other plays, Chekhov has created his images and moods in infinitely soft pastel tones. *The Seagull,* with its delicate, even fragile structure, held together by poetically symbolic images, is difficult to produce successfully, but immensely rewarding.

The next play, *Uncle Vanya,* was first performed in 1899, but by this time a number of important events and changes had taken place in the writer's life. Between April and December, 1890 he made an immense journey across Siberia by coach in order to visit the convict island of Sakhalin, returning by sea via Ceylon. On his return he published a book describing with devastating clarity and objectivity the abominable conditions in which the convicts were forced to live. This detached and scientific description made a great impression on the public and, apparently, the authorities, for in 1892 a number of significant penal reforms were introduced. For Chekhov *Sakhalin Island* was a substitute for the medical research that his literary career had, regrettably, prevented him from undertaking. These "six weeks of constant physical and mental exertion," however, weakened further his rapidly deteriorating health, and he moved to a small farm at Melikhovo, to the south of Moscow, in order to recuperate. Six years later he was forced to move still further south to the Crimea, and, from time to time, to various spas and health resorts in France, Italy and Germany. On July 2nd, 1904, he died of tuberculosis at the small resort of Badenweiler in the Black Forest.

The formation of the Moscow Theatre and their first performance of *The Seagull* were events of almost unparalleled importance in the history of the Russian theatre, and also a turning-point in the practical realisation of Chekhov's artistic demands on stage. It was essential that a new type of theatre appear if Chekhov's brilliantly heretical and original plays were to be produced, since older, traditional theatres were manifestly unable to cope with such unfamiliar material. But it was by a happy chance that the formation of the Art Theatre coincided with Chekhov's activity as a dramatist, for neither actor Stanislavsky nor producer Nemirovich-Danchenko were particularly close friends of the playwright, and it was without Chekhov's participation that the new theatre was formed. Approaching drama from different angles, they seem to have reached similar conclusions about the state of the contemporary Russian theatre and the direction it should take.

The result was that Chekhov provided the Art Theatre with material that best reflected their novel techniques and especial qualities, whilst, on the other hand, it was only in this theatre that the dramatist found an adequate response to his creative ideas. Agreement between Stanislavsky and the author was far from being total, and Chekhov often had to persuade the actor to modify his over-tragic, heavy interpretations, particularly in the matter of off-stage sound effects. It is nonetheless true that without the Art Theatre Chekhov would have had far greater difficulty in establishing his name as a dramatist, and that without Chekhov the theatre would not have earned its reputation so quickly, if at all, for some of their other, more conventional productions were quite commonplace. As it is, the names of Chekhov and the Moscow Art Theatre are inextricably linked.

Although *Uncle Vanya* was not performed until 1899 it was actually finished before *The Seagull,* but not shown to anyone or discussed by Chekhov in letters to his friends, possibly because of the play's strong connections with the ill-fated *Wood Demon,* from which it to some extent derived. In it Chekhov develops further some of the

438

6-7
Chekhov first saw his wife, Olga Knipper, when she took the
part of Irina (left) in the newly-formed Moscow Art Theatre's
1898 production of Aleksey Tolstoy's *Tsar Fyodor Ivannovich*.
The couple are shown together above.

8
The Three Sisters—a sketch of the actresses who took part in the first performance of Chekhov's play by the Moscow Art Theatre in 1901.

9-10

Chekhov reads *The Seagull,* whose first production a few years before had been a disaster, to the actors of the Moscow Art Theatre. Stanislavsky is at his right, and Olga Knipper, his future wife, stands beside Stanislavsky. Above: a scene from the first production of *The Three Sisters* in 1901.

11
A caricature of Georges Pitoëff, member of a family which did so much to introduce Chekhov and other modern dramatists to western Europe in the 1920's.

H. Tanner

themes of *The Seagull*, and also introduces some new ones that acquire even greater significance in his subsequent works. The portrayal of rustic boredom is again one of the main features of the play, and in this connection we may note that for Chekhov the problem of idleness and stagnation was not merely a Russian, but a European one. In an article of 1888 he wrote: "In our sick times, when European societies are enveloped in idleness, boredom with life, and lack of faith, when there reigns everywhere, in a strange combination, a dislike of life and fear of death, when even the best people sit doing nothing, justifying their idleness and corruption by the lack of a definite aim in life, we need active people as much as we need sunshine."

The fact remains, however, that Russian literature of the nineteenth century is particularly remarkable for its series of ineffectual, "superfluous" heroes, and so the characters of Chekhov's plays seem a logical continuation. The main difference is that Chekhov has abandoned the tradition, originating in Puškin's *Eugene Onegin* and carried on by Turgenev and Goncharov, that the weak hero be offset by a more positive heroine. He makes no distinction in this respect.

As in *The Seagull* we see the triumph of successful, but shallow and basically vulgar people over the more sensitive; the disillusionment of Vanya with the famous but mediocre "scribbling perpetuum mobile" is more than simply personal animosity aroused by disappointment; it reflects an important aspect of Chekhov's view of life, for in his works almost all the successful, satisfied people are both shallow and distasteful (for example, Trigorin in *The Seagull,* Kuligin and Natasha in *The Three Sisters* or Lopahin in the *The Cherry Orchard*). Success is the reward of mediocrity, happiness that of insensitivity. "Clearly the happy man has an easy conscience only because the unhappy bear their burden in silence, and but for this silence his happiness would be impossible. There ought to stand at the door of every self-satisfied, happy man someone with a hammer, to remind him continually by his knocking of the existence of unhappy people in the world." Sensitivity is constantly suffering defeat at the hands of vulgarity, and the fate of beauty on earth is perpetually in the balance, thanks to human indifference and carelessness.

Beauty and nature are for Chekhov symbolised by trees, and we can feel the author speaking through Astrov when he describes to a typically inattentive Yelena Andreyevna the immense and senseless destruction of the country's natural beauty and resources. The theme reoccurs in a different form in *The Three Sisters* when Natasha flounts her moral victory over the sisters by announcing plans to cut down the birch trees in their garden, whilst in *The Cherry Orchard,* of course, it has become the focal point of the play and acquired strong symbolic significance.

In the last act of *Uncle Vanya,* when the professor has departed after the unsuccessful attempt to shoot him, Sonya and Vanya begin to bury themselves in practical affairs, seeing work as the answer to their problems and unhappiness. Here the theme is still fairly muted, however, compared with *The Three Sisters,* and by the very end of the play Sonya is not expecting happiness this side of the grave. "We will rest." In the next play the idea of work as the key to a happier future is expressed very clearly by a number of the characters, but it is interesting to note that although work would seem to be the answer to many of their problems, Chekhov does not in fact show it has having this positive effect : the characters who extol the value and necessity of labour are those who have not experienced it, like Vershinin, Tusenbach and Irina, and

when, for example, Irina does begin working she soon
becomes as disillusioned as the more experienced Olga.

It is also noteworthy that quite often Chekhov's "positive" ideas are put forward by unpleasant or ridiculous
characters: in this instance both Serebryakov in *Uncle
Vanya* and Kuligin in *The Three Sisters* preach to the
other, more likeable characters the nobility and rewards
of labour. In *The Cherry Orchard* mankind's beautiful
future is proclaimed by the "eternal student" Trofimov
who considers himself above love. His speech about
mankind moving towards the highest truth is made
against the background of his ridiculous concern at
having mislaid a pair of galoshes, and only when they
are found can the party depart from the old house, Anya
crying: "Farewell, house ! Farewell, old life !" and Trofimov, triumphantly: "Greetings, new life !"

Uncle Vanya is called neither comedy nor tragedy, but
simply "scenes from country life," a description that
could be given to all the other plays except *The Three
Sisters*, which would be "scenes from provincial life,"
and this raises a number of important general questions
concerning the form and construction of Chekhov's
"plotless" and "directionless" dramas. Gorky rightly ob-
served of Chekhov that "he does not say anything that
is new, but what he does say is always amazingly convincing and simple, frighteningly simple and clear, irre-
futably true." Thus Chekhov's originality does not lie
so much in what he says as how he says it. It was the
novelty of his plays' form (or, as it seemed to some, their
formlessness) that most struck contemporary audiences
and critics. One can get some idea of the theatre-going
public's degree of sophistication from the reproach of
Shcheglov, a friend of Chekhov, who said: "One must
never, never, never disregard the laws of the stage that
have grown up logically on the lines laid down by

441

Molière and Griboyedov." It is thus not surprising that Chekhov was accused not so much of creating the "new forms" called for by Treplev in *The Seagull* as of destroying altogether the genre in which he was writing.

Contemporaries failed to realise that by deliberately shunning obviously dramatic devices and external conflicts Chekhov was strengthening the inner action of his plays; that moments like the end of the second act of *Uncle Vanya,* when the professor's refusal to allow music to be played is announced by Sonya with the words "No, we must not," symbolising Serebryakov's negative influence on the household, are infinitely more dramatic and powerful than, for example, Ivanov's suicide or Vanya's attempt to shoot the professor, to say nothing of the kind of melodrama that was the usual fare of audiences of that time. Chekhov expressed his ideas of what a play should be when he said: "Let everything on stage be as complicated and at the same time as simple as in life. People are having lunch, simply having lunch, and at the same time their happiness is being formed or their lives are being broken up."

Thus Marya Savina, an outstanding actress of the time, was quite right when she said: "All this 'new form' of Chekhov stems from his striving to be realistic, to be true to life." Chekhov was not, as some critics have suggested, destroying drama, but rather expanding its scope by discarding what was unnecessary for the faithful representation of human emotions and problems. The personal, larger themes emerge naturally from amongst the banal, everyday conversations. We learn something of the mood of the characters from their own declarations—and this is natural when there is such a striking lack of communication between them—but there is no feeling that they are making unnatural announcements, for it is from almost all their remarks, however apparently trivial, that we learn about their mental and spiritual state.

Chekhov puts into practice ideas expressed by his contemporary, Maeterlinck, in *The Tragic in Daily Life* (1896): "And indeed the only words that count in the play are those that at first seemed useless, for it is therein that the essence lies. Side by side with the necessary dialogue you will almost always find another dialogue that seems superfluous; but examine it carefully, and it will be borne home to you that this is the only one that the soul can listen to profoundly, for here alone it is the soul that is being addressed."

Chekhov's drama is not one of surprises: there are no twists in the plot, but simply a deepening of our understanding of a basic situation, generally outlined in the first few scenes. On the whole, the moods and interrelationships of the characters do not change, but rather develop along strictly natural and foreseeable lines. Similarly, physical events are anticipated, so that when they occur they are part of a logical progression rather than isolated happenings. Chekhov once said that if there is a gun on the wall in the first act it must go off before the end; thus in *The Three Sisters* the jealous Solyony promises to kill Tusenbach at the very beginning of the play, and repeats his threat in the second act, with the result that the duel and the baron's death is an event that has been feared and expected throughout the play.

The Three Sisters, first performed in 1901, is texturally the most complicated and for many people the greatest of Chekhov's plays. Written with great difficulty, the play was described by the author as "some Crimean nonsense," or again, in a letter to his wife, who created the role of Masha in the Art Theatre production, as "not a play, but a sort of muddle." It was certainly not an easy task to create three individual heroines, and all general's daughters, but it drew from the author a work of great richness in texture and emotions. The atmosphere created from the very beginning is one of neurotic frustration and gloom, and it is maintained by the widespread use of symbolic devices like Masha wearing a black dress and repeating unaccountably sinister lines from Pushkin; Chebutykin, drunk during the fire, smashing the clock belonging to the sisters' mother, whilst Andrey, Nero-like, plays on his violin, expressing not merely his alienation from the present tragic events, but from the ordinary, honourable everyday life that he lived before marrying the vulgar Natasha.

In Chekhov's stories a favourite technique is a swing in emotion, or in our attitude to a given character, and this is particularly noticeable here in our attitude to Natasha. At first we feel sorry for her, so obviously out of place amidst the cultured Prozorov family, but soon our pity turns to contempt as she proceeds to take over the house, revenging herself on her husband and the sisters for their moral and cultural superiority. Her selfishness equals that of Serebryakov in *Uncle Vanya,* and as a destructive force she is no less effective.

"To write plays one must have a special talent: one can be a first-rate prose writer and still produce atrocious drama." The curious paradox, particularly emphasized by *The Three Sisters,* with its range of brilliantly characterized individuals, is that the *dramatis personae* of Chekhov's plays are a great deal more sharply defined than the protagonists in his stories, who often seem more like vessels or vehicles for feelings and emotions, without other distinguishing features. The sisters are clearly differentiated: Masha, sensitive despite the coarsening influence of a disappointing married life to a shallow schoolteacher; Olga, the most stable temperamentally, the most resigned

12
Yalta in 1890. Chekhov took refuge in this southern resort on the Black Sea in 1899 in an attempt to regain his health, already ravaged by tuberculosis.

13
Chekhov's house at Yalta. Here the dying man entertained his celebrated friends and was besieged by hundreds of curiosity-seekers.

14-15
Chekhov's study at Yalta, and (above) his bedroom. In this house he wrote *The Three Sisters* and *The Cherry Orchard*.

16
Chekhov at Yalta with his mother and sister (left) and his wife,
Olga Knipper the actress, behind him.

to the unrewarding and soul-destroying toil of life, and yet, perhaps, the most committed to their shared dream of returning to Moscow; Irina, whose heart is "like a grand piano of which no one has the key," at first young and coquettish, but later sobered by life, eventually prepared to face the future camly and to hope for attainable happiness—only to have it taken away by Solyony's bullet. Highly individual in character, they are united by adversity, and appear as a family unit only when faced by the hostile and alien force of Natasha.

Nor are the officers stereotyped: Tusenbach, eager to please, to conform, but weakened by his background, anxious to work, but in fact capable only of high-flown philosophising; Vershinin, part hero, part woolly idealist, part figure of tragedy with a crazed wife; Solyony, ridiculous in his delusions of grandeur, destructive in his jealousy and sense of isolation; Tchebutykin, seeking escape from his problems in alcohol. None resembles another and none is a mere type. Vershinin's appearance as a representative of the Moscow life so idealised by the sisters is paralleled by Natasha, who at first seems to the naive Andrey as the embodiment of youth's charm—youth which he, like Masha and Irina, already feels slipping away from him. Andrey is in some ways the most pathetic figure in the play for he seems even more isolated from the values he believes in than do his sisters. Failure in his career and misery in married life are, as it were, crystallised in his position as a member of the Zemstvo, of which his wife's lover is chairman. With him we see the tragedy of non-communication in its clearest form, for he, not unlike Gaev in *The Cherry Orchard,* who addresses his thoughts to the bookcase, deliberately seeks out the deaf servant Ferapont as his confidant: "If you could hear properly I would probably not talk to you. I need someone to talk to; my wife does not understand me and I am somehow afraid that my sisters will laugh at me, put me to shame."

The atmosphere of obsessive preoccupation is bound to mean disillusionment for the majority of the characters. Where dreams are so important reality can have little place, for all the sisters' and officers' attempts to achieve something positive. At the end of the play, with the soldiers' departure and Tusenbach's death, the expressions of hope for a happy future ring even more hollowly than at the end of *Uncle Vanya* or *The Cherry Orchard*. As in the latter play the last scene is one of departure, and one feels here that the departure means not so much the start of a new life as an end to all illusions, to any belief in the possibility of happiness: the only contented figures are Kuligin and Natasha.

On the construction of plays Chekhov said: "The first act can last for as much as an hour, but the others must not be more than thirty minutes each. The crux of the play is the third act, but it must not be allowed to kill the last one." In *The Three Sisters* the third act is certainly the most emotionally powerful, and the events of the last seem rather pale beside the drama of the fire, but the act is not "killed," for Chekhov is showing us how life goes on, how sober day must follow tempestuous night. Tusenbach dies violently, but for the most part the tragedy is one of attrition; the characters are destroyed by their own natures rather than events or inevitable circumstances.

But if weakness is an important element in their make-up, they nonetheless retain our sympathy by their desire to lead a more positive life; they struggle in vain, and the odds seem heavily against them, but they are conscious of certain aims and they strive towards them. By comparison, Ivanov, in the earlier play, submits very easily. The tension of the play is maintained throughout, with the conflict between certain of the characters, the all-pervading atmosphere of doom, created largely by symbolic means, and the jarring juxtapositions (here stemming mainly from the obtuse Kuligin) that so characterize the work of Chekhov as a whole.

The next and last play was *The Cherry Orchard,* acclaimed by many as Chekhov's masterpiece. Written in 1903 and produced at the Art Theatre in the following year, it has a lightness and gaiety, albeit autumnal, that shocked and perplexed both Stanislavsky and Nemirovich-Danchenko. When the latter first read the play in manuscript he was "disappointed to find nothing new" and sighed for "that pearl of an early work *Ivanov.*"

It is, indeed, true that Chekhov's work, like that of Strindberg, did develop rather than change, and that, as in the plays themselves, all the author's cards are placed on the table at once: there are none of the dramatic changes in content and form that we find in Ibsen's development, for example. But when it came to the matter of staging and interpretation it was Stanislavsky and Nemirovich-Danchenko that proved conservative, for they insisted on trying to play *The Cherry Orchard* as high drama, in the manner of *Ivanov* and *The Three Sisters,* rather than as comedy—in places almost vaudeville—thus causing the now seriously ailing Chekhov a great deal of distress. Although Stanislavsky later wrote in praise of Chekhov's immense innate dramatic talent and his ability to sum up scenes merely by glancing at the sets, it took him a long time to appreciate fully and adapt himself to Chekhov's individuality, just as the playwright had difficulty in overcoming his instinctive dislike of the actor's "peacock" temperament.

An indication of the gap between this play and the preceding one is the quite different nature of the symbolism: there are no more black dresses, broken clocks or fires; Gaev is characterized by his billiard cue, Yasha by his smell of herrings and cheap cigars. In the dénouement —if one can apply the word to anything as organically continuous as a Chekhov play—it is Yasha who swigs down Lopahin's cheap champagne. Only at the very end, when Firs is abandoned and forgotten, does the dramatist reveal the melancholy always lurking behind the ridiculousness and fun. The symbolism of the cherry orchard being felled whilst the old servant is left to die in the deserted house is so explicit as to seem to some exaggerated. On the other hand, it makes a fitting conclusion to Chekhov's dramatic *opus* as a whole, combining as it does many important features of his style and themes.

Many elements in the play are continued or developed from the earlier works, and to this extent Nemirovich-Danchenko was correct. Vulgarity again triumphs over culture and sensitivity, although here the positive aspects of the vulgar Lopahin and the less commendable side of the cultured Madame Ranevsky are brought out very clearly. Once again the themes of work and belief in a happy future are introduced, albeit through Trofimov. Chekhov was dissatisfied with the way he had characterized the student, feeling him to be incomplete, and it may well be that he did not intend him to cut quite the ridiculous figure that he does in many productions nowadays: "I am mainly distressed by certain imperfections in my portrayal of the student Trofimov. After all, this Trofimov is constantly being banished or expelled from the university, but how can you show these things?" He was also disturbed by the small amount of action in the second act, although on the stage this is not felt as a shortcoming. Lack of communication is again important: Lopahin who "understands nothing" cannot, for his part, penetrate the wall of fecklessness and idealism erected by Gaev and his sister; Varya talks to the sleeping Anya, Gaev to the bookcase, whilst the comic, yet pathetic Charlotta lives a lonely life, quite cut off from the problems and aspirations of the Russian society on which she is dependent.

The prospects of Lopahin proposing to Varya are brought up by Anya as soon as she returns from abroad, as is also the parlous state of Madame Ranevsky's finances. Thus no surprises are sprung; the main elements of the play are presented at the very beginning. Once again evocative sounds, like the distant snapping of a rope, are employed, although some of them actually stem from the Art Theatre production rather than from the author himself; but despite his weak health Chekhov still had enough strength to resist Stanislavsky's over-enthusiastic use of "emotive" sounds such as, for example, bird noises, particularly when the latter were manifestly inappropriate in season and place.

In any case, he was strongly opposed to what he called "vulgar naturalism": in 1902 he wrote in a letter to his wife: "Why are you playing Gorky's play with a Volga region pronunciation? What are you doing?!! It is as despicable as when Darsky played Shylock with a Jewish accent. In *The Petty Bourgeois* they all talk in the same way as you and I do." For Chekhov realism and verisimilitude were not achieved by naturalistic gimmicks but by hints and the selective use of significant detail. Indeed, the fact that the characters in his plays, particularly those written before the establishment of the Art Theatre, have less distinguishing speech characteristics than those in the stories may possibly be a sign that he did not wish to risk giving actors material for distortion and exaggeration.

Describing *The Cherry Orchard,* he wrote to Olga in 1903: "However boring my play may be, it contains something new. There is not a single shot in it." From Ivanov's suicide to Tusenbach's death in a duel Chekhov's plays had always contained some element of violence, although

449

he deliberately restrained it, placing off-stage what other playwrights might have used for great dramatic effect. A contemporary of Chekhov described a rehearsal of the third act of *Uncle Vanya,* in which at the words, "Papa, one must show mercy," Sonya fell on her knees and kissed her father's hand. "You must not do that, it is not dramatic," said Anton Pavlovitch. "The whole significance and drama is in the life of Sonya up to this moment, and there will also be drama after it, but this is simply an event, a continuation of the shot. And after all a shot is not drama, but a happening."

For all their relative lack of action Chekhov's plays are, in fact, highly dramatic and only stand to lose by the kind of exaggerated approach that can turn genuine pathos into bathos, drama into mawkish melodrama. The continuing performances today not only of his masterpieces, *The Three Sisters* and *The Cherry Orchard,* but of all his plays, in almost every country of the world, bear witness to a dramatic talent that, though often discouraged, persevered and brought about, almost single-handed, a revolution in the Russian theatre—and that played as well an individual and important part in the transformation of Western theatre as a whole, and the creation of what is known as modern drama.

The writer and critic, D. S. Merezhkovsky wrote of Chekhov: "He is national to the highest degree, but not universal. Infinitely observant and sensitive to everything that is Russian and contemporary, he is practically blind and deaf to what is foreign or in the past. He saw Russia more clearly than anyone else but overlooked Europe and the rest of the world." The fallacy of this view is apparent when we consider his close ties with contemporary European dramatists, whom he read avidly and whose plays he sought to have staged in the Russian capitals.

17
Young Maxim Gorky, the writer, with his son in 1899. Chekhov
took a great interest in Gorky's work.

18
Tolstoy, the great Russian novelist of an older generation, who admired Chekhov's work, especially his language, but did not altogether understand it.

19-22
August Strindberg of Sweden (top, left) and Gerhart Hauptmann of Germany (top, right) were dramatists contemporary
with Chekhov. Somewhat older were Henrik Ibsen (bottom,
left), the Norwegian dramatist, and the Russian novelist, Ivan
Turgenev (right), whose work was close in style and spirit to
that of Chekhov.

23
Anton Chekhov in his garden at Yalta, not long before his death.

Chekhov may in many ways be seen to stand in clear succession to Ostrovsky, who died in 1886, a year before the first production of *Ivanov,* and to Turgenev who also had made extensive use of atmosphere, developing undercurrents of inner action and "emotional signals"; but Chekhov was no less involved with the work of Ibsen, Maeterlinck and Strindberg than he was with that of his compatriots. Who better answered the appeal of Zola, writing in 1881: "The impulse of the century is toward naturalism ... This force has abducted the novel and the drama ... I am waiting for someone to rid us of fictitious characters, of these symbols of virtue and vice that have no worth as human data ... I am waiting for everyone to throw out the tricks of the trade, the contrived formulas, the tears and what is superficial ..."? To describe Chekhov as a figure of purely national significance is to misrepresent and limit him quite unjustifiably.

How did Chekhov regard his contemporaries? Of the Russians, it was naturally in the young and promising Gorky that he took the greatest interest, for although Lev Tolstoy's didactic problem plays like *The Living Corpse, The Fruits of Enlightenment* or *The Power of Darkness* were of greater artistic merit than most of the younger writer's work, they held no mystery or promise for the future, but simply consolidated the teaching of the great novelist's controversial post-conversion period. At that time it seemed that the future lay with the iconoclastic Gorky, and Chekhov viewed his plays with concern and excitement.

The Lower Depths made him "almost dance for joy," but *The Petty Bourgeois* was criticized for its unadventurous form, although Chekhov took a very personal interest in its production, giving much advice about casting and interpretation. A play like this may have been technically unworthy of its spectacular popularity, but Gorky's significance was "not that he pleased the public, but that he was the first person in Russia, and, indeed, in the whole world, to speak of the bourgeoisie with scorn and revulsion." Aleksey Tolstoy's *Tsar Fyodor Ivannovich* (in which, incidentally, Chekhov first saw his wife-to-be perform) was praised for its "intelligent atmosphere and the genuinely artistic feeling coming from the stage." Even less important plays, like Naydenov's *Money* or Lunacharsky's *Temptation* are also mentioned favourably in his correspondence, and in general one is struck by Chekhov's catholic taste and freedom from cant: *The Petty Bourgeois* might be conservative in construction, or *Temptation* conventional in terms of plot, but Chekhov always sought out a play's positive aspects. Accordingly, Gorky is praised for his outspokenness on social issues, Lunacharsky for his work's auditory and visual qualities.

Chekhov had little use for the Symbolist poets, who had a considerable following amongst the intelligentsia at that time. He felt that they were deceiving the public with their "decadence" and obscure mysticism, but, nonetheless, he tried to get Balmont's plays performed at the Moscow Art Theatre, in order to extend the still rather limited horizons of theatre audiences and, indeed, actors. His interests were always those of the Russian theatre as a whole.

Chekhov's dislike of Ibsen is well known. Despite the Norwegian's great originality in both subject matter and form, despite his boldness in speaking out on controversial questions, Chekhov found him artificial and insincere. Both at home and abroad it was Ibsen's fate to be taken as a teacher rather than an artist, despite his refusal to explain his plays and commit himself on public questions. He joined no parties and took part in no movements—"I have been more of a poet and less of a social philosopher than is commonly supposed"—but, nonetheless, Chekhov's

452

attitude to him remained consistently hostile and short-sighted.

With other European dramatists, however, he showed the catholicity of taste that marked his attitude to compatriots. Hauptmann attracted Chekhov greatly, particularly in his early plays taken from the life of the intelligentsia, like *Michael Kramer* or *The Lonely Ones*. After the first Russian performance of the latter in October, 1901 Chekhov declared: "That is a real dramatist! I am not a dramatist, do you hear? I am just a doctor." During rehearsals of *Michael Kramer* Chekhov is said to have laughed with pleasure at the German's artistry, despite the tragic nature of the play's content, and he was genuinely surprised by the lack of success enjoyed by Hauptmann's plays on the Russian stage. The two playwrights shared an interest in hidden action behind the façade of monotonous daily life; both developed the use of banal dialogues, concealing undercurrents of psychological significance, both made extensive and effective use of pauses.

These elements were also present in the short philosophical dramas of Maeterlinck, although the Belgian's symbolic abstractions were as alien to Chekhov as were the mystical formulas of his own compatriots. It was not Maeterlinck's search for a hidden world behind the real one that attracted Chekhov, but his adventurous dramatic techniques and his ability to develop complicated internal movement and conflicts beneath a surface of deceptive simplicity. Chekhov constantly championed the work of Maeterlinck in Russia, but when Suvorin did finally put on some of his plays they enjoyed little success.

Finally one may mention Strindberg, who also fought against artificiality and "theatrical schematism." Chekhov admired much of his work, as such, particularly

Miss Julie, but wrote very critically of Strindberg's attitude to women and belief that "war is the inevitable
condition of any intimate relationship between men and
women." The picture that emerges, then, is certainly not
of Chekhov as a narrow nationalist, but as a man with
a deep concern for the basic problems of human existence, however they might be expressed, and with a
genuine love for the theatre as a form of art and an
instrument for revealing our innermost lives. He is no
more a purely national figure than, say, Dostoyevsky or
Tolstoy.

"I have not acquired a political, philosophic and religious outlook on life," wrote Chekhov in 1888. Thus
we cannot talk about themes in his work in the same way
as we can about those in Ibsen or Shaw; it is not possible
to trace, for example, a development from sociological,
reformist to philosophical plays, as we find it in Ibsen,
or a swing from Zola-type naturalism to non-representa-
tional metaphysics, as we have in Strindberg. Chekhov's
work was consistent both in form and in subject matter.
The lack of plot that accounted for so much of its unusual dramatic form links him both with his predecessors,
Ostrovsky, Nekrasov and Turgenev, and with Hauptmann and Maeterlinck. He was not alone in breaking
down the division, already weak in Russian literature, between drama and comedy, or in doing away with the
formal division of acts into scenes. Nor was he alone in
presenting whole and "breathing" characters without
"psychologising" and dissecting them. Where he was
supremely successful was in combining all these various
elements in a form of universal appeal, in creating
credible characters with problems, weaknesses and virtues
recognizable not only to Russians but to many different
people in various countries and at various periods.

The type of humane and undogmatic realism exemplified by Chekhov has suffered some harsh knocks in this century. Typical of certain influential schools of thought was Sartre, writing in 1946: "Therefore our new theatre has definitely drawn away from the so-called 'realistic theatre,' because realism has always offered plays made up of stories of defeat, laissez-faire and drifting; it has always preferred to show how external forces batter a man to pieces, destroy him bit by bit, and ultimately make him a weathervane, turning with every change of wind. But we claim for ourselves the *true* realism because we know it is impossible, in everyday life, to distinguish between fact and right, the real from the ideal, psychology from ethics" (*Forgers of Myths*).

Fortunately not all playwrights have made such arrogant claims; not all audiences seek to be bludgeoned, to have truth revealed to them arbitrarily. Recent history has shown that fact and right must be distinguished, that we must understand what is real if our ideals are to be meaningful. Today it is the plays of Chekhov rather than those of Tolstoy or Sartre that are widely performed and enjoyed.

Chekhov has achieved in his drama much more than any self-confident reformer : he has opened our eyes to the quality of the life we lead; he has shared with us some of his own humanity, sensibility and understanding.

Arnold B. McMILLIN

SOURCES OF THE ILLUSTRATIONS

Frontispiece : Anton Chekhov in 1897. Novosti Press Agency, London.

1 Chekhov with his brother, 1880. Novosti Press Agency, London.

2 Moscow in the 1880's. Mansell Collection, London.

3 Clearing snow from the streets. Mary Evans Picture Library, London.

4 Anton with his family and friends in Moscow. Novosti Press Agency, London.

5 Chekhov's house at Melikhovo. Novosti Press Agency, London.

6 Chekhov and his wife. Courtesy of the Swiss-USSR Association, Geneva.

7 Olga Knipper acting at the Moscow Art Theatre. Novosti Press Agency, London.

8 A sketch from the first performance of *The Three Sisters*. Published in the literary magazine "Neva", 1901. Bibl. de Genève.

9 A scene from *The Three Sisters,* 1901. Novosti Press Agency, London.

10 Chekhov reading *The Seagull* to actors of the Moscow Art Theatre. Courtesy of the Swiss-USSR Association, Geneva.

11 Caricature of Georges Pitoëff. Cabinet des estampes de la Bibl. de Genève.

12 Yalta. Mansell Collection, London.

13 Chekhov's house at Yalta. Novosti Press Agency, London.

14 The bedroom of Chekhov's house at Yalta. Novosti Press Agency, London.

This book, designed by
Werner Schelling
is a production of
Edito-Service S.A., Geneva

Printed in Switzerland
R 1